THE ART AND ARCHAEOLOGY OF THE MOCHE

THE Art AND Archaeology OF THE Moche

An Ancient Andean Society
of the Peruvian North Coast

EDITED BY STEVE BOURGET
AND KIMBERLY L. JONES

University of Texas Press ⟊ Austin

THE PUBLICATION OF THIS BOOK WAS MADE POSSIBLE, IN PART,
BY GENEROUS SUPPORT FROM THE POTTS AND SIBLEY FOUNDATION.

Requests for permission to reproduce material from this work
should be sent to:
    Permissions .
    University of Texas Press
    P.O. Box 7819
    Austin, TX 78713-7819
    www.utexas.edu/utpress/about/bpermission.html

♾ The paper used in this book meets the minimum require-
ments of ANSI/NISO Z39.48-1992 (R1997) (Permanence of
Paper).

LIBRARY OF CONGRESS CATALOGING-IN-PUBLICATION DATA

The art and archaeology of the Moche : an ancient Andean
society of the Peruvian north coast / edited by Steve Bourget
and Kimberly L. Jones. — 1st ed.
      p.   cm.
    Papers originally presented at a symposium at the Depart-
ment of Art and Art History at the University of Texas at Austin
in November 2003.
    Includes bibliographical references and index.
    ISBN 978-0-292-71867-8 (cloth : alk. paper)
1. Mochica Indians—Antiquities—Congresses.   2. Mochica
art—Congresses.   3. Excavations (Archaeology)—Peru—Moche
River Valley—Congresses.   4. Moche River Valley (Peru)—
Antiquities—Congresses.   I. Bourget, Steve, 1956–   II. Jones,
Kimberly L., 1979–
    F3430.1.M6A78   2008
    985'.1601—dc22
                              2008027539

14968430

Dedicated to the memory of Donna McClelland and D. J. Sibley

Contents

Preface

STEVE BOURGET

In November 2003, the Department of Art and Art History at the University of Texas at Austin hosted the Fourth D. J. Sibley Family Conference. This three-day symposium, entitled "The Art, the Arts, and the Archaeology of the Moche: An Ancient Andean Society of the Peruvian North Coast," brought together a number of scholars directly involved in Moche studies. In recent years, these and other specialists have made significant discoveries, carried out long-term archaeological projects, and implemented a variety of innovative techniques that have provided for a recent exponential increase in our understanding of Moche culture.

The main objective of this symposium was to discuss how the fields of archaeology and iconography have increasingly come to enrich and complement one another in Moche scholarship. A number of the presentations thus incorporated archaeological and iconographic analyses in the discussion of a wide range of subject matter. The papers further explored other pressing issues and concerns, such as Moche site chronologies, cultural identity, distribution of styles, the impact of ecology on north coast societies, and the visual expression of social change.

Fifteen papers were delivered at the meeting, and fourteen of them appear in this book. Christopher Donnan, David Scott, and Todd Bracken submitted a chapter on Moche metallurgy for publication that had not been presented at the meetings. Thus, the completed volume has fifteen chapters.

Support for the symposium and preparation of the book was provided by the Potts and Sibley Foundation, as well as by the Department of Art and Art History at the University of Texas at Austin. I would also like to take this opportunity to thank those who generously assisted in the organization of the symposium: Amy Bracewell, Reymundo Chapa, Kimberly Jones, Virginia Portillo, Fernando Rochaix, and Maline Werness.

Introduction

STEVE BOURGET AND KIMBERLY L. JONES

The Moche became known as a distinct cultural entity at the turn of the last century as a result of Max Uhle's excavations at the Huacas de Moche site in the Moche Valley. Since that time, Moche monumental architecture and visual culture have fascinated scholars and laypeople alike. For more than a century, Moche art, consisting of thousands of ceramic and metallic objects extracted from archaeological contexts, has been collected and disseminated throughout the world. As a result, Moche art objects currently grace the display cases of countless museums and private collections. Such objects continue to garner ever-increasing interest in and fascination with this complex culture from the Early Intermediate Period (AD 100–800) of Prehispanic Peru.

Some of the first knowledge of Moche culture, in fact, derived from increasing interest in the outstanding artistic tradition made visible by such marketed objects. Investigators approached the striking realism and visual complexity of the sculptures and paintings on Moche fineware ceramics in order to explore the information they provided with regard to religion, way of life, rituals, political institutions, and craft activities of this ancient north coast civilization. Such efforts at visual reading and interpretation continue, supplemented by continued archaeology by which to contextualize the material.

Following Max Uhle's departure from the north coast of Peru in 1899, illicit excavations, archaeological research, and iconographic analyses in the region continued throughout the twentieth century at a fairly consistent pace—that is, until the late 1980s. In 1987, the world of Andean archaeology was taken by surprise by the chance discovery of elite tombs at Sipán. The succeeding excavations at the site revealed the most elaborate and undisturbed Moche funerary contexts ever found. Their discovery and excavation have since marked the beginning of a new era of research in Moche studies. Following the work at Sipán, Moche scholars began initiating long-term archaeological projects at numerous other Moche sites, including San José de Moro, Dos Cabezas, El Brujo, and Huacas de Moche. Also, valley-wide surveys have been undertaken in the Jequetepeque, Chicama, Moche, Chao, and Santa valleys to further define the extent of Moche occupation and influence.

This book is a reflection of the present state of Moche research, its advances, and problematics. The chapters in this volume touch upon not only the major sites and regions currently under investigation, but also the major methodologies being explored in the study of Moche culture. They demonstrate an authentic range of multidisciplinary approaches. While the authors in this volume often combine archaeological research with iconographic studies in their investigations, they incorporate additional analyses and varied methodological concerns to provide for a rich tableau of scholarly explorations.

Elizabeth P. Benson appropriately sets the stage for the remaining volume in the opening chapter. She presents a complex reflection on the nature of objects depicted in Moche iconography and their material counterparts recovered from archaeological contexts. Her overriding concern is to delimit the rules of object depiction—to examine what she terms Moche visual "shorthand." Benson discusses the presence of such iconographic shorthand in the nature of sacrificial scenes, depictions of architecture, and representations of clubs and maces, among other visual themes and motifs. By surveying the current expanse of research in Moche studies and the dimensions such research continues to add to analyses of Moche ceramic iconography, Benson exhibits her impressive work in the field of Moche studies, to which the 2003 Fourth D. J. Sibley Family Conference was dedicated.

In Chapter 2, Anne Marie Hocquenghem develops more fully her long-term approach to Moche iconography, which she founds on the structuralist theory of Claude Lévi-Strauss. Hocquenghem explores how religious attitudes and ritual practices recorded for a later period—post-conquest ethnohistoric and modern ethnographic studies—may elucidate the role of Moche rituals and religion as identified in the material record. Over the past thirty years, her work has inspired many investigators, especially Spanish- and French-speaking scholars, through the establishment and elaboration of this methodological approach. This volume presents for the first time a detailed publication of her research and methodology in English.

Another long-term study by Donna McClelland (Chapter 3) provides a review and elaboration of her extended project to identify a particular fruit species commonly represented in Moche iconography, known as the *ulluchu*. This final contribution exemplifies the manner in which an investigation may actively combine iconographic and archaeological material toward species identification. In this case, McClelland seeks out the still elusive fruit, the *ulluchu*, as it is depicted and encountered in the Moche visual and material record. The chapter presented here undoubtedly provides the most detailed analysis of this plant to date, as well as its multitudinous relations in Moche iconography with images of blood sacrifice, ritual warfare, and rulership. McClelland's chapter reflects her dedication to the details of such a focused investigation, the same dedication that she devoted to her invaluable reproductions of Moche fineline paintings. Sadly, Donna McClelland passed away before this final publication. The present volume is dedicated to her memory and her overwhelming contribution to the field of Moche studies.

The remaining twelve chapters complement the preceding long-term investigations by contributing further to methodological advancements and innovative multidisciplinary techniques in the field of Moche studies. The authors and their contributions center roughly around the major sites of Dos Cabezas in the Jequetepeque Valley, Huacas de Moche in the Moche Valley, and Sipán in the Lambeyeque Valley, as well as the Santa Valley region. Studies that are more site specific intersperse with chapters of greater regional concern. In this respect, recent explorations and recently introduced technical and scientific studies find equal placement with the flow of advancing archaeological and icono-

graphic investigations, localized and regionalized. The contributions reflect prevalent themes in Moche studies such as the influence of El Niño/Southern Oscillation (ENSO) on this north coast polity, the nature of Moche warfare and sacrifice, and the role of Moche visual culture in decoding social and political frameworks. The studies further demonstrate the continued interests and diverse pursuits of the individual scholars, thus substantiating a volume of increasingly specialized approaches and their relative application to the various research problems at hand in Moche studies.

Innovative and controversial, Michael E. Moseley, Christopher B. Donnan, and David K. Keefer (Chapter 5) utilize the site of Dos Cabezas in the Jequetepeque Valley as a case study for the investigation of social change on the north coast of Peru based on the detection of extreme ecological conditions. Among other factors, they suggest that the end of Moche occupation at Dos Cabezas coincided with a series of severe environmental conditions, such as massive floods and successive aeolian sand encroachments, brought about by a mega El Niño event. Moseley and his colleagues propose that such ecological disruptions noted at Dos Cabezas may eventually be detected at other Moche sites. Their model, which reflects in part the application of ecological determinism, may thus have far-reaching implications for future Moche investigations.

The role of El Niño in Moche studies has received ever-increasing attention over the past thirty years. This geoclimatic phenomenon, which occurs every four to seven years, brings torrential rains and flooding to the north coast of Peru, with warm Pacific waters temporarily replacing the cold Humboldt Current and its ecosystem, which run along the western coastline. Recent excavations in Plaza 3a at Huaca de la Luna strongly suggest the coordination of Moche sacrificial events with the occurrence of at least two such El Niño episodes. Moche iconographic studies may further lend increasing weight to the social or political emphasis placed on the El Niño phenomenon (see the chapters by Alva and Bourget, this volume). Therefore, research into the various effects and dating of El Niño and mega El Niño events on this north coast culture may provide critical insight into Moche identity and site interaction, as proposed by Moseley, Donnan, and Keefer for the site of Dos Cabezas.

In Chapter 6, Alana Cordy-Collins and Charles F. Merbs offer a detailed and extensive analysis regarding the health, pathologies, and social roles of five Moche giants buried together at the site of Dos Cabezas. These high-ranking individuals are perhaps some of the most intriguing Moche persons excavated to date. Following a meticulous forensic analysis, Cordy-Collins and Merbs suggest not only that the individual pathologies of the five giants reflect habitual practices such as kneeling or sitting, but also that such practices correspond to their prescribed rank in burial. The giants thus reinforce a link between a recognized physical practice and its representation in both the iconography and archaeological record. Following upon comparative forensic research of Moche human sacrificial victims (see Verano, this volume), this study evinces the range of disciplinary approaches that may serve to elucidate cultural practices, social roles, and hierarchies in Moche society. That such a detailed forensic study fits well within the theme of this volume testifies to the open and innovative state of Moche research.

Framing these studies at Dos Cabezas are two more chapters by Christopher B. Donnan and colleagues discussing the creation, design, and possible significance of particular sets of Moche ceramic and metal artifacts. In a groundbreaking study, Christopher B. Donnan (Chapter 4) explores the masking traditions of the Moche. He provides a detailed examination of the composition and design of assorted mask types created and used by the Moche. Donnan compares the masks uncovered in the archaeological record with those represented in Moche iconography in order to evince their variable functions. Such a comprehensive analysis provides the material necessary to better define the specified ritual practices of this ancient north coast society.

The contribution by Christopher B. Donnan, David A. Scott, and Todd Bracken (Chapter 7) was not presented at the 2003 Sibley conference. Nevertheless, the chapter presents invaluable research on the metallurgical techniques employed by the Moche. The authors' approach is thoroughly technical and experimental. By illuminating the manner of Moche metallurgy, the study will undoubtedly facilitate future interpretations of the use and value of particular Moche metal objects. Such technical investigations are crucial for a better understanding of the inherent value and symbolism of

Moche material culture, including the items used in ritual practice.

In Chapter 8, Claude Chapdelaine shifts the regional attention briefly to the extreme south of the Moche sphere of influence. Chapdelaine explores the identification of Moche in the Santa Valley, where he has worked continuously since 2000. He examines the relationship that may have existed between the Santa Valley populations and those living in the center of the Southern Moche state, presumably in the Moche Valley, based on their comparative material culture (ceramics). Following a comprehensive discussion of the ceramic forms and their distribution, Chapdelaine suggests the presence of a more localized Santa style as expressive perhaps of the emergence of a regional identity. Chapdelaine thus addresses the nature of Moche cultural distribution, state establishment, and social identity in the southern sphere.

The Huacas de Moche site in the Moche Valley is generally considered the regional capital of this Southern Moche sphere and has witnessed considerable excavations since the time of Max Uhle at the end of the nineteenth century. In 1991, the University of Trujillo began a long-term project at Huaca de la Luna, directed by Santiago Uceda. In Chapter 9, Uceda presents a provocative analysis regarding the social identity of one class of specialized individuals buried in the site's main platform (Platform I). Uceda explores the specific social roles of this class of buried individuals based on his identification, examination, and interpretation of corresponding figures and their implements represented in certain iconographic scenes. An effigy pelt worn or carried by these individuals was uncovered in a buried cache in Platform I. As Benson references in Chapter 1, the effigy presents a one-to-one correspondence between the iconography and the archaeological record. Uceda's investigation of the burials and cached objects thus considers not only the identification of the particular class of individuals associated with such emblematic implements. He further explores their placement and role in a proposed Moche social or ritual framework, in ritual battles and human sacrifice.

Between 1995 and 2001, two key deposits of human sacrificial victims were excavated by Steve Bourget, and by John Verano and Moises Tufinio within Plazas 3a and 3c, respectively, adjacent to Platform I of Huaca de la Luna. The excavations, analyses, and forensic studies of these two arenas and their human remains have since spawned increasing interest in and debate on the nature of Moche warfare and human sacrifice. The succeeding two chapters, focusing on Huaca de la Luna, thus appropriately address the nature of Moche human sacrifice. Venturing a relatively novel form of scientific research, Izumi Shimada and his colleagues (Chapter 10) explore the social and political organization of the Moche through a genetic study of the sacrificial victims at Huaca de la Luna. Different in intent and scale than previous studies performed at the Sicán site of Huaca Loro in the La Leche Valley, Shimada and colleagues investigate and evaluate what mitochondrial DNA analyses may reveal about the biodiversity of Moche participants in sacrificial practices at the Southern Moche capital. While understandably controversial in its application, this relatively new research technique provides for an increasingly more complex and comprehensive profile of Moche rulers, sacrificial victims, and general population.

John Verano follows in Chapter 11 with an updated discussion of his forensic analyses of the sacrificial victims from both Plazas 3a and 3c at Huaca de la Luna. Verano compares the human remains found in the two plazas in order to examine the nature and sequence of sacrificial practices at the site. Based on his inspections of the skeletal material, Verano posits a series of complex Moche ritual practices and suggests their variation across time. In this contribution, Verano thus continues his investigations into and interpretations of the nature of Moche human sacrifice, as well as Moche warfare, based on the relevant forensic data.

In the following chapter, Jeffrey Quilter (Chapter 12) pursues this perhaps most elusive and actively debated topic in Moche studies—the nature of Moche warfare and militarism—through a comparatively different approach. Quilter investigates the objects of Moche militarism and the identity of warriors in the iconography and archaeological record, advancing upon previous research by Larco Hoyle. In order to tease out the meaning of Moche warfare and its representation, Quilter adopts a comparative method, referencing similar activities performed or represented by the Japanese samurai, the French and English during the Hundred Years' War, and the painted Attic vases of Ancient Greece, among

others. The controversial topic of Moche warfare and the comparative approach taken provide weight to this particular contribution, which incites discussion of the proper manner for interpreting Moche militarism through the iconographic and archaeological records.

With a comparable critical eye to methodology, Jean-François Millaire (Chapter 13) turns his gaze to the assessment of Moche social practices—in this case, Moche textile production. Millaire examines the representation of this craft production in Moche iconography, particularly in the example known as the Weaver's Scene, a fineline drawing from a Moche Phase IV *florero* currently housed in the British Museum. Based on his analysis, Millaire challenges the notion of large-scale, organized textile production proposed in recent studies. He suggests rather a revision of the methodological approach that led to the identification of such a specialized mode of production in Moche society. Notably at odds, then, in Millaire's discussion are comparative interpretations of the archaeological and iconographic data, and the methodologies taken to align these two fields properly.

The volume naturally concludes by returning to the site of Sipán in the Lambayeque Valley. As mentioned above, the tombs discovered at this site in 1987 launched the recent age and success of intensive research and investigation. At the 2003 Sibley symposium, Walter Alva, director of the Sipán excavations, presented a paper by his son Néstor, which is translated here from the original Spanish (Chapter 14). In this contribution, Néstor Alva ventures a species identification of the spider representations most common in Moche iconography. As a point of departure, Alva addresses the objects found within the high-status burial of Tomb 3 at Sipán. Rather than focus on the identity of the Tomb 3 occupant, Alva directs his attention to the biological indicators of the spider motif, which appears extensively in this funerary assemblage. His investigation examines both preceding Cupisnique representations and various contemporary Moche forms. It thus contributes to an ever-increasing body of publications exploring the concept of a ritual ecology among the Prehispanic cultures of the Peruvian north coast.

In the final chapter, Steve Bourget (Chapter 15) returns to the site of Sipán, and the occupant of Tomb 3 in particular. Bourget suggests that the social and ritual identity of the main individual buried in the third tomb may have eluded the scrutiny of previous investigators. He proposes that this tomb, in fact, may have been the resting place of an individual depicted in the Sacrifice Ceremony. As such, the proposed identification follows a series of relatively recent archaeological discoveries that have recognized Sacrifice Ceremony individuals buried at sites such as San José de Moro, Huaca de La Cruz and Sipán. Bourget's analysis of this early Sipán ruler, through a thorough evaluation of his funerary assemblage and context, contributes to a greater understanding not only of the identified persona within, but also of the overall nature of Moche rulership.

The Fourth D. J. Sibley Conference at the University of Texas at Austin in 2003 sought to bring together some of the most distinguished and innovative scholarship on Moche art, arts, and archaeology. The contributions presented in this volume reflect this goal, presenting long-standing methodologies alongside the diversity and innovation of disciplinary approaches and techniques available to Moche scholars. The contributions range from the most detailed and comprehensive evaluations of material and visual culture to the broadest interpretations of Moche social and ritual practice and identity. Following the theme of the symposium, most authors readily address and investigate the critical interpretive value at the conjunction of the archaeological and artistic records. The present volume thus offers but one of many past, and no doubt future, compiled bodies of research that are needed to eventually bring to life the Moche art of museum and private collections, as well as the vast array of archaeological contexts slowly but surely being unearthed from the sands of the Peruvian north coast.

THE ART AND ARCHAEOLOGY OF THE MOCHE

CHAPTER ONE

Iconography Meets Archaeology

ELIZABETH P. BENSON, INSTITUTE OF ANDEAN STUDIES

Abstract

For many years, attempts to understand the Moche world were largely dependent upon the rich iconography of the ceramic bottles. After the last fifteen or so years of fairly constant archaeological investigation, archaeology is now being used to explain the iconography. In some instances, archaeology has provided for the first time actual examples of objects known only from ceramic depictions. In other instances, architectural excavations have revealed structures and rooms of types that appear on the ceramics in abbreviated form. These comparisons instruct us in the ways that the Moche put their realities into compact visual expression, and they give evidence of what in the iconography actually existed and what was a gloss to express the numinous quality of the art. Archaeology has further uncovered new forms and new concepts within Moche metallurgy and mural art, and it is pointing out differences in the northern and southern regions in Moche approaches to art and iconography. Archaeology also raises many new questions as it expands and enriches our knowledge of iconography.

There is great Moche art; there are many media for Moche art; and the archaeology of the last fifteen or so years has made a critical difference in knowledge of Moche art. Beginning with Max Uhle, a little over a hundred years ago, many contributions to Moche studies have been made, but the concentration and achievement of the recent work are unparalleled.

Dependent largely on the sea and irrigation farming, the Moche people, in most of the first three-quarters of the first millennium AD, lived in river valleys that cut through expanses of sand on the desert north coast of Peru, a narrow, over 400-mile-long strip between the Pacific Ocean and some of the world's highest mountains. The Moche domain included ties with offshore islands and the sierra. Distinct northern and southern Moche regions are defined, in part, by major differences in art. The southern ceramics, with line drawing or sculptural forms, richly display gods, people, ceremonies, and environmental elements, presented usually on distinctive stirrup spout bottles. Thanks particularly to recent investigations of architecture at Huaca de la Luna (in the Moche Valley) and Huaca Cao Viejo (Chicama Valley), a quantity of striking murals and painted reliefs is now known. Moche textiles, which are expertly and inventively woven, though often poorly preserved, will not be discussed here, and I will say little about the remarkable Moche metallurgy. I would like to note that various craft workshops have been discovered and that knowledge of craft production has increased through recent excavations.

Moche architecture, murals, and fine crafts mirror developments in Moche political history, for they embody the will and the administrative and cosmological needs of rulers, for whom the arts were an important part of their politico-religious power structure. The subject matter of the ceramics sometimes seems only naturalistic—a portrait, a llama, maize, or potatoes—but it probably always has symbolic, ritual, and/or mythic significance. The rules for what was shown and how it was shown must have been quite strict, yet there was allowance—and perhaps need—for the fresh and creative spirit that gives life to any fine art; enlivening seems to have been very much a part of Moche artistic endeavor. For many years, attempts to understand the Moche world were dependent largely on the rich iconography of the ceramic bottles. After the last fifteen years of field investigation, the archaeology is beginning to explain the ceramic iconography.

Although the ceramics yield many kinds of information, it has long been obvious that certain important subjects were missing; now the tables are turned, and archaeological evidence exists for ritual activities for which there are no obvious images. For example, subjects such as the offering-room group at Pacatnamú and the room with skulls at Dos Cabezas (both Jequetepeque Valley sites) described by Alana Cordy-Collins (1997, 2001a) do not appear in ceramic scenes, nor does a burning event that took place at Pacatnamú. That funerary rites were a significant activity is obvious from the archaeology, yet ceramics tell little about them except for examples of the very late Burial Theme in the northern region (Donnan and McClelland 1979) and middle-period depictions of probable grave goods in the south. On the other hand, some depicted rites are not obvious in the archaeology. Evidence for the deer hunt, for example, a major middle-period theme (Donnan 1997; Donnan and McClelland 1999; Kutscher 1983: Abbn. 69–87), has not yet been found in excavations and would perhaps be difficult to identify; deer remains are rare. Some ceremonies are not obvious in either art or archaeology. The enthronement of a ruler was surely a major rite, but one difficult for archaeology to reveal and not distinguishable in iconography. Are effigy portrayals of an important man, seated on a platform, sometimes with a small feline, condensed/shorthand descriptions of accession? Is one of the depicted rites an unrecognized accession ceremony—the ritual chewing of coca leaves, for example, or a sacrificial libation rite?

The confrontation of archaeology and iconography raises new sets of questions and categories. Indeed, archaeological discoveries rarely match exactly what we are seeking on the basis of the iconography, which has special symbolic-language rules. This very observation teaches us something about the Moche mind. I would like to explore this subject, first noting some instances of matching iconography and recent archaeology.

Correspondences

Twenty years ago, in a manuscript for the *Metropolitan Museum of Art Bulletin* (Benson 1984a), I wrote that certain sacrifice-associated figures in the art wear a tunic of metal platelets sewn onto cloth. Julie Jones, the Metropolitan curator, looking at the manuscript, asked if I had ever seen such a garment. I had seen an actual Chimu example, but not a Moche one; I could not prove that was what it was. I was relieved to learn soon afterwards that Walter Alva had found one at Sipán, the first example known (Alva and Donnan 1993: figs. 57, 245).

A correspondence noted by many people is that between a figure in a sacrificial rite that Christopher Donnan first described in 1975 as the Presentation Theme, a figure identified by several people (Berezkin 1980 [1981]; Hocquenghem and Lyon 1980) as a woman, whom I believe to be a supernatural being. She wears a variable but distinctive headdress with a projection at either side. In 1991, Donnan and Luis Jaime Castillo (1992, 1994; see also Donnan, this volume) excavated at San José de Moro (Jequetepeque Valley) the burial of a priestess with the same accessories; the following year they excavated another.

The supernatural woman—I think that she is a moon goddess (Benson 1985)—is also depicted seated in a crescent that is sometimes a raft. The many examples of this scene excavated at San José de Moro fit Donna McClelland's (1990) finding of an increase in marine subject matter in her sample of Late Moche vase drawings. The late marine scenes show supernatural beings on possibly sacrificial missions; the "hold" of the raft is often occupied by captives. Unlike earlier scenes, in which anyone in a raft usually has a fishing line, almost no one in the last Moche phase is fishing. Drop nets are often attached to the goddess's raft, and Cordy-Collins (2001b) points out the probability that a weight for a net is attached to the goddess's garment. A possible argument against the weight interpretation is that, as far as I know, fishing gear has not been excavated in female burials. Nevertheless, this female was a goddess strongly associated with the sea, and in one Late Moche-Huari scene, she is fishing (Donnan and McClelland 1999: fig. 5.39). Instead of the weight, or in addition to it, she can have what looks like a small, wrapped and tied gift, or she holds a cloth or bag in which there is an object not yet tied (Donnan and McClelland 1999: figs. 5.19, 5.58). We now know that many burial offerings were wrapped or tied. If her raft trip relates to the voyage to the other world through the sea, these images are appropriate to her journey. In fineline ceramic scenes, apparent grave goods are tied together. Dancers holding a cord or cloth (Donnan 1982: figs. 7–12) may belong to the funerary rite; this fiber or cloth is possibly intended for burial

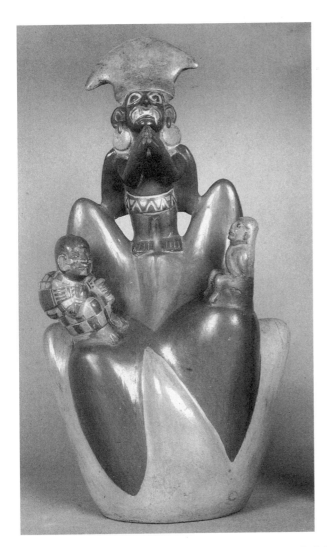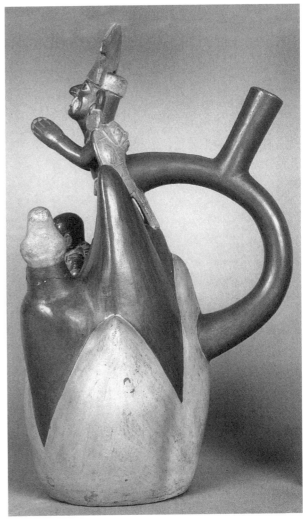

FIGURE 1.1. Middle Moche stirrup spout bottle with the god of the coca rite wearing the pendant. With him are a captive and a man holding a lime gourd for use in the coca rite. Courtesy of the National Museum of the American Indian (23/4865).

offerings. As for the wrapping, cloth was precious and added preciousness. Wrapping gave an offered object a special ambience.

An object previously known only on ceramics appears usually in scenes related to the coca-chewing rite, where it is suspended on a cord around the neck of a figure that I take to be the patron god of the rite. The object has a metal-platelet body, arms, wings, or hands, and a feline or batlike head (Donnan and McClelland 1999: figs. 4.19, 4.90; Uceda, this volume). On fineline bottles, it usually swings out to the back from the god's body or floats in space; on a modeled bottle, it lies against the

god's back (Figure 1.1) or, in at least one case, the side (Figure 1.2). I had surmised that it was a bag, because coca leaves are carried in a bag and because the object looks like a god's superbag.

In 1999, the Museo Arqueológico de la Universidad Nacional de Trujillo exhibited the contents of a burial cache excavated in Platform I of Huaca de la Luna that included the first actual example known of the pictured pendant (Morales, Asmat, and Fernández 2002; Uceda, this volume). It is much more complex than the pottery drawings, but it is clearly the same object, and it is not a bag (Figure 1.3). It has a gold-encased, wooden feline

FIGURE 1.2. Modeled god with the pendant and coca rite attributes. Staatliche Museen zu Berlin—Preussischer Kulturbesitz, Ethnologisches Museum (VA-17573).

head; the long body with four clawed feet is made of hide and cotton cloth with gilded silver, gilded copper, sea shells, feathers, cinnabar, and resin. A step design—a symbol of importance—is formed in its center.

On the ceramics, the pendant is normally worn by the god, but it can appear on a human. One human effigy wearing this object has a bag and Maltese-cross face paint (Donnan and Donnan 1997: fig. 43), both associated with the coca rite, and another has a raised-hands headdress, which also belongs to the rite (Figure 1.4; see Benson 1979). In some coca scenes (Bourget 1994: fig. 3.29; Hocquenghem 1987: fig. 70), the god wears a headless version, and a simpler example may float before the enthroned human ritualist on the other side of the

vessel. A bottle in the British Museum depicts a human with this object on his back but no other coca traits (Figure 1.5). His unusual headdress and a similar object can appear in another ceremony (the "waterlily" or "badminton" rite [De Bock 1998: fig. 3; see also Donnan 1978: fig. 114]). Ordinarily, the two ritual complexes do not share traits. When one problem is solved, another puzzle appears. The excavated object, however, exhibits a reasonably simple relationship between archaeology and iconography.

In comparing archaeology and ceramic imagery, it becomes clear that the iconography usually speaks in a kind of shorthand: the ceramics do not reproduce scenes or objects in detail; they present certain basic material

FIGURE 1.4. A man with facial hair and raised-hands headdress wearing the pendant in front. Museo Nacional de Arqueología, Antropología, e Historia del Perú, Lima. Photograph by author.

FIGURE 1.3. Multimedia pendant from burial cache in Huaca de la Luna. Photograph by Steve Bourget, with thanks to Ricardo Morales and Miguel Asmat.

FIGURE 1.5. Middle Moche effigy bottle of man wearing a pendant. By kind permission of the Trustees of the British Museum. Photograph by author.

information and certain basic numinous information, often quite minimally. Moche images seem not intended to describe, explain, or explore, but to convey core meaning. I find that I have used the term *shorthand* in the past without seeing its implications. Now I realize that it is significant in terms of how the Moche were thinking and how we are to read their art. (One must not forget, of course, that the archaeological object is also iconographic, but the iconography is somewhat different from that of its ceramic depiction.)

Architecture

Now I would like to enter a more complicated maze. Architectural depictions are a frequent ceramic theme, drawn in fineline scenes or modeled in fired or raw clay; examples exist also in stone and wood. Some may have been models for, or of, actual structures (Castillo 2001: fig. 8; Castillo and Donnan 1994; Castillo, Nelson, and Nelson 1997; see also Donnan 1978: figs. 132–139; Donnan and McClelland 1999; Franco and Murga 2001). There are elaborate Early Moche examples of effigy architecture, often in a compressed form (see Morales 2003: fig. 14.2). Effigies with provenience come mostly from late burials. Some appear to depict temples, some tombs. All may be cosmic models.

A high official (or perhaps an ancestor), seated in a structure at the top of a pyramid or platform in a small space just large enough for him, is portrayed in ceram-

FIGURE 1.6. Middle Moche temple vase with maces on roof and a figure inside. American Museum of Natural History (41.2/8022). Photograph by Christopher B. Donnan.

ics, sculptural or fineline, often those depicting sacrifice (Figure 1.6). Actual structures generally resembling the ceramic ones have been excavated at Huaca de la Luna and Huaca Cao Viejo (Figures 1.7, 1.8). What the ceramics do not show is that the small spaces like those on bottles were part of a much larger architectural scheme. There are no huge structures or plazas in the ceramic art. Again, we learn something about ceramic shorthand. A reconstruction drawing of Luna shows a large area adjacent to the node space (Figure 1.7). The node space has been called an altar. If it is an altar, it points out a drastic difference between archaeology and iconography, for the latter does not depict altars but does show a ruler or a supernatural being seated in such a space on ceremonial occasions.

Until recent excavations, Moche architecture had not been much studied, certainly not sacred precincts like those at la Luna and Cao Viejo with their successive building stages. The ceramic representations give little idea of architectural complexity and of the process of ritually "burying" and re-creating sacred structures. Santiago Uceda has written: "We now feel that the rebuildings were linked to veneration of ancestors, and that the architectural renovations served to reinforce ancestral and priestly power at Huaca de la Luna" (2001:62). This building activity, discussed particularly by Uceda (1997, 2001) and also by the Cao Viejo team (Franco, Gálvez, and Vásquez 1998a, 1999a, 2001), is not obvious in the iconography.

FIGURE 1.7. Huaca de la Luna. Reconstruction drawing of the upper platform of Platform I, with the "royal pavilion" at the upper left. Photograph courtesy of Proyecto Puesta en Valor Huacas de Moche.

FIGURE 1.8. Huaca Cao Viejo, showing the upper structure. Photograph by Steve Bourget.

Roofs of ceramic buildings often have motifs that likely relate to ritual activity. The step motif is easy to form with adobes; the practice probably existed but might be hard to identify from fallen structures or eroded adobes. Foxes or felines occasionally prowl roofs or ramps (Donnan and McClelland 1999: fig. 4.48); these likely express a numinous concept not to be found in excavation. Moche art uses not only shorthand but additional glosses on subjects; it is often hard to know whether the reality was more than meets the eye—or less.

The Mace, or War Club, As a Symbol

On Moche ceramics, the roofs of temples and sacred precincts, where a lord sits or sacrifice takes place, are often lined with mace heads (Figures 1.6, 1.7). Maces may symbolize sacrificial offerings. A large copper scepter from Sipán displays a striking example of maces lining the roof of a sacred, elite-structure model (Alva

1994: Láms. 79–82; Alva and Donnan 1993: figs. 47, 48). A question used to be asked: Were maces put into the picture to symbolize the associations of the structure or the rite, or were they real architectural features? Clay maces from structures have now been found as offerings in a very early level (Edifice E) at Huaca Cao Viejo (Franco, Gálvez, and Vásquez 2002:95) and at Sipán, Dos Cabezas, and Huaca de la Luna in building remains and offering caches. From evidence at Huaca de la Luna and Huaca Cao Viejo, important buildings atop the platforms probably had maces on the roof (which could be seen from afar); the pavilion with the Complex Theme murals in the plaza at Huaca Cao Viejo also had them (Figures 1.8, 1.9; Franco, Gálvez, and Vásquez 2001; Uceda 2001).

The motif is a war club; men with clubs and shields march or face each other in murals at Huaca de la Luna and Huaca Cao Viejo, in earlier-published paintings at Pañamarca (Bonavia 1985), and on fineline bottles,

FIGURE 1.9. Huaca Cao Viejo. Reconstruction drawing of the pavilion with Complex Theme murals. Courtesy of Régulo Franco Jordán and the Programa Arqueológico Complejo El Brujo.

where warriors carry clubs of varying proportions and sometimes use them. Modeled-ceramic kneeling warriors hold a club and a shield. Hunters in ritual deer and sea lion hunts wield a club. I use the word *mace*, however, because the implement is much more than a club; it is a symbol of power or office, a kind of scepter, and all that a scepter signifies. The mace is one of the most important symbols in Moche iconography and a recurring theme in this book.

Steve Bourget found a hefty wooden mace in a tomb in the sacrificial area that he excavated at Huaca de la Luna (Bourget 1997, 2001; Bourget and Newman 1998). Tests revealed that it had been "repeatedly drenched" with human blood, vivid evidence for the realism of ceramic images of warriors hitting opponents on the skull. Other wooden maces, some of which had been sheathed in copper, have turned up in excavations—in a grave at Dos Cabezas, for example (Donnan 2003:62). Some wooden ones look sturdy; others are long and thin, useful in ritual but not for serious bashing. At Huaca Cao Viejo, wooden maces were offerings (Figure 1.10). Basing their study on shape and manufacture, Franco, Gálvez, and Vásquez (1999b) established a chronological sequence of maces at Huaca Cao Viejo. The authors call them emblematic clubs, noting that they are objects of command and magico-religious power; a mace is the principal ritual baton.

In the tomb of the Lord of Sipán, Alva excavated one metal knife-scepter bearing a large mace at either side of a shaft, which displays warrior garments in relief; another scepter with a figure standing over a captive, holding a prominent mace; and a pair of intricately made ear ornaments, remarkable pieces of gold work, featuring a man holding a mace and a shield (Alva 1994: Láms. 39–41, 79–83; Alva and Donnan 1993: cover and figs. 86–88, 104–106). At the bottom of the tomb lay miniature copper maces, along with miniature shields and spears. Maces appeared also in other Sipán tombs (Alva 2001).

A major motif in fineline ceramics consists of a mace as the center and support of a "weapons bundle," which commonly contains emblematic Moche weapons (Hocquenghem 1987: figs. 84–93). A weapons bundle may show a captured mace hanging upside down from an erect Moche one. The bundle can be the center of a ritual scene or the only motif on a bottle; many of the fineline bottles that appeared in Late Moche at San José de Moro have a weapons bundle on the spout above the primary design (Castillo 2003: fig. 18.17). It seems to be a kind of logo for that site in the late period. Indeed, it may be a logo for the Moche.

Some mace heads in fineline scenes have human-like heads. The human-headed mace is often stuck into the sand in scenes of the presentation of captives for sacrifice; it also appears in supernatural scenes. An effigy bottle in the form of a mace may have a god or animal head. Sometimes a mace is additionally animated with legs and arms. A human-headed mace may even take a captive. No actual human-headed mace has been found. It was likely a philosophical concept; the head was a

FIGURE 1.10. Wooden mace from Huaca Cao Viejo. Photograph by author.

gloss to enliven the mace, to express spirit and power, and probably to indicate sacrifice—by beheading or throat-slitting—that achieved that spirit and power.

Many writers have commented on the face-to-face battle depicted in Moche art (see Verano 2001a:112). This may have been an actual fighting method, especially in what was surely ritualized battle. But this might be another example of a kind of metonymy in Moche art. Slings and spear-throwers are shown but not used. This rather fits the pattern of other shorthand depictions. It probably should not be an argument against serious warfare.

Sacrifice and the Disposition of Body Parts

"Until recently most of our information on the subject of human sacrifice in the Moche culture came from the study of its iconography," Bourget has said (2001:89). Evidence of sacrifice is seen in Early Moche ceramics. In the larger scenes of the middle period, a depicted ritual sequence begins with a battle in which captives are taken; the stripped captives are then led to be presented before rulers, captains, or priests. Two victims often appear in a scene, but little archaeological evidence has been found for this pairing. It may reflect Andean dualism; it may be an abbreviated depiction of larger-scale sacrifice. Warriors and priests work together in these scenes, and warriors often wear some priestly garment. It is interesting that Alva (2001:242) has found priest and warrior types interred in somewhat different parts of the same burial mound at Sipán. In this sacrificial rite, a throat was slit for blood to be offered to the gods or ancestors. Throat-slitting or decapitation is performed by an anthropozoomorph or a disguised or transformed human in warrior garments. A normal mortal is never pictured in this act, but remains of what seem to be mortal sacrificers have been found at Huaca de la Luna and Dos Cabezas (Bourget 1997, 1998; Bourget and Millaire 2000; Cordy-Collins 2001a). Human victims in ceramic scenes are sometimes placed in the context of a mythic event—the Presentation Theme, or Sacrifice Ceremony—with gods who hold and pass a stemmed cup, or goblet, presumably filled with blood. The process can also be shown with humans (all but the sacrificer); an enthroned ruler holds the cup or is presented with it. A cup of this kind from the Museum für Völkerkunde, Berlin, proved, on testing, to be positive for human blood

(Bourget 2001; Bourget and Newman 1998). Whether the blood was drunk or offered in some way, whether some cups held blood and some *chicha*, or when the libations or offerings might have been performed is still unknown. A cup of this type, apparently bloodless, was excavated at San José de Moro; painted on it is a series of human-headed clubs holding cups like the one on which they appear (Castillo 2001:314; Donnan and McClelland 1999: fig. 5.21). The cup is sometimes held to the face of a human-headed mace, or the mace holds it to its own mouth (Kutscher 1983: Abb. 269). Apparently, no other figure in these scenes is shown drinking the contents of the cup. In the last period, the goddess in the raft may hold such a cup to her mouth (Donnan and McClelland 1999: figs. 6.163, 6.166).

The first known large-scale Moche sacrifices were found in 1995 in Plaza 3a, Huaca de la Luna, by Bourget (1997, 1998, 2001; Bourget and Millaire 2000; see also Uceda 2001; Verano 1998, 2001a, 2001b, and this volume). The site includes part of a rock outcrop that was surely sacred. Embedded in clay around it, associated with El Niño rains, the approximately 70 individuals, from at least five sacrifice episodes, were males with an average age in the mid-twenties; there were few complete skeletons but many partial skeletons and isolated bones. The victims had been strong and physically active, with fractures that were well healed; some had recent injuries. The skeletons show traces of torture, throat-cutting, and dismembering of arms, legs, and feet. The use of rocks and metal knives is indicated. Ceramics picture supernaturals using crescent-shaped knives; a few scenes show human rock-throwers.

In some ceramic scenes with a sacrificial victim or victims (and in certain scenes without a victim), cut-off arms, legs, and heads (often with rope ties) float in space, seeming to indicate what happened or will happen. In at least one instance, detached limbs are the sole, repeated motif on a vessel (Figure 1.11). The excavation of Plaza 3a and burials and offerings at several sites provide new data: the Moche moved body parts from one burial to another, the entombed as well as the sacrificed (Alva 2001; Bourget 1997, 2001; Cordy-Collins 1997; Franco, Gálvez, and Vásquez 1998a, 1999a; Hecker and Hecker 1992; Uceda 1997:186; 2001; Verano 1997, 2001a). Some burials have extra skulls; some are missing an arm or a leg, or have an extra limb. Mandibles in burials might have been removed, since disarticulated mandibles were found in Plaza 3a.

Bone mixing and offering had many variations. Uceda and Tufinio (2003:218) have written that the offering of bones from old burials was related to the renovation of the temple, and that burial of officials in a temple was tied to renovation of ancestors in the world of the living. Bones and burials were offered for renewal of power and legitimacy. The Plaza 3a remains roughly match ceramic scenes of captured-warrior sacrifice, but the iconography barely hints at scattering.

Pottery also was found broken up and distributed in excavated burials—a sherd here, most of a bottle there (Donnan 2001, 2003; Franco, Gálvez, and Vásquez 1998a:13, 1999a). With the human remains in Plaza 3a, Bourget (1997, 1998) found at least fifty shattered, unfired clay effigies of seated, nude, human males with ropes around the necks and painted designs on the body and face, including the mandible. The effigies are exceptionally well made, detailed, and sometimes quite beautiful; the heads are idealized or portrait-like. In ceramic iconography, whole vessels appear in most ritual scenes, possibly marking the scene as funeral- or sacrifice-related. Pottery was itself an iconographic symbol. Breaking it and moving broken pieces would be a part of its symbolism and part of a rite, but the iconography gives no indication of breaking ceramics.

Skeletons, treated somewhat differently from those in Plaza 3a, were encountered in a nearby, earlier (but more recently excavated) sacrificial site at Huacade la Luna, Plaza 3c (Orbegoso 1998; Uceda 2000; Verano 1998, 2001a, this volume). The victims in both plazas had cervical and other cut marks and healing injuries; several weeks had passed between injury and death. Both groups had sherds of ceramic captives with them. The Plaza 3c bodies had received intentional, complicated postmortem treatment. Bodies had been flayed, partially disarticulated, and arranged; in some instances, bones had been tied together with rope. Plaza 3c was sealed over when Plaza 3a was in use. There was no obvious tie with an El Niño event in Plaza 3c.

Both excavation and iconography indicate that there was more than one occasion for, or one type of, sacrifice, but the archaeological remains do not exactly match the depicted rites. The awkward fit may be a matter of shorthand or of chronology. An apparent acceleration of sac-

FIGURE 1.11. Early Moche bottle with cut-off "running" legs. Museo Nacional de Arqueología, Antropología, e Historia del Perú, Lima.

rificial rites occurred during the last decades of Moche power, when the Moche were confronted not only with serious El Niño events but also with periods of drought (see Moseley, Donnan, and Keefer; Quilter; and Verano, this volume). Most of the examples of depicted sacrifice are earlier. The ceramics show, in addition to sacrifices related to the Presentation Theme and its human version, a probable sacrificial occasion with captives who have attributes of the coca rite, pendant-disk ear ornaments or Maltese-cross face paint (Benson 1984b; Uceda, this volume).

A different interpretation relates to a ceramic subject often called the Dance of the Dead, commonly rendered in relief technique: partially skeletal figures, accompanied by skeletal musicians, dance in a line. Uceda

(2000:211, 213) sees a possible relationship between these figures and the manipulable, rigged skeletons from Plaza 3c. (The unarranged Plaza 3a skeletons are sometimes found in postures that suggest dancing, a curious parallel.) In a modern Day of the Dead rite at Mórrope, in Lambayeque, skulls and long bones are placed in small chapels outside the cemetery to signify the presence of the dead (Vreeland 1992). Descendants of the dead come to feast, drink, visit, and chat. Many Andean ethnographic accounts describe a gradual process from living to dead and the ritual stages that go with this. The idea that the dances belong to funerary procedures or the continuing life of the dead has long been present (Arsenault 1993; Benson 1975; Hocquenghem 1987:138). The idea that skeletons were manipulated is new.

In the past, the only archaeological evidence for sacrifice consisted of bodies of those buried with the important dead. Huaca de la Cruz (Virú Valley) and, more recently, Sipán, Dos Cabezas, and San José de Moro have yielded bodies that accompanied an elite burial (Alva 1994; Alva and Donnan 1993; Donnan 2003; Donnan and Castillo 1994; Strong and Evans 1952; Verano 2001b). Such burials are apt to contain the primary corpse accompanied by a guardian or priest (who often lacks feet or has his feet tied), one or two women, and a child. This pattern is basically the cast of characters of the Dance of the Dead, where a frontal figure with the two-disk headdress of certain important live figures can appear, a little more prominently than the other figures; he looks like the primary burial. There is at least one woman, a child, and a priestly figure. Daniel Arsenault (1993), noting a prosthesis on the priest in some scenes, concludes that foot-removal mutilation marked a special escort of the nobility in this world and the other.[1]

Sacrificial acts and funerary activities form a node for the meeting of archaeology and iconography. Both areas, however, are complex, and much of the relationship has yet to be clarified. Do the dance scenes, for example, represent activity of a newly dead group? Do they depict a ritual performance using bones of sacrifice victims? Or are these two concepts merged?

Dynastic Possibilities

I would like to finish with a few subjects that are superficially simpler but, I think, suggestive. Portrayals on ceramics generally have certain headgear that is informative of status and activity. The archaeology, however, reveals some distinctive headgear that is seemingly peculiar to a site, which suggests that they might symbolize dynastic power and lineages. Burials at Dos Cabezas, excavated by Donnan and Guillermo Cock (Donnan 2001, 2003), contain multiple examples of a fairly tall, straight-sided crown not yet found elsewhere. An Early Moche–style bottle in one of the tombs portrays a man with a generally similar headdress (Donnan 2003: Lám. 2.2c). At Huaca Cao Viejo, the Complex Theme murals are late and very differently composed from other murals there and elsewhere, although they include motifs familiar from ceramics: priests, animals, vegetation, nets, and boats (Franco, Gálvez, and Vásquez 1994, 1998b; Franco and Vilela 2003; Gálvez and Briceño 2001: fig. 21).[2] A candidate for a lineage symbol in the murals is unusual headgear, topped with tapered projections ending in circles, that resembles a medieval European crown; it is worn by a recurring figure who might be an ancestor introduced toward the end of occupation of the site by a new ruling family (Figure 1.12).

An earlier, large human figure on a post, all carved from a single piece of *lúcumo* wood (Figure 1.13), was buried, probably as an offering, in a new construction stage at Huaca Cao Viejo (Franco and Gálvez 2003; Franco, Gálvez, and Vásquez 2003: Lám. 19.4). It would seem to be a previous ancestor standing under the protection of two large-scale, facing images of a mythical creature that goes by many names (Figure 1.14). Most commonly referred to as the Moon animal or crested animal, it has long been known on ceramics, including several early bottles in the Museo Arqueológico Rafael Larco Herrera that likely came from the Chicama Valley, where the Larco collection was formed (Benson 2003: Láms. 15.2, 15.3; Larco 2001).[3] The creature is prominent in Early Moche. The lineage of Huaca Cao Viejo and the surrounding El Brujo site may have considered it ancestral. Small wooden scepters excavated at Cao Viejo show the creature with shell inlay at the top (Figure 1.15; Franco, Gálvez, and Vásquez 2001:161, foto 25), and recent work at the site revealed a wall of repeated images of the motif in an early phase of the structure (Figure 1.16). The animal appears as a design on the rear wall of the temple bottle in Figure 1.6[4] and on the rear wall of the copper architectural staff from Sipán (could this have been a mace captured from Huaca Cao Viejo?); in both

FIGURE 1.12. Huaca Cao Viejo. Detail of Complex Theme mural showing crowned figure. Photograph by author.

FIGURE 1.13. Wooden sculpture excavated in Huaca Cao Viejo, seen on exhibit in Banco Wiese, Trujillo, Peru. Photograph by Steve Bourget.

FIGURE 1.14. Detail of the crested animal pair above the head seen in Figure 1.13. Photograph courtesy of Régulo Franco Jordán and the Programa Arqueológico Complejo "El Brujo."

FIGURE 1.15. Small wooden staff with crested animal in shell, seen on exhibit in Banco Wiese, Trujillo, Peru. Photograph by Steve Bourget.

FIGURE 1.16. Detail of wall in Huaca Cao Viejo (Edificio D), showing one of the repetitions of the crested animal. Photograph by Steve Bourget.

instances, the animal is associated with multiple maces. The image has a wide distribution, however. It is seen in the form of effigy bottles excavated by Donnan at Dos Cabezas (Donnan 2001, 2003) and on many objects without provenience; it is prominent in Recuay art (uphill from the Moche region). Widespread as a ceramic design, it appears on murals and large sculpture only at Huaca Cao Viejo, as if it had special significance there.

North and South

Finally, I would like to speak briefly to differences between north and south. The complex fineline iconography of the middle period appears only in the southern region. The sequence of ceramic chronology devised by Larco (1948) indicates how form, technique, and subject matter developed in the south (Benson 2003). If the middle-period dates that Donnan (2003) has found for Early Moche–style ceramics at the northern site of Dos Cabezas are correct (and I hope that they are), the anachronism tells a great deal about north-south differences and fills the gap created by the dearth of middle-period fineline. The north was little known until recent times, but it clearly did not require the complex development of human-ritual ceramic iconography, which was closely involved with the power of southern rulers, the political and ecological problems they encountered, and the artistic exuberance that expressed their power. Late dates for the early ceramic style in the north may imply less need for change and a particular kind of respect for the ancestral in the north. Northern pottery is generally simple; elaborate iconography was not called for. Instead of stirrup spout bottles with fineline scenes, northern ceramics tend to be globular jars with a face in relief at the neck, simple figure vessels, or bottles with two small suspension hooks at the neck and sometimes a painted design on the body (Alva and Donnan 1993; Castillo 2001, 2003; Donnan and McClelland 1997; Makowski et al. 1994). Only in Late Moche times do fineline narratives appear in the north.

Northern middle-period iconography was displayed mostly in metallurgy and usually dealt with mythic characters and occasions. Most known metallurgy comes from the north, from excavations at Sipán and from looting at Loma Negra (farther north, in the Piura Valley), a region that produced exceptionally handsome Early Moche ceramics (Makowski et al. 1994). The open-

ing of the Sipán graves was a dramatic eye-opener. Rich tombs produced quantities of spectacular metalwork and many quickly produced crude ceramic vessels, along with a few fine ones (Alva 1994, 2001; Alva and Donnan 1993). There was surely exceptional metalwork in the south—a few examples exist, after looting since Colonial times—but there may have been more emphasis on metal in the north, where metal sources may have been better (see Shimada 1994:200–202).

Among regional differences is the prevalence of mural painting in the south. There are many possible reasons for its comparative scarcity in the north. Pacatnamú and San José de Moro, for examples, had long post-Moche occupations that surely would have destroyed what murals there might have been. Murals existed at Pampa Grande (Shimada 1994), and fragments of painting from Sipán are on exhibit at the Museo Tumbas Reales de Sipán.

New Kinds of Iconography

Some murals were discovered in the past and are well published by Duccio Bonavia (1985), but the murals unearthed at Huaca de la Luna and Huaca Cao Viejo in the last fifteen years are perhaps the most exciting recent discoveries in Moche art (Figures 1.16, 1.17). With architectural excavation, not only have murals been found, context has been found for them. The extent of their presence on walls, ceilings, and columns is exhilarating; the painted north facade of Platform 1 is spectacular (Figure 1.17). The mural art also opens new worlds for scholarship. Ricardo Morales and others, through meticulous examination of the murals, are revealing not only technical information but evidence of new dimensions of iconography, including large scale, the symbolic value of color (instead of the usual bichrome or trichrome of the ceramics), structures of the painting/relief surface, and the chemistry of the painting procedure. Color change in the overpainting of a god's face is one example of the new kind of information. Perhaps significant is the apparent use, as a binder for pigment, of the psychoactive San Pedro cactus or a relative (Morales, Solorzano, and Asmat 1998). Morales points out that referring to the murals as "wall decoration" is incorrect, for they employ an ideographic language closely related to the liturgical connotations of the space of which they are a vital part (Morales 2003;

FIGURE 1.17. Huaca de la Luna, detail of north facade mural. Photograph by Steve Bourget.

Morales et al. 1998). Figure 1.17 is a partial view of the last phase of the horizontal panels on the north facade of the Huaca de la Luna; a line of monsters fills the tier below the snake on the upper part of the ramp. Seen for the first time in many centuries, all of this is wonderful to look at, loaded with new questions and answers, contributing to a growing sense of who and what the Moche people were.

Today careful and knowledgeable excavation of buildings and tombs shows (or does not show) relationships with known iconography. Moreover, a new iconography is growing out of the archaeology based on interpretation of various kinds of technical examination, including osteological and geological evidence. We are not only acquiring a new view of ceramic iconography, but also learning about new kinds of iconography. John Verano has earned appreciation for his reading of the skeletal material—and sometimes of the iconography. In addition to his analytical work and that of Morales are the vitally significant findings of Izumi Shimada and his group (this volume) in solving mysteries of mitochondrial DNA identification of human remains, which will support a quantum jump in interpretation, leading into another depth of iconography. Work like that of Michael Moseley (this volume) points out some causes for change in the iconography. Ceramic iconography no longer exists in a vacuum with dashes of excavation; it is beginning to be seen as a response to known, postulated, or implied natural and political events. These are indeed exciting times to work with Moche art and archaeology. Between archaeology and ideology, and the synergy of their encounter, we are coming much closer to a re-creation of the Moche world.

Notes

1. Verano's 2003 article on foot amputation relates to this.

2. Since this was written, almost-identical murals have been excavated at Huaca de la Luna, which implies a very close relationship between the two sites.

3. Rafael Larco Hoyle did some of the earliest Moche archaeology and was arguably the first Moche iconographer.

4. As far as I know, this bottle has no provenience.

Bibliography

Alva, Walter

1994   *Sipán.* Colección Culturas y Artes del Perú, Lima.

2001   The Royal Tombs of Sipán: Art and Power in Moche Society. In *Moche Art and Archaeology in Ancient Peru,* 223–245. Edited by Joanne Pillsbury. National Gallery of Art and Yale University Press, Washington, D.C.

Alva, Walter, and Christopher B. Donnan

1993   *Royal Tombs of Sipán.* Fowler Museum of Cultural History, University of California, Los Angeles.

Arsenault, Daniel

1993   El personaje del pie amputado en la cultura mochica del Perú: Un ensayo sobre la arqueología del poder. *Latin American Antiquity* 4 (3):225–245.

Baessler, Adolf

1902–1903   *Ancient Peruvian Art: Contributions to the Archaeology of the Empire of the Incas.* Translated by A. H. Keene. Dodd, Mead and Co., New York, and A. Asher, Berlin.

Benson, Elizabeth P.

1975   Death-associated Figures on Mochica Pottery. In *Death and the Afterlife in Pre-Columbian America,* 105–144. Edited by Elizabeth P. Benson. Dumbarton Oaks Research Library and Collections, Washington, D.C.

1979   Garments as Symbolic Language in Mochica Art. *Actes du XLIIe Congrès International des Américanistes* Vol. VII:291–299.

1984a   A Moche «Spatula.» *Metropolitan Museum of Art Bulletin* 18:39–52.

1984b   The Men Who Have Bags in their Mouths. *Indiana* 9 (1):367–381.

1985   The Moche Moon. In *Recent Studies in Andean Prehistory and Protohistory,* 121–135. Edited by D. Peter Kvietok and Daniel H. Sandweiss. Cornell Latin American Studies Program, New York.

2003   Cambios de temas y motivos en la cerámica moche. In *Moche: Hacia el Final del Milenio,* Tome I, 477–495. Actas del Segundo Coloquio sobre la Cultura Moche, Trujillo, 1 al 7 de agosto de 1999. Edited by Santiago Uceda and Elías Mujica. Universidad Nacional de Trujillo and Pontificia Universidad Católica del Perú, Lima.

Berezkin, Yuri E.

1980 [1981]   An Identification of Anthropological Mythological Personages in Moche Representations. *Ñawpa Pacha* 18:1–26.

Bonavia, Duccio

1985   *Mural Painting in Ancient Peru.* Translated by Patricia J. Lyon. University of Indiana Press, Bloomington.

Bourget, Steve

1994   Bestiaire sacre et flore magique: Écologie ritualle de l'iconographie de la culture Mochica, côte nord du Perou. Ph.D. dissertation, Université de Montréal.

1997   Las excavaciones en la Plaza 3a de la Huaca de la Luna. In *Investigaciones en la Huaca de la Luna 1995*, 51–59. Edited by Santiago Uceda, Elías Mujica, and Ricardo Morales. Universidad Nacional de Trujillo, Perú.

1998   Excavaciones en la Plaza 3a y en la Plataforma II de la Huaca de la Luna durante 1996. In *Investigaciones en la Huaca de la Luna 1997*, 43–64. Edited by Santiago Uceda, Elías Mujica, and Ricardo Morales. Universidad Nacional de Trujillo, Perú.

2001   Rituals of Sacrifice: Its Practice at Huaca de la Luna and Its Representation in Moche Iconography. In *Moche Art and Archaeology in Ancient Peru*, 88–109. Edited by Joanne Pillsbury. National Gallery of Art and Yale University Press, Washington, D.C.

Bourget, Steve, and Jean-François Millaire

2000   Excavaciones en la Plaza 3a y Plataforma II de la Huaca de la Luna. In *Investigaciones en la Huaca de la Luna 1997*, 47–60. Edited by Santiago Uceda, Elías Mujica, and Ricardo Morales. Universidad Nacional de Trujillo, Perú.

Bourget, Steve, and Margaret E. Newman

1998   A Toast to the Ancestors: Ritual Warfare and Sacrificial Blood in Moche Culture. *Baessler-Archiv*, Neue Folge, 46:85–106. Berlin.

Castillo, Luis Jaime

2001   The Last of the Mochicas: A View from the Jequetepeque Valley. In *Moche Art and Archaeology in Ancient Peru*, 307–332. Edited by Joanne Pillsbury. National Gallery of Art and Yale University Press, Washington, D.C.

2003   Los últimos Mochicas en Jequetepeque. In *Moche: Hacia el Final del Milenio*, Tome II, 65–124. Actas del Segundo Coloquio sobre la Cultura Moche, Trujillo, 1 al 7 de agosto de 1999. Edited by Santiago Uceda and Elías Mujica. Universidad Nacional de Trujillo and Pontifícia Universidad Católica del Perú, Lima.

Castillo B., Luis Jaime, and Christopher B. Donnan

1994   La ocupación Moche de San José de Moro, Jequetepeque. In *Moche: Propuestas y perspectivas*, 93–146. Actas del Primer Coloquio sobre la Cultura Moche, Trujillo, 12 a 16 de abril de 1993. Edited by Santiago Uceda and Elías Mujica. Travaux de l'Institut Français d'Études Andines 79. Universidad Nacional de la Libertad, Trujillo, Perú.

Castillo, Luis Jaime, Andrew Nelson, and Chris Nelson

1997   "Maquetas" Mochicas de San José de Moro. *Arkinka* 1 (22):120–128. Lima.

Cordy-Collins, Alana

1997   The Offering Room Group. *The Pacatnamu Papers*, Vol. 2: *The Moche Occupation*, 283–292. Edited by Chris-

topher B. Donnan and Guillermo A. Cock. Fowler Museum of Cultural History, University of California, Los Angeles.

2001a   Decapitation in Cupisnique and Early Moche Societies. In *Ritual Sacrifice in Ancient Perú*, 21–34. Edited by Elizabeth P. Benson and Anita G. Cook. University of Texas Press, Austin.

2001b   Blood and the Moon Priestesses: Spondylus Shells in Moche Ceremony. In *Ritual Sacrifice in Ancient Peru*, 35–53. Edited by Elizabeth P. Benson and Anita G. Cook. University of Texas Press, Austin.

De Bock, Edward

1998   The Waterlily Ritual: An Andean Political and Religious Ceremony of the Moche Culture. *Journal of the Steward Anthropological Society* 26:1–18.

Donnan, Christopher B.

1975   The Thematic Approach to Moche Iconography. *Journal of Latin American Lore* I (2):147–162.

1978   *Moche Art of Peru: Pre-Columbian Symbolic Communication*. University of California, Museum of Cultural History, Los Angeles.

1982   Dance in Moche Art. *Ñawpa Pacha* 20:97–120.

1997   Deer Hunting and Combat: Parallel Activities in the Moche World. In *The Spirit of Ancient Peru: Treasures from the Museo Arqueológico Rafael Larco Herrera*, exhibition catalogue, 51–59. Edited by Kathleen Berrin. Fine Arts Museum of San Francisco, Thames and Hudson, New York.

2001   Moche Burials Uncovered. *National Geographic* 199 (3):58–73.

2003   Tumbas con entierros en miniatura: Un nuevo tipo funerario moche. In *Moche: Hacia el Final del Milenio*, Tome I, 43–78. Actas del Segundo Coloquio sobre la Cultura Moche, Trujillo, 1 al 7 de agosto de 1999. Edited by Santiago Uceda and Elías Mujica. Universidad Nacional de Trujillo and Pontificia Universidad Católica del Perú, Lima.

Donnan, Christopher B., and Luis Jaime Castillo B.

1992   Finding the Tomb of a Moche Priestess. *Archaeology* 45 (6):38–42.

1994   Excavaciones de tumbas de sacerdotisas Moche en San José de Moro, Jequetepeque. In *Moche: Propuestas y perspectivas*, 415–424. Actas del Primer Coloquio sobre la Cultura Moche, Trujillo, 12 a 16 de abril de 1993. Edited by Santiago Uceda and Elías Mujica. Travaux de l'Institut Français d'Études Andines 79. Universidad Nacional de la Libertad, Trujillo.

Donnan, Christopher B., and Sharon G. Donnan

1997   Moche Textiles from Pacatnamu. In *The Pacatnamu Papers*, Vol. 2: *The Moche Occupation*, 215–242. Edited by

Christopher B. Donnan and Guillermo A. Cock. Fowler Museum of Cultural History, University of California, Los Angeles.

Donnan, Christopher B., and Donna McClelland

1979   *The Burial Theme in Moche Iconography.* Studies in Pre-Columbian Art and Archaeology 20. Dumbarton Oaks Library and Collections, Washington, D.C.

1997   Moche Burials at Pacatnamu. In *The Pacatnamu Papers*, Vol. 2: *The Moche Occupation*, 17–187. Edited by Christopher B. Donnan and Guillermo A. Cock. Fowler Museum of Cultural History, University of California, Los Angeles.

1999   *Moche Fineline Painting: Its Evolution and Its Artists.* Fowler Museum of Cultural History, University of California, Los Angeles.

Franco Jordán, Régulo, and César Gálvez Mora

2003   Un ídolo de madera en un edificio Mochica temprano de la Huaca Cao Viejo, Complejo El Brujo. *Arkinka* 8 (93):94–105.

Franco Jordán, Régulo, César Gálvez Mora, and Segundo Vásquez Sánchez

1994   Arquitectura y decoración Mochica en la Huaca Cao Viejo, Complejo El Brujo: Resultados preliminares. In *Moche: Propuestas y perspectivas*, 147–180. Actas del Primer Coloquio sobre la Cultura Moche, Trujillo, 12 a 16 de abril de 1993. Edited by Santiago Uceda and Elías Mujica. Travaux de l'Institut Français d'Études Andines 79. Universidad Nacional de la Libertad, Trujillo, Perú.

1998a   Desentierro ritual de una tumba Moche: Huaca Cao Viejo. *Sian* 3 (6):9–18.

1998b   Un cielorraso Moche polícromo en la Huaca Cao Viejo, El Brujo. *1/2C: Media de construcción* 144:37–42.

1999a   Tumbas de cámara Moche en la plataforma superior de la Huaca Cao Viejo, Complejo El Brujo. *Boletín Programa Arqueológico Complejo "El Brujo"* 1.

1999b   Porras Mochicas del Complejo El Brujo. *Sian* 4 (7):16–23.

2001   La Huaca Cao Viejo en el Complejo El Brujo: Una contribución al estudio de los Mochicas en el valle de Chicama. *Arqueológicas* 25:123–173.

2002   La Huaca El Brujo: Architectura y iconografía. *Arkinka* 8 (85):86–97.

2003   Modelos, función y cronología de la Huaca Cao Viejo, Complejo El Brujo. In *Moche: Hacia el Final del Milenio*, Tome II, 125–177. Actas del Segundo Coloquio sobre la Cultura Moche, Trujillo, 1 al 7 de agosto de 1999. Edited by Santiago Uceda and Elías Mujica. Universidad Nacional de Trujillo and Pontificia Universidad Católica del Perú, Lima.

Franco Jordán, Régulo, and Antonio Murga Cruz

2001   Una representación arquitectónica en piedra en el Complejo Arqueológico El Brujo, Valle de Chicama. *Arkinka* 8 (70):92–99.

Franco Jordán, Régulo, and Juan V. Vilela Puelles

2003   Aproximaciones al calendario ceremonial Mochica del Complejo El Brujo, valle Chicama. In *Moche: Hacia el Final del Milenio*, Tome I, 383–423. Actas del Segundo Coloquio sobre la Cultura Moche, Trujillo, 1 al 7 de agosto de 1999. Edited by Santiago Uceda and Elías Mujica. Universidad Nacional de Trujillo and Pontificia Universidad Católica del Perú, Lima.

Gálvez Mora, César, and Jesús Rosario Briceño

2001   The Moche in the Chicama Valley. In *Moche Art and Archaeology in Ancient Peru*, 141–157. Edited by Joanne Pillsbury. National Gallery of Art and Yale University Press, Washington, D.C.

Hecker, Gisela, and Wolfgang Hecker

1992   Huesos humanos como ofrendas mortuarias y uso repetidas de vasijas. *Baessler-Archiv* n.s. XL (1):171–195.

Hocquenghem, Anne Marie

1987   *Iconografía Mochica.* Fondo Editorial de la Pontificia Universidad Católica del Perú, Lima.

Hocquenghem, Anne Marie, and Patricia J. Lyon

1980   A Class of Anthropomorphic Supernatural Females in Moche Iconography. *Ñawpa Pacha* 18:27–48.

Kutscher, Gerdt

1983   *Nordperuanische Gefässmalereien des Moche-Stils.* Verlag C. H. Beck, Munich.

Larco Hoyle, Rafael

1948   *Cronología Arqueológica del Norte del Perú.* Sociedad Geográfica Americana, Buenos Aires.

2001   *Los Mochicas.* 2 vols. Museo Arqueológico Rafael Larco Herrera, Lima.

Makowski, Krzysztof, Christopher B. Donnan, Ivan Amaro Bullon, Luis Jaime Castillo, Magdalena Diez Canseco, Otto Elespuru Revoredo, and Juan Antonio Murro Mena, eds.

1994   *Vicús.* Banco de Crédito del Perú, Colección Arte y Tesoros del Perú, Lima.

McClelland, Donna

1990   A Maritime Passage from Moche to Chimu. In *The Northern and Southern Dynasties: Kingship and Statecraft in Chimor*, 75–106. Edited by Michael Moseley and Alana Cordy-Collins. Dumbarton Oaks Library and Collection, Washington, D.C.

Morales Gamarra, Ricardo

2003   Iconografía litúrgica y contexto arquetectónico en Huaca de la Luna, Valle de Moche. In *Moche: Hacia el Final del Milenio*, Tome I, 425–476. Actas del Segundo Coloquio sobre la Cultura Moche, Trujillo, 1 al 7 de agosto de 1999. Edited by Santiago Uceda and Elías Mujica. Universidad Nacional de Trujillo and Pontificia Universidad Católica del Perú, Lima.

Morales Gamarra, Ricardo, Miguel Asmat Valverde, and Arabel Fernández López

2002 Atuendo ceremonial Moche: Excepcional hallazgo en la Huaca de la Luna. *Iconos* 3:49–53.

Morales Gamarra, Ricardo, Jorge Solórzano Solano, and Manuel Asmat Sánchez

1998 Superficies arquitectónicas: Tipología, tecnología, y materiales. In *Investigaciones en la Huaca de la Luna 1997*, 211–219. Edited by Santiago Uceda, Elías Mujica, and Ricardo Morales. Universidad Nacional de Trujillo, Perú.

Orbegoso, Clorinda

1998 Excavaciones en el sector sureste de la Plaza 3c de la Huaca de la Luna durante 1996. In *Investigaciones en la Huaca de la Luna 1996*, 67–73. Edited by Santiago Uceda, Elías Mujica, and Ricardo Morales. Universidad Nacional de Trujillo, Perú.

Shimada, Izumi

1994 *Pampa Grande and the Mochica Culture*. University of Texas Press, Austin.

Strong, William Duncan, and Clifford Evans, Jr.

1952 *Cultural Stratigraphy in the Virú Valley, Northern Peru: The Formative and Florescent Epoch*. Columbia Studies in Archaeology and Ethnology 4. Columbia University Press, New York.

Uceda [Castillo], Santiago

1997 El poder y la muerte en la sociedad Moche. In *Investigaciones en la Huaca de la Luna 1995*, 177–188. Edited by Santiago Uceda, Elías Mujica, and Ricardo Morales. Universidad Nacional de Trujillo, Perú.

2000 Los ceremoniales en la Huaca de la Luna: Un análisis de los espacios arquitectónicos. In *Investigaciones en la Huaca de la Luna 1997*, 205–214. Edited by Santiago Uceda, Elías Mujica, and Ricardo Morales. Universidad Nacional de Trujillo, Perú.

2001 Investigations at Huaca de la Luna, Moche Valley: An Example of Moche Religious Architecture. In *Moche Art and Archaeology in Ancient Peru*, 47–67. Edited by Joanne Pillsbury. National Gallery of Art and Yale University Press, Washington, D.C.

Uceda, Santiago, and Moisés Tufinio

2003 El complejo arquitectónico religioso Moche de Huaca de la Luna: Una aproximación a su dinámica ocupacional. In *Moche: Hacia el Final del Milenio*, Tome II, 179–228. Actas del Segundo Coloquio sobre la Cultura Moche, Trujillo, 1 al 7 de agosto de 1999. Edited by Santiago Uceda and Elías Mujica. Universidad Nacional de Trujillo and Pontificia Universidad Católica del Perú, Lima.

Verano, John W.

1997 Physical Characteristics and Skeletal Biology of the Moche Population at Pacatnamu. In *The Pacatnamu Papers*, Vol. 2: *The Moche Occupation*, 189–214. Edited by Christopher B. Donnan and Guillermo A. Cock. Fowler Museum of Cultural History, University of California, Los Angeles.

1998 Sacrificios humanos, desmembramientos y modificaciones culturales en restos osteológicos: Evidencias de las temporadas de investigaciones 1995–96 en la Huaca de la Luna. In *Investigaciones en la Huaca de la Luna 1996*, 159–171. Edited by Santiago Uceda, Elías Mujica, and Ricardo Morales. Universidad Nacional de Trujillo, Perú.

2001a War and Death in the Moche World: Osteological Evidence and Visual Discourse. In *Moche Art and Archaeology in Ancient Peru*, 111–125. Edited by Joanne Pillsbury. National Gallery of Art and Yale University Press, Washington D.C.

2001b The Physical Evidence of Human Sacrifice in Ancient Peru. In *Ritual Sacrifice in Ancient Peru*, 165–184. Edited by Elizabeth P. Benson and Anita G. Cook. University of Texas Press, Austin.

2003 Avances en la bioantropología de los Moche. In *Moche: Hacia el Final del Milenio*, Tome I, 15–32. Actas del Segundo Coloquio sobre la Cultura Moche, Trujillo, 1 al 7 de agosto de 1999. Edited by Santiago Uceda and Elías Mujica. Universidad Nacional de Trujillo and Pontificia Universidad Católica del Perú, Lima.

Vreeland, James M., Jr.

1992 Day of the Dead. *Archaeology* 45 (6):43.

CHAPTER TWO

Sacrifices and Ceremonial Calendars in Societies of the Central Andes

A Reconsideration

ANNE MARIE HOCQUENGHEM, CENTRE NATIONAL DE RECHERCHES SCIENTIFIQUES

Abstract

In the Prehispanic iconography of the central Andes, two particular forms related to human death draw particular attention: prisoners with their throats cut, and supplicating men and women. Returning to a method of iconographic analysis and interpretation proposed in the 1970s, in this chapter I attempt to demonstrate the sacred character of these images, to identify the main actors, and to reconstruct the circumstances and significant features of these acts. Such features relate to rites of propitiation and of expiation in central Andean society, and likely Prehispanic Moche society as well.

Without entering into a grand debate over the nature of sacrifice, this ritual act can be considered as an offering to animate or inanimate divinities, and as consecrated and placed continually outside of profane use between that of immolation and destruction. The sacrificial act can be thought of as expressing a dependant relationship between humans and mythical beings. The communications established through the sacrifice, between the sacrificers and the supernatural beings, further can be understood as an act of submission and homage, which humans perform to obtain favors from or divert the wrath of powerful immortals. Sacrifice thus has two potential frameworks. On one hand, a person offers what they have. On the other, a person deprives himself of something with the objective of obtaining in exchange for the offering a counter-gift, one that relates to the vital force. Within this model of exchange, it can be supposed that the sacrifice will be better received and more effective if the offering has high value. It is in this sense that the immolation of human beings can best be understood. Yet sacrifice does not have to pertain to a particular type of rite but rather consists in generic forms that include many sacrificial acts in various social contexts. These acts can be distin-

guished by their offerings, by their nature, by the form of immolation, by the circumstances, and by the particular objects of established communications between the sacrificers and the entities upon which they depend.

In order to explore the sacrificial theme in the societies of the central Andes, I will address the corpus of Prehispanic iconography in Peru, centering my attention upon the highly representational Moche images. The majority of Moche representations appear on objects from funerary contexts located in and around administrative and ceremonial centers along the north coast of Peru, which date between AD 200 and 700. Among many visual themes, the images illustrate diverse ways of killing human beings: men, women, and children.

In the context of this work, I will take into account the scenes that reference or depict the decapitation of prisoners and those that illustrate human punishment. I intend to demonstrate the sacred character of these images, to identify the actors, and to reconstruct the circumstances and particular objects of these ritual acts. In order to accomplish this task, I will apply a method of analysis and interpretation to the iconography that I proposed in the 1970s (Hocquenghem 1973, 1977a, 1977b, 1987).

The Sacred and Ceremonial Character of Moche Iconography

From the materials preserved in European and Peruvian collections and museums, I have constituted a photographic corpus of painted, modeled, sculpted, etched, and woven representations on more than 4,000 objects of clay, ceramic, stone, metal, bone, shell, vegetable fibers, and animal fur. From analyses upon this corpus, I have evinced some of the internal structure and sacred character of the iconography. In sum, the corpus has yielded the following observations:

1. The different representations were reproduced in large number through the same techniques over similar supports or through various mediums of artistic expression on objects of diverse forms and qualities. They present reproductions of parts or details of the complex scenes.
2. The complex scenes were also reproduced in large number and with variant forms, whether complete, in parts, or in detail. They represent a limited number of specific actions that refer to the communication between the real world and the supernatural world— or which develop in parallel in these two worlds. The real world is populated by human beings, while the supernatural world is inhabited by the deceased, whose bodies are skeletons, and by the anthropomorphic and zoomorphic mythological beings, whose attributes are fangs and serpents.
3. The different complex scenes are not independent from each other. The actors are the same, and the actions are organized in temporal sequences.

In addition to the above observations derived from independent studies, the Moche corpus has been compared with other visual programs from Prehispanic Peru. These derive from the coast and central Andes, and they date from the first millennium before the Common Era until the Spanish conquest in the sixteenth century. Such comparative studies have further yielded the following assumptions:

1. Although styles differ across regions and epochs, the structure of the Andean visual systems of representation and the represented actions themselves remain similar.

2. The internal structure of the visual programs and their themes indicate that the diverse representations illustrate, across time and space, a specific discourse enunciated and replayed in parts or details. This repeated discourse does not relate to the sphere of the profane and quotidian but rather to the sacred and ceremonial.

By accepting these above observations and assumptions, I am thus accounting for the sacred and ceremonial character of all the Prehispanic visual systems, including that of the Moche. As such, the Moche images of prisoners with their throats cut and of tortured men and women can be considered representations of sacrificial acts. In order to understand the particular significance of these scenes, it is necessary to try to reconstruct the meaning and function of the iconographic group of which they form part.

The Iconography and the Andean Ceremonial Calendar

In order to reconstruct the meaning and function of this group of Moche images, I will first compare them with the texts that, since the sixteenth century, have addressed the discourses and customs related to the sacred and the ceremonial, to the myths and rites of the central Andes. This method seems justified by applying a structuralist approach. For example, Claude Lévi-Strauss writes in his article "The Serpent with Fish inside His Body":

> We can no longer doubt that the key to so many heretofore incomprehensible motifs is directly accessible in myths and tales which are still current. One would be mistaken to neglect these means which enable us to gain access to the past. Only the myths can guide us into the labyrinth of monsters and gods when, in the absence of writing, the plastic documentation cannot lead us any further. By reconstructing the connections between distant areas, various historical periods, and cultures at different stages of development, this king of research documents, illuminates— and, perhaps, one day will explain—the vast syncretism that has persistently frustrated Americanists in their search for the historical antecedents of specific phenomena. (1963:272–273)

From the texts of the Spanish chroniclers and the extir-pators of idolatry, such as Juan de Betanzos ([1550] 1987), Piedro Cieza de León ([1553] 1967, 1987), Cristóbal de Molina ([1575] 1959), Juan de Acosta ([1590] 1954), Felipe Guamán Poma de Ayala ([1615] 1936), and Inca Garcilaso de la Vega ([1609] 1985), I composed and analyzed a corpus of accounts about the rites and myths of the Inca. I then compared these ethnohistoric accounts with the Moche visual representations. The results have suggested that each one of the different Moche iconographic scenes relates to one of the ceremonies that constituted the Incan ceremonial calendar (Hocquenghem 1987, 1997).

The Incan ceremonial calendar established parallels between the cycles of natural phenomena, the celestial bodies and the seasons, the animal and vegetal repro-ductive cycles, and the reproduction of humans and their institutions. It established homologies and marked the passage of one age to another in the natural and social cycles. The Incas celebrated sacrifices to mark each one of the twelve ceremonies related to one of the twelve months of the lunar and solar calendar. The nature of the sacrificial offerings varied according to the type of ceremonies. The offerings could have been men, women, children, llamas, coca, precious metal objects, gold, silver, shell of *Spondylus* or *Strombus*, textiles, first fruits of the harvests, or some part of all that was pro-duced during the course of the year.

The Quechua manuscript that describes the rites and traditions of the Huarochirí, as well as the commentar-ies upon the translated text offered by Gerald Taylor ([1608] 1987a), offer the most direct glimpse of how the sacrificial offerings functioned. They elucidate how the life force was transmitted through the medium of sacrifices between a strong animate (*camac*); an ances-tor, predecessor, or sacred entity (*huaca*); and a being or animated object (*camasca*). According to the manuscript, the perception of the *camac* during the seventeenth century was that of an effective force that animated and sustained not only humans but also animals and plants so that each could realize its full natural potential. The ancestors possessed different capacities to animate and sustain. Some *camac* were more effective than others depending on their rank and on the quality of their cult—on the quality of the sacrifices that their *camasca* offered to them. The existence of a powerful *camac* did not exclude the others, whose strengths could have

been complementary. The *camasca*, who received their existence from and paid tribute to different sources, could increase the quality of the *camac* and reanimate it (Taylor [1608] 1987a; Garcilaso de la Vega [1609] 1985).

In his vocabulary of the general language of Peru, called Quechua ([1608] 1952), Diego Gonzáles Holguín associated *camac* to *hucha*: a demand, transaction, or plea. Taylor observes that, in the less acculturated pas-sages of the Huarochirí manuscript, *hucha* corresponds above all to *falta;* that is to say, to the lack of observing a ritual obligation, the consequence of which is inevitably the sickness or death of the guilty party or one of his next of kin. *Falta* implies obligation, and in the series of *camac* definitions from the same dictionary, there are expressed varying shades of "dues" and "duty." *Pleito* is a disputed and recovered fee, while *negocio* in this context seems to signify "task or function associated with some-one" (Taylor [1608] 1987a:29–30).

It is further noteworthy that the Huarochirí distin-guished between three aspects of vital force, or three different forms of power (Taylor [1608] 1987a). An intel-lectual power, *callpa*, was related to communication, memory, and knowledge, which the priests obtained through effort and constant work. The priests repeated the gestures of their predecessors in order to acquire the ancestral arts that permitted them to see and avoid evil. A physical power, *sinchi*, was related to valor and bravery, which the leaders developed during an extended and rigorous process of initiation in order to confront and overcome all adversities. Finally, a political power, *capac*, was related to wealth, opulence and generosity, which respected individuals acquired and demonstrated in order to impose and maintain order.

With the goal to maintain the circulation of vital force, the Incas sacrificed to the most powerful mythical ancestors. First they sacrificed to Viracocha Pachaca-mac, the *camac* that animated and sustained space and time (*pacha*) from their beginning until their end. Next, they sacrificed to Inti Viracocha, the sun and father of the Incas, followed by those that accompanied him and had designated rooms in his temple. These included (1) Mama Quilla, the moon, wife, and sister of the sun and mother of the Inca; (2) Venus, the light of dawn and dusk, together with the seven Pleiades and the stars, models of all things existing; (3) Inti Illapa, the light-ning-thunder-hail entity, both opposite and complementary to the sun; and (4) Cuichu, the arc of the sky, so grand that it occupied both walls of the temple with all its vivid colors, and so venerated that, when they saw it, the Incas closed their mouths and placed their hands over them. If the teeth were discovered, they would be lost or would rot. The fifth room of the Temple of the Sun was that of the highest priest, who sacrificed to the mythical ancestors and to the mummies of the founding ancestors of the diverse Incan lineages (Garcilaso de la Vega [1609] 1985, L. 3:127–129).

Based on these accounts and their interpretations, I consider the maintenance of the vital force as a form of negotiation between the immortal leaders and the humans that performed the sacrificial acts. On one hand, the capacity to animate and sustain the ancestors depended on the nature of the offerings that they received and on the earnestness of their descendents in fulfilling their ritual obligations. On the other hand, the quantity and quality of vital force that the *camasca* received were relative to the treatment that they offered to their *camac*. This relationship suggests that from month to month, from year to year, and from generation to generation through the medium of sacrifices, the Inca ceremonies had to maintain the circulation of vital force between humans and their ancestors, mythical and real. The ceremonial calendar was thus the institution that actuated the cult of the ancestors and, by recalling the myths and reenacting them through ritual, assured the social production and reproduction of the central Andes.

Returning to the discussion of Moche iconography, I would argue that if the established parallel between the

Moche scenes and the Inca ceremonies is justified, then Moche iconography functioned to establish an ancestral order through the medium of the image. In order to identify the actors and to discriminate between the circumstances and particular objects of the two forms of human sacrifice in this study, I will next demonstrate, using some of the Incan rites and certain survivals of an Andean ceremonial calendar, how these different images could be interrelated.

Decapitation and the Rites of Propitiation

In Moche iconography there exists a sequence of complex scenes that depict some form of ritual battle. The warriors often confront one another in pairs and strike at each other with clubs (Figure 2.1). Blood runs, and the defeated are captured (Figure 2.2). The prisoners, deprived of their attire and with ropes around their necks, are presented to important individuals (Figure 2.3). Afterwards, their hands bound, they are beheaded by zoomorphic mythic beings, and their blood is offered to anthropomorphic beings that possess fangs and serpents (Figure 2.4). A grand bicephalus serpent divides the scenes of the sacrifice and the offering of blood (Figure 2.5). Finally, together with their charge of objects, the sacrificed individuals embark on boats to navigate the ocean (Figure 2.6) (Hocquenghem 1978, 1979a, 1979b, 1987).

Ethnohistoric accounts, in particular those of Cristóbal de Molina, refer to a similar sequence of Inca ritual acts that can be placed in parallel with the above Moche iconographic sequence. Molina describes a ritual battle

FIGURE 2.1. Warriors in combat. Private collection. Drawing by Donna McClelland.

FIGURE 2.2. Warriors and prisoners, Museo Amano, Lima. Drawing by Donna McClelland.

FIGURE 2.3. Warriors and prisoners. Private collection. Drawing by Donna McClelland.

FIGURE 2.4. Fineline painting of the Presentation Theme. Museo Nacional de Arqueología, Antropología e Historia del Perú, Lima. Drawing by Donna McClelland.

FIGURE 2.5. Fineline painting of the Presentation Theme. Staatliches Museum für Völkerkunde, Munich. Drawing by Donna McClelland.

FIGURE 2.6. Bottle in the form of fish-boat. Museo del Banco Central de Reserva del Perú, Lima (ACE-2975). Photograph by Steve Bourget.

that was celebrated in Cuzco after the December solstice ([1575] 1943). Following the battle but before the March equinox, a dance was sung with a large rope, and a major sacrifice was performed. The remains were tossed into the waters of the river that passed through the ceremonial and administrative center of the Inca. In order to better grasp its eventual comparison to Moche visual representations, I will describe these ethnohistoric accounts in greater detail.

In the new moon following the summer solstice in January, at the beginning of the humid season when nature demonstrates its vital force and when the plants grow and the animals fatten, the Incas celebrated the ritual combat of *Camay*. The combatants, young warriors recently initiated, represented the two halves of Cuzco: *hanan* and *hurin*. They would confront each other in the plaza, throwing heavy fruits with all their might. Eventually the Inca would stop the combat and reconcile the two parties (Molina 1959). The individual warriors presumably were demonstrating their vital force, valor, bravery, and physical strength—their individual *sinchi*. Their participation in the battle perhaps served as a reminder that those who completed their ritual obligations would come to be very animated (*ancha camasca*) by their different *camac*. As indicated by its name, this rite would have been related to the transmission of the vital force, specifically through the form of physical prowess.

During the full moon, the Inca men and women of Cuzco would sing and dance the *taqui Yanayra*. During this performance, they would carry in their hands a long rope of four colors: black, white, red and tawny. They would take this rope, which they called *moro urco*, from a house of the same name located next to the House of the Sun. Dancing in turns around the plaza, the Inca would deposit the rope on the ground in the form of a spiral, rolled up in the manner of a snake. Those in charge of the rope would then return it to its room (Molina 1959). The *moro urco*, which had its room in the Temple of the Sun, together with the most powerful ancestors, was none other than the arc of the sky, Cuichu, mentioned by Garcilaso de la Vega and known to have had the power of corruption; that is, the power to deprive someone of his vital force. In the following study concerning the *taqui* song and dance, I intend to demonstrate that these ritual performances related to the transmission of

vital force from the *camac* to the *camasca* that celebrated it (Hocquenghem 1996).

The Inca song and dance with the rope-serpent corresponds closely with earlier Moche representations of men and women dancing with a large rope (Figures 2.7, 2.8). In some of these images, the Moche dancers also wear different face masks (Figure 2.7). This attribute may correspond to another related act described in the ethnohistoric accounts. The Quechua manuscript of the Huarochirí mentions that the Checas Indians preserved the facial skin of an ancestor (*Namsapa*) and transformed it into a mask. When the Checas celebrated the harvest as a victory over the negative vital and adverse physical forces, they would sing and dance with this relic, which conserved the vitality, as well as the valor and bravery, of the ancestor (Taylor [1608] 1987a). The Huarochirí would also cut off the facial skin of their principal enemies and preserve them in the form of masks, with which they would dance and sing, thus appropriating the vital force and physical prowess of their enemies (Taylor [1608] 1987b). Drawing upon such related sources and actions, I would argue that the *taqui Yanayra*, celebrated after the combat of *Camay*, was a ritual act related to transmitting the vital force through the particular form of physical strength, or *sinchi*. Such power would have animated and sustained not only the warriors but the whole of society. It would have been intended to confront and overcome all of the obstacles to social production and reproduction.

In February, the lunar month that succeeds the rites of *Camay* and *Yanayra,* and the month when the rivers are strongest and most abundant, the Incas celebrated the rites of *Mayocati*. The objective of these rituals was to transport to Viracocha Pachacamac all the carbon and ashes that remained from the enacted sacrifices, along with a portion of the production and yield of the entire year. These elements would be tossed into the waters of the river that runs through Cuzco so that it would carry them to its confines, to the center of the world. The Incas would supplicate themselves, asking that the sacrifices be received as a sign of gratitude for all that had been bestowed upon them, with the hope of obtaining more throughout the coming year (Molina 1959). I would suggest that, before the equinox of the humid season, the Incas gave to the water the whole of their sacrifices in order to return to its source the vital force under all its forms of power that had been conceived throughout the annual cycle, with the hope of it returning in excess the following year. The name of this ceremony supports this interpretation: *mayo* or *mayu* means "river," while *cati* or *cuti* means "to return." The sacrifices presented in this context would have had the significance of rites of propitiation.

The ethnographic accounts further attest to certain continuities in the form and significance of the Inca rites of *Camay* and *Mayocati* and the performances of modern Andean groups. For example, between the holidays of the Virgen de la Candelaria and Carnaval in January, certain indigenous ceremonies involve the demonstration of force and the offering of sacrifices to the entities that animate and sustain the Andean world. Furthermore, many indigenous groups continue celebrating ceremonial combats between the two halves of the community. The bloodshed and, in some cases, the lives of the victims of these sacred confrontations are offered to the earth and to the guardian divinities in order to assure continued production. These ceremonial confrontations and their consequences preserve the significance of such ancient rites of propitiation (Alencastre and Dumézil 1953; Contreras 1955; Gorbák, Lischetti, and Muñoz 1962; Hartmann 1972).

By comparing the sequence of Moche visual representations with the sequence of ethnohistoric and ethnographic data, and by assuming that the ritual acts have preserved over time some of their forms and meanings (although the nature of the offerings changes), I further propose an interpretation of the Moche representations of sacrifice by decapitation. The recently initiated Moche warriors would have represented the two halves of the society. In the first new moon following the summer solstice, they would have undertaken a ritual combat to demonstrate the vital force, in particular the physical power, of their lineages (Figure 2.1). All of the Moche would have propitiated this vital force in the full moon, dancing with a large rope and wearing the masks of their ancestors (Figure 2.7). In the following moon, the month preceding the equinox of the humid season, the defeated warriors would have been consecrated as sacrificial victims and decapitated (Figure 2.5). The beheaded bodies and the rest of the year's sacrifices were then shipped on boats for a trip across the ocean, a trip intended to return them to the confines and

origin of the Andean world, to the source of vital force (Figure 2.6). This sacrifice, part of the exchange of vital force between the Moche and their ancestors, would have been celebrated with the goal of obtaining for the upcoming year the vital force—in particular, physical strength—which would ensure social and economic reproduction. This sequence of sacred acts would have had the significance of rites of propitiation.

In this model of interpretation, then, who are the mythical anthropomorphic beings who figure into the scenes of sacrifice, and whose attributes are fangs and serpents (Figures 2.4, 2.5)? I would argue that these attributes represent the immortal power and absolute authority, the *camac,* of these sacred beings, or *huaca,* sources of the vital force that animates and sustains the Andean world (Hocquenghem 1983a, 1987). The Moche illustrated three masculine and one feminine entity with such attributes (Figure 2.9). These would have been the Moche predecessors of Viracocha Pachacamac—the auspicious master of life and death in the Central Andes—of Inti Viracocha, of Inti Illapa, and of Mama Quilla.

The zoomorphic mythical beings would have been the ancestors of the diverse lineages that composed Moche society (Hocquenghem 1987, 1998). The serpent with two heads—the grand, mythic boa—would have been the Moche predecessor of the Inca *Cuichi,* the arc of the sky (Figure 2.5). It should be recalled here that the enthnohistoric and ethnographic accounts regarding Andean beliefs and customs suggest a relationship between ophidians, the circulation of water, and the circulation of vital force (Hocquenghem 1983a, 1983b, 1987).

The diurnal arc of the sky is the rainbow, and the nocturnal arc is the Milky Way: the *mayu,* or celestial river. These arcs continue to be extremely feared and respected in the Andes. They should not be looked at or signaled to directly so as not to risk becoming sick—that is, losing one's vital force. I would further recall here that the Andeans feared and respected the terrestrial river, *mayu,* because its currents returned the vital force of all that it carried to the origin of water, the sea or *mamacocha,* mother of the high Andean lagoons. It is likely that the Andeans established a relation between the circulation of water and the circulation of the vital force. As the fertility or sterility of the valleys depends upon the quantity and nature of water that flows in the rivers between the Andean peaks and the Pacific littoral,

FIGURE 2.7. Moche dancers. Redrawn by Christopher B. Donnan from Lavalle 1985, page 58.

FIGURE 2.8. Dancers holding a long rope. Redrawn from Kutscher 1983, Figure 152.

FIGURE 2.9. Detail of the Presentation Theme. Staatliches Museum für Völkerkunde, Munich. Drawing by Donna McClelland.

so does human reproduction or annihilation in the Andean world depend upon the abundance and quality of the vital force that flows in the arc of the sky between the world's origin and its confines. The large Moche mythic boa, the Inca arc of the sky, would then have represented the circulation of vital force that animates and sustains the Andean world.

The Punishments and Rites of Expiation

Moche iconography represents punishments inflicted on human individuals. In some cases, they were left exposed on mountain peaks (Figure 2.10), with the skin of their faces pulled away and hanging. Others were stoned to death, and their physical remains abandoned to the vultures (Figure 2.11). Some were decapitated and dismembered (Figure 2.12) (Hocquenghem 1980, 1987). Here I must admit that, as Steve Bourget signaled to part (1994:92–93), in 1987 I committed an error in considering these "mountain sacrifice scenes" as separate scenes without noting the bodies of sacrificial victims that often lie decapitated and dismembered like those of the punished (Hocquenghem 1987:180–185). In the more complex scenes of torture, the executions relate to the offering of *Strombus* shells to mythical beings, individuals often seated in the interior of a temple structure (Figure 2.13). On the roof of the temple, part deer, serpent, and jaguar zoomorphic beings emerge from other *Strombus* shells. The acts of punishment relate to activities around an open tomb. Ethnohistoric accounts also provide evidence of the celebration of Inca rituals that involved such suffering, as I discuss below.

The texts and drawings of Guamán Poma de Ayala indicate that corporal punishments formed part of the ritual acts of the ceremony of *Uma raimi quilla,* celebrated during the lunar month that follows the month of equinox and the dry season in October, when water is scarce. In the "moon ceremony of the water" *(quilla* [moon] + *raimi* [ceremony] + *uma* [water]), the Incas lashed and struck at their llamas and dogs in the plaza while they and their children cried. Through this ritual, they expressed great pain in order to call the attention of Viracocha Pachacamac by exposing their sufferings and those of their animals. They pleaded to the most powerful of the *camac* to concede to them the vital liquid (Guamán Poma de Ayala [1615] 1936:254–255). Guamán Poma de Ayala also states that the Incas stoned pairs

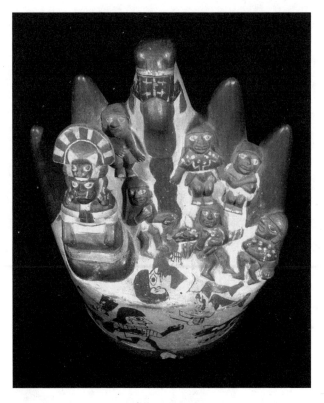

FIGURE 2.10. Stirrup spout bottle in the form of a mountain. Staatliche Museen zu Berlin—Preussischer Kulturbesitz, Ethnologisches Museum (VA-48095). Photograph by Steve Bourget.

FIGURE 2.11. Skeletal being tied to a tree and pecked by a black vulture. Museo Larco, Lima (ML-001478).

FIGURE 2.12. Fineline painting of sacrificial victims. Moche Archive, UCLA. Drawing by Donna McClelland.

FIGURE 2.13. Burial Theme. The sacrificial victim eaten by vultures is located in the upper left corner. Moche Archive, UCLA. Drawing by Donna McClelland.

of adulterers, hung those who maintained prohibited sexual relationships, whipped the sorcerers, and delivered traitors to savage animals (Figures 2.14, 2.15).

The punished, condemned to atrocious deaths, were individuals who had allied themselves with inappropriate people, used their knowledge to wrongful ends, or did not fulfill their obligations. Those who failed to comply with their ritual obligations would lose the respect of the ancestral order, and the inevitable consequence was sickness or death of the guilty or his next of kin (Taylor 1999:xxvi–xxvii). The punishments inflicted upon the transgressors of order were intended to calm the ancestral wrath, to offer the powerful immortals the sufferings of those who had offended them. Indeed, the fury of the *camac* threatened to block the circulation of vital force. Their anger could also manifest in the form of a disaster, natural or social, whose extreme and terri-

fying consequence could be the eventual annihilation of space and time, and the return to order of a new cycle-state of the Andean world: a *pachacuti*. It is noteworthy that when a natural or social catastrophe occurred, the Incas celebrated the ritual acts of *Uma raimi quilla* in an exceptionally grave manner and in the marking of an extraordinary ceremony, the *Itu* (Acosta [1590] 1954; Cobo [1653] 1956; Guamán Poma de Ayala [1615] 1936). The ritual acts of *Uma raimi quilla* and the sacrifices celebrated in these contexts would have had the significance of rites of expiation.

Ethnographic accounts make it possible to propose certain continuities regarding the form and significance of the rites at the end of the dry season. A few examples should suffice. Around the mid-twentieth century, some Aymara communities, in order to terminate the drought, forced the toads, which are associated with Pachamama

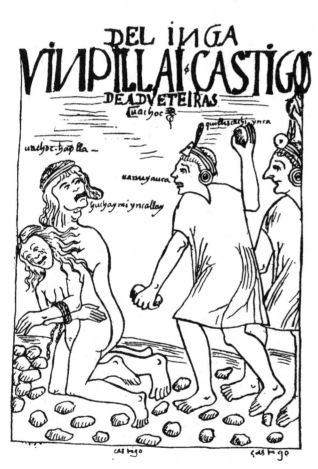

FIGURE 2.14. Scene of lapidation. Redrawn from Adorno and Boserup 2003, Figure 1b.

FIGURE 2.15. Scene of sacrifice. Redrawn from López-Baralt 1993, Figure 10.

or Mother Earth, to suffer by leaving them out to dry in the sun. The Aymara inflicted this punishment with the intent of calling attention from the ancestors, so that they would take pity on the sufferings of the earth and of its beings—animals, plants, and humans—greatly in need of more water. If the rains still did not come, the Aymara would search out a scapegoat, a person who had committed a mistake, and force him or her to atone for it (Tschopik 1946).

In the Peruvian Andes, the month of October has continued to be the month of grand processions in honor of the Señor de los Milagros, the Señor Cautivo, the Señor de los Temblores, the Señor de Luren, and the Christs of the Passion, bloodied prisoners who carried their crosses and were crucified to atone for the sins of men. According to the Catholic Church calendar, there is no reason why these Christ figures appear in October, when they are traditionally related to the rites of Semana Santa, which is celebrated in March, after the equinox of the humid season. Nevertheless, at the end of the dry season, the popular fervor brings forth these images from the churches, some associated with sources of water and others with terrestrial events, invoking the divine will and entreating God to free the world of all the evil that threatens and afflicts mankind: droughts, floods, famines, earthquakes, epidemics, wars, aggressions, repressions, robbery, and other natural and social calamities. Many people dress in purple during October and make oaths of penitence in front of these tormented figures of the cross. These Christian rituals and processions suggest the survival of a syncretism between Andean and Christian rites.

Based on the parallel established between the iconography and the ethnohistorical and ethnological accounts, I propose an interpretation of the Moche representations of torture. The humans left exposed on the mountain summits, flayed and lapidated, would have been transgressors of the ancestral order. They would have suffered the punishments leading to death in a ceremony celebrated during the month following dry season or when extraordinary circumstances demanded. The Moche would tear away the flesh of the faces, leaving it hanging, in order to deprive the victims of, and also to destroy, the malevolent vital force—the bad physical strength, the wrongful actions, the insolence—that caused them to ignore their ritual obligations and lose

the respect of the mythic ancestors. Their bodies, decapitated and dismembered, were exposed to the elements and abandoned to the vultures. Deprived of the funerary rites that would have assured the circulation of vital force between life and death, they were thus condemned to disappear. These sacrificial rites of expiation were intended to calm the wrath of the powerful immortals and avoid their consequences.

Moche representations also highlight the relationship between the punished and the offerings of *Strombus* shells (Figures 2.16, 2.17). In 1975, John Murra reunited accounts concerning the sacrifices of snails and marine conchs, daughters of *mamacocha*, the source of vital force. Murra argued that they were presented to the high Andean lagoons when drought threatened with the aim of receiving rain. I propose that this offering would have been made not only to reestablish the circulation of water but, above all, to restore the circulation of vital force.

The deer-serpent-jaguar being, which surges from the *Strombus* shells, remains to be identified. In certain images, it accompanies the female ancestor the moon—who does not stop transforming throughout the monthly cycle or passing through the sky, day and night—without losing her identity (Figure 2.18). Therefore, in Moche iconography the *Strombus* appears to be one of the attributes of the mythic ancestors. Comparatively, in the Huarochirí tales, the *camac* animate and sustain, convene and order their *camasca* by blowing a shell trumpet (Taylor [1608] 1987a:77). These accounts suggest that the being with feline potency, serpent vitality, and the majesty of a deer surging forth from a *Strombus* possesses vital force through its three aspects: *sinchi*, *callpa*, and *capac* (Figure 2.19). The being is the manifestation of immortal power and absolute authority, and of those who govern the Andean world. It would likewise represent the *camac*, or animate, by way of the ancestral spirit that resonates from the shells.

Indigenous myths tell of a mythic being, or *amaru*, that lives in the high Andean lagoons. Every so often, the *amaru* emerges with extraordinary violence, similar to the fury of the savage bull, and destroys everything in its path, thereby recording in the landscape the sign of its passage. The *amaru*'s appearance announces the disorders that provoke ancestral wrath, whose consequences are natural and social disasters that last until the restoration of order in a new cycle-state of the world,

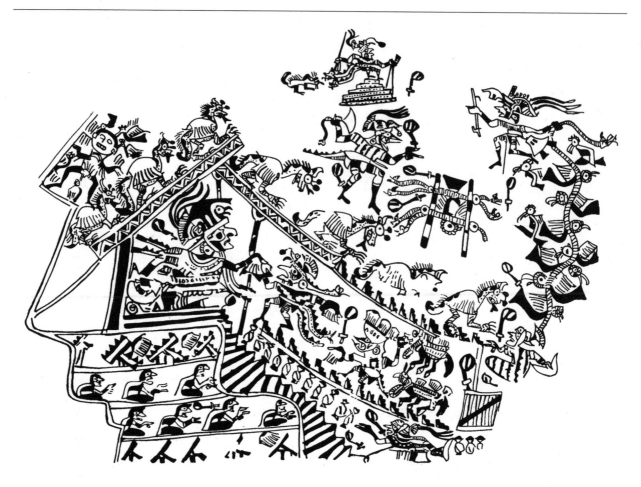

FIGURE 2.16. Offering of *Strombus* shells. Detail from a Burial Theme (Figure 2.13). Moche Archive, UCLA. Drawing by Donna McClelland.

FIGURE 2.17. Woman pecked by vultures. Detail from a Burial Theme (Figure 2.13). Moche Archive, UCLA. Drawing by Donna McClelland.

FIGURE 2.18. Drawing of the moon and the lunar fox. Redrawn from Kutscher 1954, Figure 44b.

FIGURE 2.19. Detail of warrior sitting in front of a *Strombus* Being. By kind permission of the Trustees of the British Museum, London. Drawing by Donna McClelland.

a *pachacuti*. The *amaru*'s features recall the calamities occasioned by lack of respect for ritual obligations (*hucha*). The Moche deer-serpent-jaguar arguably represents the predecessor of the *amaru*, the feared manifestation of the eternal return—under diverse forms and in different contexts—of the ancestral order (Hocquenghem 1983b, 1987).

If the first rains in the mountains and the swellings of the rivers can be considered signs of reconciliation between humans and their ancestors, and the reestablishment of the circulation of vital force, I suggest that the open tomb in Moche iconography signifies the punishments related to the offerings of *Strombus* (Figure 2.13). Upon completing the rites of *Uma raimi quilla*, offerings were made to the deceased, who would return to their origins and establish communication between the real and mythic worlds (Guamán Poma de Ayala [1615] 1936; Hocquenghem 1979, 1987).

The Archaeological Testimonies: The Rites of Expiation in Huaca de la Luna

Archaeological research since the 1950s has increasingly suggested that the Moche iconographic scenes represent actual rites of a type practiced at the ceremonial and administrative centers. In 1987, Walter Alva, Susana

Meneses, and Luis Chero discovered the tomb of the Lord of Sipán and excavated this Moche site over the next eight years (Alva and Donnan 1993). These excavations confirmed the existence of the personages, attributes, ornaments and objects represented on funerary artifacts and temple walls (Alva 1994). Following this discovery, what remained to be found was archaeological evidence of the ceremonies, the sacrificial locations, and the features of the sacrificers and of the sacrificed (Bourget 1995).

In 1995, Steve Bourget located and excavated a sacrificial site in Plaza 3a within the highest platform of Huaca de la Luna, the Moche's administrative and ceremonial center. Bourget exposed the remains of men who apparently were sacrificed. Some were sacrificed in the manner of rites of expiation celebrated in the context of an extraordinary ceremony similar to that of the *Inca Itu*, while others appear to have been killed as in rites of expiation celebrated in the context of an annual ceremony similar to that of *Uma raimi quilla*.

These excavations in Plaza 3a, the studies and results of which have been published by Steve Bourget (1997, 1998a, 1998b) and John Verano (1998), brought to light a series of skeletons preserved in two levels of mud (Figure 2.20). The mud had accumulated from the disintegration of the enclosure's adobe walls during a period of extraordinary rains, the consequence of an uncommon but powerful natural event, El Niño, also known as the El Niño/Southern Oscillation (ENSO) (Hocquenghem 1998; Hocquenghem and Ortlieb 1992; Ortlieb and Machare 1993). The archaeological excavations revealed that the bodies fell over wet soil. As they decomposed, wind-blown sand penetrated into the thoracic cavities, indicating that the bodies remained exposed to the elements. Some time after, a second series of bodies fell, this time over a cap of sand that had dried, enclosed, and cracked. In this case, the remains of fly casings on the skeletal remains and the whiteness of the bones attest to the open-air exposure of the bodies before they too were eventually covered by fine sand. Dogs, foxes, and other carnivores apparently did not have access to the plaza; however, vultures could still account for the disorder of some of these skeletal remains.

The study of the Plaza 3a human remains revealed that all of the individuals were male and died between the ages of 15–39 years, the average age being 23. These men, who ought to have been robust, active, and of good health, suffered from repeated face-to-face combat. The skeletal remains exhibited ante mortem lesions such as fractures of the nose, ribs, and long bones, among others (Verano 1998). At the time of death, at least eleven individuals had lesions that were healing, suggesting a period of up to one month between infliction of the injury and death. The perimortem lesions include cuts on the cranium indicating facial cuts, cranial fractures that could have been caused by mace hits, and cuts in the cervical vertebrae indicating decapitation. Finally, in some cases the sacrificed individuals had cuts to the long bones and phalanges, indicating dismemberment.

The positions of the skeletons suggest that the bodies fell one by one, some over others, after being struck by

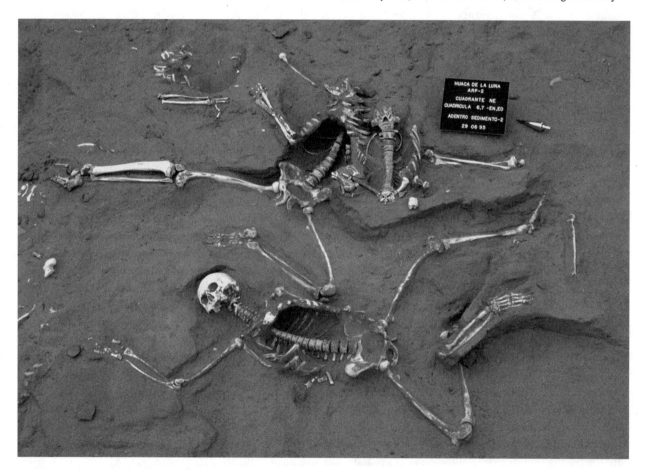

FIGURE 2.20. Sacrificial victims in Plaza 3a, Huaca de la Luna. Photograph by Steve Bourget.

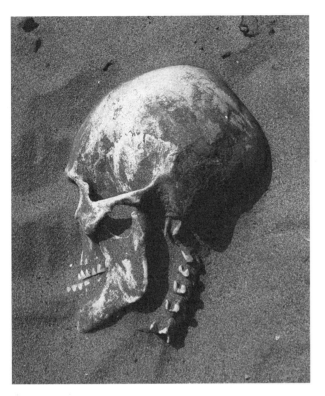

FIGURE 2.21. Human cranium, Plaza 3a, Huaca de la Luna. Photograph by Steve Bourget.

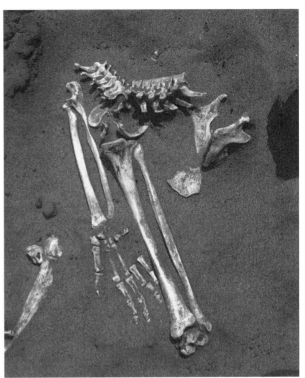

FIGURE 2.22. Human remains, Plaza 3a, Huaca de la Luna. Photograph by Steve Bourget.

clubs. The bodily positions, with arms and sometimes legs wide open, further suggest that these individuals were firmly tied or held to the ground at the moment of execution. Indeed, there remained in the mud the imprint of a rope at the height of a wrist (Bourget 1998b). Various bodies were decapitated, with the heads located here and there throughout the sacrificial arena, and with the inferior mandible sometimes separated (Figure 2.21). Other bodies were dismembered with apparently savage cuts to the skin and muscles. The two sequences of sacrifices could have been partially mixed given that most of the remains of the first act were only partially covered by the layer of soil, whose thickness did not surpass 10 cm. Articulated arms and legs and groups of vertebrae in anatomical position cover the site (Figure 2.22). It can be supposed that the sacrificers returned to the sacrificial site to manipulate the skeletal remains.

Recent mitochondrial DNA analyses show that all of the victims were related to the same group that lived in the ceremonial center (Shimada et al., this volume). Therefore, they cannot be considered the remains of enemies. Instead, and without doubt, they are the remains of warriors representing the two halves of the society, who had just confronted one another in ritual combat. They were then consecrated as sacrificial victims and executed.

The parallels between Moche iconography and the ethnohistoric and ethnographic information thus serve to reinforce further the identification of Plaza 3a as a sacrificial site and the executed bodies as the remains of sacrificial victims. I would even venture that the warriors whose skeletons lie in the mud were subjected to mistreatment during the ritual combat of the first lunar month after the December solstice—during the humid season. These particular humid seasons apparent in sediment layers of the plaza were marked by abnormal rains created by a mega El Niño event. The rivers overflowed, destroying the ceremonial center and some houses, damaging irrigation systems, and inundating fields.

The sacrificial victims were thus designated as scapegoats. Burdening the offenses, the debts of all of the community in front of the ancestors, they were tortured

FIGURE 2.23. Sacrificial victims in Plaza 3a, Huaca de la Luna. Photograph by Steve Bourget.

during a ceremony of extraordinary expiation, similar to the *Inca Itu*. This ceremony was intended to calm the wrath of those who animated and sustained the Moche world, which had manifested in the form of a flood. In contrast, I would argue that the skeletons lying over the cracked clay had been tortured some months after the rains, at the end of the dry season after the September equinox, during a ceremony of annual atonement similar to the Inca *Uma raimi quilla* (Figure 2.23). The ceremony presumably had an exceptional character since the consequences of the recent flood would still have been felt.

As one final note, some broken ceramic sherds and clay sculptures representing naked men seated with their legs crossed and ropes around their necks were found among the tortured bodies (Figure 2.24) (Bourget 2001). These sculptures bear some presumed similarities with the victims deposited in the plaza. I would even propose that the deposition of such material between these unburied bodies could be interpreted as a form of harassment rather than physical torture.

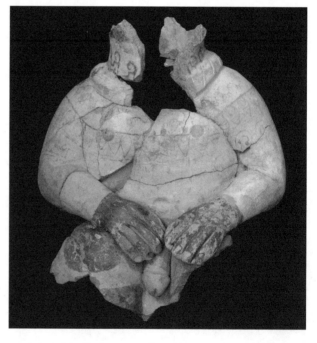

FIGURE 2.24. Clay statuette from Plaza 3a, Huaca de la Luna. Photograph by Steve Bourget.

Conclusion

By establishing relations between the independent but complementary sources of information—iconographic, ethnohistoric, ethnographic, and archaeological—I have tried to demonstrate how it is possible to reconstruct the meaning and function of Moche and Prehispanic iconography, as well as the circumstances and objects of the represented scenes. I cannot conclude this chapter without trying to communicate the emotional burden of confronting the remains of the atrociously mutilated bodies in Huaca de la Luna, as well as in the imagery of the Moche and others of martyred men and women or of decapitated young warriors. Nor can I conclude without expressing the impossibility of considering human sacrifice without it bringing to mind recollections of all the executions committed in the name of implacable divine justice, some infinitely given. All the massacres and all the common graves—in all times, here and in other places—attest to the atrocity of the sufferings imposed with the goal of establishing and maintaining social order.

Bibliography

Acosta, Juan de

[1590] 1954   *Historia natural y moral de las Indias*. BAE, Madrid.

Adorno, Rolena, and Ivan Boserup

2003   *New Studies of the Autograph Manuscript of Felipe Guaman Poma de Ayala's Nueva corónica y buen gobierno*. Museum Tusculanum Press, Copenhagen.

Alencastre, Andrés, and Georges Dumézil

1953   Fêtes et usages des indiens de Langui. *Journal de la Société des Américanistes*. T. XLII:22–118.

Alva, Walter

1994   *Sipán*. Colección Cultura y Artes del Perú, Lima.

Alva, Walter, and Christopher B. Donnan

1993   *Royal Tombs of Sipán*. Fowler Museum of Cultural History, University of California, Los Angeles.

Betanzos, Juan de

[1550] 1987   *Suma y narración de los incas*. Atlas, Madrid.

Bourget, Steve

1994   Los sacerdotes a la sombra del Cerro Blanco y del arco bicéfalo. *Revista del Museo de Arqueología, Antropología e Historia* 5:81–125. Trujillo, Perú.

1995   Éros et Thanatos: Relations symboliques entre la sexualité, la fertilité et la mort dans l'iconographie mochica. *Recherches Amérindiennes au Québec*, Vol. XXV (2):5–20.

1997   Excavaciones en la plaza 3a de la Huaca de la Luna. In *Investigaciones en la Huaca de la Luna 1995*, 51–59. Edited by Santiago Uceda, Elías Mujica, and Ricardo Morales. Universidad Nacional de la Libertad, Trujillo, Perú.

1998a   Pratiques sacrificielles et funéraires au site moche de la Huaca de la Luna, côte nord du Pérou. *Bulletin de l'Institut Français d'Etudes Andines* 27 (1):41–74.

1998b   Excavaciones en la plaza 3a y en la plataforma II de la Huaca de la Luna durante 1996. In *Investigaciones en la Huaca de la Luna 1996, Proyecto Arqueológico Huacas del Sol y de la Luna*, 43–64. Edited by Santiago Uceda, Elías Mujica, and Ricardo Morales. Universidad Nacional de la Libertad, Trujillo, Perú.

2001   Rituals of Sacrifice: Its Practice at Huaca de la Luna and Its Representation in Moche Iconography. In *Moche Art and Archaeology in Ancient Peru*, 88–109. Edited by Joanne Pillsbury. National Gallery of Art and Yale University Press, Washington, D.C.

Cieza de León, Pedro

[1553] 1967   *El señorío de los incas*. IEP, Lima.

[1553] 1984   *Crónica del Perú*, Primera Parte. Lima.

[1553] 1987   *Crónica del Perú*, Segunda Parte. Lima.

Cobo, Bernabé

[1653] 1956   *Historia del nuevo mundo*. BAE, Madrid.

Contreras, M. A.

1955   Las guerrillas indígenas del Chyaraque y del Toqto. *Archivo Peruano de Folklore* 1 (1):110–119. Cuzco.

Garcilaso de la Vega, Inca

[1609] 1985   *Comentarios reales de los incas*. Banco de Crédito del Perú, Lima.

Gonzáles Holguín, Diego

[1608] 1952   *Vocabulario de la lengua general de todo el Perú llamada quichua o del inca*. Universidad Nacional Mayor de San Marcos, Lima.

Guamán Poma de Ayala, Felipe

[1615] 1936   *Nueva corónica y buen gobierno*. Travaux et Mémoires de l'Institut d'Ethnologie, Paris.

Gorbák, C., M. Lischeti, and C. Muñoz

1962   Batallas rituales del Chiriaje y del Tocto de la provincia de Canas (Cuzco, Perú). *Revista del Museo Nacional*, T. XXXI:245–304.

Hartmann, Roswith

1972   Otros datos sobre las llamadas batallas rituales. *Actas y memorias del XXXIX Congreso Internacional de Americanistas*, 125–135. Lima.

Hocquenghem, Anne Marie

1973   *Code pour l'analyse des représentations figurées sur les vases mochicas*. Institut d'Ethnologie, Paris.

1977a   Une interprétation des vases portraits mochicas. *Ñawpa Pacha* 15:131–146.

1977b   Quelques projections sur l'iconographie mochica. *Baessler-Archiv* 25:163–191.

1978   Les combats mochicas: Essai d'interprétation d'un matériel archéologique à l'aide de l'iconologie, de l'ethno-histoire et de l'ethnologie. *Baessler-Archiv* 26:127–157.

1979a   L'iconographie mochica et les rites andins: Les scènes en relation avec l'océan. *Cahiers des Amériques Latines* 20:113–129.

1979b   Rapports entre les morts et les vivants dans la cosmovision mochica. *Les hommes et la mort: Objets et mondes* 19:85–95.

1980   L'iconographie mochica et les représentations de supplices. *Journal de la Société des Américanistes* T. LXVII:249–260.

1983a   Les crocs et les serpents: L'autorité absolue des ancêtres mytiques. *Visible Religion, Annual for Religious Iconography.* V. II:58–74.

1983b   The Beauty of the Deer-Serpent-Jaguar. *Camak beilage I, Mexicon:* 4–7. Berlin.

1987   *Iconografía mochica.* Fondo Editorial de la Pontificia Universidad Católica del Perú, Lima.

1996   Relación entre mito, rito, canto y baile e imagen: Afirmación de la identidad, legitimación del poder y perpetuación del orden. In *Actas del simposio interdisciplinario e internacional "Cosmología y música en los Andes",* 137–173. Edited by Max Peter Baumann. Vervuert, Iberoamericana, Frankfurt-Madrid.

1997   Como una imagen del otro lado del espejo: Una memoria para el futuro, una visión del orden del mundo andino. In *Pensar América: Cosmovisión mesoamericana y andina,* 215–247. Edited by A. Garrido Aranda. Coedición Obra Social y Cultural Cajasur, Ayuntamiento de Montilla, Cordoba.

1998   *Para vencer la muerte: Piura y Tumbes: Raíces en el bosque seco y en la selva alta, horizontes en el Pacífico y en la Amazonia.* CNRS, IFEA, INCAH, Lima.

Hocquenghem, Anne Marie, and Luc Ortlieb

1992   Eventos El Niño y lluvias anormales en la costa del Perú. *Bulletin de l'Institut Français d'Etudes Andines* 21 (1):197–278.

Kutscher, Gerdt

1954   *Nordperuanische Keramik : Figürlich Verzierte Gefässe der Früh-Chimu.* Gebr. Mann, Berlin.

1983   *Nordperuanische Gefässmalereien des Moche–Stils.* Materialien zur Allgemeinen und Vergleichenden Archäologie, 18. C. H. Beck, Munich.

Lévi-Strauss, Claude

1963   *Structural Anthropology.* Translated by Claire Jacobson and Brooke Grundfest Schoepf. Basic Books, New York.

López-Baralt, Mercedes

1993   *Guaman Poma, autor y artista.* Pontificia Universidad Católica del Perú, Lima.

Molina, Cristóbal de

[1575] 1943   Fábulas y ritos de los incas. *Las crónicas de los molinas,* 7–84. Lima.

1959   Ritos y fabulas de los inca. Editorial Futuro, Buenos Aires.

Murra, John

1975   El tráfico de mullu en la costa del Pacífico. *Formaciones económicas y políticas del mundo andino,* 255–267. Instituto d'Etudes Peruanos, Lima.

Ortleib, Luc, and Jose Machare, eds.

1993   Registro del fenómeno El Niño y de eventos ENSO en América del sur. *Bulletin de l'Institut Français d'Etudes Andines* 22 (1):406.

Taylor, Gérald

[1608] 1987a   *Ritos y tradiciones de Huarochirí del siglo XVII.* Instituto d'Etudes Peruanos and Institut Français d'Etudes Andines, Lima.

1987b   Cultos y fiestas de la comunidad de san Damián (Huarochirí) según la carta anua de 1609. *Bulletin de l'Institut Français d'Etudes Andines* 16 (2–4):85–96.

1999   *Camac, Camay, y Camasca y otros ensayos sobre Huarochirí y Yanyos.* Lima SFEA; Cuzco: Centro de Estudios Regionales Andinos «Bartolomé de las Casas.»

Tschopik, Harry

1946   The Aymara. *Handbook of South American Indians,* Vol. 2:501–573. Washington, D.C.

Verano, John

1998   Sacrificios humanos, desmembramientos y modificaciones culturales en restos osteológicos: Evidencias de las temporadas de investigación 1995–1996 en la Huaca de la Luna. In *Investigaciones en la Huaca de la Luna 1996,* 159–171. Edited by Santiago Uceda, Elías Mujica, and Ricardo Morales. Universidad Nacional de la Libertad, Trujillo, Perú.

CHAPTER THREE

Ulluchu: An Elusive Fruit

DONNA McCLELLAND, MOCHE ARCHIVE, UNIVERSITY OF CALIFORNIA, LOS ANGELES

Abstract

The ulluchu *appears in so many Moche images that it seems to have been an important part of Moche ceremonies. Yet what special properties does it contain? This chapter continues the research begun over thirty years ago to identify the* ulluchu *plant. Since the 1970s, the Moche Archive at the University of California, Los Angeles, has expanded its photographic collection of* ulluchu *depictions, and archaeological excavations have uncovered the remains of real* ulluchus.

In the early 1970s, I became intrigued with an image of what appeared to be a comma-shaped fruit that appears frequently in Moche art (Figure 3.1). Rafael Larco Hoyle referred to the plant as *ullucho* or *ulluchu* (2001:52, 149–150).[1] The latter spelling is more widely used today. I wrote to several botanists in an attempt to obtain a botanical identification. I shopped in the outdoor markets of Trujillo and Cajamarca in September 1972, looking for the fruit in the stalls of *curanderos*, or shamanic folk healers (Figure 3.2). At that time, I was not even sure if the plant existed or was mythical. I was able to eliminate several plants including pepino (*Solanum muricatum*), aji (*Capsicum* sp.), bean (*Phaseolus* sp.), gourd (*Lagenaria siceraria*), and avocado (*Persea americana*). Pepinos and gourds (Figure 3.3) are clearly depicted in Moche art and do not resemble *ulluchus*. Although I was unsuccessful in identifying the plant or actually seeing one, I knew that if I ever saw a real one, I would recognize it from its images in Moche art. Since the publication of the first study in 1977, the Moche Archive at the University of California, Los Angeles, has greatly expanded and has acquired additional photographs of Moche objects that are significant to this research. In addition, archeological excavations have revealed important information about the plant.

The *Ulluchu* in Moche Art

Depictions of *ulluchus* in fineline paintings exhibit a wide range of variations (Figure 3.4). I have defined the diagnostic features of the fruit by comparing these drawings with a modeled *ulluchu* (Figure 3.5). The fruit has a comma-shaped body with an exaggerated round calyx. Lines on the body in the paintings correspond to grooves on the modeled fruit.

A cursory look at Moche art leads to the impression that *ulluchus* can be found in almost every aspect of the art from Phase III through Phase V.[2] They are common in the backgrounds of many types of fineline paintings such as anthropomorphized clubs (Figure 3.6), badminton scenes (Figure 3.7),[3] anthropomorphized hawk warriors (Figure 3.8), and Muscovy duck warriors (Figure 3.9). Over 50 percent of the belts worn by figures in fineline paintings are decorated with *ulluchus*. Smaller images such as those on belts have the typical comma shape but generally do not show the grooves or calyxes (Figures 3.10, 3.11). An exception is a painting of hawk runners (Figure 3.12), which clearly shows the calyxes on the runners' belts. In the first of two scenes from the Warrior Narrative (Donnan and McClelland 1999:69, 130, 178), three warriors are fighting (Figure 3.13).

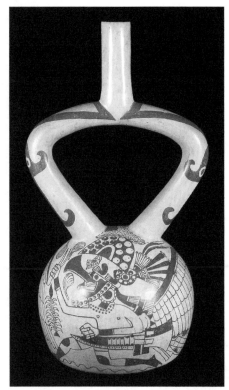

FIGURE 3.1. Anthropomorphized Muscovy duck runner and *ulluchu* fruits. Private collection. Drawing by Donna McClelland.

FIGURE 3.2. Outdoor shaman market, Trujillo, Peru. Photograph by Donna McClelland.

FIGURE 3.3. Modeled pepino and gourd. Private collection. Photographs by Christopher B. Donnan.

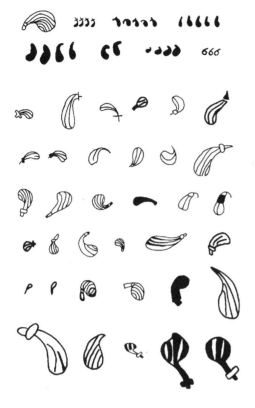

FIGURE 3.4. Images of *ulluchus* from fineline drawings. Drawing by Donna McClelland.

FIGURE 3.5. Modeled *ulluchu* bowl. Courtesy of Museo Nacional de Antropología, Arqueología e Historia, Lima (C-16589).

FIGURE 3.6. Anthropomorphized war clubs. Private collection. Drawing by Donna McClelland.

FIGURE 3.7. Ceremonial Badminton scene. Museo Nacional de Antropología, Arqueología e Historia, Lima. Drawing by Donna McClelland.

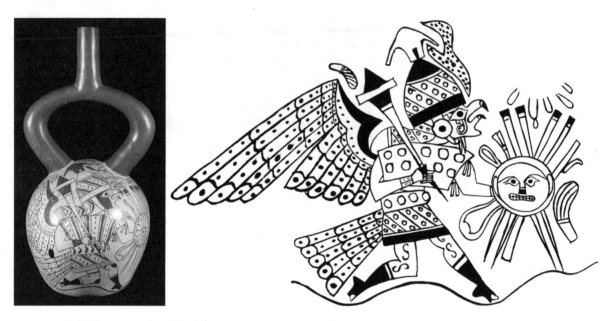

FIGURE 3.8. Anthropomorphized hawk warrior. Private collection. Drawing by Donna McClelland.

FIGURE 3.9. Anthropomorphized Muscovy duck warriors. Fowler Museum of Cultural History, UCLA. Drawing by Donna McClelland.

FIGURE 3.11. Anthropomorphized animal runners with *ulluchus* on belts. Völkerkundlichen Sammlungen der Stadt Im Reiss-Museum, Mannheim. Drawing by Donna McClelland.

FIGURE 3.10. Anthropomorphized monkey with *ulluchus* on belt. Museo Bruning, Lambayeque, Peru. Photograph by Christopher B. Donnan.

FIGURE 3.12. Anthropomorphized hawk runners. *Ulluchus* on belts have visible calyxes. The Art Institute of Chicago. Drawing by Donna McClelland.

FIGURE 3.13. Three fighting warriors, two with *ulluchus* on their belts and one with a backflap. Private collection. Drawing by Donna McClelland.

FIGURE 3.14. Captives bleeding and warriors holding the blood in goblets. Private collection. Drawing by Donna McClelland.

FIGURE 3.15. Supernatural figure holding lime gourd and wearing a double *ulluchu* headdress. Private collection. Photograph by Christopher B. Donnan.

FIGURE 3.16. Supernatural figure in a coca scene wearing a double *ulluchu* headdress. Private collection. Drawing by Donna McClelland.

Two have *ulluchus* on their belts. One of those also displays *ulluchus* on his backflap. In the second painting, *ulluchus* fill the background of a scene in which captives are bleeding, and warriors are holding the blood in goblets (Figure 3.14).

Double *ulluchus* are used as headdress ornaments on figures that either hold a lime gourd (Figure 3.15) or participate in the coca ceremony (Figure 3.16). Some of the headdresses are almost abstract (Figure 3.17). The identification of the double ornaments as *ulluchus* is suggested by the headdress worn by a supernatural coca chewer (Figure 3.18). *Ulluchu* fruits hanging from limbs are painted on each of the modeled *ulluchu* ornaments.

The *ulluchu* fruit is held in goblets in several types of depictions. They were carved on a calabash in a crescent boat scene (Figure 3.19). The occupants of the four boats

FIGURE 3.17. Two figures wearing abstract double *ulluchu* headdresses. Private collection. Photograph by Christopher B. Donnan.

FIGURE 3.18. Supernatural figure seated and holding lime gourd. *Ulluchus* are painted on modeled double *ulluchu* headdress. Private collection. Photograph by Christopher B. Donnan.

each hold a goblet, two of which contain an *ulluchu*. An anthropomorphized feline holding a *tumi*[4] also carries a goblet containing *ulluchus* in Figure 3.20, and *ulluchus* are pictured on anthropomorphized war clubs in weapon bundles (Figure 3.21). A mural at Huaca Facho also depicts anthropomorphized weapons bundles holding the fruit in goblets (Figure 3.22) (Donnan 1972). In a detail from a particularly complex fineline painting, a seated figure inside a ceremonial structure holds a goblet with an *ulluchu* (Figure 3.23). It appears in so many different ritualistic scenes that it must have been an important part of Moche ceremonies.

Our photographic sample contains eleven *ulluchu* trees with the fruit on the limbs. The tree has a splayed

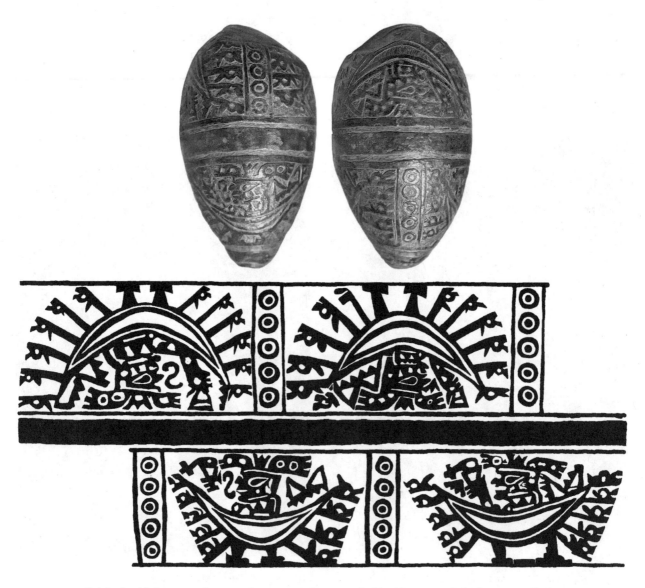

FIGURE 3.19. Calabash with four carved crescent boat scenes. Occupants hold goblets, two of which contain *ulluchus*. Private collection. Photograph by Christopher B. Donnan. Drawing by Donna McClelland.

FIGURE 3.20. Anthropomorphized feline holding a *tumi* and a goblet containing two *ulluchus*. Private collection. Drawing by Donna McClelland.

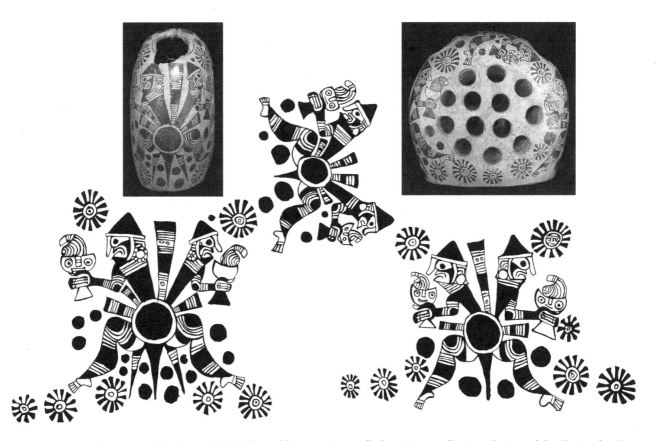

FIGURE 3.21. Anthropomorphized war clubs holding goblets containing *ulluchus*. Private collection. Photograph by Christopher B. Donnan. Drawing by Donna McClelland.

FIGURE 3.23. Detail from complex fineline painting. Figure in ceremonial structure holds a goblet containing an *ulluchu*. Private collection. Photograph by Christopher B. Donnan. Drawing by Donna McClelland.

FIGURE 3.22. Anthropomorphized war club holding goblet containing *ulluchu*. Panel from mural at Huaca Facho. Drawing by Patrick Finnerty.

FIGURE 3.24. Monkey with bag collecting *ulluchus* from tree. Private collection. Photograph by Christopher B. Donnan.

symmetry with variously shaped leaves. The fruit hangs from the limbs by its smaller pointed end (Figure 3.24). All trees but one have monkeys in the branches. The monkeys seem to be trained to climb the tree and pick the fruit, and some carry bags in which to collect the fruit (Figure 3.25). In one polychrome fineline painting, the monkeys wear tethers, but they are not attached to the tree (Figure 3.26).

Monkeys are modeled on two spout and handle bottles. On one, the monkey holds the spout, with its body forming the handle (Figure 3.27). Its tail is painted below the handle on the chamber. On the other bottle, the monkey clings to the spout (Figure 3.28), with its modeled tail lying on top of the fineline painting on the chamber below.

The spout and handle bottle in Figure 3.29 suggests that monkeys may also transport bags of *ulluchus*. What appears to be a harvest scene on the upper part of the

FIGURE 3.25. Scene on low-relief bottle. Monkeys with bags collecting *ulluchus* from trees. Private collection. Photograph by Christopher B. Donnan. Drawing by Donna McClelland.

FIGURE 3.26. Polychrome painting of tethered monkeys collecting *ulluchus* from trees. Museo Arqueológico "Horacio H. Urteaga," Cajamarca, Peru. Photograph by Christopher B. Donnan. Drawing by Donna McClelland.

FIGURE 3.27. *Ulluchu* tree on spout and handle bottle. A modeled monkey forms the handle of the bottle. Museo Rafael Larco Herrera, Lima. Photograph by Christopher B. Donnan. Drawing by Donna McClelland.

FIGURE 3.28. *Ulluchu* tree on spout and handle bottle. Modeled monkey grasps spout. Private collection. Photograph by Christopher B. Donnan. Drawing by Donna McClelland.

FIGURE 3.29. Harvest scene. Museo Arqueológico Rafael Larco Herrera, Lima. Drawing by Donna McClelland.

chamber features food plants such as corn, cactus, manioc, and beans. The figure at the right holds an *ulluchu* in one hand and points with the other hand to several bags around the handle. The gesture may indicate that the bags contain *ulluchus*. Below, monkeys in a procession carry net bags. They are followed by a figure with a whip. This may suggest that *ulluchus* were a part of this agricultural ritual. Several similar low-relief vessels in our sample display this scene with slight variations.

The association of monkeys with *ulluchu* trees continues in Chimu. A colorful Chimu textile published by Lavalle (1998:258) illustrates three trees. Each tree has three layers of branches, and each layer has three monkeys.

Plant Depictions in Moche Art

Although the *ulluchu* has not been identified, other fruits or seeds depicted in Moche paintings have been botanically identified, including *maichils* (yellow oleanders) and *espingos (Nectandra* spp.*)*. Our understanding of their physical and chemical properties enables us to make conjectures about the significance of these plants to the Moche.

The known properties of the yellow oleander, *Thevetia peruviana* (Towle 1961:77–78), suggest how it may have been used by the Moche (Figure 3.30). It is not a true oleander, but has the same poisonous properties. The plant contains a substance, thevetin, that is similar to digitalis. Its seeds are used in the manufacture of medicine for heart conditions. Although we have no idea whether the Moche were aware of its medicinal properties, the iconography suggests another use. Its drupe dries to a hollow, woody, triangular endocarp, called a *maichil* in Peru. Clustered together, the seeds produce a pleasant rattle sound. In a fineline painting of a musical procession, eleven of the participants wearing leggings strung

FIGURE 3.30. Yellow oleander plant, known as *maichil* in Peru. Photograph by Donald McClelland.

FIGURE 3.31. Triangular endocarps of yellow oleander (*maichils*) and fineline drawing of musical procession with participants wearing *maichils* on their leggings. Private collection. Photograph by Donald McClelland. Drawing by Donna McClelland.

with *maichils* (Figure 3.31) march towards the principal figure, who also wears these leggings.

Margaret Towle, a botanist, suggested that *espingos* are members of the genus *Nectandra* (1961:40). She describes a Moche ceramic figure holding strands of *espingo* seeds. It was illustrated by Yacovleff and Herrera (1935:89), who suggest that the seeds are the cotyledons of *N. pichurim*. The anthropomorphized owl in Figure 3.32 holds similar strands. Towle mentions archaeological specimens from Ancón that may be *N. reticulata* or *N. mollis*. She also describes archaeological specimens from Chuquitanta and Hacienda Grana in the Chancay Valley, but without identifying the species. The seeds on the three strands in Figure 3.33 differ in size and shape, and may represent more than one species of *Nectandra*.

The *espingo* (*Nectandra*) has an overpowering odor similar to curry that does not disperse or evaporate rapidly. Professor Henry Wassén (1976), at Gothenburg

Ethnographic Museum in Sweden, investigated the psychotropic, intoxicating, and medicinal properties of *espingo*. He reported that powdered *espingo* was added to drinks such as *chicha* both for medicinal and psychotropic purposes. Pablo José de Arriaga (1968:41) also reported that the Incas ground the *espingo* into a white powder and added it to *chicha* drinks. The sorcerers who drank them acted "as if mad," indicating that *espingos* were psychotropic and intoxicating.

An Identification?

The *ulluchu* has not yet been identified, so we currently have no way of assessing its significance beyond what is shown in the iconography. The botanical identification of the *ulluchu* may hinge on images of the tree. Monkeys are busy picking fruit in an *ulluchu* tree that seems to emanate from a copulating couple (Figure 3.34). The male is supernatural and holds an *ulluchu*. He looks like Wrinkle

FIGURE 3.32. Anthropomorphized owl holding strands of *espingos*. Private collection. Photograph by Christopher B. Donnan.

FIGURE 3.33. Strands of *espingos*. Photograph by Donald McClelland.

FIGURE 3.34. Erotic scene with *ulluchus* and *espingos*. Private collection. Drawing by Donna McClelland.

FIGURE 3.35. Low-relief erotic scene. The copulating couple is under an *ulluchu* tree and an *espingo* tree. Museo Arqueológico Rafael Larco Herrera, Lima. Drawing by Percy Fiestas.

Face, a well-known figure in Moche art. His companion, Iguana, faces him, and his spotted dog stands behind him. Additional *ulluchus* and *espingo* seeds float in the background. To the right, two people are blowing through tubes into a kiln, where drilled seeds of *espingo* are drying.

The association of *ulluchus* and *espingos* is demonstrated even more clearly on a low-relief spout and handle bottle that also features two copulating mythical figures. Two trees grow together out of the union (Figure 3.35). The tree on the right is an *espingo,* and that on the left is an *ulluchu.* Again, the male holds an *ulluchu.*[5] The *espingo* is the only plant that is clearly associated with the *ulluchu* in Moche art.[6]

These two trees provide an interesting clue about where the *ulluchu* tree might grow. A Peruvian botanist, Weberbauer (1945:587–592), mentions two areas east of the crest of the Andes in which *Nectandra pichurim* (*espingo*) grows. One is in the Mayo Valley, around Moyobamba (northeast of Chiclayo). The other is in the Monzón Valley (east of Chimbote) at an altitude of 900 to 1,800 m. In both cases, he calls the zone "Monte siempre verde, subxerófilo, de hojas más o menos duras" (1945:586). This may be the zone in which both trees grow.

After my research was published in 1977, I received a letter from Professor Wassén informing me of his interest in identifying the *ulluchu* botanically. He contacted botanists from Europe, North America, and South America. After considering numerous possibilities, he concluded that the *ulluchu* is a *Carica candicans*, a papaya (Wassén 1987:66–67). He also coauthored an article with two professors at Stockholm University (Hultin, Wassén, and Bondeson 1987) describing the enzyme papain, a chemical component of papaya.[7] Papain is extracted

from the unripe papaya fruit and can be used to keep the blood protein, fibrin, from coagulating. Hultin and his colleagues proposed that the enzyme was used in the Sacrifice Ceremony to prevent the coagulation of blood collected from sacrificed captives and later consumed by priests. The idea that the papaya was used to keep sacrificial blood from congealing was so appealing that it was wholeheartedly accepted, and the identification of the *ulluchu* as a papaya was not questioned.

Nevertheless, the *ulluchu* cannot be a papaya, which belongs to a group of plants called "cauliflory" (Armstrong 1999).[8] The papaya flowers and fruit grow on the trunk of the tree, not on its limbs (Figure 3.36). When papayas are picked or fall off, they leave triangular scars on the trunk. *Ulluchus* depicted in Moche art, however, hang from limbs. Furthermore, papaya leaves do not resemble *ulluchu* leaves, which are simple triangular, ovoid, or boomerang shapes hanging from limbs. Each large palmate papaya leaf grows on a stem from the top of the tree. Unfortunately, the idea that the *ulluchu* is a papaya still persists.

Archaeological Excavations

At the time of the original publication of this research, no archaeological excavations had turned up any real *ulluchus,* but since 1977, two excavations at Sipán and Dos Cabezas have recovered real ones. Two others, at San José de Moro and Huaca de la Luna, have found carved *ulluchu* beads (Figure 3.37).

SIPÁN

In the 1980s, Walter Alva directed the excavation of the royal Moche tombs containing large amounts of

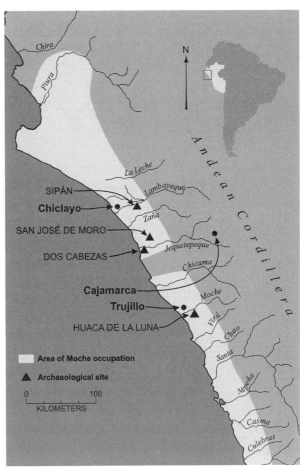

FIGURE 3.36. Papaya tree. Photograph by Donald McClelland.

FIGURE 3.37. Area of Moche occupation and archaeological sites. Map by Donald McClelland.

gold and gilded copper objects in a small pyramid near the village of Sipán in the Lambayeque Valley (Alva 1994; Alva and Donnan 1993). A bivalve shell offering was excavated from the ramp leading to the top of the pyramid. Inside the shell were several desiccated *ulluchus* (Figure 3.38). They were easily identified by their grooved comma shape and enlarged calyx. Their composition was like cigarette ash, but Christopher Donnan was able to photograph them before they collapsed. This was the first evidence that the *ulluchu* was definitely a real and not a mythical fruit.

The Royal Tombs contained several rectangular banners covered with gilded copper platelets attached to a textile backing. *Ulluchus* are embossed on the platelets bordering the banners (Figure 3.39). When the platelets were lifted, a real *ulluchu* was found under each one (Fig-

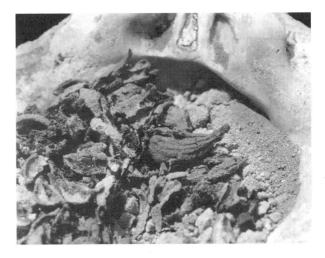

FIGURE 3.38. *Ulluchu* cache at Sipán. Photograph by Christopher B. Donnan.

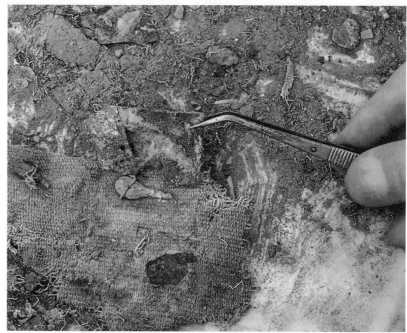

FIGURE 3.39. Sipán banner with platelets embossed with *ulluchus*. From Alva and Donnan 1993, Figure 62.

FIGURE 3.40. Lifting platelet on banner to reveal real *ulluchu* underneath. From Alva 1994, page 179.

ure 3.40; Alva 1994:179). A hole had been drilled through each *ulluchu*, which was secured to the textile backing with a thread to maintain the fruit's position when the banner was held aloft.

DOS CABEZAS

Between 1997 and 1999, Christopher Donnan excavated three elite male tombs with rich grave goods at Dos Cabezas, a pyramid near the mouth of the Jequetepeque River.[9] The burials were dated to approximately AD 400. Three mud brick tombs were built on a platform in a line next to the outer southwest wall of the pyramid. The individual in the middle tomb had a small mound of *ulluchus* near his right side (Figure 3.41). They were also desiccated and fragile, but less so than the ones in the shell cache offering at Sipán. They appear to be the same shape and size as the Sipán examples: approximately 2.5

to 3 cm long. The actual *ulluchus* that have been found so far are smaller than they appear in fineline paintings. Moche artists may have painted them larger than life-size to make them recognizable.

The three skeletons in the three tombs are giants compared to the average Moche male. A Phase IV fine-line painting may illustrate two giant Moche warriors in a fighting scene (Figure 3.42). All of the combatants wear *ulluchu* designs on their belts. The long legs and large heads of the two giant warriors are similar to those of the skeletons in the Dos Cabezas tombs (Figure 3.41).

A perspective view of the pyramid shows the south-west side corner, where the burial platform was located (Figure 3.43). When the front of the pyramid was cleared, a cache of *ulluchus* was found on a dais near the base at the northwest corner (Figure 3.44).

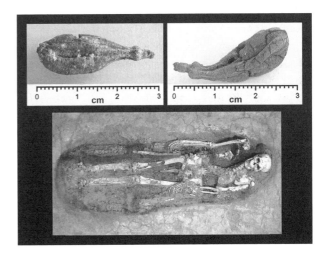

FIGURE 3.41. *Ulluchus* recovered from Dos Cabezas burial. Photographs by Donald McClelland (*ulluchus*) and Christopher B. Donnan (burial).

FIGURE 3.42. Fighting scene involving two giant warriors. Museo de la Nación, Lima. Drawing by Donna McClelland.

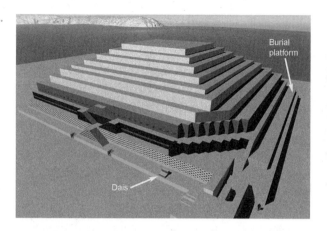

FIGURE 3.43. Perspective view of Dos Cabezas pyramid. Computer rendering by Christopher B. Donnan.

FIGURE 3.44. Dais at front of Dos Cabezas pyramid where a cache of *ulluchus* was found. Photograph by Christopher B. Donnan.

SAN JOSÉ DE MORO

In 1992, Christopher Donnan and Luis Jaime Castillo excavated the site of San José de Moro in the Jequetepeque Valley near the Chaman River. An elite burial of a female was found in a large room tomb; and near the upper sidewall of the chamber, a Moche infant was buried in a shaft tomb (Figure 3.45). Around the neck of the infant was a necklace of very small, carved and drilled *Spondylus* shell beads in the shape of *ulluchus* (Figure 3.46). They are approximately 1 cm in length.

HUACA DE LA LUNA

Steve Bourget excavated the Phase IV Tomb 2/3 on Platform II at Huaca de la Luna in the Moche Valley. In the tomb were carved bone *ulluchu* beads drilled for stringing (Figure 3.47). They are approximately 1.3 to 1.7 cm in length. These beads, as well as the *Spondylus* shell beads from San José de Moro, are somewhat smaller than the real *ulluchus* found at Sipán and Dos Cabezas.

Recent Attempts at Identification

The discovery of the desiccated *ulluchus* confirmed that the plant was real; however, we still have not identified it or determined what properties it has that would have been of value to the Moche. It has been suggested that the *ulluchu* is a *Meliaceae*. Unfortunately, *Meliaceae* is a large plant family that includes at least nine cedars plus many other trees and plants. The *ulluchu* may be a *Meli-*

FIGURE 3.45. Infant burial above an elite room tomb. Photograph by Christopher B. Donnan.

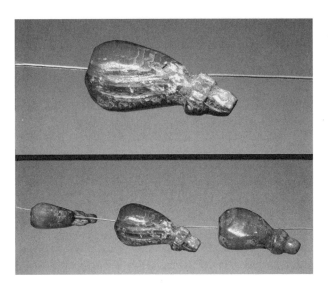

FIGURE 3.46. *Spondylus* shell *ulluchu* beads found around the neck of buried infant. Photograph by Donald McClelland.

FIGURE 3.47. Necklace of bone beads in the form of *ulluchus* from Huaca de la Luna. Photograph by author.

aceae, but we need a specific identification of the plant to locate it and determine whether it has special properties that would explain its omnipresence in Moche art.

I have attempted to obtain an identification of the *ulluchu* by contacting several botanists who specialize in Peruvian plants. I included a photograph of real, desiccated *ulluchus* and the iconographic evidence of a possible geographic zone where it may grow. So far, none of these botanists has suggested an identification.

Conclusions

Although the botanical identification of the *ulluchu* remains elusive, recent fineline paintings provide a valuable clue about where to search for the growing plant, as well as insights about its importance and role in Moche society. The use of trained monkeys to pick and transport *ulluchus* reveals an interesting aspect of Moche culture. Monkeys are almost exclusively associated with *ulluchus* rather than with other plants. The only plants more frequently depicted in Moche art are beans. *Ulluchus* appear in so many different ritualistic scenes, such as the runners in Figure 3.48, that they must have been an important part of Moche ceremonies.

Archaeological excavations have found actual *ulluchus* in elite tombs at two sites. These real *ulluchus,* with their grooved, comma shape and thick calyx, look exactly like the Moche images and were easy to identify.

FIGURE 3.48. Five runners with *ulluchus* in background. The Art Institute of Chicago. Drawing by Donna McClelland.

We could finally determine their actual size. Apparently, they were considerably smaller than they appear in Moche art.

The value of knowing the *ulluchu's* properties is demonstrated in the discussion of other plants such as *espingo* and yellow oleander. If we knew the properties of the *ulluchu,* we might be able to explain its omnipresence in Moche art. The biggest challenge remains: an identification.

Addendum

Since I presented this paper at the Sibley Conference at the University of Texas, November 2003, the Larco Museum in Lima has made their online catalog (catálogo en línea) available to the public on the Internet (*http://catalogomuseolarco.perucultural.org.pe*). It displays many ceramics with *ulluchus* that I have never seen before. The most interesting to me are the seated anthropomorphized *ulluchus*. I am grateful to the Larco Museum for their generosity in making images of this large group *ulluchu* ceramics available.

Notes

Thanks to Chris for lugging heavy photographic equipment all over Europe, North America, and South America on many trips in all kinds of weather to take photographs of fineline paintings for me to draw.

1. This study continues the search for the identification of a plant in Moche art called an *ulluchu*. The first study was published in 1977 (McClelland 1977). Both studies were conducted in the Moche Archive created by Christopher B. Donnan at the University of California, Los Angeles.

2. Rafael Larco Hoyle (1948) divided Moche vessels into a five-phase chronology.

3. Gerdt Kutscher (1956) described these scenes as Badminton because of the resemblance of the flowerlike objects to shuttlecocks. Edward de Bock (1998) described this scene as a waterlily ritual.

4. *Tumis* are ritual knives with curved blades used only by supernatural beings.

5. Many cultures have a mythical tree, but what the tree represents is different from culture to culture. Some are called the Tree of Life. The Judeo-Christian Bible describes the tree of knowledge in the garden of Eden on which grew the forbidden fruit tasted by Adam and Eve. In Norse mythology, Yggdrasil is a giant ash tree that is the foundation of the universe. The Maya sacred tree, *Yaxhe*, is a tall ceiba that represents the *axis mundi*, a stable world center for the three layers of the earth: underworld of death, the middle world of life, and the upper world of heaven.

6. *Ulluchus* and *espingos* are also associated in two fineline paintings of the Sacrifice Ceremony (Donnan and McClelland 1999: figs. 4.29, 4.102).

7. Today the enzyme papain is commonly used as a meat tenderizer.

8. *Cauliflory* translates as "stem flower."

9. In their search for gold, the Spanish cut through the center of the pyramid leaving two high pyramidal structures on either side of the cut resembling two heads, thus the site's name of Dos Cabezas.

Bibliography

Alva, Walter

1994   *Sipán*. Colección Culturas y Artes del Perú, Lima.

Alva, Walter, and Christopher B. Donnan

1993   *Royal Tombs of Sipán*. Fowler Museum of Cultural History, University of California, Los Angeles.

Armstrong, Wayne P.

1999   The Truth about Cauliflory. Wayne's Word Noteworthy Plants: May. http://waynesword.Palomar.edu/plmay99.htm.

Arriaga, Pablo José de

1968   *La extirpación de la idolatría en el Perú*. University of Kentucky Press, Lexington.

De Bock, Edward K.

1998   The Waterlily Ritual: An Andean Political and Religious Ceremony of the Moche Culture. *Journal of the Steward Anthropological Society* 26 (1–2):1–18.

Donnan, Christopher B.

1972   Moche-Huari Murals from Northern Peru. *Archaeology* 25 (2):85–95.

Donnan, Christopher B., and Donna McClelland

1999   *Moche Fineline Painting: Its Evolution and Its Artists*. Fowler Museum of Cultural History, University of California, Los Angeles.

Hultin, Eskil, Henry Wassén, and Wolmar Bondeson

1987   Papain in Moche Blood Ceremonies. *Journal of Ethnopharmacology* 19 (2):227–228.

Kutscher, Gerdt

1956   Das Federball-Spiel in der Alten Kultur von Moche. *Bassler-Archiv, Neue Folge*, Band IV, 173–184. Berlin.

Larco Hoyle, Rafael

1948   *Cronología arqueológica del norte del Perú*. Sociedad Geográfica Americana, Buenos Aires.

2001   *Los Mochicas*. Vol. I. Museo Arqueológico Raphael Larco Herrera, Lima.

Lavalle, José Antonio de

1998   *Culturas precolumbinas: Chimu*. Colección Arte y Tesoros del Perú, Banco de Crédito del Perú, Lima.

McClelland, Donna

1977   The *Ulluchu*: A Moche Symbolic Fruit. In *Pre-Columbian Art History, Selected Readings*, 435–452. Edited by Alana Cordy-Collins and Jean Stern. Peek Publications, Palo Alto, California.

Towle, Margaret A.

1961   *The Ethnobotany of Pre-Columbian Peru*. Wenner-Gren Foundation for Anthropological Research and Aldine Publishing Company, Chicago.

Wassén, S. Henry

1976   Was *Espingo* (*Ispincu*) of Psychotropic and Intoxicating

Importance for Shamans in Peru? In *The Realm of the Extra-Human: Agents and Audiences*, 511–520. Edited by Agehananda Bharati. Mouton Publishers, The Hague/Paris.

1987   *"Ulluchu" in Moche Iconography and Blood Ceremonies: The Search for Identification.* Göteborgs Etnografiska Museum, Annals 1985/86, Göteborg.

Weberbauer, August

1945   *El mundo vegetal Andes Peruanos estudio fitogeográfico.* Estación Experimental Agrícola de la Molina, Dirección de Agricultura, Minsterio de Agricultura, Lima, Perú.

Yacovleff, Eugene, and Flavio L. Herrera

1935   *El mundo vegetal de los antiguos peruanos.* Revista del Museo Nacional 3. Lima, Perú.

CHAPTER FOUR

Moche Masking Traditions

CHRISTOPHER B. DONNAN, UNIVERSITY OF CALIFORNIA, LOS ANGELES

Abstract

To understand how the Moche made and used masks, evidence must be assembled from several sources: the artistic depictions of Moche masks being used, the Moche masks that are in museums and private collections, and the instances of Moche masks that have been excavated archaeologically. No one of these sources alone could elucidate Moche masking traditions; however, when combined, they indicate that the Moche made and used at least three different types of masks. Each type had a distinct form and function: (1) masks that were to be worn by the living, (2) masks that were to be worn by the dead, and (3) masks that were to animate cane coffins. After Moche society ended around AD 800, these masking traditions changed dramatically.

The Moche made and used a variety of masks. To classify the different types, and to appreciate their distinct function, evidence must be assembled from the Moche artistic depictions that show masks being used, the Moche masks that are in museums and private collections today, and the Moche masks that have been excavated archaeologically. No one of these sources alone could elucidate Moche masking traditions, but when combined, they indicate that the Moche made and used at least three different types of masks, each with a distinct form and function.

Type 1: Masks Worn by the Living

There are five Moche objects that clearly portray individuals wearing masks. Three of these are cast copper finials on the handles of bladed spatulas (Figures 4.1–4.3). Each of the finials depicts a standing human figure with a large, fanged face. The face, however, is actually a mask with loop hinges that allow it to be swung up above the figure's head, thus revealing a fully human face underneath.

One of the copper finials (Figure 4.1) portrays an individual holding a club with a star-shaped mace head in his left hand. In his right hand, he holds a rattle with

four lobes at its lower end. His mask, which appears to be a feline or fox face with an extended tongue, has inlaid eyes and a crescent-shaped headdress ornament.

The second copper finial (Figure 4.2) depicts an individual holding a standard Moche war club in his left hand and rattle in his right hand. The mask is badly corroded, but it appears to be a human face with large fangs. The mask has a crescent-shaped headdress ornament similar to the one on the copper finial in Figure 4.1.

The third copper finial (Figure 4.3) also portrays an individual holding a war club in his left hand. But the upper part is bent back at the point where he grasps it, and the club head is behind the individual's neck. The pointed bottom of the club is bent down in front of his left arm. The club head may be star-shaped, like the one in Figure 4.1, but this is difficult to determine because it is heavily corroded. Like the other two finials, the figure holds a rattle his right hand. His mask is similar to that of the second finial (Figure 4.2), depicting a human face with large fangs. This mask has a headdress that is not crescent-shaped like the other two examples.

In addition to the three copper finials, the ceramic vessel illustrated in Figure 4.4 clearly portrays an individual wearing a mask. It is a stirrup spout bottle with

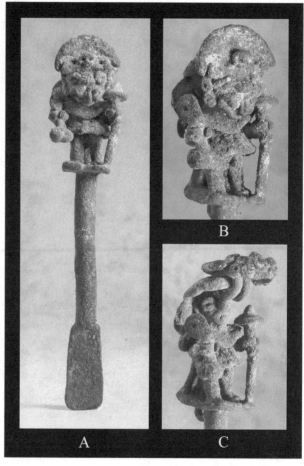

FIGURE 4.1. Copper finial (*A*) with a masked human figure. *B*, detail of finial; *C*, detail of hinged mask lifted to show face. Private collection. Photographs by Christopher B. Donnan.

FIGURE 4.2. Copper finial (*A*) with a masked human figure. *B*, detail of finial; *C*, detail of hinged mask lifted to show face. Private collection. Photographs courtesy of José Antonio Lavalle.

figures on top of the chamber. The principal figure is seated, leaning against a backrest, and holding a rattle in his right hand. He has a circular shield on his left wrist. On the right of the principal figure is a human head and a standard Moche war club. In front and to the left of the principal figure is another seated individual. A scar on the upper surface of the chamber opposite him suggests that there was originally a similar seated figure.

The principal figure wears a mask in the form of a large owl face with a human head in its beak. The mask is attached with a loop hinge similar to those on the copper finials, and thus can be swung up to reveal the face.[1] In addition to these sculptural representations of masks being worn, there is one fineline painting that provides

clear evidence of individuals wearing masks (Figure 4.5). Painted on the chamber of a stirrup spout bottle, the scene is divided into an upper and lower register. In the upper register the primary figure (who is larger and more elaborately dressed than the others) is being approached from the left by a smaller figure, a drummer, and three *queña* players. The primary figure has rattles tied to his legs and holds a ribbon, which is also held by the smaller figure standing behind him. In Moche art, dancers are generally portrayed either holding onto long ribbons or holding hands. They often have rattles tied to their legs and are accompanied by musicians (Donnan 1982).

The lower register of this scene depicts a procession of ten individuals. Their long garments suggest that

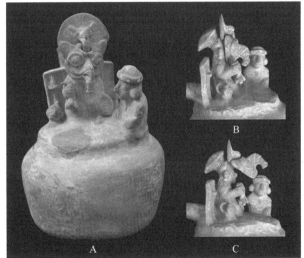

FIGURE 4.3. Copper finial with a masked human figure. C, detail of hinged mask lifted to reveal face. The Metropolitan Museum of Art, New York. Photographs by Christopher B. Donnan.

FIGURE 4.4. Ceramic vessel with an individual wearing a mask. Private collection. Photographs by Christopher B. Donnan.

FIGURE 4.5. Fineline painting of masked dancers. Redrawn from Lavalle 1985, page 58.

FIGURE 4.6. Ceramic mask of an individual with portions of his lip and nose missing. Staatliche Museen zu Berlin—Preussischer Kulturbesitz, Ethnologisches Museum (VA-18056).

they are females. The first three, as well as the last, are dressed in black and hold rattles in their right hands. The other six, dressed in white, hold hands as though dancing. Each wears a different mask. The mask worn by the second individual, for example, is the only one with a nose ornament. The mask worn by the third individual is an animal face. The fifth individual wears a skeleton mask, and the sixth individual's mask is the only one with a headdress. All of the masks are suspended by cords from above, as though tied to the individuals' headdresses. The suspension from above is similar to the loop hinges used on the copper and ceramic masked figures discussed above; located at the upper edge of the mask, they would have allowed it to be swung up above the person's head.

Some Moche masks in museums and private collections are remarkably similar to those being worn by masked individuals portrayed in Moche art. Nearly all are ceramic. Figure 4.6 illustrates a mask of an individual who is missing portions of his lip and nose. The mask in Figure 4.7 portrays a fanged figure wearing an animal head ring and serpent earrings. These features, along with the pronounced wrinkles and large circular eyes,

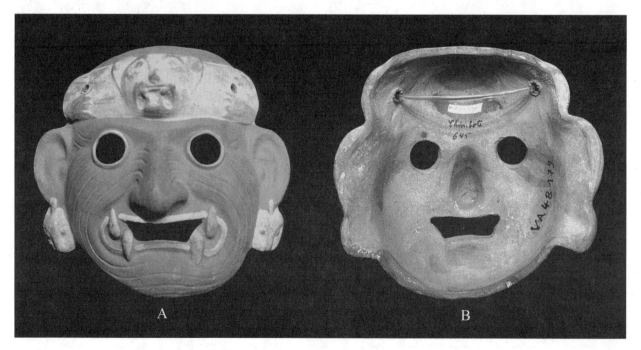

FIGURE 4.7. Ceramic mask of Wrinkle Face. Staatliche Museen zu Berlin—Preussischer Kulturbesitz, Ethnologisches Museum (VA-18057).

FIGURE 4.8. Scene on a ceramic vessel of Wrinkle Face hunting a deer. The Art Institute of Chicago. Drawing by Donna McClelland.

FIGURE 4.9. Ceramic mask. Private collection. Photograph by Christopher B. Donnan.

FIGURE 4.10. Copper mask. Museo Nacional Brüning de Lambayeque, Peru. Photograph courtesy of the Soloman R. Guggenheim Museum.

indicate that the mask is of Wrinkle Face, an important supernatural figure in Moche iconography (Figure 4.8) (Donnan and McClelland 1979:6, 31; 1999:64). Each of these ceramic masks has two perforations near its upper edge that could have been used to suspend it with cords from above, precisely as shown in the fineline dance scene of people wearing masks (Figure 4.5).

Two other masks of this type are unusual. One would have covered only the upper part of the face, leaving the chin and mouth exposed (Figure 4.9). The perforations are on the sides rather than the top of the face, but could still have allowed the mask to be suspended from above. The other mask (Figure 4.10) is unusual because it is copper rather than ceramic.

Moche masks that were made to be worn by the living have two consistent features: (1) the eyes are open so the person wearing them could see, and (2) the mouths are open, suggesting that the individuals wearing them were expected to speak or sing. This correlates well with the fineline painting portraying this type of mask being worn in a dance procession. The open eyes on the masks would have allowed the dancers to see and thus move about freely. Meanwhile, the open mouth would have allowed them to speak or sing.

FIGURE 4.11. Copper mask with inlaid shell eyes. Private collection. Photograph courtesy of José Antonio Lavalle.

FIGURE 4.12. Copper mask with inlaid shell eyes. Private collection. Photograph courtesy of José Antonio Lavalle.

It is noteworthy that all of the individuals portrayed wearing masks either hold rattles in their right hands or are flanked by individuals with rattles in their right hands (Figures 4.1–4.5). In the fineline painted scene, the six mask wearers are holding hands, indicating that they are dancing. There are also dancers and musicians in the upper register of the painting, suggesting that Moche masks were worn in rituals that involved dancing and music, or were worn by individuals who were chanting or singing to the accompaniment of a rattle.

Mask-wearing also appears to have had a strong association with warriors. All three of the masked figures depicted on the copper finials hold war clubs in their left hands (Figures 4.1–4.3). Similarly, the seated figure wearing a mask on the ceramic vessel has a circular shield on his left wrist, and on his right side there is a war club leaning against the backrest (Figure 4.4). In the fineline painted scene (Figure 4.5), both of the figures holding the ribbon in the upper register are dressed as warriors, with conical helmets. The principal figure also wears a warrior's backflap.

The existing evidence of Moche masks worn by the living indicates that they were made to be worn by both males and females, and by individuals of different roles and status. Moreover, masks depicting both human and animal figures, as well as both living and dead figures, could be worn by individuals engaged in the same ritual.

The essence of masking in all human societies is to bring about transformation. This first type of Moche mask, which was worn by the living, would have transformed the wearer into a different being such as an animal, a skeleton, or a supernatural figure such as Wrinkle Face.

Type 2: Masks Worn by the Dead

A second type of Moche mask has very different characteristics from the type worn by the living. Neither the eyes nor mouths have openings, suggesting that they were not to be worn by people who were moving about, or who were speaking or singing. They are consistently made of sheet metal. Most examples have the eyes inlaid with shell (Figures 4.11, 4.12).[2]

Evidence for the function of this type of mask comes from archaeological excavation, with two examples having been found in Moche tombs. The first to be excavated was in a royal tomb at Sipán (Alva 1994:186; Alva and Donnan 1993:189–191). The deceased was lying fully extended on his back. Inside his funerary bundle, a copper mask had been placed over his face (Figures 4.13, 4.14). The mask has a human face. Its right eye is inlaid with shell; the inlay of the left eye is missing.

A second mask worn by the dead was excavated in a tomb at Dos Cabezas (Donnan 2001, 2003). Here again the deceased was lying fully extended on his back. Inside his funerary bundle a large copper bowl had been placed upside down over his head (Figure 4.15). Beneath the bowl, the mask was lying directly over his face (Figure 4.16). It is made of copper, with gilded copper elements added to form a band over the nose and above the eyes to create a geometric band across the headdress, and to accentuate portions of the lower face (Figure 4.17). The mask has a gilded copper nose ornament, and both eyes are inlaid with shell. Numerous wires project from the chin and cheeks, with a gilded copper disc suspended from each. These probably represent a beard.

Some Moche masks with inlaid shell eyes have large fanged mouths (Figure 4.18). Although none of these

FIGURE 4.13. Masked individual in Tomb 3 at Sipán. Photograph by Christopher B. Donnan.

FIGURE 4.14. Detail of masked individual in Tomb 3 at Sipán. Photograph by Christopher B. Donnan.

FIGURE 4.15. Funerary context at Dos Cabezas. Photograph by Christopher B. Donnan.

FIGURE 4.16. Copper mask from Dos Cabezas. Instituto Nacional de Cultura, La Libertad. Photograph by Christopher B. Donnan.

have been excavated archaeologically, it is likely that they were made as funerary masks and placed over the faces of deceased individuals.

The large inlaid eyes on Moche masks made for the dead give the appearance of a fully alert, living individual. Thus, these masks would have served to transform the dead into the living, effectively giving the deceased the appearance of eternal life. Although only two examples of this type of mask have been found archaeologically, in both cases they were found in extremely elaborate tombs. It may be that this type of mask was restricted to the burials of individuals of the highest echelon of Moche society.

Although the masks worn by the dead were normally made as a single object, one unusual variation should be noted. The principal individual in the tomb of the Warrior Priest at Sipán (Tomb 1) was buried with two eyes, a nose, and a mouth that were placed over these parts of his face (Figure 4.19, Alva 1994:72–75; Alva and Donnan 1993:89–90). Each was made separately of sheet gold. Together, they would have served the same function as a burial mask, transforming the dead into the living and thus giving the deceased the appearance of eternal life.

A

B

FIGURE 4.17. Copper mask from Dos Cabezas. Instituto Nacional de Cultura, La Libertad. Photograph by Christopher B. Donnan.

FIGURE 4.18. Copper mask. Private collection. Photograph by Christopher B. Donnan.

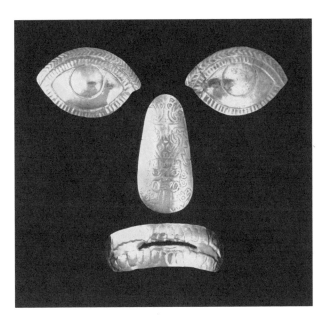

FIGURE 4.19. Separate mask elements from the tomb of the Warrior Priest (Tomb 1) at Sipán. Museo Tumbas Reales de Sipán. Photograph courtesy of José Antonio Lavalle.

In this case, the Moche simply divided the traditional burial mask into its basic elements and used them to achieve the same function.

Type 3: Masks to Animate Coffins

A third type of Moche mask is similar to the type worn by the dead. There are no openings for the eyes or mouth, implying that this type of mask was not worn by living individuals. All known examples are made of sheet metal and are larger than life-size (Figures 4.20, 4.21).

The eyes have a very unusual construction. Instead of being inlaid, each eye is created with a slightly convex, eye-shaped piece of sheet metal that is attached with

FIGURE 4.20. Copper mask. Private collection. Photograph by Christopher B. Donnan.

FIGURE 4.21. Copper mask. Instituto Nacional de Cultura, La Libertad. Photograph by Christopher B. Donnan.

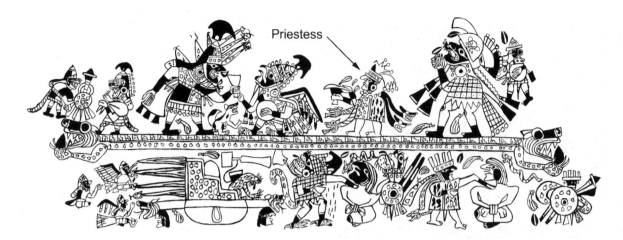

Priestess

FIGURE 4.22. Scene on a vessel of the Sacrifice Ceremony. Staatliches Museum für Völkerkunde, Munich. Drawing by Donna McClelland.

FIGURE 4.23. Priestess tomb at San José de Moro. Photograph by Christopher B. Donnan.

tabs to the surface of the mask. This piece has a large hole near its center, with a disc of sheet metal suspended inside to represent the iris of the eye. Because the disc is suspended on two wire loops, it swings when the mask is moved, thus making the eyes appear to be looking about.

The function of this type of mask became clear when examples were excavated archaeologically in two high-status tombs at the site of San José de Moro (Donnan and Castillo 1992, 1994). The tombs were of adult females, each of whom was buried with two large plumes and a distinctive goblet that identified her as having served in the role of Priestess at the Sacrifice Ceremony (Figures 4.22–4.24). Each female was buried in a large cane coffin wrapped in a textile (Figure 4.25). The mask was then sewn to the textile exterior of the coffin at the head end, human arms and legs of sheet metal were sewn to the sides along with sheet metal objects depicting jars with ropes around their necks, and two sheet metal plumes were stuck into the top (Figure 4.26).

The mask and other metal objects sewn to the exterior of these coffins have a direct correlation with fineline paintings of the Priestess in a reed boat (Figure 4.27). These paintings are from ceramic vessels that are contemporary with the two Priestess tombs excavated at San José de Moro, and they were probably painted at or near that site. They portray the Priestess, with her two-tasseled headdress, standing in a reed boat with jars that have ropes around their necks. The boat is animated with heads at the bow and stern, as well as human arms and legs.

Reed boats closely resemble cane coffins. Both have long elements that are bound together intermittently along their length with sedge rope. They are made entirely from plant material and are yellowish brown. Apparently, the Moche made an analogy between reed boats and cane coffins, and they buried the Priestesses in cane coffins as though placing them in their reed boats. To underscore this analogy, they anthropomorphized the cane coffins in the same way they anthropomorphized her reed boat in fineline paintings: with arms and legs along the sides, and a face at the end. They even added sheet metal depictions of jars with ropes around their necks, analogous to the jars shown on the reed boats transporting the Priestess (Figures 4.26, 4.27). The two plumes in the top of the coffin would have

FIGURE 4.24. Priestess tomb at San José de Moro. Photograph by Christopher B. Donnan.

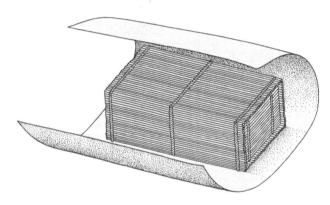

FIGURE 4.25. Image of the Priestess's coffin depicting textile exterior. Drawing by Patrick Finnerty.

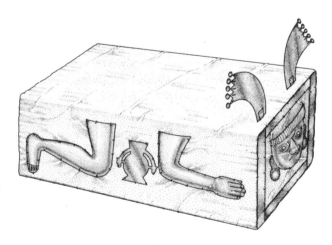

FIGURE 4.26. Image of the Priestess's coffin depicting elements sewn on textile exterior. Drawing by Patrick Finnerty.

FIGURE 4.27. Scene from a vessel of the Priestess in a reed boat. Museo Amano, Lima. Drawing by Alana Cordy-Collins.

clearly indicated that it contained a Priestess, for this is a unique characteristic of her ritual attire.

To date, these are the only two cane coffins archaeologically excavated that have sheet metal objects on their exterior. There are, however, several other masks of this type in museums and private collections, along with other sheet metal arms, legs, and plumes that are very similar in size and form to those excavated in the Priestess burials at San José de Moro.[3]

Ubbelohde-Doering (1983:112–120) excavated a disturbed shaft tomb at Pacatnamú containing sheet metal arms that are nearly identical to the ones attached to the coffins at San José de Moro (Ubbelohde-Doering 1983:112–120), suggesting that it was the coffin of another Priestess. It was associated with Phase V ceramic vessels, and almost certainly pertains to this phase. The cane coffins containing Priestesses excavated at San José de Moro also are associated with Phase V. Furthermore, the fineline painted depictions of the Priestess in her anthropomorphized reed boat only occur in Phase V. Thus, it would appear that all of the examples of this type of mask occur in Phase V. There are no known antecedents for either its form or function.

The form of the masks used to animate cane coffins

closely conforms to their function. The fact that the eyes and mouths are not open implies that they were not worn by the living. Yet the intricate means of making the eyes move, combined with the fact that the masks were sewn to the exterior of the coffins, suggests that they were to be seen in motion, with the eyes moving to give the appearance that the mask was animated. Perhaps the coffin was carried through the community as part of the funerary ritual, with the eyes of the mask appearing to look about. Again, this type of Moche mask served to transform the cane coffin of a Priestess into the animated reed boat in which she is portrayed in fineline paintings.

Although the masks made to animate coffins were normally made as a single object, there is one unusual variation. At San José de Moro there was a large tomb similar to the two that contained Priestess burials. Its principal occupant, however, was a child between six and eight years of age (Figure 4.28). Like the Priestesses, the child was buried in a cane coffin that had a mask sewn to the exterior of the head end. This mask, however, consisted of a mouth, a nose, eyes, eyebrows, and ears with circular ear ornaments (Figure 4.29). Each element was made separately of sheet copper, with perfora-

land 1999:17), has turned the mask so it can be clearly recognized. Thus, the cane coffin in this scene appears to have been animated with a mask. It is not possible to say whether the coffin contained the body of a Priestess. It is noteworthy, however, that all of the sixteen known bottles painted with the Burial Theme are Phase V, thus providing additional evidence that masks used to animate coffins pertain to that phase of the Moche style.

The three types of Moche masks defined in this study probably do not include the full inventory of masks that were made by the Moche. They do, however, provide a beginning for understanding Moche masking traditions.

FIGURE 4.28. Tomb of a masked child at San José de Moro. Photograph by Christopher B. Donnan.

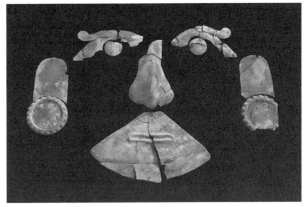

FIGURE 4.29. Separate mask elements of sheet copper from child's tomb at San José de Moro. Instituto Nacional de Cultura, La Libertad. Photograph by Christopher B. Donnan.

tions that allowed it to be sewn to a textile. The style of the mask was clearly derived from those used to animate the Priestess coffins. Even the eyes were made so the pupils would move about when the mask was in motion. Together, they would have transformed the inanimate coffin into an animated one. Like the burial mask in Tomb 1 at Sipán (Figure 4.19), this mask had been divided into its basic elements, which were then used to achieve the same purpose as the conventional mask.

One final observation should be made about the Moche masks created to animate coffins. In the Burial Theme in Moche iconography (Donnan and McClelland 1979) there is a clear portrayal of a cane coffin being lowered with ropes into a deep burial chamber (Figure 4.30). The face portrayed at one end of the coffin is almost certainly a burial mask, which would have been attached to the head end of the coffin. The artist, following typical Moche artistic canons (Donnan and McClel-

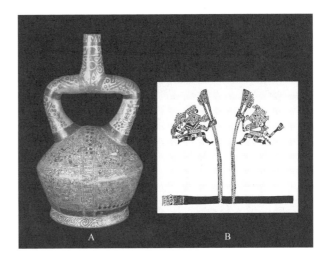

FIGURE 4.30. Stirrup bottle with Burial Theme. Private collection. Detail drawing (B) by Donna McClelland. Photograph by Christopher B. Donnan.

As more evidence becomes available, it is hoped that additional types of Moche masks can be identified on the basis of their form and function.

Notes

1. Of the tens of thousands of ceramic vessels photographed for the Moche Archive at the University of California, Los Angeles, this is the only one with a hinged element.

2. Other examples of this type of mask are illustrated in Lapiner 1976: figs. 323, 333, 349; and Lavalle 1985:227, 229.

3. There are similar arms, legs, and masks in the Museo de Oro Peruano in Lima. A pair of sheet metal legs is illustrated in Carcedo Muro 1999:362.

Bibliography

Alva, Walter

1994   *Sipán*. Colección Culturas y Artes del Perú, Lima.

Alva, Walter, and Christopher B. Donnan

1993   *Royal Tombs of Sipán*. Fowler Museum of Cultural History, University of California, Los Angeles.

Carcedo Muro, Paloma

1999   *Cobre del antiguo Perú*. APF Integra, Lima.

Donnan, Christopher B.

1982   Dance in Moche Art. *Ñawpa Pacha* 20:97–120.

2001   Moche Burials Uncovered. *National Geographic* 199 (3):58–73.

2003   Tumbas con entierros en miniatura: Un nuevo tipo funerario Moche. In *Moche: Hacia el Final del Milenio,* Tome I, 43–78. Actas del Segundo Coloquio sobre la Cultura Moche, Trujillo, 1 al 7 de agosto de 1999. Edited by Santiago Uceda and Elías Mujica. Universidad Nacional de Trujillo and Pontificia Universidad Católica del Perú, Lima.

Donnan, Christopher B., and Luis Jaime Castillo

1992   Finding the Tomb of a Moche Priestess. *Archaeology* 45 (6):38–42.

1994   Excavaciones de tumbas de sacerdotistas moche en San José de Moro, Jequetepeque. In *Moche: Propuestas y perspectivas*, 415–424. Actas del Primer Coloquio sobre la Cultura Moche, Trujillo, 12 a 16 de abril de 1993. Edited by Santiago Uceda and Elías Mujica. Travaux de l'Institut Français d'Études Andines 79. Universidad Nacional de la Libertad, Trujillo, Perú.

Donnan, Christopher B., and Donna McClelland

1979   *The Burial Theme in Moche Iconography*. Studies in Pre-Columbian Art and Archaeology 21. Dumbarton Oaks, Washington, D.C.

1999   *Moche Fineline Painting: Its Evolution and Its Artists*. Fowler Museum of Cultural History, University of California, Los Angeles.

Lapiner, Alan

1976   *Pre-Columbian Art of South America*. Harry N. Abrams, New York.

Lavalle, José Antonio de, ed.

1985   *Moche*. Colección Arte y Tesoros del Perú, Banco de Crédito del Perú, Lima.

Ubbelohde-Doering, Heinrich

1983   Vorspanische Graber von Pacatnamu, Nordperu. *Materialien zur allgemeinen und vergleichenden Archaologie 26*. Munich.

CHAPTER FIVE

Convergent Catastrophe and the Demise of Dos Cabezas

Environmental Change and Regime Change in Ancient Peru

MICHAEL E. MOSELEY, UNIVERSITY OF FLORIDA

CHRISTOPHER B. DONNAN, UNIVERSITY OF CALIFORNIA, LOS ANGELES

DAVID K. KEEFER, U.S. GEOLOGICAL SURVEY

Abstract

Greatly exceeding twentieth-century El Niño norms, exceptionally severe erosion damage has been documented at the Jequete-peque Moche center of Dos Cabezas and its agrarian hinterland. Flooding was followed by massive sand dune incursions, which contributed to the site abandonment. The dating and variable effects of these collateral natural disasters are reviewed and then assessed in other areas of the Moche realm.

The archaeological complex of Dos Cabezas (long 7°21.031"S lat 79°34.753"W) was a regional hub of Peru's prehistoric Moche culture. Situated immediately south of the Jequetepeque River mouth, the site was apparently the largest administrative center in this irrigated valley between about AD 300 and 650 (Figure 5.1). The Moche regime at Dos Cabezas, however, collapsed in the wake of convergent natural catastrophes. This chapter thus examines the relationships between that environmental change and cultural change.

Late in its history, the urban center of Dos Cabezas and its agrarian hinterlands experienced an episode of exceptionally severe El Niño rainfall and runoff that resulted in pervasive landscape stripping. Shortly after the metropolis was rebuilt, a collateral catastrophe struck the region in the form of expansive sand dunes advancing inland from the sea and burying much of the landscape. Despite Herculean efforts by the inhabitants to mitigate the unrelenting sands, Dos Cabezas became uninhabitable, and abandonment ensued.

After describing the lower valley, Dos Cabezas, and the disasters that struck it, we model relationships between rainfall, runoff, and sand dune formation by drawing upon analogies from recent severe El Niño

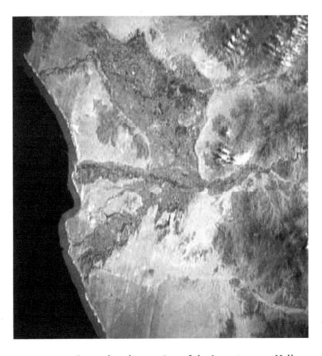

FIGURE 5.1. Space shuttle overview of the Jequetepeque Valley showing the location of Dos Cabezas; the northern, central, and southern lobes of irrigated land; and the normally dry drainage known as the Cupisnique Quebrada. Modified from and courtesy of NASA.

events and their contributions to marine and aeolian movement of sediments. We then assess the magnitude of the Moche flood event and aeolian sediment activity. We propose that a mega El Niño event produced severe erosion and abundant sediment supplies for the extensive formation of sand dunes, and that this phenomenon constituted a geoarchaeological horizon marker that should be evident elsewhere in the region.

Environmental Setting

Similar to other desert valleys, our study area is very arid with pauperous vegetation. Historically, all incidents of significant rainfall and flooding have occurred only in association with El Niño/Southern Oscillation (ENSO) events. Typically, strong long-shore currents flow northward along the coast, and strong winds blow inland off the ocean on a daily basis except during heavy winter fogs (Figure 5.2). Thick quaternary coastal alluvium forms plains or pampas that are typically truncated along the littoral by wave-cut sea cliffs approximately 55 m high. Nearing the coast, the river has down-cut through the pampas.

The Jequetepeque River is one of Peru's largest desert drainages, and it supplies water to three separate lobes of irrigated land (Figure 5.1). Situated behind a narrow range of hills, the northern lobe occupies inland alluvial plains that also receive intermittent runoff from the small Río Chaman. Today this forms the biggest expanse of Jequetepeque farmland, but it was largely undeveloped during the Dos Cabezas regime. A narrow, central band of farming occurs along the down-cut river. A somewhat larger, southern lobe descends an older, wider valley created by a former course of the river. Grading into the south side of this lobe is the wide, flat floodplain of a normally dry drainage, the Cupisnique Quebrada. With an extensive catchment basin in the desert foothills, the Cupisnique flows north to the former river course and then descends the old channel to the sea. The region where the wide quebrada and old valley merge has extensive tracts (> 20 km²) of flat land that were attractive for agriculture. When Dos Cabezas flourished, this region was extensively irrigated, and the expanse of southern farming likely matched or exceeded that of today's northern Chaman region. The southern heartland of early Moche farming was subject to a great deal of northward blowing sand. Irrigation entrained and deposited large quantities of aeolian sediment that contributed to the formation of unusually thick agricultural soils. Later, massive dune fields and sand seas inundated much of the south, curtailing its agricultural potential.

Site Description

Between about AD 300 and 650, Dos Cabezas apparently was the most important religious and administrative center in the Jequetepeque Valley and held a major place in the political structure of northern Peru. It was built atop a low (2 m high) terrace remnant about 500 m south of the Jequetepeque River and 400 m inland from the Pacific shoreline (Figure 5.3). The surviving core of the sprawling archaeological complex extends over approximately 1 km² and is dominated by a large platform mound flanked by spacious courts, corridors, and palace complexes made of adobe bricks. Surrounding the urban core are non-elite residential areas indicative of a large population that was highly stratified, with proletariat farmers and fisher folks supporting cadres of skilled crafts personnel who produced a wealth of fine arts for priests and potentates at the pinnacle of power.

Late Natural Disasters

The principal platform mound and attendant monumental facilities were remodeled, added to, and enlarged incrementally over time. If they ever suffered earthquake damage followed by reconstruction, it cannot be distinguished from normal architectural modifications and improvements. This is not the case for ENSO-induced flood damage. Excavations indicate that the impact of one ENSO episode was unprecedented in the long occupation of Dos Cabezas, and there are no indications of a comparable event after abandonment. The large scale and scope of erosional damage to the capital is commensurate with the pervasive destruction of Moche agricultural systems documented on the south side of the valley (Eling 1986). In both cases, impact magnitude greatly exceeded that of the very strong 1997–1998 ENSO, considered the most severe of the twentieth century.

Evidence of prehistoric erosion is dramatic at the towering platform mound that dominates the old urban core. Called Huaca Dos Cabezas, the structure measures more than 230 m by 165 m at its base and has a summit elevation of more than 30 m. Constructed over time, with interspersed episodes of use and build-

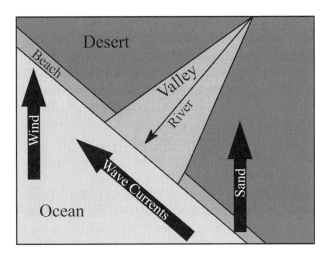

FIGURE 5.2. Schematic overview of an idealized coastal valley illustrating directions of river flow, near-shore coastal currents, winds, and sand movement.

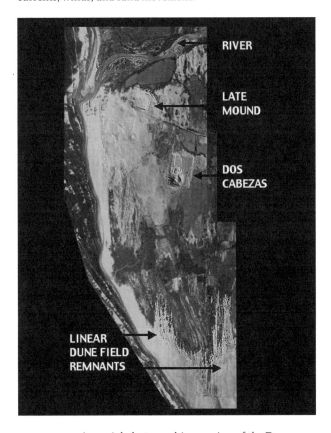

FIGURE 5.3. An aerial photographic overview of the Dos Cabezas area showing the Jequetepeque River, the late prehistoric platform mound, Huaca Dos Cabezas, and its downwind dune fields. Compiled and modified from an image courtesy of SAN.

ing, it became the largest single edifice ever built in the Jequetepeque Valley. Made of mud bricks, it had terraced sides that apparently stepped up to a flat-topped summit, destroyed by Spanish Colonial looting. During the prehistoric ENSO event copious runoff flowed down the sides of Huaca Dos Cabezas, cutting rills and concavities. Figures 5.4–5.6 illustrate the southwest corner of the platform after it was enlarged with solid adobe masonry prior to destruction (Figure 5.4); immediately following severe ENSO scouring (Figure 5.5); and after the enlargement of two erosional concavities to create chambers for tombs (Figure 5.6). Two tombs, Tombs 2 and 3, were richly accompanied high-status burials (Donnan 2001, 2003). Once the chambers were transformed into roofed mausoleums, the damaged platform was repaired and put back in use.

Two radiocarbon dates were obtained from material excavated in Tomb 2. Sample 1 was desiccated organic material from inside the cranium of the principal individual, while Sample 2 was from a fragment of textile from his funerary bundle. These produced the following results:

> Sample 1: Beta-129542
> > Conventional radiocarbon: 1530+/-60 BP
> > Calibrated 2 Sigma (95% probability): Calibrated AD 410–645
> Sample 2: Beta 129543
> > Conventional radiocarbon: 1580 +/- 50 BP
> > Calibrated 2 Sigma (95% probability): Calibrated AD 390–600

These results indicate that Tomb 2 dates between AD 390 and 645, and there is good evidence that the Tombs 2 and 3 are contemporary.[1] Other radiocarbon dates obtained from Moche material at Dos Cabezas cluster between AD 420 and 610 (calibrated) and thus are consistent with the dates from Tomb 2. It is likely that Tomb 2 dates toward the later part of this occupation, sometime around AD 600. Therefore, the erosional concavity that was enlarged to form the burial chambers would have originated shortly before this date.

After the tombs were completed and extensive settlement repairs to the settlement were made, aeolian sand began to inundate Dos Cabezas. The sand arose as a beach-side linear dune field directly upwind of the civic

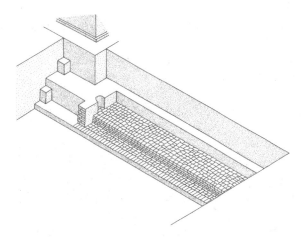

FIGURE 5.4. Diagram of the southwest corner of Huaca Dos Cabezas prior to El Niño.

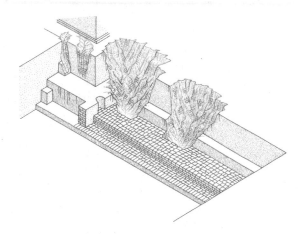

FIGURE 5.5. Diagram of the southwest corner of Huaca Dos Cabezas after destructive erosion.

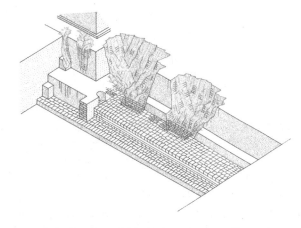

FIGURE 5.6. Diagram of the southwest corner of Huaca Dos Cabezas with modification of erosional concavities to create tomb chambers.

center, with the sediment propelled inland by strong daily winds blowing northeast off the sea (Figures 5.3, 5.7). Once the dune field began to form, salinizing sands invaded all areas of the civic center on a prolonged basis, accumulating on the lee side of major buildings and in high-walled courts and plazas. Among other ill effects, the airborne sediment would have often impaired vision between approximately 9 a.m. and 5 p.m., when daily winds are in force—to judge from our experience with active coastal dune fields.

The sand was certainly detrimental to the capital's pomp, ceremony, and business, and Herculean efforts were devoted to dealing with it. The inhabitants may have first attempted to remove the sand by simply transporting it off-site; however, as ever-larger quantities of sediment continued to accumulate in the civic center, workers spread it out over the floors of spacious rooms and large patios and then capped it with new clay floors. In some buildings, this occurred on multiple occasions, resulting in as many as four superimposed clay floors with aeolian sand between each. Eventually, sand disposal strategies shifted to employing aeolian sediment in adobe case and loose fill construction. Nearly all of the large platform mounds at Dos Cabezas began as a solid matrix of mud bricks, and throughout most of the Moche occupation they were enlarged using only solid brick masonry. Near the end of the capital's occupation, however, enlargements entailed construction of large retaining walls of mud brick filled with aeolian sand and capped with adobe bricks. In essence, dune inundation caused construction techniques to shift from solid brick to case-and-fill structures because the latter would sequester invasive sediment.

Despite the prodigious efforts to deal with the relentless sand inundation, the inhabitants of Dos Cabezas were unable to stop its onslaught. Ultimately, they chose to abandon the site. This appears to have happened rather suddenly. In some domestic areas, people left complete cooking and storage vessels on the floors, along with a variety of fishing and weaving implements (Figure 5.8). These were soon buried with sand. The wood pillars and roof beams in one palace complex were removed, and the roof was deliberately collapsed over the floor. This left the walls of rooms, which were plastered and painted white, exposed to the elements. Aeolian sand subsequently filled the rooms to a height of

FIGURE 5.7. Oblique aerial photograph of Huaca Dos Cabezas and shoreline dune fields. Photograph courtesy of Kenneth Garrett.

FIGURE 5.8. Cooking and storage vessels left on the floor of an abandoned room at Dos Cabezas. After abandonment the floor was quickly buried by windblown sand. Photograph courtesy of Christopher B. Donnan.

2 m, so quickly that the plaster and paint did not experience significant weathering (Figure 5.9).

A small number of people continued to live at Dos Cabezas after its abandonment. Since Huaca Dos Cabezas no longer served as a major religious structure, squatters built rudimentary structures adjacent to its north side, where they would have had some protection from the prevailing winds. They also occupied some of the patio areas in abandoned palace complexes. Yet even they must have found it difficult to continue residing at Dos Cabezas, for the archaeological evidence indicates that the occupation was very brief.

Sand dune inundation did not simply impact the administrative capital but was widespread south of the river in agricultural areas that had been the Dos Cabezas breadbasket. Therefore, people residing beyond the capital were also impacted. Where they could seek relief was, in part, determined by the fact that dune fields invading the south sides of coastal valleys cannot readily cross large, active river courses, such as the Jequetepeque. This is because flowing rivers entrain encroaching sand and disgorge the invasive sediment to the sea. Therefore, the northern sides of coastal valleys are relatively less perturbed by episodic sand invasion than southern sides. Consequently, when Dos Cabezas was rendered uninhabitable, many former residents are inferred to have moved immediately across the river to establish a new settlement at Pacatnamú on a high pampa overlooking the ocean on the west and the cultivated valley floor

FIGURE 5.9. Excavation of adobe architecture at Dos Cabezas that had been rapidly filled up to its roof line by aeolian sand. Photograph courtesy of Christopher B. Donnan.

on the south and east. Located less than 4 km north of Dos Cabezas, Pacatnamú would have been a relatively sand-free location where the relocated people would have been close to their fishing grounds and farmland. Others may have moved into the northern Chaman region, where refugees from the south side of the valley likely joined them.

The discovery of an inland elite tomb at La Mina (Narváez 1994), constructed of adobes quarried from Dos Cabezas and accompanied by ceramics and metal objects that are nearly identical to those in the Dos Cabezas tombs, suggests that elements of the old order persisted after the capital was lost. Yet this must have

FIGURE 5.10. Large yardangs. Photograph by Michael E. Moseley.

been brief because everything distinguishing the former regime, from its fine arts to the form of its mud bricks, disappeared in the Jequetepeque region shortly after Dos Cabezas was abandoned. The ensuing occupation of the valley is associated with people using a different style of Moche ceramics.

After the Moche abandonment of Dos Cabezas, the site remained unoccupied for several centuries. During that time, the coastal dune field gradually became less active, reducing the supply of inland sands. Then, around AD 900, Lambayeque people began to occupy the northern part of the site. They built several small temples, large walled enclosures, and one very large platform mound that today is called Huaca La Mesa, 528 m north of Huaca Dos Cabezas (Figure 5.3)

Modeling Sediment Movement

To model processes that impacted Dos Cabezas, we use a modern analogue from the Río Santa, some 200 km to the south (Moseley et al. 1991). The Río Santa demonstrates that desert rivers annually disgorge geological debris into the sea, where it is entrained and reworked into smaller clasts and sand by strong long shore currents. While heavier material is lost in deep waters, the northwest-flowing currents deposit sand along beaches, where it is then subject to inland transport by winds off the ocean, depending on shoreline topography. To judge from the Río Santa analogue, rendering cobble-size clasts into sand requires approximately 20 to 25 km

of abrasive marine movement. Normally, the sediment transport and processing system is in relative balance, with annual debris from one river contributing a certain amount of sand to beaches on the south side of the next valley up the coast to the north (Figure 5.2).

The system, however, is swamped with material when the rainfall and runoff from strong El Niño events increase the competency of rivers and normally dry drainages to disgorge debris into the sea. Once the erosional capabilities of long shore currents are exceeded, ENSO-induced sediment overloads generate coastal progradation. Seaward building of the shorelines is particularly pronounced immediately north of river mouths. Thus, the shoreline immediately north of the Río Jequetepeque delta, which is normally rocky, built outward approximately 30 m during the 1982–1983 and 1997–1998 ENSO events. Subsurface deposition was even more extensive, and it was possible to walk out into the ocean for more than 100 m before the depth was shoulder high. In less than three years, marine currents removed this backlogged material, bringing the shoreline back to its pre-ENSO condition.

Synergistic Disasters

Drawing on the Río Santa analogue, we hypothesize that Dos Cabezas was struck by exceptionally severe El Niño flooding that washed massive amounts of debris into the sea. The debris was then entrained by strong, northward-moving long shore currents that deposited reworked

FIGURE 5.11. Yardangs with furrows capping sun-cracked flood wash and overlying Late Moche sherds. Photograph by Michael E. Moseley.

sediment and sand along beaches. New supplies of beach sand were then moved inland by daily winds off the sea. Aeolian sediment inundating Dos Cabezas came from shoreline dune fields directly upwind of the capital. Long shore currents moving sediment from south to north fed sands provisioning the liner dunes. To the south, the nearest large source of El Niño debris was material expelled from the mouth of the southern valley lobe and the Cupisnique basin. Here coastal progradation was certainly massive because ENSO flood scouring literally lowered the inland landscape.

Eling (1986) documents the remains of two prehistoric agricultural regimes in the south. Dating after about AD 900, the later one consists of relatively well-preserved remnants of canals and planting surfaces. These works surround and abut scattered elevated remnants of the earlier Moche regime. The remnants include thin, high terrace-like deposits banked against bedrock hills and occasional yardangs on open flat lands. Yardangs resemble small geological mesas 1 to 5+ m high, with steep sides and flat summits (Figure 5.10). Within the southern region of Dos Cabezas' reclamation, these erosional remnants were formed from thick, sandy agricultural soils consolidated by irrigation. The flat tops of most have been wind deflated.

Eling (1986), however, discovered two remnants with very well-preserved summit furrows located far inland in the Canoncillo area (Figure 5.11). We carefully exam-

ined the two yardangs and found no ceramic sherds incorporated in the soils exposed on the side profiles of these structures. Significantly, the summit planting surfaces—both furrows and ridges—were capped by a thin (> 1 cm) deposit of sandy silt with pervasive sun cracks and drying curls. Whereas irrigation leads to deposition in furrows, but not planting ridges, the capping deposit overrides both and completely covers the former planting surfaces. We therefore attribute the capping deposits to El Niño–induced sheet wash inundating the planting surfaces and depositing fine scree. This was followed by sediment drying, sun cracking, and curling (Figure 5.11). This process is typical because sheet wash is the most pervasive form of El Niño–induced erosion and deposition. It is also the first impact of ENSO runoff. The accumulated runoff then feeds into progressively larger quebradas and drainages, providing them with the hydraulic heads required to erode and strip landscapes (Moseley and Keefer n.d.). In other words, as El Niño rains fell on all land surfaces, runoff first eroded and deposited silt, sand, and fine gravel. The slurry then entered successively larger drainages with ever-increasing competency to entrain ever-larger cobbles and boulders, inducing landscape erosion. Once the surface of the old Moche landscape was deeply incised by ENSO flood cuts, remnants of the former breadbasket were subjected to ensuing centuries of more normal erosion by wind and physical elements (Figure 5.12). Therefore, we do not

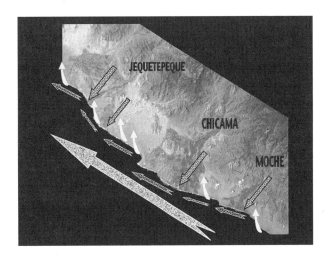

FIGURE 5.12. Overview of north coast valleys schematically illustrating major river sources of El Niño sediment outwash and ensuing sand input to the adjacent valley.

know the amount of sediment that was initially flushed out to sea, but it was certainly an exceptional load. Nor do we know why the megaflood triggered a long-term, down-cutting regime.

Due to imprecise chronological constraints, we cannot conclusively prove that the ENSO erosion at Dos Cabezas and its southern agricultural hinterland were products of one and the same disaster. Nevertheless, two separate flood disasters of exceptional magnitude seem very improbable. While examining the yardangs with preserved furrows, we observed a number of loose Late Moche sherds atop and overlying the sun-dried, curled capping deposits (Figure 5.11). Because the ceramic fragments were atop—not within or below—the capping sheet wash, we attribute them to scattering from a large post-flood Late Moche occupation on a hill approximately 330 m away that also left similar remains on surfaces below the yardangs that are more recent than the higher relic planting surfaces.[2]

Modeling

Eling (1986) was a pioneer in identifying massive El Niño destruction of former farmland in the Jequetepeque region. Drawing upon subsequent advances in Peruvian paleo-flood studies, it is now possible to propose that the catastrophe began with severe storms unleashing extraordinary torrential rains throughout the region. Runoff on sloping topography initially entrained fine sediment, generating rill wash and sheet wash that inundated lower, flatter areas, including farmland, where it sometimes survives as a thin capping deposit atop inland yardangs with preserved planting surfaces. Runoff then fed into higher-order drainages, increasing erosional competency and ability to transport cobbles and boulders. It is not clear if the highest-order drainage, the Jequetepeque River, overflowed its central channel and spilled into its former southern channel during the height of the river flood surge. Nonetheless, the flood surge descending the Cupisnique Quebrada from its very large catchment basin was the primary destructor of the formerly expansive southern agricultural system and resulted in down-cutting and stripping of the agrarian landscape.

Sediment Movement

Observation of recent El Niño events indicates that

runoff becomes progressively more viscous as it descends successively larger drainages, with growing power to entrain more sediments and ever larger clasts (Moseley and Keefer n.d.). This transforms floodwaters into debris flows composed of about 60 percent solid matter. Therefore, when Cupisnique ENSO runoff flowed to the sea through the old southern river channel, it released exceptional loads of coarse and fine geological debris. The material disgorged from the old river mouth must have prograded the adjacent coastline and built the shoreline seaward with a massive overload of unconsolidated sediment. After El Niño conditions abated, the return of normal conditions and long shore currents began a very long process of eroding back the debris overload. This started with northward transport of small particles and sand, followed by the longer process of reworking of larger rocks. Later, smaller El Niño outwashes undoubtedly renewed supplies of disgorged debris. Therefore, the process of returning the shoreline to stasis was lengthy and measured in centuries.

Debris flow from the Cupisnique provided the nearest large supply of sediment to the dune fields that inundated Dos Cabezas, yet outwash from other areas also contributed copious sediment to the sea. Although we believe that erosional stripping of loosely consolidated surface sediment was very widespread in the Jequetepeque region and elsewhere along the coast, this proposition is difficult to verify because most areas lack tell-tale yardangs.

Landscape alteration, however, may be evident in settlement pattern preservation. Currently, there appears to be a paucity of Jequetepeque sites known to be contemporary with Dos Cabezas. If this is confirmed by systematic survey, then it may reflect an El Niño–induced preservation pattern. While loss of landscape sediment is difficult to detect, ensuing dune formation is a recognizable consequence of massive erosion. Dating aeolian incursions on the basis of buried or superimposed archaeological features is essential, however, because dune fields have arisen episodically in the past.

El Niño Magnitude

Geoarchaeological transformations in the Jequetepeque region that began late in the Dos Cabezas regime are compatible with propositions that the Peruvian desert coast has been subject to Holocene cycles of radical landscape alteration in which large-scale sand incursions follow severe ENSO erosion that can, in turn, be preceded and exacerbated by seismic or tectonic events (Moseley et al. 1991). Although identification of tectonic input remains elusive at Dos Cabezas, repetitive long-term cycles of landscape buildup and catastrophic deflation are now well documented in the Jequetepeque region (Dillehay and Kolata 2004; Dillehay, Kolata, and Pino 2004). In the absence of evidence of prior earthquake activity, the flood damage to the old Moche capital and its hinterlands implicates exceptional quantities of ENSO-induced rainfall and runoff that significantly exceeded historic El Niño cases.

Rare but recurrent events of broadly comparable magnitude are documented in long-term Andean paleo-flood sequences. The first Mega-Niño event to be identified geoarchaeologically was one that struck the north coast during Chimu times and is variously dated at about AD 1100 or 1300 (Keefer et al. 2003). Stratified deposits with Chimu debris flow overlying Moche debris flow have not been securely identified and dated. Consequently, their relative magnitudes must be assessed indirectly. Significantly, larger ENSO flood events, such as those of 1997–1998, tend to rework, obfuscate, and destroy the deposits of earlier, smaller events, such as those of 1982–1983 (Moseley and Keefer n.d.). This biases preservation, and paleo-floor records are dominated by very large debris flows, while more normal strong El Niño flood deposits, including those of 1982–1983 and 1997–1998, are infrequently represented. Therefore, in light of relative preservation, we speculate that the magnitude of the Chimu Mega-Niño event did not exceed that of its earlier Moche counterpart. Indeed, the latter may prove to have been the larger if stratified deposits of the two can be found and compared.

Events and Processes

The number of storms and quantity of rainfall involved in paleo-flood episodes are difficult to identify. As with recent El Niño events, the number and intensity of past ENSO storms probably varied both along the desert and between the coast and low sierra (Moseley and Keefer n.d.). Strong ENSO events of the twentieth century have typically endured about 18 months, but the duration of exceptionally severe prehistoric events is poorly understood. Nonetheless, the washout of Dos Cabezas, modi-

fication of erosional concavities for tombs, and ensuing reconstruction indicates that the severe Moche El Niño was a single climatological event of relatively short length in terms of archaeological and geological time scales. The dates of the tombs imply that the calamity transpired around or shortly after AD 600. While the El Niño was a disastrous "event," the ensuing sand incursions were a catastrophic "process" that endured for generations. The process began with the flood outwash of sediments, preceded first by their marine processing and deposition as shoreline sand and then by their inland aeolian transport, eventually culminating in inland repose and consolidation. The shoreline supplies of sand that impacted Dos Cabezas seem not to have stabilized until about AD 900, when people began to reoccupy the region of the former capital and to again farm in the southern lobe area. Significantly, the magnitude and duration of the catastrophic aeolian sand process is commensurate with the exceptional magnitude of the triggering ENSO disaster. Thus, the Jequetepeque region provides consistent erosional and depositional evidence of a singular Moche episode of landscape alteration. Yet there were clearly earlier episodes of transformation as well (Dillehay and Kolata 2004).

Discussion

The Dos Cabezas Mega-Niño event should constitute a geoarchaeological horizon marker detectable in other coastal areas. Some Moche sites in the Chicama, Moche, and Virú valleys do exhibit evidence of severe ENSO impact. Available dates, though, are not closely aligned; at best they bracket the event as transpiring sometime between about AD 450 and 750. This is expectable given the standard deviations of radiocarbon assays. Furthermore, paleo-flood deposits are notoriously difficult to date directly, and most age calculations come from cultural remains that shortly pre- or post-date the ENSO activity. Nonetheless, as chronological constraints improve, the age of the Moche disasters will draw into sharper focus.

Due to imprecise dating, we are reticent to draw conclusions about different regional responses to the convergent catastrophes. Nonetheless, if all Moche centers exhibiting severe El Niño impact pertain to the same geoarchaeological horizon, then regional reactions were highly varied. They seemingly ranged from immediate post-flood abandonment, through abandonment during dune incursion, to prolonged continued occupation. Perhaps some of this variability may relate to whether centers and their respective agrarian hinterlands were located north or south of their respective coastal rivers. The Moche Mega-Niño event certainly exerted exceptional stress on coastal societies. As with recent ENSO events, there were no doubt fatalities from drowning as well as from pestilence brought on by the outbreak of tropical diseases and the loss of potable water, stored food, and other infrastructure. The reconstruction of Dos Cabezas is testimony to a remarkable post-disaster resilience. Indeed, life might have returned to normal, and the southern agricultural system might have returned to production, had it not been for the ensuing collateral catastrophe of aeolian sediment incursion. Ultimately, it was the massive dune incursions that rendered the administrative capital and much of its southern hinterland uninhabitable. To the degree that natural disaster contributed to cultural change, it is significant that the demise of Dos Cabezas and its regime were ultimately brought about by excessive sand rather than by excessive water. Perhaps this is because that flood was a short-lived but extreme event, whereas the incursion of dunes was an abrasive process that endured for generations.

Ultimately, Dos Cabezas provides a well-documented case of environmental and cultural change, but relationships of the two must be critically appraised. Massive El Niño–induced flooding was certainly a major destabilizing factor. The ensuing incursion of aeolian sand rendered much of the agrarian landscape unproductive and made the capital uninhabitable. Regime change, however, was ultimately a cultural decision. Perhaps people decided that gods and leaders of the former system had failed and that a new order offered better prospects for coping with the altered social environment and the transformed landscape.

Conclusions

During the seventh century AD, an exceptionally severe episode of desert rainfall and runoff damaged the prehistoric Moche capital of Dos Cabezas and destroyed much of its agrarian hinterlands in the Jequetepeque Valley. The scope of landscape alteration implicates a Mega-Niño event exceeding the magnitude of the worst twentieth-century ENSO flood events. The synergistic consequence of this disaster was yet another catastrophe in the form of massive sand dune incursions. Fed by flood debris that the El Niño washed to the sea, copious supplies of beach sand were blown inland, where they inundated the capital and contributed to its abandonment. Although infrequent, the convergent flood and sand catastrophes that struck Dos Cabezas were driven by recurrent environmental processes that have episodically resculpted the desert landscape during Holocene times.

Notes

1. The ceramics associated with these tombs would clearly be assigned to Phase I of Larco's chronology (Larco 1948), which we would expect to date to between AD 100 and 200. The date of AD 390 to 645 is therefore surprising. Although Larco's chronology has been effective for the southern Moche region, it has been shown to be less applicable for the northern Moche region, which includes the Jequetepeque Valley (Castillo and Donnan 1994).

2. The ceramics found atop the yardang capping deposit and with the nearby hilltop occupation are stylistically affiliated with Phase V of the Larco (1948) chronology.

Bibliography

Castillo, Luis Jaime, and Christopher B. Donnan
1994   Los Moche del norte y los Moche del sur. In *Vicús*, 143–181. Edited by Krzystof Makowski, Christopher B. Donnan, Ivan Amaro Bullon, Luis Jaime Castillo, Magdalena Diez Canseco, Otto Elespuru Revoredo, and Juan Antonio Murro Mena. Colección Arte y Tesoros del Perú, Lima.

Dillehay, Tom D., and Alan L. Kolata
2004   Long-Term Human Response to Uncertain Environmental Conditions in the Andes. *Proceedings of the National Academy of Science* 101 (12):4325–4330.

Dillehay, Tom D., Alan L. Kolata, and Mario Pino Q.
2004   Pre-Industrial Human and Environment Interactions in Northern Peru During the Late Holocene. *Holocene* 14 (2):272–281.

Donnan, Christopher B.
2001   Moche Burials Uncovered. *National Geographic* 199 (3):58–73.

2003   Tumbas con entierros en miniatura: Un nuevo tipo funerario moche. In *Moche: Hacia el Final del Milenio,*

Tome I, 43–78. Actas del Segundo Coloquio sobre
la Cultura Moche, Trujillo, 1 al 7 de agosto de 1999.
Edited by Santiago Uceda and Elías Mujica. Universidad Nacional de Trujillo and Pontificia Universidad Católica del Perú, Lima.

Eling, Herbert H., Jr.
1986   Pre-Hispanic Irrigation Sources and Systems in the
Jequetepeque Valley, Northern Peru. In *Andean Archaeology: Papers in Memory of Clifford Evans*, 130–149.
Edited by Ramiro Matos M., Solvieg A. Turpin, and
Herbert H. Eling, Jr. Monograph 27. Institute of Archaeology, University of California, Los Angeles.

Keefer, David K., Michael E. Moseley, and Susan D. DeFrance
2003   A 38,000-year Record of Floods and Debris Flows in the
Ilo Region of Southern Peru and Its Relation to El Niño
Events and Great Earthquakes. *Paleogeography, Paleoclimatology, Paleoecology* 194:41–77.

Larco Hoyle, Rafael
1948   *Cronología arqueológica del norte del Perú.* Sociedad
Geográfica Americana, Buenos Aires.

Moseley, Michael E., Robert Feldman, and Charles Ortloff
1981   Living with Crises: Human Perception of Process and
Time. In *Biotic Crises in Ecological and Evolutionary*

Time, 231–267. Edited by M. Nitecki. Academic Press,
New York.

Moseley, Michael E., and David K. Keefer
n.d.   Deadly Deluges in the Southern Desert: Modern and
Ancient El Niños in the Osmore Region of Peru. In *El
Niño, Catastrophism, and Culture Change in Ancient
America*. Pre-Columbian Symposium at Dumbarton
Oaks, October 12–13, 2002. Edited by Daniel Sandweiss
and Jeffrey Quilter. Dumbarton Oaks, Washington, D.C.

**Moseley, Michael E., David Wagner, and James B.
Richardson III**
1991   Space Shuttle Imagery of Recent Catastrophic Change
along the Arid Andean Coast. In *Paleoshorelines and
Prehistory: An Investigation of Methods*, 215–235. Edited
by Lucille L. Johnson and Melanie Straight. CRC Press,
Boca Raton.

Narváez, Alfredo V.
1994   La Mina: Una tumba Moche I en el valle de Jequetepeque. In *Moche: Propuestas y perspectivas*, 59–92. Actas
del Primer Coloquio sobre la Cultura Moche, Trujillo, 12
a 16 de abril de 1993. Edited by Santiago Uceda and Elías
Mujica. Travaux de l'Institut Français d'Études Andines
79. Universidad Nacional de la Libertad, Trujillo, Perú.

CHAPTER SIX

Forensic Iconography

The Case of the Moche Giants

ALANA CORDY-COLLINS, UNIVERSITY OF SAN DIEGO

CHARLES F. MERBS, ARIZONA STATE UNIVERSITY

Abstract

"Forensic iconography" is a term coined by the authors to signify a new approach to the study of individuals from archaeological cultures. The focus of this study is a group of five remarkable men who were part of Moche Norteño culture in the middle of the first millennium AD. All were young when they died, and exhibited both extraordinary stature and pathological skeletal abnormalities. This study profiles each of the individuals from a forensic perspective and identifies their occupations via iconographic analysis.

The Archaeological Evidence

The discoveries between 1977 and 2000 of five male giants at the site of Dos Cabezas, a Moche settlement situated in the delta of the Jequetepeque River valley (Figure 6.1), are the first reported cases of gigantism from prehistoric Peru (Cordy-Collins 2003). Of the myriad issues that surround these finds, two critical questions are: Who were these men? What role did they play in the life of Dos Cabezas? Based on the archaeological data, we form a hypothesis. All of the men were buried in a cemetery platform located at the southwest corner of the most imposing structure at the site, the eroded mud-brick edifice that has given the site its name, Dos Cabezas. Although the entire huaca—including the cemetery—has been heavily vandalized over the centuries since its construction, scientific excavation has shown (Donnan and Cock 1995, 1998, 1999, 2000, 2001) that the platform served as a sepulcher for elites. Judging by stratigraphic and architectural evidence, as well as comparative grave goods analysis (Donnan 2001:64–66, 2003:75–76, fig. 2.4), we are certain that four of the five giants were contemporaries. They were interred so closely in time that we may suppose they knew each other by name. The stratigraphic evidence also allows

us to establish the relative chronology of their burial (Donnan and Cock 2001:33–35). Three tombs, each with a miniature annex (Donnan 2003), were constructed in a north-south line, with the most lavishly accoutered, Tomb 2, centered between Tomb 1 on the south and Tomb 3 on the north. Based on the intersecting data of tomb layout and relative quantity and quality of the three graves, we hypothesize that the individual buried in Tomb 2, Giant 2, occupied the highest rank. This supposition conforms to a pattern for elite burial in the northern Moche region, which may be formalized as the following hypothesis: *The Moche Norteño Standard Elite Burial Pattern places the highest-ranked individual in the center, flanking that person with the same type of individual, but ones of lesser rank.* This pattern has been observed since early Moche times at Sipán, where the Lord of Sipán was buried with a high-ranking adult male at each side (Alva and Donnan 1993), and in the terminal Moche period at San José de Moro, where the burial of two Priestesses were each bordered by a high-ranking adult female, and the burial of an elite child was flanked by high-ranking children (Castillo and Donnan 1992). The Dos Cabezas Giants, with their dates squarely in the middle (AD 390–645), suggest that the Sipán and

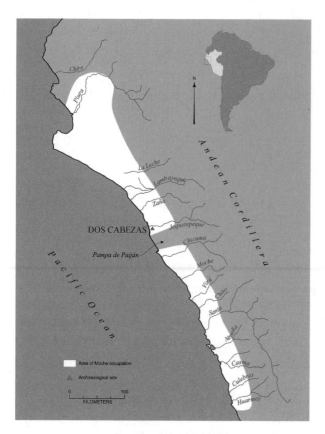

FIGURE 6.1. Map of the north coast of Peru highlighting the area of Moche occupation and the location of Dos Cabezas. Cartography by Donald McClelland.

San José de Moro burials are not isolated incidents, but rather examples of a Moche Norteño pattern.

Thus, we interpret that Giant 2 outranked Giant 3 to his north, Giant 1 to his south, and certainly Giant 4—the youngest—buried beneath him. In fact, the limited amount of grave goods recovered in association with Giant 4 suggests that he was himself an offering to the tomb's main occupant, Giant 2.

The Osteological Data

Beyond the fact that all these men were young (17–22 yrs) and particularly tall (165.5–180 cm), they suffered from an array of abnormal developmental or genetic skeletal defects, many of which would have caused them considerable pain of movement. One of the most striking abnormalities of their bones is extreme cortical thinning, coupled with enlarged medullary chambers, made so by a diminished trabecular structure.

Giant 1 was the most pathologically deformed of the group. Stature based on femur length yields 177 cm, or 5'10" (Genovés 1967). A sixth lumbar vertebra, however, may have added 2.3 cm of height, bringing him closer to 6' tall. This is far above the norm for Moche males, whose height range was 148.2–168.8 cm, or 4'10"–5'6" (Verano 1993:318–319). Compression fracturing of approximately half of his vertebrae, though, resulted in pronounced kyphosis. Therefore, it seems unlikely he was ever able to rise to his full height, at least in his later years. This conclusion is supported by the anatomical relationship of his vertebrae to the rest of his postcranial skeleton as seen in his burial posture (Figure 6.2).

Giant 2, though lacking the extreme pathology of Giant 1, evinced a similar abnormal height and diseased skeleton (Figure 6.3). All of the long bones were too fragile to measure with an osteometric board, but rather were taped in situ. Applying the Genovés regression formula (1967) to the taped measurements, the man's height was estimated at 170–175 cm (5'7"–5'9"). In contrast, a direct taping of the skeleton from the highest point on the cranial vault to the bottom of the calcaneus yielded the slightly greater measure of 180 cm (5'11"). Moreover, his bone cortex was extremely thin and fragile, undoubtedly a significant factor contributing to the poor state of bone preservation.

Giant 3 was also abnormally tall and thin-boned (Figure 6.4). He is estimated to have stood 175 cm, or 5'9". Like Giants 1 and 2, his bone cortex was fragile and the medullary cavities of the long bones were virtually empty of trabeculae.

The Giant 4 skeleton, buried beneath Giant 2, is also characterized by extremely thin, fragile bones, some of which appear to have been still growing rapidly at time of death (Figure 6.5). As the youngest of the five, about 17 years of age, he was also the least tall (165.5–167 cm, or 5'5"–5' 5.75"), but still at the upper range for normal adult Moche males.

Giant 5 was interred in an older part of the burial platform, to the west of Tombs 1–3 (Figure 6.6). This individual, also a young adult male (18–20), exhibits the same primary characteristics of the other four men: extreme height (175 cm, or 5'9") and thinned bone with little trabecular structure.

All of the complete skeletons share important characteristics, most notably their abnormal height and

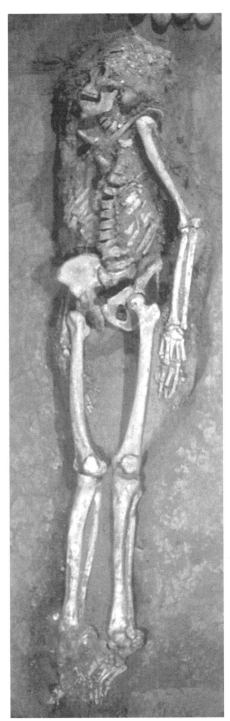

FIGURE 6.2. Giant 1 in situ. Dos Cabezas, Jequetepeque Valley, 1997. Photograph by Christopher B. Donnan.

FIGURE 6.3. Giant 2 in situ. Dos Cabezas, Jequetepeque Valley, 1998. Photograph by Christopher B. Donnan.

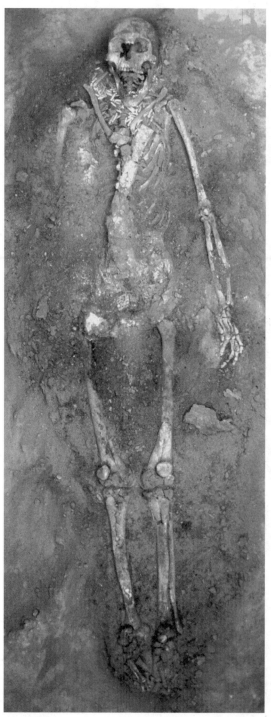

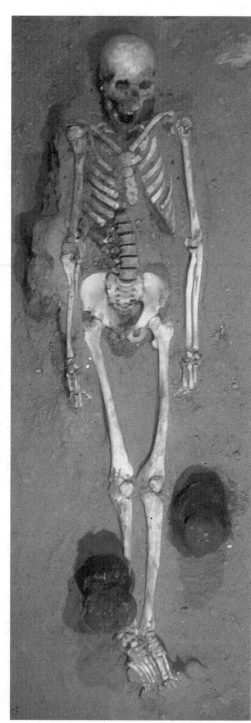

FIGURE 6.4. Giant 3 in situ. Dos Cabezas, Jequetepeque Valley, 1999. Photograph by Christopher B. Donnan.

FIGURE 6.5. Giant 4 in situ. Dos Cabezas, Jequetepeque Valley, 2000. Photograph by Christopher B. Donnan.

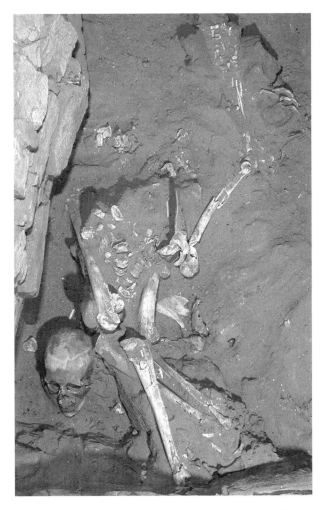

FIGURE 6.6. Giant 5 in situ. Dos Cabezas, Jequetepeque Valley, 2000. Photograph by Alana Cordy-Collins.

thinned cortical bone, accompanied by "latticed" trabeculae of the medullary cavities of the long bones. What is also common to all five is that their bones were growing and aging rapidly. Clearly, the five giants constitute a remarkable group of individuals, not only to modern-day researchers, but certainly to their contemporaries at Dos Cabezas as well. In an attempt to get closer to how they were seen in their own time, a particular sort of skeletal analysis is extremely useful: forensics.

The Forensic Approach

A forensic approach to human skeletal remains generally focuses on the individual rather than a group, with one of the primary objectives being individual identification.

Toward this end, the remains are analyzed for information pertaining to age at death, sex, size, pathology, occupation, and other relevant characteristics. The forensic approach also attempts to determine cause and manner of death. This approach is as relevant to ancient remains as it is to recent cases, with the understanding that the individual characteristics obtained are usually aimed at profiling an individual rather than actually identifying that individual by name.

In the case of the five giant skeletons from Dos Cabezas, considerable osteological information of a forensic nature had already been gathered during earlier studies, information such as age, sex, size (stature), pathology (still under analysis), and cause and manner of death (unknown). What they had not been examined for was evidence pertaining to occupation.

Occupational Analysis

The term *occupation* is used broadly in a forensic context to refer to behavior patterns that are repeated over a significant period of a person's lifetime, significant enough to leave an identifiable imprint on the skeleton. This could include positions assumed and sustained over an extended period of time if they resulted in identifiable skeletal imprints. An occupational imprint may take many forms. Typical imprints include patterns of degenerative joint pathology, facet development in response to unusual bone contact, unusual muscle development reflected in muscle attachment sites, bone fracture patterns, dental wear or loss, changes in cortical cross-sectional shape and thickness in response to stress, and trabecular realignment.

Given the relatively young ages of the Dos Cabezas giants, it seemed unlikely that enough time had elapsed to produce identifiable imprints of occupation, so it came as a surprise to find them present, and present in abundance. This could be due to the intense nature of the occupation involved. But it is likely that the pathology that produced the large stature in these individuals, a process that accelerated the aging process, also produced occupational markers at an earlier age than expected.

Four categories of skeletal evidence of occupational stress were utilized in the study of the Moche giants: degenerative joint changes, new facet development, unusual muscle development, and fracture patterns.

Most degenerative joint changes fall under the heading of osteoarthritis (or osteoarthrosis) and occur due to repeated stressing of a joint or sustained stress that ultimately causes cartilage and underlying articular bone damage. New bone (osteophyte) may develop around the margins of articular surfaces, and, with complete cartilage loss, parts of articular surfaces may become polished (eburnated). A classic example of this approach is the association of a particular pattern of osteoarthritis in the elbow with use of an atlatl (Angel 1966). Evidence of osteoarthritis was also used for multiple joint analysis in a study of Canadian Inuit (Merbs 1983).

The second category involves the development of new facets on bones through frequent or sustained bone-on-bone contact. Hyperflexion of a joint, for example, could bring the bones involved into a pressure-contact situation that, if sustained over a long enough period, could cause the bones to develop contact facets on the affected parts. A classic example of this is the so-called squatting facet, a feature of the tibia and talus ascribed to squatting, that was first described in the nineteenth century (Charles 1893–1894; Thompson 1890). This trait has also been related to anterior flexion of the feet while kneeling, the position assumed by Pueblo women in the American Southwest while grinding corn on a metate (Merbs and Euler 1985). Another example is Poirier's facet on the anterior surface of the femoral neck (Kostick 1963; Poirier and Charpy 1911) and the corresponding flange lesion on the superior dorsal margin of the acetabulum of the pelvis (Stirland 1991), indicators of anterior hyperflexion of the leg at the hip.

Muscle development is reflected in the development of the site at which the muscle attaches to bone: the greater the development of the muscle, the more robust the attachment site. In skeletons from South Asia, unusually robust development of the supinator crest and the attachment area for the anconeus muscle has been attributed to the throwing of weapons (Kennedy 1983). A particularly violent stress on a muscle or ligament could produce a pit-like lesion in the bone at its attachment site, a condition associated with Inuit kayaking (Hawkey and Merbs 1995). Muscle function may also alter the shape of a bone. Unlike nearly every other bone in the postcranial skeleton that develops from cartilage or membrane, the patella develops in the tendon of the femoral quadriceps muscles. It thus reacts to stresses

involving this muscle group, particularly the pressure of vastus lateralis during sustained contraction associated with flexion of the knee. The presence of an impression on the superior lateral margin of a patella, referred to as a "vastus impression" or "vastus notch," is associated with chronic knee flexion (Messeri 1961). General muscle stress on a bone can also be reflected in bone size. For example, greater stress on a person's dominant side will produce a shorter clavicle on that side (May, Steele, and Ford 1999).

The relationship between bone fractures and activity is sometimes reflected in the name of the fracture (Merbs 1989). The parry fracture of the ulna, for example, is associated with parrying a blow with the forearm, and the boxer's fracture of a metacarpal with delivering a blow with the fist. An occupational activity is associated with the clay-shoveler's fracture of a lower cervical or upper thoracic vertebra. These name relationships are merely generalizations, however, and the etiology in a particular case may be different than that implied by the fracture name. Other fractures may be associated with a particular traumatic event, such as the Colles fracture of the radius, which occurs when a person falls onto the hand with the force transmitted to the distal end of the radius (Schultz 1990).

Occupational Markers on the Giants' Skeletons
GIANT 1
This was the oldest giant at time of death, and the skeleton displays the most extreme example of the pathology that produced the unusually tall stature of these men.

Shoulders: In general, muscle attachments involving the shoulders are well-developed. The right clavicle is shorter than the left, but the costal tuberosity on this side is better developed than on the left, appearing as a depression with a slight marginal ridge. The right clavicle is also extremely wide in its lateral half. These features suggest that this individual was right-handed. The width of the right clavicle may also reflect pathology as a deep groove in the shaft may indicate a healed fracture.

Both shoulders show evidence of osteoarthritis. The glenoid articular area of the scapula in each case has marginal osteophytes, but with different parts affected: the anterior-superior part on the right side, and the anterior-inferior part on the left side. Slightly raised

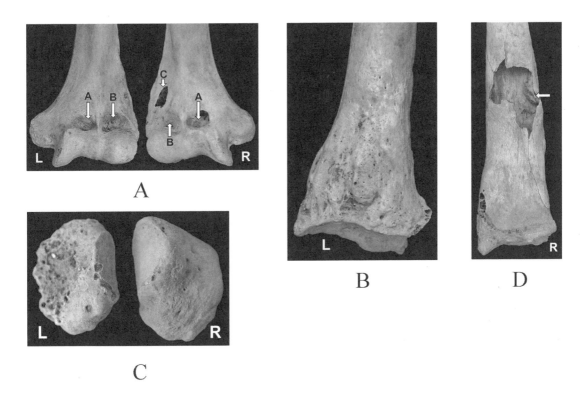

FIGURE 6.7. Giant 1. *A*, left and right humeri: anterior view of distal ends showing deep coronoid fossa (Arrow A) and radial fossa (Arrow B); postmortem damage (Arrow C) reflects the extremely thin cortex of these bones. *B*, left radius: posterior view of distal end showing well-healed Colles fracture of the wrist. *C*, left and right pisiforms showing distortion of left pisiform. *D*, right radius: anterior view of distal end showing possible fracture of the shaft; postmortem damage (arrow) reflects extremely thin cortex.

nodules on the posterior-inferior part of the glenoid surface indicate a lack of pressure in this region. All of this suggests a behavioral pattern in which the right arm was held higher and more forward than the left. Both humeral heads have a roughened surface with several small holes, and the lesser tubercles present a rough pitted surface.

Elbows: The radial fossa of the humerus is unusually deep on both sides, but particularly the left side, and the floor of the left fossa presents a porous appearance (Figure 6.7a). The coronoid fossa is also deep on both sides, particularly the right side, where a deep depression opens upward into the shaft. The appearance of this region suggests sustained flexion, or even hyperflexion, of both elbows. In contrast, there is no evidence of hyperextension in either elbow. Articular bone destruction is evident on the head of the radius, involving just the ventral margin on the left radius, but both the ventral and dorsal margins on the right radius. The radial

tuberosity is well-developed, especially on the left side, reflecting a well-developed biceps muscle.

Wrists: A Colles fracture of the radius affected the left wrist of this individual (Figure 6.7b). This is a typical falling fracture in which the weight is transferred from the flattened hand to the wrist. Characteristic of this type of fracture, some dorsal displacement of the distal end of the radius has occurred. The fracture is well healed, and some remodeling of bony callus has taken place. The traumatic event that produced this fracture is likely responsible for the severe distortion of the left pisiform and the styloid process of the left ulna, either being caused directly by the trauma, or indirectly through disruption of normal wrist function resulting from the fracture (Figure 6.7c). The head of the left ulna shows evidence of osteoarthritis, as does the corresponding articulation of the radius.

An irregularity of the right radius may be evidence of another fracture (Figure 6.7d), one that occurred earlier in this individual's life. This fracture involved the distal third of the radial shaft rather than the distal end as on the left side. Considerable remodeling has taken place, and postmortem damage in this area has exposed the extreme cortical thinning characteristic of this skeleton.

Hands: Osteoarthritic bone destruction at the elbow on the ventral margin of both radial heads in line with the radial tuberosity indicate that the hands were habitually turned with the thumb side upward, as though holding an object in a vertical position. A second area of destruction on the right radial head indicates a second sustained position for the right hand, in this case with the thumb positioned downward.

Hips: Both femora show asymmetrical development of the neck region, which indicates sustained anterior flexion of the right leg at the hip. The left femur shows some postmortem damage in this region, but enough is present to indicate that the asymmetry is real, not an artifact. The quadriceps attachments on the femoral shafts are more developed on the right side than the left, indicating greater flexion with the pelvis on this side. These features indicate a sustained or habitual position in which the right leg was flexed at the knee at a much greater angle than the left.

Knees: The attachment for the gastrocnemius muscle at the distal end of the femur presents an asymmetrical pattern, appearing as a raised circular area on the left femur, but being barely visible on the right femur. Osteoarthritic destruction of the articular surface is observable on the lateral condyle of the right femur. This condition suggests repeated or habitual hyperflexion of the right knee, with localized destruction of cartilage and articular bone from joint pressure. The right patella has a vastus impression, but the left patella does not. This trait is associated with the tendon of the vastus lateralis of the femoral quadriceps complex and reflects habitual hyperflexion of the right knee.

The lateral condyle of the left tibia sustained a mild depression fracture (Figure 6.8a). This type of fracture usually results from a fall while the leg is straightened at the knee. The vertical force produced drives the lateral condyle of the femur into that of the tibia, resulting in a fracturing of the weaker tibia. Today, this fracture is seen most frequently in skiers.

A rim of osteophyte has developed on the anterolateral margin of the lateral condyle of the left tibia. This bone also shows osseous development into the patellar ligament, more like a small osteophyte than typical "whiskering." These conditions are more likely related to the fracture in this region than behavior.

Ankles: The left fibula suffered a fracture or multiple fractures of the distal third of its shaft above the ankle (Figure 6.8b). An abundance of irregular callus development in this area suggests recent trauma, in which the

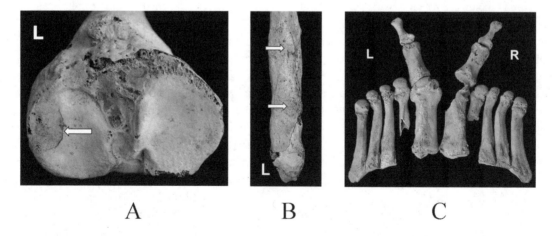

A   B   C

FIGURE 6.8. Giant 1. *A*, left tibia: superior view of proximal end showing fracture of lateral condyle (arrow). *B*, left fibula: medial view of distal end showing healed fractures (arrows) of the shaft. *C*, left and right metatarsals and phalanges of the first toe: superior view showing lateral deviation. The right first proximal and distal phalanges are actually seen in inferior view.

separated parts are firmly united but with little remodeling at the fracture site. Very slight squatting facets are evident on both tali; however, the corresponding parts of the tibiae are too damaged to assess tibial involvement. ·

Feet: A pattern of lateral deviation involving the metatarsal bones and metatarsophalangeal joints is observable in this individual (Figure 6.8c). The shafts of metatarsals 2, 3, and 4 on the right side and 3 and 4 on the left side curve laterally toward their distal end, with the condition being most extreme in the fourth metatarsals. The forces that produced this distortion were likely already in place while this individual was young and these bones were still developing. The metatarsophalangeal joints show evidence of osteoarthritis that also indicates marked lateral deviation, suggesting that the forces remained in place during the latter years of this individual's life. Particularly dramatic in this regard is the first metatarsophalangeal joint on each side, where the big toe has been forced laterally, resulting in gross distortion of the metatarsal head. Lateral deviation of the toes has been observed in other series where it was attributed to restrictive footwear (May 2005). In this case, the cause is more likely restrictive positioning of the foot for long periods of time. Habitual or sustained hyperextension of the toes relative to the foot, and of the toe segments relative to each other, has produced ridging on the superior margins of the articular surfaces. This positioning of the toes is also reflected by an eburnated area on the inferior surface of the head of the first metatarsal produced by pathological contact with the sesamoid.

GIANT 2

This skeleton is in the poorest condition of the five in terms of bone preservation, but most major articulations are available for observation. Except for the ankles, these joints show little indication of occupational pathology.

Shoulders: The scapular spine is unusually broad on both sides, but the clavicles are not unusual.

Elbows: A small septal aperture is present in the right humerus, but not in the left. This is unusual as the septal aperture more often occurs in gracile individuals, particularly females, and more often on the left side.

Hips: There is no evidence of osteoarthritis in the hip, and neither femur shows extension of faceting onto the neck.

Knees: There is a suggestion of degenerative pathology on the medial surface of the left patella and the lateral condyle of the right femur. Much or all of this may be due to postmortem damage.

Ankles: Both tali show medial expansion of the articular surface for the medial malleolus of the tibia (squatting facet), but it is much more pronounced on the right side than the left (Figure 6.9a). There is a corresponding facet on the right tibia. The left tibia has an osteophytic ridge on the anterior margin where it was in contact with the talus. When the tibia is positioned with the talus in maximum flexion for the two feet as determined by their skeletal anatomy, the angle between the leg and foot is less on the left side than the right. In fact, the angle on the left side appears as small as the anatomy of the bones will allow. This suggests that the presence of squatting facets indicates habitual squatting, but not maximum flexion, the latter producing little or no actual faceting. Two toe phalanges (medial and distal) are fused.

GIANT 3

Shoulders: Both clavicles appear unusually long. The left is longer than the right, but the right is distinctly broader over the distal 40 percent of the bone than the left. The right clavicle shows greater development of the conoid tuberosity, and there is a deep groove on its inferior surface. All of this suggests right-handedness. The glenoid of the right scapula shows more osteoarthritis than the left, which also suggests greater use of the right arm.

Both scapulae show evidence of glenoid osteoarthritis with the pattern of involvement different on the two sides (Figure 6.9b). Osteophyte development is most prominent on the superior margin of the right glenoid and the inferior margin of the left. The right glenoid also shows involvement of the articular surface toward its upper end. Overall, the pathology is more pronounced on the right side, suggesting greater strain on the right shoulder. The involvement of the superior margin also suggests habitual or sustained raising of the right arm. The humeral heads show no evidence of degenerative pathology.

Both scapulae have an extremely convex vertebral border, indicating strong development of the back muscles that attach to the blade of the scapula (Figure 6.9c). No obvious side difference was identified.

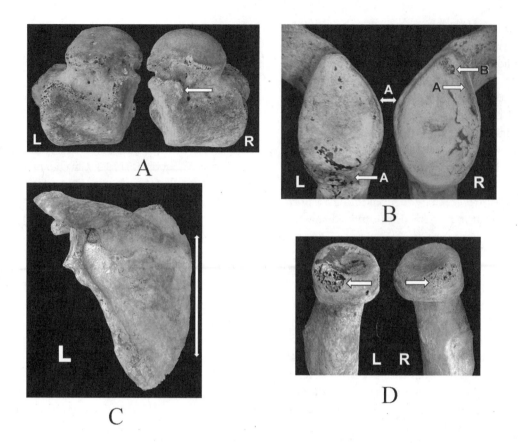

FIGURE 6.9. *A*, Giant 2: left and right taluses; superior view showing well-developed tibial facet (squatting facet) on right side (arrow). *B*, Giant 3:left and right scapulas; medial view of glenoid articular surfaces showing different patterns of osteoarthritis on the two sides (arrows), osteophyte development (Arrow A) and cortical defect (Arrow B). *C*, Giant 3: left scapula; posterior view showing convex vertebral border (arrow). *D*, Giant 3: left and right radii; anterior view, proximal end, showing osteoarthritis (arrows).

Elbows: Both humeri show a deep depression (resembling a septal aperture, but not completely perforating the bone) in the coronoid fossa, with that on the left side covering a much larger area than that on the right. Both humeri also show osteophyte development of osteoarthritis in the elbow region, but in general the right side is more severely affected than the left. Similarly, the right side shows osteophyte development on the margin of the capitulum, while none is evident on the left side. The coronoid fossa, however, is deeper on the left side. Osteoarthritic destruction is evident on the ventral margin of the head of both radii, with more on the left side than the right (Figure 6.9d). An osteophyte has developed on the olecranon and coronoid margins of the ulna with no observable side difference.

Hands: The articular bone destruction seen on the ventral margin of the head on both radii occurred while these bones were in a position with the hands turned vertically, thumbs upward. This would result from habitually holding an object in a vertical or near vertical position.

Hips: Both femora show faceting on the surface of the neck from contact with the rim of the acetabulum, but the condition is much more pronounced on the right side than the left (Figure 6.10a). This condition was likely produced by anterior flexing at the hip on the right side. There is a corresponding lesion on the margin of the right acetabulum of the pelvis (acetabular flange lesion) (Figure 6.10b). The right femoral head also shows more degenerative change around the fovea capitis, another indication of greater stress on the right side.

Knees: Indications of osteoarthritis are evident in

both knees. This consists of osteophyte development on the medial margin of the medial condyle and articular surface destruction of the anterior surface of the lateral condyle of the femur (Figure 6.10c). The posterior superior surface of the lateral condyle of the left femur is rough, indicating cartilage destruction caused by prolonged hyperflexion of the left knee. The attachment area of the gastrocnemius muscle, however, shows the opposite pattern: that on the right side being large, rough and pitted, while that on the left is barely discernible (Figure 6.10d). Both patellae show arthritic destruction corresponding to that on the femoral condyles (Figure 6.11a). A vastus notch is present on the right patella, but not the left. The left patella shows more osteophyte development on the superior margin and has a prominent osteophyte extending downward from the inferior margin of the lateral surface. In general, the pathology is concentrated more toward the top of the right patella and the bottom of the left patella. Both tibiae show a trace of osteoarthritis on the superior surface, involving the margins of the condyles on the right side and a small area on the medial part of the lateral condyle on the left side. All of this is consistent with this individual spending long periods of time kneeling on his left knee with the right leg flexed forward at the hip and the right foot flat to the ground.

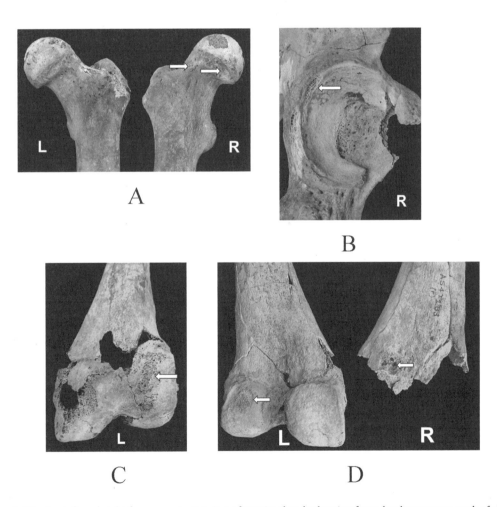

FIGURE 6.10. *A*, Giant 3: left and right femurs; anterior view of proximal ends showing facet development on neck of right femur (arrows). *B*, Giant 3: right pelvis (coxa); lateral view of acetabulum showing flange lesion (arrow). *C*, Giant 3: left femur; anterior view of distal end showing severe osteoarthritis (arrow). *D*, Giant 3: left and right femurs; posterior view of distal ends showing osteoarthritis (*L*, arrow) and well-developed attachment for the gastrocnemius muscle (*R*, arrow).

Ankles: There is no evidence of squatting facets on either side.

Feet: Both calcanei have a bony extension known as a heel spur.

GIANT 4

This individual is the youngest of the five giants and thus the least likely to show degenerative skeletal changes associated with sustained or frequently repeated activity. For example, the skeleton exhibits virtually no evidence of osteoarthritis. The first and second sternebrae of the body of the sternum are not fused, an unusual condition for someone of this age, but due to a developmental lag rather than behavior.

Shoulders: The right clavicle is shorter than the left, an indication of right-handedness. Both clavicles show prominent development of the attachments for the conoid ligament and the deltoid muscle, indicating strong shoulder development. The area of attachment for the subclavian muscle on the left clavicle is deeply grooved, and the sternal end of the right clavicle is notched. The glenoid facet of the right scapula has a small beveled and slightly notched area on the lower anterior corner of its margin, a condition not present on the left scapula. These features may be related to the dislocation noted below.

Elbows: The dominant feature of the right arm is an unreduced dislocation of the radius at the elbow. As a result, the capitulum on this side appears continuous with the trochlea, and the radial fossa is unusually large, reflecting the fact that it had to accommodate the dislocated radial head (Figure 6.11b). The elbow portion

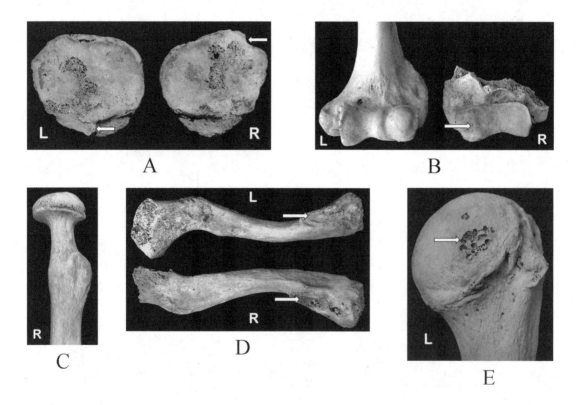

FIGURE 6.11. *A*, Giant 3: left and right patellas; posterior view showing osteoarthritis on both sides, with osteophyte on left patella (arrow) and vastus notch on right patella (arrow). *B*, Giant 4: left and right humeri; anterior view of distal end showing poorly developed right capitulum (arrow) indicating dislocation of the radial head. *C*, Giant 4: right radius; distal end showing poor development of the head and neck resulting from dislocation. *D*, Giant 5: left and right clavicles; inferior view showing well-developed, deeply pitted costal tuberosities (arrows). *E*, Giant 5: left humerus; anterior view of proximal end showing osteoarthritis.

of the right radius is much more gracile in appearance than that on the left side, the head is small and poorly developed, and the radial neck is unusually long (Figure 6.11c). Although the right radial head still contains a depression for the capitulum of the humerus, it is poorly developed. The right ulna has no facet for the radial head. The rotational aspect of the right elbow appears to have been undergoing modification at the time of death. Although radial dislocation is often associated with a Monteggia fracture of the ulna, radiographs of the right ulna in this case show no clear evidence of fracture.

A small depression similar to a septal aperture is present in the floor of the coronoid fossa of the left humerus, but it does not communicate with the olecranon fossa. The coronoid margin of the left ulna is unusually sharp and fits into the depression in the fossa when the elbow is hyperflexed.

Hands: The fifth finger on the right hand was completely missing in life. The first (proximal) phalanx of the second finger on the right side also was habitually hyperflexed relative to the second (middle) phalanx. It is possible that this was due to a fracture of the first phalanx because this bone is shorter in length than that on the left side. The first phalanx of the fifth finger on the left side also shows evidence of habitual hyperflexion relative to the second phalanx. This could also be the result of a fracture of the left first phalanx.

Hips and knees: No behavioral markers were observed at the hips or knees.

Ankles: A small squatting facet is present on the left tibia and talus, indicating hyperflexion of the left ankle. Although the right talus is damaged in this region, the right tibia lacks a facet. An extension of the medial tuberosity of the right calcaneus (but not the left) indicates that this individual suffered from a heel spur on the right foot.

GIANT 5

This body was apparently removed during an ancient looting of the tomb and the parts, some still articulated, some not, were later returned to the tomb. Some important bones were broken or not recovered, but overall the preservation is quite good.

Shoulders: The right clavicle is slightly shorter than the left but more rugose overall, signifying right-handedness. The vertebral border of the right scapula

is convex, indicating well-developed back muscles. No information is available for the left side.

Both clavicles show a deeply pitted costal tuberosity and a well-developed conoid tubercle (Figure 6.11d). Both features reflect considerable stress on the shoulder region, with the right side showing greater stress than the left. The glenoid fossa of the scapula presents an asymmetrical picture of osteoarthritis on the two sides. On the left side, the anterior superior margin of the rim is raised above the articular surface, and the anterior inferior margin is slightly raised. On the right side, the anterior inferior margin is distinctly raised, whereas the superior posterior border is actually depressed. There is also an area of cortical remodeling on the superior margin of the right acromion. The lesser tubercle on both humeri has an irregular porous surface, and there is an area of arthritic destruction near the anterior margin of the left humeral head (Figure 6.11e). The right humeral head has an area of destruction along the posterior margin, but this may be postmortem damage. The left deltoid tuberosity is well developed; the right is too fragmentary for an observation.

Elbows: Both humeri show osteophyte development on the margins of the articular surfaces, indicative of slight to moderate osteoarthritis with no significant side difference noted. The olecranon fossae show no evidence of stress pathology that would reflect hyperextension of the elbow. Both humeri, however, have a shallow radial fossa with a rough articular surface and a deep coronoid fossa. The left coronoid fossa has two small holes in the cortex that do not communicate with the olecranon fossa, and the superior margin has developed a sharp ridge in contrast with a smooth margin on the right side. The head of the left radius has a small area of arthritic destruction along the anterior margin, as would occur when the left elbow was in a tightly flexed position (Figure 6.12a). The right radius was not recovered. The overall picture for this individual is thus one of frequent or sustained hyperflexion of the elbows.

Wrists: A Colles fracture of the left radius with moderate dorsal displacement has united with moderate callus remodeling (Figure 6.12b). The external appearance suggests two distinct fracture lines, but this could not be verified on radiographs. The fracture appears to have affected skeletal changes that might otherwise be related to activity. For example, osteoarthritic changes on the

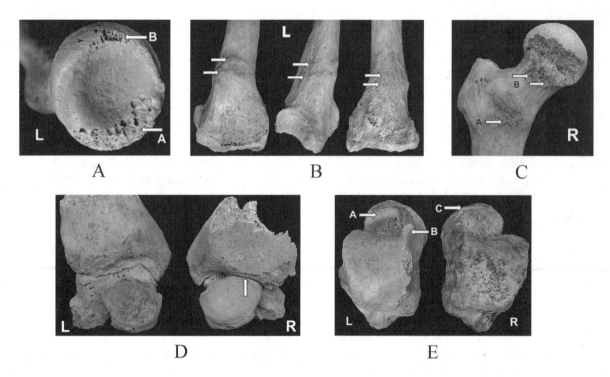

FIGURE 6.12. *A*, Giant 5: left radius; superior view of proximal end showing osteoarthritis (Arrow A); Arrow B indicates postmortem damage. *B*, Giant 5: left radius; anterior, posterior, and ulnar views of distal end showing healed Colles fracture with two possible fracture lines (arrows). *C*, Giant 5: right femur; anterior view of proximal end showing unusually well-developed attachment for the quadriceps muscle (Arrow A) and rough faceting on the femoral neck (Arrow B). *D*, Giant 5: left and right tibias and taluses; anterior view showing right ankle locked in vertical position and left ankle with tibia-talus contact (arrow) producing an angle of less than 90 degrees. *E*, Giant 5: left and right taluses; superior view showing anterior (Arrow A) and medial (Arrow B) contact facets with tibia on left talus, and anterior ridge (Arrow C) on right talus.

articular surface of the styloid of the left radius are probably related directly to the fracture. The same is true of a small articular area of destruction on the left fifth metacarpal, pisiform, and triangular bones. The pisiform on the right side is severely distorted, perhaps the result of additional trauma focused directly on this bone.

Hands: The location of osteoarthritic destruction on the left radial head is consistent with the left hand holding something in a vertical position. This observation is not available for the right hand.

Hips: A prominent feature of the asymmetry at the hip involves the attachment areas for the quadriceps muscle: well-developed on the right side and poorly developed on the left side (Figure 6.12c). Although both femora have faceting with an irregular articular surface on the neck, the condition is more extreme on the right side. The right femoral head also has a circular area

of arthritic destruction near its center, while the left femoral head is normal. Both pelves are fragmentary with parts missing. The observable parts, the ischium part of the right acetabulum and the pubis part of left acetabulum, show evidence of osteoarthritis. Unfortunately, missing parts make a complete side comparison impossible. All of the observed features reflect sustained or repeated anterior flexion of the right leg at the hip.

Knees: Osteoarthritic destruction of the articular surface is evident on the right patella, but not the left. A small vastus notch also is present on the right patella, but not the left. Both femora are affected by osteoarthritis at the knee, with the right side showing greater involvement than the left. The anterior surface of the lateral condyle is involved on both sides, but the right femur also shows marginal osteophyte development on the posterior parts of both condyles, particularly the medial condyle. The lateral condyles of both tibiae also show some surface destruction and marginal osteophytosis, with the right side showing greater involvement than the left. This asymmetrical pattern of osteoarthritis indicates greater flexion stress at the right knee than the left.

Ankles: The appearance of the articular facets of the tibia and talus on the two sides is also markedly asymmetrical. The right side shows no evidence of hyperflexion. In fact, when the tibia and talus on this side are fitted together, they appear almost locked at an angle approximating 90 degrees (Figure 6.12d). In sharp contrast, prominent facets on the anterior margin of the tibia and the superior surface of the talar head on the left side indicate sustained contact between these parts (Figure 6.12e). When placed in this contact position, the angle formed at the ankle is well under 90 degrees, indicating habitual hyperflexion of the foot relative to the lower leg on this side. There is also an area of osteoarthritic destruction on the distal articular surface of the left fibula that matches a similar area on the lateral articular surface of the left talus.

The observations from the hip, knee, and ankle are consistent with this individual spending considerable time kneeling on his left knee with the left foot tightly flexed against the leg. In contrast, the position of the right foot with the leg would have approximated a right angle, suggesting that the right leg was bent at the hip and knee with the foot firmly planted on the ground.

Discussion

The giant skeletons from Dos Cabezas yield interesting information regarding joint degeneration, new facet formation, muscle attachment development, and bone fracturing relevant to occupation. The amount of data obtained is surprising given the young ages of these individuals. Not all of these data present a simple interpretation, but where interpretation does seem possible, the results are intriguing.

The pattern of occupational markers in the upper limbs is asymmetrical, although some of this may simply be due to dominant handedness. The shorter clavicles on the right side along with the generally greater bone robusticity on this side indicate that all four of the individuals for which the information is available (1, 3, 4, 5) were right-handed.

Giants 1, 3, and 5 show evidence of hyperflexion at both elbows, sometimes with small differences between the sides. In contrast, they show no evidence of hyperextension. This suggests that these individuals did not engage in any strenuous activities requiring a full range of flexion and extension at the elbow, but rather that the arms were held for long periods in a tightly flexed position. Osteoarthritic destruction of the radial head, where it occurs, further indicates that the hands were habitually held in a position with the thumbs upward. This is consistent with something held in the hands in a vertical position. The picture is more complicated in Giant 1, whose right radius has two areas of osteoarthritic change, suggesting the hand was also sometimes held in the opposite position, with the thumb downward.

The overall pattern of upper limb skeletal trauma in the giants includes two classic Colles (falling) fractures of the radius (one a possible double fracture), an unreduced elbow dislocation, a probable radial shaft fracture, two possible finger fractures and a missing fifth finger, and two deformed (likely crushed) pisiforms. The fractures are all united but show varying degrees of remodeling, indicating they occurred at varying times before death. None of the trauma involving the upper limb appears to reflect occupation. More likely it is due to random accidents, perhaps reflecting poor bone quality and the general awkwardness of these unusually tall individuals. Only two fractures of the lower limb were observed, these involving the knee and lower leg, and they also can more easily be attributed to accidents than occupation.

Markers on the bones of the lower limb present a more distinctive picture than those on the upper limb. Again Giants 1, 3 and 5 show the most interesting patterns, with markers generally absent in Giant 2, perhaps due to inactivity, and in Giant 4, probably because of relative youth. The only distinct markers on the skeleton of Giant 2 involve the ankles and indicate greater flexion on the right side than the left. This contrasts with the picture presented by Giants 1, 3 and 5, where the greater flexion was on the left side. The absence of any faceting on the neck of the femur on either side and any stress pathology at the knees suggests that Giant 2 did not spend time in a kneeling position, but instead sat or stood much of the time. The faceting on the talus indicates that sitting was more likely than standing, with the right foot forward and the left foot back, thus increasing the angulation between the leg and foot on the left side.

The picture presented in Giants 1, 3, and 5 is consistent with an individual spending considerable time on the left knee with the right leg bent forward at the pelvis. In this position, the right knee would have been bent at something less than 90 degrees. The bottom of the right foot would have been in contact with the ground, but the left foot could have been bent forward, producing a sharp angle between the foot and the leg, or bent backward, putting the top of the foot in contact with the ground. The clearest evidence for positioning of the left foot is found in Giant 5. Here the anterior part of the tibia was in contact with the talus enough to produce distinct faceting, indicating that the foot was bent forward, not backward. This, in fact, appears to be the case for all five Giants, although for the others the evidence is less clear.

Of particular interest are the feet of Giant 1. Their extreme lateral deviation probably began to develop at an early age and was later accentuated by degenerative changes. Turning the feet outward while kneeling on one knee for long periods of time would increase an individual's stability, especially when the heel is raised from the ground, making the tendency to fall to either side less likely. This tendency of keeping the heels raised and extending the toes may have been a personal behavior of this particular individual.

The occupation imprinted on the skeletons of Giants 1, 3, and 5 appears to be that of maintaining a particular position for long periods of time, a position that involved kneeling on the left knee and holding objects in both hands with the elbows bent to maximum flexion. Beyond this basic pattern we find individual variations, some of which lend themselves to logical interpretation, and some not. The asymmetry seen in the shoulders of Giant 5, for example, suggests that the right arm was held in a somewhat different position than that used by Giants 1 and 3.

The Iconographic Evidence

Iconography, or more properly iconology, is the study of symbols and how they are or were employed in individual cultures. Symbols can be religious or secular; in either case, they encode behaviors or beliefs. Being able to interpret an iconographic symbol correctly usually means that one must be a participant in the culture that uses it or, at least, be privy to the nuances of that culture. Yet even when a researcher is distant from the inner workings of another culture, some spectacular results are possible by employing careful analogies. Iconographic investigations can be particularly informative when they are employed within archaeological cultures lacking a writing system but possessing a vibrant art tradition. Obviously, the Moche culture is ideal for such an approach. Over the past thirty years, iconographic studies of Moche art have been so widely used and so successful that it would congest the bibliography to list them all. Following in that tradition, but expanding thereon, it has been possible to compare the osteo-forensic conclusions of the Dos Cabezas Giants' study with the body of Moche art.

As has been noted repeatedly, Moche art is largely concerned with scenes and individual images of battle and its aftermath. In fact, so pervasive is this theme that it can characterize almost the entire corpus of Moche hieratic culture. Therefore, it is not too surprising that the occupation or role of some of the Dos Cabezas Giants is best interpreted as that of a warrior. In fact, the description of the skeletal evidence from Giants 1, 3, and 5 exactly matches the pose of the "Kneeling Warrior." At least forty examples are known of modeled ceramic figurines that are identified by their accoutrements of loincloth, club, and shield as male warriors. Thirty-six such examples were tallied in the photographic collection of the Archive of Moche Art at UCLA, where it was found that thirty were posed with the left knee on the ground and the right knee raised at a 90 degree angle, right foot flat to the ground. In four examples, the pose was reversed, and two figures had both knees on the ground. All thirty-six had their arms bent at the elbow, but raised at slightly different elevations. Of the intact figures, sixteen held a shield on the left arm and grasped a club in the right hand (Figure 6.13). Two more figures had a shield on the left arm, but the right hand was broken away. Only one warrior held just a club, but in his right hand. The remaining examples show a kneeling warrior, a shield on one arm (usually the left) and with the opposite hand empty, but with its thumb and fingers curled around empty space. In other words, there was something removable in that grasping hand, most

FIGURE 6.13. Kneeling Warrior with a feline effigy on his back. Courtesy of the Cleveland Museum of Art, Andrew R. and Martha Holden Jennings Fund (1989.90).

likely a club. Some of the Kneeling Warrior figures have inlays in the form of eyes and decoration on clothing and shield. Excavations at the contemporaneous Moche site of La Mina yielded a seated figurine with removable carved bone ear rods (Narváez 1994). Therefore, it seems reasonable to postulate that the Kneeling Warrior figurines with an empty clenched hand originally held a removable club. Not only does the general kneeling posture of the figurines match the forensic data from the giants, but the details do as well. The sharp foot flexion of many ceramic examples matches well with the squatting facets observed on the giants' ankle bones. So, too, does the pose of the hands, which are shown in the figurines with the thumb either raised directly above the

fingers (on the shield side) or slightly above the curled fingers (on the club side).

Giants 2 and 4, as discussed above, do not evince the same skeletal pattern as Giants 1, 3, and 5—with the possible exception of squatting facets. It has been suggested that Giant 4 was too young at death to have any occupation mark his skeleton. But Giant 2 was in the same age range as the others, so the lack of skeletal markers in his case must be addressed. He does not appear to have been a kneeling warrior. In fact, we speculate that he may have spent considerable time doing very little other than standing or sitting. There are many examples of figures in Moche art shown standing or seated, but one type of seated figure is suggestive. These individuals appear not simply sitting down, but seated in an elevated position on a dais (Berrin 1997: figs. 70, 72; Donnan 1978: color plate, p. 84; fig. 141). Such individuals are commonly referred to as "rulers" or men seated on a "throne" because of their elaborate garments and elevated pose. Actual "thrones" or elevated daises have been found at archaeological sites, including two at Dos Cabezas (Donnan and Cock 2002:35–39). Painted scenes show elites seated and carried in litters, some of which also have throne-like backs (Donnan and McClelland 1999, fig. 3.27).

Was Giant 2 so important that he did virtually nothing that would mark his bones? Such an interpretation is supported by the material remains of his tomb. Giant 2 was buried much more elaborately than his contemporaries, Giants 1 and 3. Furthermore, the suggestion that Giant 2's importance relieved him of physically stressful practices is in accord with the physiognomy of the most elite Moche male ever examined osteologically, the Lord of Sipán, whose bones were delicate and showed no signs of heavy muscle development (Alva and Donnan 1993:105).

What this study has shown is that a forensic examination of individuals from a culture long extinct can not only shed light on the stresses (or lack thereof) imposed on them by their daily lives, but, when conjoined with archaeological and iconographic data, can lead to a clearer understanding of cultural machinations. For example, although the Kneeling Warrior figurines have been recognized as a ceramic type for many years, not until this study could it be said that the pose was actually assumed by real Moche people. Even if it had been presumed that the kneeling position reflected reality, there was no way to know that individuals practiced it so repeatedly and sustainedly that it imprinted their bones. This forensic study also is consistent with the Moche Norteño Standard Elite Burial Pattern hypothesis. Giant 2 was like the two individuals flanking him in death—they were all giants, but Giant 2 was of superior rank.

Bibliography

Alva, Walter, and Christopher B. Donnan
1993   *Royal Tombs of Sipán*. Fowler Museum of Cultural History, University of California, Los Angeles.

Angel, J. Lawrence
1966   Early Skeletons from Tranquility, California. *Contributions to Anthropology* 2 (1):1–18. Smithsonian Press, Washington, D.C.

Berrin, Kathleen, ed.
1997   *The Spirit of Ancient Peru: Treasures from the Museo Arqueológico Rafael Larco Herrera*. Thames and Hudson, Fine Arts Museums of San Francisco.

Castillo Butters, Luis Jaime, and Christopher B. Donnan
1992   *Primer informe parcial y solicitud de permiso para excavación arqueológica Proyecto San José de Moro*. 1ra Temporada de Excavaciones (junio–agosto de 1991), Lima.

Charles, R. H.
1893–1894   The Influence of Function, as Exemplified in the Morphology of the Lower Extremity of the Punjabi. *Journal of Anatomy and Physiology* 28:1–18.

Cordy-Collins, Alana
2003   Five Cases of Prehistoric Peruvian Gigantism. In *Mummies in a New Millennium: Proceedings of the 4th World Congress on Mummy Studies, Nuuk, Greenland, September 4th to 10th, 2001*. Edited by Niels Lynnerup, Claus Andreasen, and Joel Berglund. Greenland National Museum and Archives and Danish Polar Center, Copenhagen.

Donnan, Christopher B.
1978   *Moche Art of Peru: Pre-Columbian Symbolic Communication*. Fowler Museum of Cultural History, University of California, Los Angeles.
2001   Moche Burials Uncovered. *National Geographic* 199 (3):58–73.
2003   Tumbas con entierros en miniatura: Un nuevo tipo funerario moche. In *Moche: Hacia el Final del Milenio*, Tome I, 43–78. Actas del Segundo Coloquio sobre la Cultura Moche, Trujillo, 1 al 7 de agosto de 1999. Edited by Santiago Uceda and Elías Mujica. Universidad Nacional de Trujillo and Pontificia Universidad Católica del Perú, Lima.

Donnan, Christopher B., and Guillermo A. Cock Donnan
1995   *Informe parcial: Proyecto arqueológico Dos Cabezas*. 1ra temporada de trabajo de campo, Lima.
1998   *Cuarto informe parcial: Proyecto arqueológico Dos Cabezas*. 4ta temporada de excavaciones (junio–julio 1997), Lima.
1999   *Quinto informe parcial: Excavaciones en Dos Cabezas, valle de Jequetepeque, Perú*. 5ta temporada de excavaciones (julio–agosto 1998), Lima.
2000   *Sexto informe parcial: Excavaciones en Dos Cabezas, valle de Jequetepeque, Perú*. 6ta temporada de excavaciones (junio–julio 1999), Lima.
2001   *Sétimo informe parcial: Excavaciones en Dos Cabezas, Valle*

de Jequetepeque, Perú. 7ma temporada de excavaciones (junio–julio 2000), Lima.

2002   *Informe: Excavaciones en Dos Cabezas, valle de Jequetepeque, Perú. 8va temporada de excavaciones* (junio–agosto 2001), Lima.

Donnan, Christopher B., and Donna McClelland

1999   *Moche Fineline Painting: Its Evolution and Its Artists.* Fowler Museum of Cultural History, University of California, Los Angeles.

Genovés, Santiago

1967   Proportionality of Long Bones and Their Relation to Stature among Mesoamericans. *American Journal of Physical Anthropology* 26:67–77.

Hawkey, Diane E., and Charles F. Merbs

1995   Activity-induced Musculoskeletal Stress Markers (MSM) and Subsistence Strategy Changes among Ancient Hudson Bay Eskimos. *International Journal of Osteoarchaeology* 5:324–338.

Kennedy, Kenneth A. R.

1983   Morphological Variations in Ulnar Supinator Crests and Fossae, as Identifying Markers of Occupational Stress. *Journal of Forensic Science* 28:871–876.

Knowles, A. Keith

1983   Acute Traumatic Lesions. In *Disease in Ancient Man*, 61–83. Edited by Gerald D. Hart. Clarke Irwin, Toronto.

Kostick, E. L.

1963   Facets and Imprints on the Upper and Lower Extremities of Femora from a Western Nigerian Population. *Journal of Anatomy* 97:393–402.

May, Simon A.

2005   Paleopathological Study of the Hallus valgus. *American Journal of Physical Anthropology* 126:139–149.

May, Simon A., James Steele, and Mark Ford

1999   Direction Asymmetry in the Human Clavicle. *International Journal of Human Osteology* 9:18–28.

Merbs, Charles F.

1983   *Patterns of Activity-induced Pathology in a Canadian Inuit Population.* National Museum of Man Mercury Series, Archaeological Survey of Canada Paper No. 119, Ottawa.

1989   Trauma. In *Reconstruction of Life from the Skeleton*, 161–189. Edited by Mehmet Yaşar İşcan and Kenneth A. R. Kennedy. Liss, New York.

Merbs, Charles F., and Robert C. Euler

1985   Atlanto-occipital Fusion and Spondylolisthesis in an Anasazi Skeleton from Bright Angel Ruin, Grand Canyon National Park, Arizona. *American Journal of Physical Anthropology* 67:381–391.

Messeri, Piero

1961   Morfologia della rotula nei neolitici della Liguria. *Archivio per l'Antropologia e l'Etnologia* 91:1–11.

Narváez V., Alfredo

1994   La Mina: Una tumba Moche I en el valle de Jequetepque. In *Moche: Propuestas y perspectivas*, 59–92. Edited by Santiago Uceda and Elías Mujica. Universidad Nacional de La Libertad, Trujillo, Perú.

Poirier, Paul, and A. Charpy

1911   *Traité d'anatomie.* 2nd ed. Masson et cie Editeurs.

Schultz, Robert J.

1990   *The Language of Fractures.* Williams & Wilkins, Baltimore.

Stirland, Ann

1991   Diagnosis of Occupationally Related Paleopathology: Can It Be Done? In *Human Paleopathology: Current Syntheses and Future Options*, 40–47. Edited by Donald J. Ortner. Smithsonian Institution Press, Washington, D.C.

Thompson, A.

1890   Additional Note on the Influence of Posture on the Form of the Articular Surfaces of the Tibia and Astragalus in the Different Races of Man and in the Higher Apes. *Journal of Anatomy and Physiology* 24:210–217.

Verano, John W.

1993   Características físicas y biología osteológica de los Moche. In *Moche: Propuestas y perspectivas*, 307–326. Actas del Primer Coloquio sobre la Cultura Moche, Trujillo, 12 a 16 de abril de 1993. Edited by Santiago Uceda and Elías Mujica. Travaux de l'Institut Français d'Études Andines 79. Universidad Nacional de la Libertad, Trujillo, Perú.

CHAPTER SEVEN

Moche Forms for Shaping Sheet Metal

CHRISTOPHER B. DONNAN, UNIVERSITY OF CALIFORNIA, LOS ANGELES

DAVID A. SCOTT, COTSEN INSTITUTE OF ARCHAEOLOGY, UNIVERSITY OF CALIFORNIA, LOS ANGELES

TODD BRACKEN

Abstract

The Moche were extremely skilled at shaping sheet metal into low-relief or three-dimensional depictions of people, plants, animals, and supernatural figures. They created these objects by carefully hammering sheet metal over solid forms made of either copper alloy or wood. Thus they were able to efficiently transform sheet metal into complex shapes and produce objects that were nearly identical in size and form.

The Moche were among the most sophisticated metallurgists of the ancient world. They were extremely skilled at casting, utilizing both open molds and the lost wax technique. But most objects were made of sheet metal, skillfully shaped into low-relief or three-dimensional depictions of people, plants, animals, and supernatural figures. Until recently, it was not understood how Moche sheet metal objects were shaped. This chapter demonstrates that the Moche used solid metal or wood forms over which sheet metal was carefully hammered. In this way, sheet metal was transformed efficiently into the desired shape, and duplicate objects of nearly identical size and form could be produced.

Anthropomorphized Owl Form

Our first recognition of a form for shaping sheet metal was an anthropomorphized owl figure with detached arms (Figures 7.1, 7.2). The figure wears a simple headdress, a loincloth, and a tunic with triangular elements decorating the hem. The main body stands 11.2 cm high and weighs 660 grams. It was a solid cast of metal in an open mold. The flat back (Figure 7.1c) exhibits the rippled texture characteristic of the upper, exposed surface of an open mold casting. The undercuts on the face and

body would have necessitated breaking the mold in order to remove the casting. The mold, which may have been of stone or fired ceramic, was therefore a unique product that would have produced only one casting.

The surface of the casting is slightly corroded to a gray-green patina, but in most areas it retains a good likeness of the original form. The only notable exceptions are the concretion of corrosion at the proper left side of the headdress and along the outer flange of the proper left ear (Figure 7.1a).

The two arms are separate from the body. They are bent at the elbows, with the hands closed (Figure 7.2). Slight depressions around the wrists indicate bracelets. The proper right arm has a maximum dimension of 3.12 cm and weighs 24 grams. The proper left arm has a maximum dimension of 3.9 cm and weighs 30 grams. Seam lines bisect each arm along the length, indicating that the arms were cast in enclosed two-piece molds. No signs of any casting sprues remain on the arms.

A nondestructive X-ray fluorescence analysis was used to determine the composition of the form's exposed surface.[1] The spectrum taken from the front of the torso (Figure 7.3) reveals the presence of copper with slight traces of nickel, silver and iron. A similar spectrum was

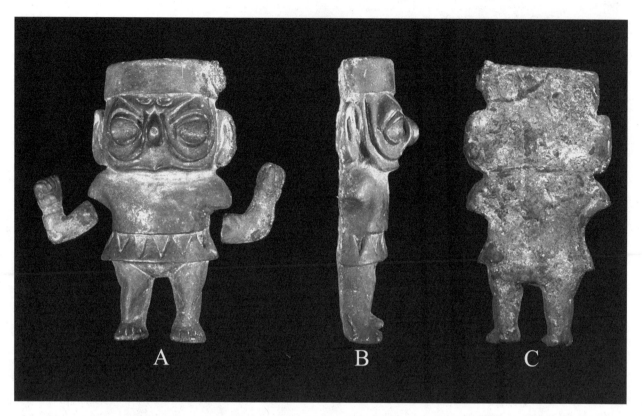

FIGURES 7.1. Anthropomorphized owl form used to mold sheet metal. Private collection. Photograph by Christopher B. Donnan.

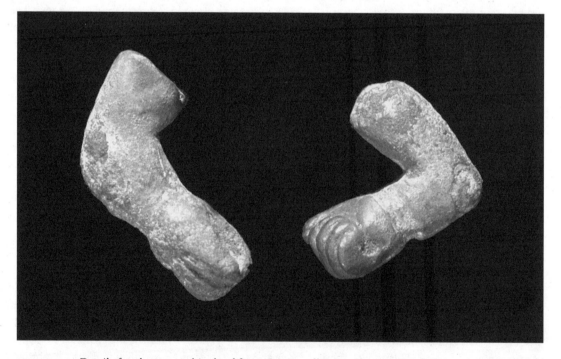

FIGURE 7.2. Detail of anthropomorphized owl form. Private collection. Photograph by Christopher B. Donnan.

FIGURE 7.3. Spectrum taken from anthropomorphized owl form.

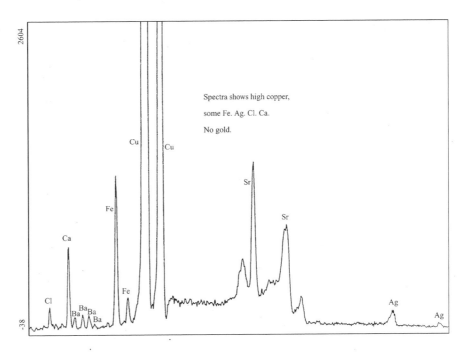

Table 7.1: Anthropomorphized Owl Form

ICP-MS Analytical Data in Parts per Million (ppm)

ELEMENT	PPM	DETECTION LIMIT
Barium	0.7	0.5
Bismuth	10.6	0.5
Boron	8	2
Calcium	680	100
Cobalt	1.1	0.5
Copper	977,000	1
Gold	148	0.5
Lead	46.9	0.5
Nickel	91.5	0.6
Palladium	29.1	0.5
Phosphorus	19.100	1,000
Platinum	0.7	0.5
Rhodium	5.7	0.5
Selenium	33	10
Silver	3,210	0.5
Strontium	2.2	0.5
Tellurium	3.6	0.5
Tin	21	0.8
Tungsten	9.9	0.9

NOTE: Elements not detected: Al, As, Sb, Be, Br, Cd, Ce, Cs, Cr, Dy, Er, Eu, Gd, Ga, Ge, Hf, Ho, I, Ir, Fe, La, Li, Lu, Mg, Mn, Hg, Mo, Ny, Ni, Os, K, Pr, Re, Ru, Sa, Si, Na, Ta, Th, Tu, Ti, U, V, Yt, Yb, Z, Zr.

obtained from each of the arms, showing that all three parts of the form were made essentially of copper. Further analysis of the composition was made using inductively coupled plasma-mass spectrometry (ICP-MS) on 20 mg of clean metal drillings that were removed from one side of the torso. The results are shown in Table 7.1.[2]

Although copper-arsenic alloys were used by the Moche, no arsenic was detected in either X-ray fluorescence analysis or by ICP-MS. The use of smelted copper can be inferred from the elemental composition; the pattern of impurities clearly matches the criteria required for smelted copper (Hancock et al. 1994; Wayman et al. 1985).[3] This indicates that Moche metalsmiths had available to them copper ores for smelting which were free of arsenic, and like later Lambayeque (Sicán) metalsmiths, produced copper-arsenic alloys by deliberately adding arsenic-rich minerals to oxidized copper ore sources (Merkel et al. 1994).

A sheet metal figure that was probably made over the anthropomorphized owl form is shown in Figure 7.4a–c.[4] It is 11.4 cm in height (0.2 cm taller than the form) and demonstrates how the sheet metal was shaped over the surface of the form and wrapped around its back side. Although the proper right arm is missing, the upper part of the proper left arm remains fastened to the torso with a metal staple.

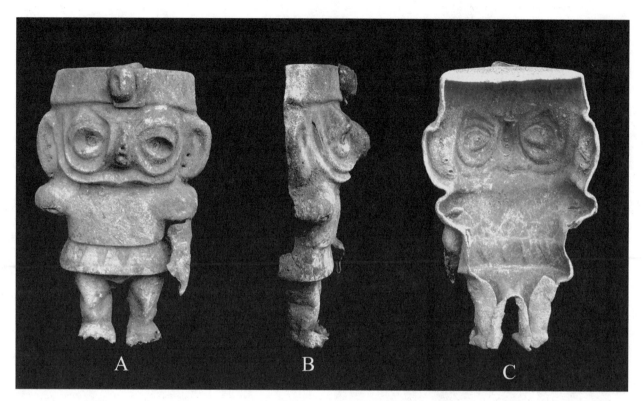

FIGURE 7.4. Anthropomorphized owl figure, probably made from owl form in Figures 7.1 and 7.2. Private collection. Photograph by Christopher B. Donnan.

FIGURE 7.5. Human warrior figure. Museo Tumbas Royales de Sipán, Lambayeque. Photograph by Christopher B. Donnan.

This sheet metal figure probably held a war club diagonally across his chest, like the human warrior shown in Figure 7.5. The anthropormorphized owl form, with its arms in similar position, is illustrated in Figure 7.6. Since the arms on these figures were rendered in full round and would have extended in front of the torsos, they had to be made separately and subsequently attached.

The sheet metal face at the center of the headdress (Figure 7.4a) was probably part of a large headdress ornament. It was attached to the figure with a staple. Two perforations in the central part of each of the figure's ears suggest that he originally wore ear ornaments, and another pair of holes at the tip of the nose suggests that there was originally a nose ornament.

Frog Form

A frog form, 5.7 cm long and weighing 158 grams, was also used to shape fine sheet metal (Figure 7.7a–c). Like the arms of the anthropomorphized owl form, it was cast of solid metal in an enclosed two-piece mold; the seam line along the sides of the body can be seen in some areas. No signs of any casting sprues remain.

The frog is unusual in having a flat, curving element projecting from its mouth. The shape of this element

FIGURE 7.6. Anthropomorphized owl form. Private collection. Photograph by Christopher B. Donnan.

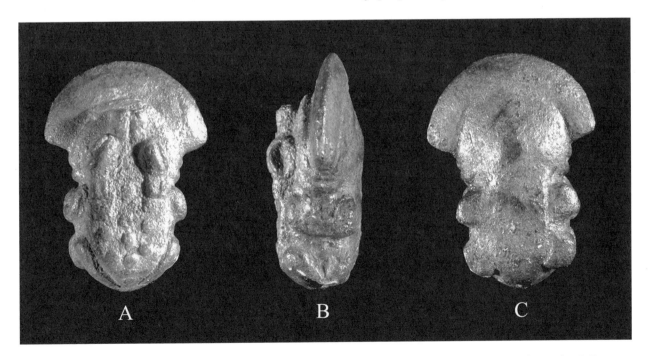

FIGURE 7.7. Frog form used to mold sheet metal. Fowler Museum of Cultural History, UCLA. Photograph by Christopher B. Donnan.

FIGURE 7.8. Scene of combat with sacrificial knives. Drawing by Donna McClelland.

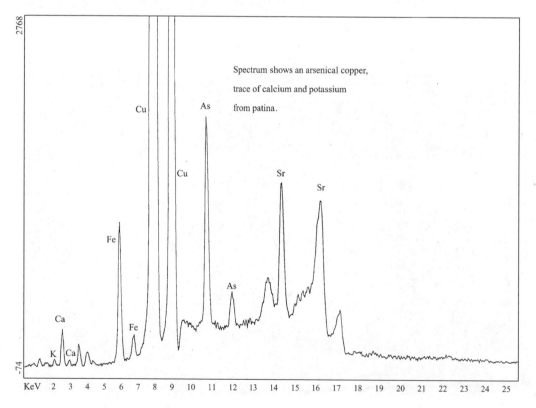

Spectrum shows an arsenical copper,
trace of calcium and potassium
from patina.

FIGURE 7.9. Spectrum taken from frog form.

Table 7.2: Frog Form
ICP-MS Analytical Data in Parts per Million (ppm)

ELEMENT	PPM	DETECTION LIMIT
Aluminium	5	2
Antimony	219	0.9
Arsenic	17,700	2
Bismuth	21.2	0.2
Calcium	35	20
Cobalt	1.2	0.2
Copper	Matrix	
Gold	7	0.2
Iron	189	10
Lead	39.8	0.2
Nickel	21.2	0.2
Selenium	80	20
Silver	657	0.5
Strontium	0.3	0.1
Tellurium	3.6	0.2
Tin	7.2	0.3
Vanadium	0.5	0.2
Zinc	14	0.5

NOTE: Elements not detected: Ba, Be, B, Br, Cd, Ce, Cs, Cr, Dy, Er, En, Gd, Ga, Ge, Hf, Ho, I, Ir, La, Li, Lu, Mg, Mn, Hg, Mo, Ny, Nb, Os, Pd, Pt, Pr, Re, Rh, Rb, Ru, Sa, Ta, Th, Tu, Tm, W, U, Yb, Yr, Zr.

resembles the blade of a *tumi*, a sacrificial knife frequently seen in Moche art (Figure 7.8).[5]

Analysis of the frog form utilizing X-ray fluorescence (Figure 7.9) and ICP-MS (Table 7.2) detected the presence of seventeen elements, including significant amounts of arsenic (1.7 percent), and small amounts of antimony, bismuth, iron, lead, nickel, selenium and silver. This form was therefore made of a copper-arsenic alloy.

Although we have been unable to identify a sheet metal frog that was made on this particular form, other Moche frogs of sheet metal are known.[6] The one shown in Figure 7.10 is 6.8 cm long, approximately 1 cm longer than one made on the frog form would have been. Moreover, it lacks the knife blade in its mouth and bumps on its back, and it has prominent "ears" and manioc tubers on its flanks. Nevertheless, it was almost certainly made over a form similar to the one illustrated in Figure 7.7, with one sheet of metal for the top half of the frog and one sheet for the bottom half. The halves were subsequently soldered together around the periphery.

Feline Head Form
Another form depicts the head of a feline projecting frontally from the center of a thick disc (Figure 7.11). It is 4.3 cm in height and weighs 142 grams. Like the body

FIGURE 7.10. Frog figure. Private collection. Photograph by Christopher B. Donnan.

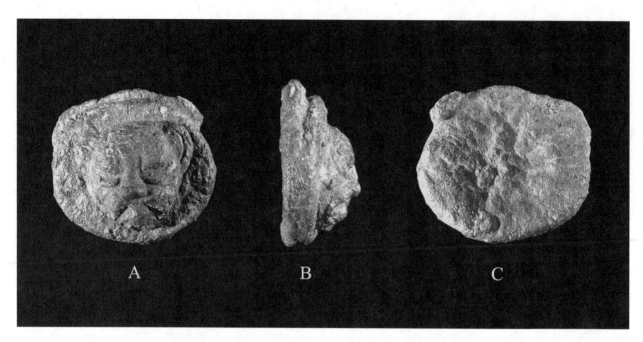

FIGURE 7.11. Feline head form. Fowler Museum of Cultural History, UCLA. Photograph by Christopher B. Donnan.

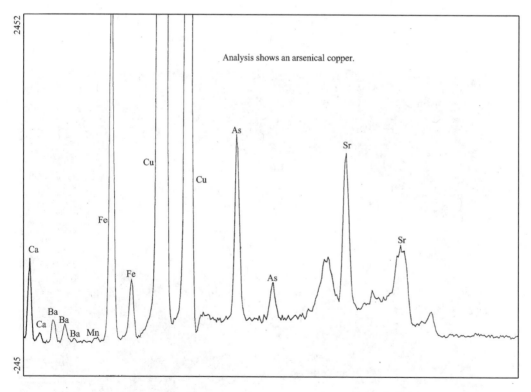

FIGURE 7.12. Spectrum taken from the feline head form.

of the anthropomorphized owl form, it was cast of solid metal in a one-piece open mold. The back has the ripple texture characteristic of the upper, exposed surface of an open mold casting (Figure 7.11c). Details of the face have lost some definition through corrosion, but the features can still be discerned.

X-ray fluorescence (Figure 7.12) and ICP-MS (Table 7.3) analysis detected twenty-one elements, including significant amounts of arsenic and trace amounts of antimony, bismuth, iron, lead, nickel, selenium and silver. This pattern of trace elements is very similar to that of the frog form, indicating that the feline head form was also made of a copper-arsenic alloy.

A feline head bead, similar to the feline head form, is shown in Figure 7.13. It is hollow, with the front made from one sheet of copper, and the back from another. The front and back were soldered together around the edge of the bead. Its size is similar to the size of the feline head form, but the mouth and eyes of the feline on the bead are depressed to receive shell and green stone inlay, whereas the mouths and eyes on the feline head form are raised. Thus, the front of the feline head bead was probably not made over this form, but over one very similar to it.

The back of the feline head bead is flat, and the edge is round so that it would fit the round edge of the front of the bead. The rippled back of the feline head form, as well as its irregular back edge, would not have been suited to forming the back of a bead like the one illustrated in Figure 7.13. Perhaps this form was meant to shape only the front of the bead, and another form was used to shape the back. The front and back, each made on different forms, would then have been soldered together around the periphery. Alternatively, the form may have been cast imperfectly, and its back was to have been smoothed and made more symmetrical prior to being used as a form. If so, this form may never have been used.

Warrior Form

One form depicts a standing warrior wearing a loin-cloth, shirt, headdress that ties under the chin, and large circular ear ornaments (Figure 7.14a, b). The sunken eyes suggest that sheet metal figures made over this form were to have inlaid eyes.

The position of the warrior's arms and hands suggest that he was meant to hold a war club diagonally across

Table 7.3: Feline Head Form
ICP-MS Analytical Data in Parts per Million (ppm)

ELEMENT	PPM	DETECTION LIMIT
Aluminium	58	5
Antimony	43	2
Arsenic	8,710	0.3
Barium	6.2	0.9
Bismuth	82.6	0.3
Calcium	1,520	40
Chromium	1.4	1
Cobalt	3.6	0.4
Copper	Matrix	
Gold	54.3	0.3
Iron	203	20
Lead	79.4	0.3
Molybdenum	5	1
Nickel	79	1
Selenium	146	40
Silver	439	0.3
Strontium	2.7	0.3
Tellurium	2.3	0.3
Tin	21.9	0.3
Tungsten	1.5	0.3
Zinc	10	3

NOTE: Elements not detected: Be, B, Br, Cd, Ce, Cs, Dy, Er, Eu, Gd, Ga, Ge, Hf, Ho, I, Ir, La, Li, Lu, Mg, Mn, Hg, N, Nb, Os, Pd, Pt, Pr, Rh, Rd, Ru, Sm, Na, Ta, Th, Tl, Ti, U, V, Yb, Yt, Zr.

FIGURE 7.13. Feline head bead. Private collection. Photograph by Christopher B. Donnan.

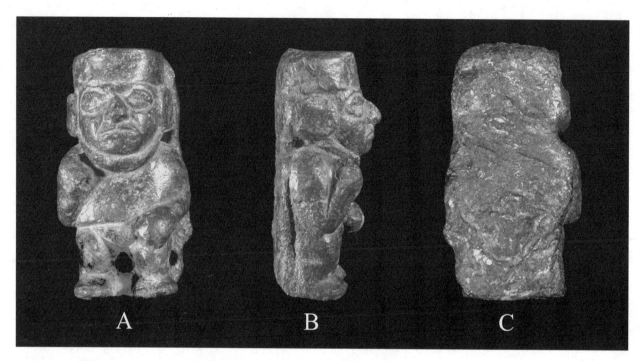

FIGURE 7.14. Warrior form. Fowler Museum of Cultural History, UCLA. Photograph by Christopher B. Donnan.

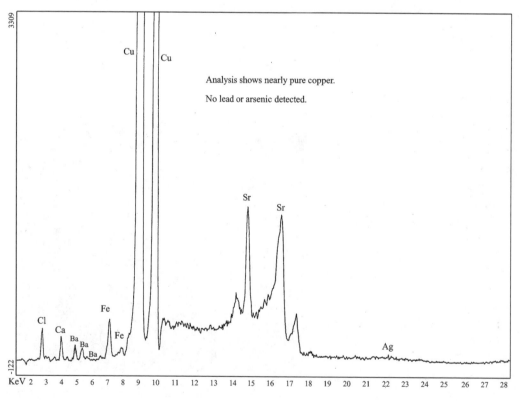

Analysis shows nearly pure copper.

No lead or arsenic detected.

FIGURE 7.15. Spectrum taken from the warrior form.

Table 7.4: Warrior Form
ICP-MS Analytical Data in Parts per Million (ppm)

ELEMENT	PPM	DETECTION LIMIT
Aluminium	118	3
Barium	5.3	0.3
Bismuth	19.4	0.2
Cadmium	0.5	0.2
Calcium	508	40
Cobalt	1.5	0.2
Copper	Matrix	
Dysprosium	0.6	0.2
Gold	201	0.2
Iron	160	20
Lead	42.4	0.3
Manganese	8.6	0.6
Molybdenum	8.6	0.7
Nickel	180	2
Platinum	0.7	0.2
Rhodium	1.3	0.2
Silver	371	0.6
Sodium	210	200
Strontium	6.1	0.2
Tin	9	3
Tungsten	9.6	0.2
Zinc	10	2

NOTE: Elements not detected: As, Sb, Be, Br, Ce, Cs, Cr, Er, Eu, Gd, Ga, Ge, Hf, Ho, I, Ir, La, Li, Lu, Mg, Hg, Ny, Os, K, Pr, Re, Ru, Sa, Si, Ta, Th, Tu, Ti, U, V, Yt, Yb, Z, Zr. Elements not analyzed: All gasses, C, P, S, K, Si, Sc, In, Tb.

his chest, like the anthropomorphized owl figure discussed above (Figure 7.6). In contrast to the owl figure, however, the arms on this form are in low relief rather than full round. Thus, a sheet metal figure shaped on this form would have the arms created directly on the form rather than made separately and attached with staples. Once a sheet metal figure was shaped over this form, the hands would have been perforated so that a war club could be slid through them.

The warrior form is 5.5 cm in height and weighs 152 grams. It was cast of solid metal in an open mold. The back has the ripple texture characteristic of the upper, exposed surface of an open mold casting (Figure 7.14c). The back is wider than the warrior, indicating some overfilling of the mold with molten metal at the time the form was cast. Two hollow portions, one between the legs (Figure 7.14a) and the other along the proper left side, resulted from imperfect casting.

X-ray fluorescence (Figure 7.15) and ICP-MS (Table 7.4) analysis detected twenty-two elements, not including arsenic or antimony. The gold content is too high for native copper, but the generally low level of other diagnostic elements suggests that the metal was probably obtained from the smelting of copper oxide ore.

Owl Head Form
In addition to the solid metal forms discussed above, there is one wood object that we believe was used as a form for shaping sheet metal. Its front is carved like the

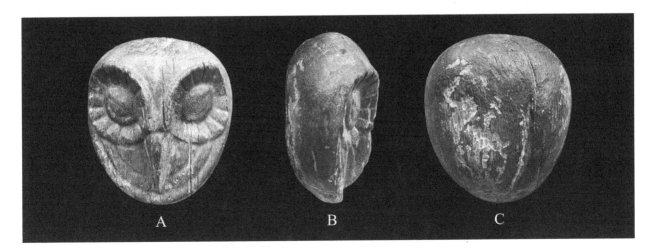

FIGURE 7.16. Owl head form of carved wood. Private collection. Photograph by Christopher B. Donnan.

face of an owl (Figure 7.16a), but it is lenticular in cross section (Figure 7.16b) and has a rounded back (Figure 7.16c). It is 14 cm high and weighs 689 grams. Superbly carved from dense hardwood (probably algarrobo, *Prosopis chilensis*), the surface shows no signs of having been painted.

This is an unusual piece of Moche woodcarving. It has no socket or tenon to attach it to another object, nor any holes for suspension. Moreover, since it is rounded at the base, it cannot stand upright without being supported. Thus its function is enigmatic.

It does, however, resemble owl heads of sheet metal (Figure 7.17) that were found in a Moche tomb at Sipán (Alva and Donnan 1993: fig. 43). Moreover, its size is similar to that of the large feline head beads from Sipán (Figure 7.18). Thus, it was probably a form for producing large, sheet metal beads.

But if it was a form, like the other four examples discussed above, why was it not cast of solid metal? The answer may be its size. It is considerably larger than the other forms, and would have required approximately 4,000 grams of metal. Since the Moche used blowtubes to create a forced draft of air in their metalworking furnaces, there would have been limits to the amount of heat, and thus to the volume of molten metal, that

they were able to produce. The amount of metal required to cast an owl head of this size (467 ml) may well have exceeded the amount of metal they were able to make molten, and was thus beyond the limits of their casting technology.

Alternatively, they may have opted for a hardwood rather than a metal form because metal was precious, and the amount of metal required to make a solid casting of this size was excessive for something that was simply to serve as a tool for metalworking. The disadvantage of a wood form is that it would not hold up as well as a metal form under repeated hammering. Moreover, a small form made of wood would not have the weight and the inertia of a solid metal form, and thus would not function as well for shaping sheet metal. But at the scale of this owl head, the weight and density of the hardwood has sufficient inertia to function very effectively.

Experimental Replication

In an effort to understand how metal forms were used to create sheet metal objects, a duplicate of the anthropomorphized owl form was cast in silicon bronze and subsequently used to create an owl figure in sheet copper (Figure 7.1). We chose the anthropomorphized owl form because it provided the challenge not only

FIGURE 7.17. Sheet metal owl head from tomb in Sipán. Private collection. Photograph by Christopher B. Donnan.

FIGURE 7.18. Feline head bead. Museo Tumbas Royales de Sipán, Lambayeque. Photograph by Christopher B. Donnan.

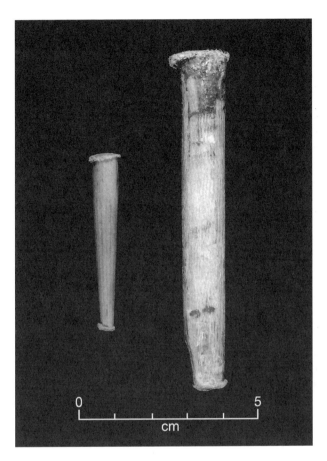

FIGURE 7.19. Wooden punches. Fowler Museum of Cultural History, UCLA. Photograph by Christopher B. Donnan.

FIGURE 7.20. Shaping of sheet metal. Fowler Museum of Cultural History, UCLA. Photograph by Christopher B. Donnan.

of fabricating the body, but also the attachable arms. Moreover, since we had photographs of a sheet metal figure that Moche metalworkers actually made over the original form, we knew the result that they sought to achieve when using it.

To duplicate the owl warrior form, three silicon rubber molds were made: one for the body, and one for each of the arms. The body mold was one piece, and each of the arm molds was two pieces with a pouring channel attached. A beeswax impression was cast from each of these molds. The wax impressions were subsequently cast in silicon bronze, and the pouring channels were removed.[7]

Attempts were then made to hammer sheet copper over the new forms to create an image similar to that in Figure 7.4. The best tools for shaping the sheet metal proved to be a hammer and an assortment of variously

shaped hardwood punches with blunt tips (Figure 7.19). The advantage of wood punches is that they do not cut the metal. Punches with metal tips may have been used for adding or enhancing details, but if metalworkers used punches for general shaping, they would have risked cutting or poking through the soft copper sheet.

In shaping the sheet metal, we found that the best results could be obtained by working from the center of the figure outward, forcing the sheet copper into the general contours of the form first (Figure 7.20) and then repeatedly going back over the surface to stretch the metal into the deeper recessed areas. The most difficult part was forming the metal downward over the top portion of the figure (Figure 7.21a). This required an extreme amount of stretching over the sharp edge of the headdress.

The original thickness of the copper sheet was very

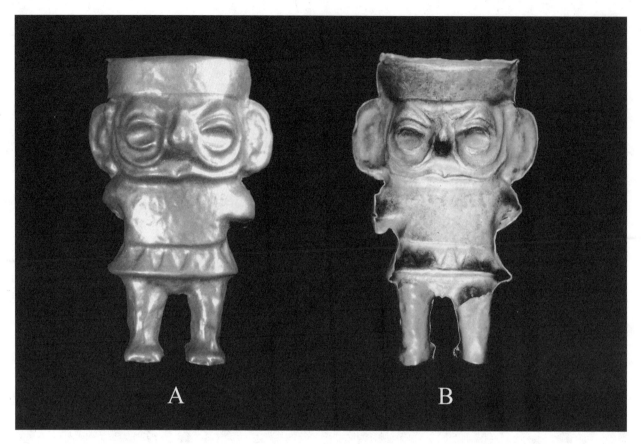

A

B

FIGURE 7.21. Incomplete anthropomorphized owl figure. Fowler Museum of Cultural History, UCLA. Photograph by Christopher B. Donnan.

important. It had to be thin enough so that it could be hammered into small recesses in the surface of the form, and thus obtain all of the detail. On the other hand, if the metal sheet was too thin, it had a tendency to wrinkle as it was being shaped or to tear in areas where it was stretched very thin, either over highly raised areas like the owl's beak, into deep depressions like the eye sockets, or beneath the owl's chin. We found that it was optimum to begin with sheet metal approximately 0.40 mm thick.[8] Although it was thinned by hammering and stretching to as little as 0.25 millimeters in some areas of the finished figure, it did not tear. It was also thin enough so that it did not wrinkle while shaping and could be hammered into all recesses of the form.

An important factor in successfully shaping sheet metal over the forms was repeated annealing. The increasing hardness of the metal as it was worked over the form became apparent by the increased springing

action felt in the hammer blows, as well as a gradual change toward higher frequency in the sound resulting from successive hammer blows. When the sheet metal became hard, it was much more susceptible to tearing. Annealing was achieved by heating the sheet metal evenly to a dull red color, and subsequently quenching or allowing it to cool slowly. This caused the metal to revert to its softer state so that shaping could continue. Producing the body of the owl shown in Figure 7.21 required annealing on eight occasions during the process of shaping.

If one compares the ears of the owl warrior on the original form (Figure 7.1a) with the ears on the sheet metal figure made by Moche metalsmiths (Figure 7.4a), it is clear that the ears on the form are smaller and closer to the head. To make them appear as they do on the sheet metal figure, we found that it was necessary to first shape the ears as they are rendered on the form,

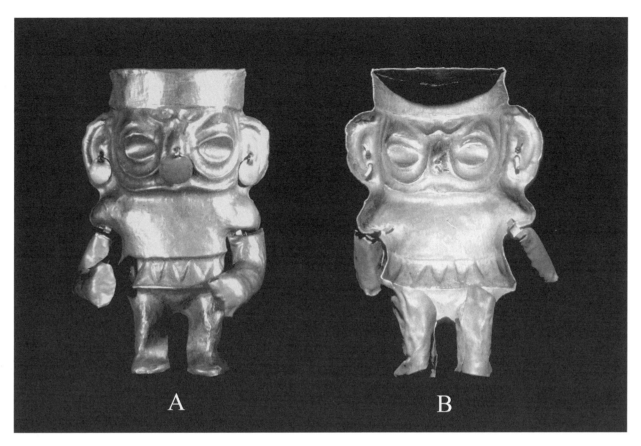

FIGURE 7.22. Completed anthropomorphized owl figure. Fowler Museum of Cultural History, UCLA. Photograph by Christopher B. Donnan.

then put the form to one side and work the sheet metal from behind the ears to enlarge them and to fill out their outer rims (Figure 7.21b). It may be that the ears on the metal form were deliberately made close to the head so they would not break off when sheet metal was hammered over them, even though the sheet metal images made over the form were to have large, flared ears.

When the figure was well along in the shaping process, the legs were divided by cutting between them with a metal chisel. The sheet metal was then worked around the inside of the thighs, calves, and ankles. Finally, the form was removed, and the sheet metal was bent around in back of the legs to make them three-dimensional (Figure 7.21b). It is noteworthy that the ears and legs were the only parts of the figure that required working from the back side without the form; all other parts were worked exclusively from the front, with the sheet metal on the form.

Creating the sheet metal arms was particularly challenging because they were so small, and thus difficult to hold in position. The process was facilitated by carving a recess in a block of wood to support an arm form while pounding the sheet metal over it, one half at a time. Given the small size of the arms, it is unlikely that the process could have been facilitated by another worker attempting to hold them in position. Once the arms were complete, they were attached to the body with copper staples cut from trimmed portions of the original sheet (Figures 7.22a, b).

The experimental replication of the sheet metal owl figure clearly demonstrated the effectiveness of solid forms for shaping metal. It is hoped that additional Moche forms will be identified in museums and private collections, and ultimately paired with sheet metal objects that were made over them.

Notes

1. The instrument used was a Kevex 0750A X-ray fluorescence spectrometer, employing either a molybdenum or barium/strontium secondary target at 50KV, 3.3mA.

2. Figure 7.4 provides data for sixty-eight sought elements; the only omissions which might be of interest in terms of smelting, extraction, or casting being sulfur and oxygen. Nineteen elements were detected, and of these, only eight have any significance at the present time. These are bismuth, gold, lead, nickel, phosphorous, selenium, silver and tin. The phosphorous content of 1.9 percent is exceptionally high and suggests infiltration of corrosion products such as copper phosphates from the burial environment, often associated with burial in a tomb. This could have resulted from the breakdown of adjacent bone material and the combination of bone phosphorous with corroding copper (Geilmann and Meisel 1942).

3. Research has shown that smelted pure copper may contain gold concentrations between 0.7 and 7 ppm, silver from about 800 to 2,000 ppm, and quantities of arsenic, nickel, selenium, and antimony between 10 and 600 ppm. The analysis showed that the copper warrior matrix contained 3,210 ppm of silver, 92 ppm of nickel, 148 ppm of gold, and 33 ppm of selenium. It is interesting to note that arsenic and antimony were not detected.

4. The sheet metal owl figure in Figure 7.4 was photographed and measured in 1987. At that time it was in a private collection in Lima, Peru. It is no longer in that collection, and its current location is unknown. Thus it has not been possible to study it in detail, nor to make a chemical analysis of its metal.

5. Two of these knives, one of gold and the other of silver, were found in a royal tomb at Sipán (Alva and Donnan 1993:96).

6. Mujica Gallo (1959:C111, CX1) illustrates gold sheet metal frogs from the north coast of Peru, but they are said to be "Chimu, 12th or 13th century AD." They appear to be somewhat smaller than the solid metal frog form.

7. On the original forms, some surfaces of the torso were corroded, and thus had a gritty texture that had to be removed from the cast duplicates by buffing. The corrosion concretion on the owl figure's forehead and ear also required removal by filing and buffing. Presumably, when the original forms were cast, they were sufficiently smooth so that no filing or buffing was required.

8. It must have been difficult to make copper sheet uniform in thickness utilizing only stone hammers. Nevertheless, measurements of Moche sheet metal indicate that the metalworkers were extremely skilled at producing sheet metal of remarkably even thickness.

Bibliography

Alva, Walter, and Christopher B. Donnan

1993   *Royal Tombs of Sipán*. Fowler Museum of Cultural History, University of California, Los Angeles.

Geilmann, W., and K. Meisel

1942   Rontgenographische Untersuchungsmethoden in der Vorgeschichtsforschung: Libethenite ein Mineral der Patinabildlung. *Nachrichtenblatt fur Deutsche Vorzeit* 18:208–212.

Hancock, R. G. V., L. A. Pavlish, R. M. Farquhar, P. J. Julig, and W. A. Fox

1994   Chemical Seriation of Northeastern North American Archaeological Sites Using Copper Artifacts. In *Archaeometry of Pre-Columbian Site and Artefacts*, 255–266. Edited by David A. Scott and Pieter Meyers. The Getty Conservation Institute, Los Angeles.

Merkel, J. F., I. Shimada, C. P. Swann, and R. Doonan

1994   Pre-Hispanic Copper Alloy Production at Batan Grande, Peru: Interpretation of the Analytical Data for Ore Samples. In *Archaeometry of Pre-Columbian Site and Artefacts*, 199–228. Edited by David A. Scott and Pieter Meyers. The Getty Conservation Institute, Los Angeles.

Mujica Gallo, Miguel

1959   *The Gold of Peru*. Aurel Bongers, Germany.

Wayman, M. L., R. R. Smith, C. G. Hickey, and M. J. M. Duke

1985   The Analysis of Copper Artifacts of the Copper Inuit. *Journal of Archaeological Science* 12 (5):367–375.

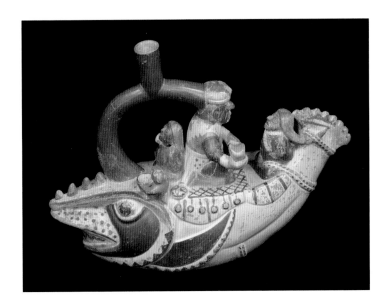

Bottle in the form of fish-boat. Museo del Banco Central de Reserva del Perú, Lima (ACE-2975). Photograph by Steve Bourget.

Skeletal being tied to a tree and pecked by a black vulture. Museo Larco, Lima (ML-001478).

Modeled *ulluchu* bowl. Courtesy of Museo Nacional de Antropología, Arqueología e Historia, Lima (C-16589).

Ritual activity under bicephalous arc. Linden-Museum, Stuttgart. Drawing by Donna McClelland.

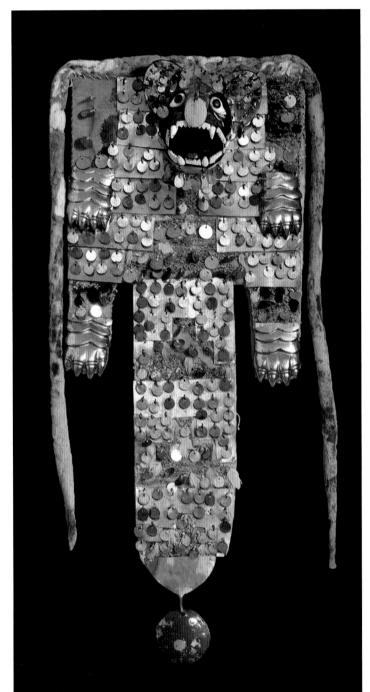

Feline effigy from Platform I, Huaca de la Luna. Photograph by Steve Bourget.

Figure holding a tunic. Museo Nacional de Antropología, Arqueología e Historia, Lima (C-61527).

Spider being, North Wall, Huaca de la Luna. Photograph by Steve Bourget.

Spider modeled on a stirrup spout bottle. Museo del Banco Central de Reserva del Perú, Lima (ACE-593). Photograph by Steve Bourget.

Bottle in the form of a Wrinkle Face with spider attributes and an octopus headdress. Museo del Banco Central de Reserva del Perú, Lima (ACE-507). Photograph by Steve Bourget.

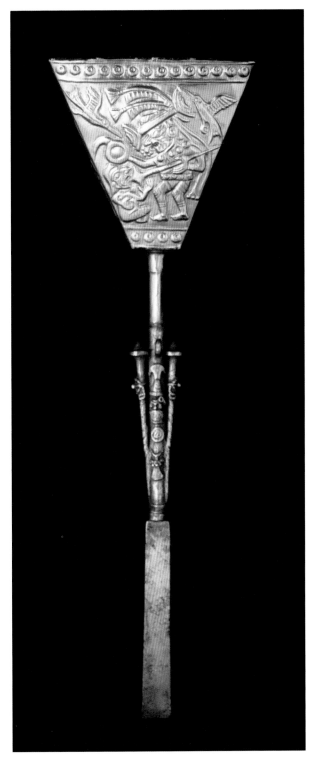

Rattle-chisel from Tomb 1, Sipán. Photograph by Christopher B. Donnan.

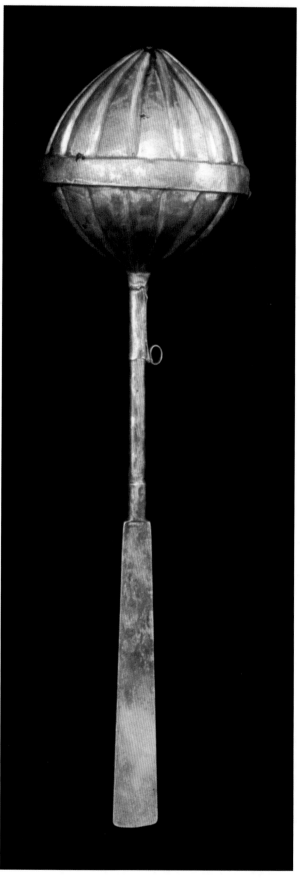

Wooden club with a sculpture of a woman sitting in front of two smaller figures. Museo Nacional de Antropología, Arqueología e Historia, Lima (MO-0879).

Rattle-chisel from Tomb 3, Sipán. Photograph by Christopher B. Donnan and Donald McClelland.

Nose ornament with a depiction of a swimming crab (*Callinectes arcuatus*) from the site of La Mina. Private collection. Photograph by Christopher B. Donnan.

Stirrup spout bottle with strombus shell (*pututo*) player standing on top and scene of Sacrifice Ceremony below. Museo Nacional de Antropología, Arqueología e Historia, Lima (C-03315). Photograph by Steve Bourget.

CHAPTER EIGHT

Moche Art Style in the Santa Valley

Between Being "à la Mode" and Developing a Provincial Identity

CLAUDE CHAPDELAINE, UNIVERSITY OF MONTREAL

Abstract

The Moche developed a multi-valley state, and the incorporation of the Santa Valley presented a determinant factor supporting the expansionist character of the Moche polity centered at the Huacas de Moche site. The physical presence of a Moche popula-tion—large or small—has been proposed on the basis of the striking resemblance between the ceramic production in the Santa, Moche and Chicama valleys. At a general level, the comparison of the well-known ceramic categories is suggesting a similar stylistic evolution between the involved valleys and the maintenance of close ties through various socioeconomic processes, including migration. At a more detailed level, slight, recorded differences are discussed within the perspective of an emerging provincial identity that may have had some direct influences on the sociopolitical organization of the Southern Moche State. The observed differences between the Santa ceramic production and the style popular in the homeland valleys of Moche and Chicama may be associated with a new autonomy of the Moche leaders ruling the frontiers. The Moche ceramic production in the Santa Valley thus followed a general Moche style, with some decorative elements indicating a provincial identity.

The Moche are considered the first cultural group to attain a complexity that resembles a state-level organization on the Peruvian north coast. In such a complex society, the elite generally sponsor the produc-tion of goods, with material symbols created to project their strength. The production of such symbolic goods might be massive, as it was for the Moche, with the capacity to produce large quantities of molded and mod-eled ceramic vessels. These ceramics are thus the best material element by which to study the Moche style, and then to analyze such styles within a state organiza-tion perspective.

What is the exact nature of the Moche state? Nowadays, it is more and more difficult to propose the existence of a single Moche state covering the whole territory where the Moche ceramic style was abundant (Quilter 2002). The idea of distinguishing two Moche cultural spheres is now solidly supported by several lines of evidence (Castillo 2001, 2003; Castillo and Donnan 1995); however, the independent presence of a Northern Moche state during the Phase III and Phase IV stylistic periods has not yet been demonstrated (Figure 8.1). In this chapter, I will thus refer to the Southern Moche state, which corresponds to the central valleys of Chicama and Moche, as well as to the southern val-leys. The Moche site, or Huacas de Moche, is the single dominant site in the Moche Valley (Bawden 1994, 1996; Billman 1996). The situation is different in the Chicama Valley, with two major sites: El Brujo (Franco, Gálvez, and Vásquez 1994, 2001, 2003), located closer to the Pacific Ocean but occupying a position similar to the Moche site; and Mocollope, which is situated further inland and may have shared a comparable power. Mocollope has been badly disturbed; however, an inter-esting ceramic workshop has been documented that indicates the importance of this second major Moche settlement in the Chicama Valley (Russell and Jackson 2001; Russell, Leonard, and Briceño 1994, 1998).

Without being able to ascertain whether the Chicama or the Moche polities assumed the dominant power, both had close cultural ties and were engaged in a very similar cultural evolution. Under the possible control of both polities, the Southern Moche state started a southward expansion with probably the Santa Valley as one of their prime targets. A very particular ceramic tradition found at Huancaco, the presumed Moche capital or regional center in the Virú Valley (Willey 1953), suggests that the Virú Valley may have kept its autonomy during this

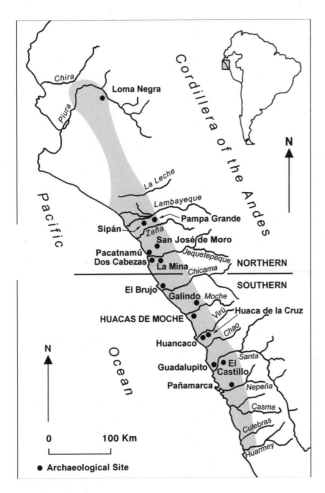

FIGURE 8.1. Northern and southern divisions of Moche territorial expansion. Map by author.

expansion (Bourget 1998, 1999, 2000, 2003). This situation is also supported by a strong Gallinazo occupation at Huaca Santa Clara that may be contemporaneous with the early phase of Moche expansion (Millaire 2004).

Research is needed to identify a Moche regional center in the Chao Valley, although this valley likely supported a center of a smaller scale than those recorded for the Santa and Nepeña Valleys because of its limited agricultural productivity. The Moche power was concentrated in the lower Santa Valley. El Castillo is considered the first Moche regional center, and it dates to Phase III. A new Moche capital with two large huacas was then constructed at Guadalupito, which dates to Phase IV. The site of Pañamarca in the middle Nepeña Valley is the southernmost regional capital of the Southern Moche

state (Proulx 1968, 1973). South of this valley, architectural and artifactual evidence of a Moche occupation is less abundant (Bonavia 1982; Pozorski and Pozorski 1996; Prümers 2000; Wilson 1995). Thus the Casma, Culebras, and Huarmey valleys could be lumped into an area of minimal Moche influence until new data are available to establish clearly the southern limit of the Southern Moche state.

If the supreme ruler at Huacas de Moche achieved political unity, and if the ruling descendants were capable of maintaining such unity through several generations, the Southern Moche state could thus be identified as a large territorial state with access to a minimum of six valleys. Through time, fragmentation of this political unity would have favored autonomy of local elites, would have reduced the central power, and might have permitted the rise of small independent polities at the valley level (Demarrais, Castillo, and Earle 1996). As we shall see, the Santa Valley style was always very close to the Moche style, being "à la mode" in the Moche Valley; however, several minor differences support the idea of an emerging provincial style. This possible emergent style must be studied to understand the social implications underlying these stylistic developments.

The Moche Presence in the Santa Valley

The popular technique or logical step in assessing the provenance of a particular type of artifact is usually the abundance criteria (see Druc 1998:24). In our case, the overwhelming quantity of Moche artifacts in the Santa Valley were and still are interpreted as the major evidence arguing for the physical presence of the Moche in this southern valley. Numerous cemeteries were found in association with habitation sites (Donnan 1973; Wilson 1988). Most of the known Moche centers are single component sites where the vast majority of the recovered artifacts are considered Moche in style (Figure 8.2). In this chapter, it is thus a basic assumption that the Moche physically occupied the Santa Valley, and that trade and diffusion alone cannot explain the presence of these abundant and diversified assemblages. Artifacts made of ceramic, metal, stone, textile, shell and wood, as well as architectural remains and burials, are all attributable to the Moche culture. In a very practical sense, an individual and its group can be identified as Moche if most of the cultural remains and mortuary patterns on a site can be associated with this culture. When applied to the lower Santa Valley, this total culture approach allows us to consider the Moche physical presence as the most reasonable explanation for the abundance of Moche style artifacts within the region.

The conquest theory was formulated long ago to explain the Moche presence in the Santa Valley (Collier 1955; Donnan 1973; Strong and Evans 1952; Willey 1953). While it has remained an adequate explanation for such a massive cultural intrusion (Wilson 1988, 1999), a more gradual takeover of the lower Santa Valley during Moche Phase III is more in line with recent data (Chapdelaine, Pimentel, and Bernier 2003). These data indicate the maintenance of the local Gallinazo population and its coexistence with Moche intruders during the early phase of the Moche expansion. It was during Moche Phase IV that the leaders from the Huacas de Moche site took over the land and started extensive irrigation projects. They allowed Moche colonists to migrate into this attractive southern valley in order to solve internal problems in the Moche Valley and to allow members of the elite to augment their benefits at lower costs.

The Santa Valley Project and Its Research Goals

Most of the previous data on the Santa Valley were obtained through surface collection and limited test pits (Donnan 1973; Wilson 1988). From 2000 to 2003, the Santa Valley Project of the Université de Montréal (PSUM) was oriented toward a better understanding of the Moche presence in the lower Santa Valley through excavations at major sites. The objectives were to reveal an occupational chronology from pre-Moche to Moche and post-Moche, and to date the arrival of the Moche, their establishment, their conquest of the valley, and the length of their occupation. To better understand the presumed cultural integration of the Santa Valley into the Moche realm, we had to look for data that could shed light on the relations between the conquerors and the conquered.

Excavations at Major Moche Sites

Our excavations were either of a small-scale nature— as at sites such as Huaca China, Guad-88, Guad-91, Guad-121 and Guad-186 (Figure 8.2)—or more extensive—as at Guadalupito (Guad-112 corresponds to the urban sector built along the eastern slope of Cerro La

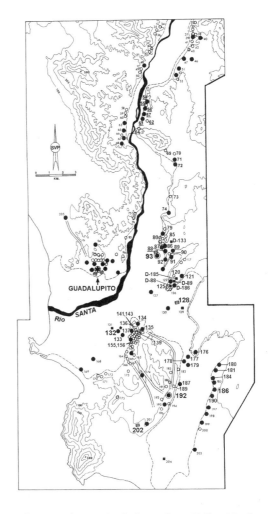

FIGURE 8.2. Moche sites in the lower Santa Valley. Map by author, modified from diverse maps in Wilson 1988.

Colina) and Guad-192 (Hacienda San José). Our major efforts were concentrated at El Castillo (Figure 8.3), where we worked for three consecutive years. Guadalupito was selected for the obvious reason of being the predominant Moche polity in Santa, and its presumed regional capital, with the largest monumental buildings and an extensive urban sector. Hacienda San José was chosen to test the idea proposed by Wilson (1988:206–207) that it was a local center in the Quebrada Lacramarca sector. El Castillo was singled out for two reasons. First, Christopher Donnan had identified this site to be of the Moche III phase (1973:39–41). This was exactly the period of site construction needed to determine the time of Moche arrival into the lower Santa Valley and to understand the type of establishment at the site, whether for elite, administrative, or production purposes. Second, following up on information gathered by Donnan (1973:40–41), the depth of cultural refuse would likely provide data on the occupation sequence that would help to verify the relationship between the Moche and the local Gallinazo culture in the lower strata. This site was thus very promising for our research goals. El Castillo turned out to be a very complex site at the horizontal level, as well as the vertical level. The results were surprising from the start, and each year the interpretations at this site changed depending upon where we conducted new excavations.

To summarize briefly, the site can be divided into five major areas (Figure 8.4):

1. Sector Alto, the hill summit
2. The Northern Terrace
3. The Eastern Terrace
4. The Western Terrace
5. The Southern Terrace

Of major importance was the construction of a massive stone wall that delimited the hill summit on its north side and served as the architectural division between the summit and the Northern Terrace. The largest huaca is located on the hill summit, positioned near the center of the built landscape; a second, smaller huaca was erected on the Northern Terrace near the foot of the abrupt flank that is covered by the massive stone wall. At the southeastern end of the Eastern Terrace stand the remains of a tapia wall with two

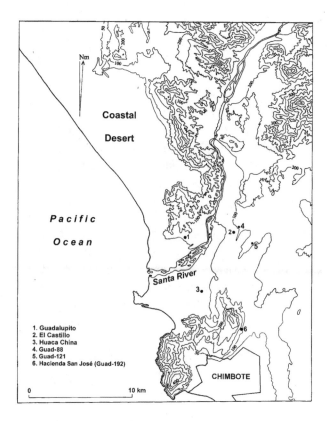

FIGURE 8.3. Location of excavated sites in the lower Santa Valley. Map by author.

segments delimiting an indirect entrance. This wall indicated the presence of a Middle Horizon occupation, which was mentioned by Donnan (1973). The horizontal occupation of these different sections is complex, and the major cultural identifications are summarized in Table 8.1.

These identifications illustrate the complexity of El Castillo. For the moment, it is difficult to identify the major or dominant occupation on the Eastern Terrace, with the Gallinazo occupying the upper sectors, and the Tanguche, or Middle Horizon local culture, and the Moche prevailing on the lower levels. The hill summit is associated with the Gallinazo and apparently remained absent of a Moche occupation since not a single Moche sherd has been recovered from the surface. Donnan (1973:40–41) also signals this absence, as well as the possible attribution of the major huaca on the hill summit to the local culture prior to Moche occupation. From our limited excavations, the major huaca should not be con-

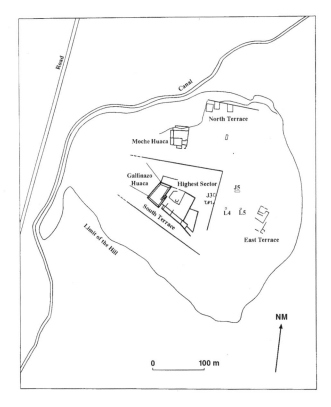

FIGURE 8.4. Plan of El Castillo. Map by author.

sidered Moche, as had been previously assumed (Chapdelaine and Pimentel 2002; Wilson 1988). The size and shape of the adobes and the presence of deep and narrow cane marks are rather indicative of Gallinazo production. The stairs that extend to the top of the structure are also not common to Moche huacas.

The Northern Terrace appears to represent the seat of power of the prominent Moche rulers at this site. This proposition is based not only on the type of architecture, the massive huaca with a painted panel of shields and war clubs (Wilson 1988:206–207, 210–211), but also on the quality of construction of the administrative compounds in the southwestern corner of the Northern Terrace system—that is, on the length of the occupation determined by four or five visible construction phases— and on the material culture (Chapdelaine and Pimentel 2001, 2002; Chapdelaine, Pimentel, and Bernier 2003). Throughout this chapter, I shall refer to the Moche occupation of the Northern Terrace when I reference data from El Castillo, which is considered here as the most important Moche Phase III site in the lower Santa Valley. Guadalupito will then be used to illustrate Moche Phase IV.

Table 8.1. Regional Cultural Sequences on the North Coast of Peru

DATE (UNCALIBRATED)	LAMBAYEQUE VALLEY	JEQUETEPEQUE VALLEY	CHICAMA VALLEY	MOCHE VALLEY	VIRÚ VALLEY	SANTA VALLEY
<1200 BP	Sicán /	Transicional Lambayeque	Chimu	Chimu Temprano ?	Tomaval Temprano	Tanguche
1300–1200 BP	Moche V /	Moche V Gallinazo	Moche IV / V	Moche IV / V	?	Moche IV / V
1500–1300 BP	Moche IV	Moche III (IV ?)	Moche IV	Moche IV	Moche IV / Gallinazo	Moche IV / Gallinazo
1700–1500 BP	Moche III	Moche III	Moche III	Moche III	Moche III? / Gallinazo	Moche III / Gallinazo
1900–1700 BP	Moche I–II /	Moche I–II / Gallinazo	Moche I–II / Gallinazo	Moche I–II / Gallinazo	Gallinazo Gallinazo	Gallinazo
2100–1900 BP	Gallinazo	Gallinazo	Gallinazo	Gallinazo	Gallinazo	Gallinazo
>2100 BP	Salinar ?	Salinar	Salinar	Salinar	Salinar	Salinar

0   10 cm

FIGURE 8.5. Early type of Moche Phase III stirrup spouts. Photograph by author.

The Timing of the Moche in the Santa Valley

After excavating at three sites—El Castillo, Hacienda San José, and Guadalupito—the development of a revised chronology is now possible with the support of twenty-eight new radiocarbon dates. As yet, there is no substantial evidence of a Moche presence in the Santa Valley earlier than Phase III. Only a few artifacts—namely, fragments of ceramic spouts—may be associated with a very early Phase III or late Phase II influence or presence (Figure 8.5). Not a single Moche Phase I artifact has yet been recovered. It is thus with confidence that I propose a chronological framework for the Moche arrival around AD 300 with the typical Moche Phase III ceramic tradition or style.

Several radiocarbon dates obtained from Moche Phase III contexts are in accordance with the dates from the Moche site (Table 8.2). It should also be mentioned that dates coming from secure Gallinazo contexts are statistically contemporaneous with Moche Phase III dates, indicating without any doubt that both groups may have concurrently occupied the site. The dates associated with ceramics of the Moche Phase IV at Guadalupito, Hacienda San José, and Guad-121 suggest that the Moche presence in the lower Santa Valley lasted as long as in the Moche Valley (Chapdelaine 2000, 2001, 2002, 2003). This new chronological framework, which indicates a long Moche occupational history of the Santa Valley, will force us eventually to reconsider the role of the Moche provinces in the decline of the Southern Moche state and in the collapse of the Huacas de Moche site.

The Moche Style in Santa

The analysis of the Moche style is a very large and commanding task that is well beyond the scope of this chapter (see Donnan 1978, 2001; Donnan and McClelland 1999). Considering the length of the Moche occupation and the abundance of Moche vessels in the lower Santa Valley, the presence of local production should be logical, and less emphasis should be placed on trade. Differences between this local production and that of Moche centers might have emerged; however, these distinctions likely remained within a limited range to keep within a Moche style that would be tolerated by the Santa Valley elite. The identification of several production centers in the lower Santa Valley, based essentially on the discovery of ceramic molds, supports this presumed local pro-

Table 8.2. PSUM Radiocarbon Dates for 2000, 2001, 2002

PSUM SAMPLE	ISOTRACE	MATERIAL	CONTEXT	DATE BP	CAL 2 SIGMA	CAL 1 SIGMA	REMARKS
2000-EC-01	TO-8967	Charcoal	C#1, R-6, floor #11, B2	2000±90	200 BC–220 AD	95 BC–80 AD	Possible old wood effect
2000-EC-04	TO-8968	Maguey	C#1, R-1, Floor #5, B2	1240±50	660 AD–895 AD	755 AD–780 AD	Wood contaminated by termites
2000-EC-05	TO-8969	Charcoal	Under last floor in B4	2310±140	795 BC–40 BC	520 BC–200 BC	Could date a Salinar occupation
2000-EC-06	TO-8970	Reed (caña)	Storage bin, B4	1540±50	410 AD–635 AD	430 AD–595 AD	Roof of a niche
2000-EC-07	TO-8971	Charcoal	Eastern Terrace, C#1, hearth R-1	980±60	975 AD–1190 AD	995 AD–1060 AD	Tanguche occupation
2001-G-121	TO-9736	Maize	C#1, floor #2	1210±50	685–900 AD	770–890 AD	Walled enclosure site
2001-G-192	TO-9737	Maize	C#2, floor #2	1540±80	375–655 AD	425–605 AD	Under the earliest floor
2001-G-192	TO-9738	Charcoal	C#4, hearth	1360±60	595–775 AD	640–685 AD	Large feature
2001-ECA-1	TO-9739	Maize	Plaza, floor #2	1540±50	410–635 AD	430–595 AD	Gallinazo context
2001-ECA-2	TO-9740	Maize	East Platform, floor #1	2410±100	800–350 BC	600–390 BC	Gallinazo context
2001-ECA-3	TO-9741	Maize	West Platform, hearth floor #1	1410±50	555–685 AD	600–660 AD	Intrusive feature, Moche?
2001-EC-1	TO-9742	Charcoal	C#2, hearth on floor #8	1480±50	525–655 AD	535–640 AD	Moche III context
2001-EC-2	TO-9743	Maize	C#2, R-5, floor #11	1600±50	375–565 AD	410–535 AD	Moche III context
2001-EC-3	TO-9744	Maize	C#2, R-5, floor #1	1420±50	540–685 AD	600–660 AD	Moche III, near surface
2002-G-88-1	TO-10579	Charcoal	Hearth in central sector	1250±60	655–895 AD	685–780 AD	Ceramic production site
2002-G-112-1	TO-10580	Maize cob	C#4, northwest bench	1360±60	595–775 AD	640–685 AD	Last modification
2002-G-112-2	TO-10581	Maize cob	C#1, R-5, between floors #1–#2	1340±60	635–775 AD	655–690 AD	Last built compound
2002-G-112-3	TO-10582	Maize cob	C#4, northwest bench	1610±50	320-595 AD	395–535 AD	Between last floor and bedrock
2002-G-112-4	TO-10583	Maize cob	C#5, R-10, below floor #2b	1490±60	425–660 AD	535–640 AD	Below first construction phase
2002-G-112-5	TO-10584	Maize cob	C#3C, R-2, between floors #2–#3	1390±60	555–720 AD	635–675 AD	Ceramist compound?

Table 8.2. PSUM Radiocarbon Dates for 2000, 2001, 2002 (continued)

PSUM SAMPLE	ISOTRACE	MATERIAL	CONTEXT	DATE BP	CAL 2 SIGMA	CAL 1 SIGMA	REMARKS
2002-G-112-6	TO-10585	Maize cob	C#6, R-2a, between floors #2-#3	1350±50	605–775 AD	650–685 AD	Southeastern compound
2002-ECA-1	TO-10586	Maize cob	Top of the hill sector, near bedrock	3000±80	1430–1000 BC	1320–1125 BC	contaminated
2002-ECE-1	TO-10587	Maize cob	Plaza, F3, between floors #3a-#3b	1560±50	400–615 AD	425–540 AD	Moche context
2002-ECE-2	TO-10588	Maize cob	J5, R-7, between floors #3-#4	1560±50	400–615 AD	425–540 AD	Gallinazo context
2002-ECE-3	TO-10589	Maize cob	L5, hearth, between floors #5-#6	1650\50	315–535 AD	375–430 AD	Gallinazo context
2002-ECE-4	TO-10590	Maize cob	L4, R-1, between floors #2-#3	1580±50	385–600 AD	420–540 AD	Gallinazo context
2002-ECH-1	TO-10591	Maize cob	Huaca, NE corner, R-5, between floors #1-#2	1530±50	415–640 AD	525–600 AD	Moche context
2002-ECH-2	TO-10592	Maize cob	Huaca, Eastern side, R-5, between floors #2-#3	1670±50	240–470 AD	335–425 AD	Moche context

NOTE: EC= El Castillo Northern Terrace; ECE= El Castillo Easthern Terrace; ECA= El Castillo Top of the Hill; ECH= El Castillo Huaca Moche on Northern Terrace; G-112= Urban Sector of Guadalupito; G-121= Guad-121; G-88= Guad-88

FIGURE 8.6. Location of Moche ceramic production centers in the Lower Santa Valley. Map by author.

ductivity (Figure 8.6). The local production of Moche goods may have started as early as Phase III to satisfy local demand. It was thus inevitable that a Santa style would become progressively more visible on the finished products. Our goal is to present a general overview of the pottery encountered at Santa Valley Moche sites in order to demonstrate its diversity within the perspective that style played a significant role in the Moche ethnic identification.

The importance of ethnicity and the origin of ethnic groups are central issues for the study of complex societies (Emberling 1997). Exotic and prestige goods are generally used to identify the rank or status of individuals in a community or cultural group. Style is linked intimately to this ethnic identification. In that particular sense, style is not only decorative (and passive) but bears a clear sociopolitical function (Hill 1985). This function was true for the Moche since a considerable portion of decorated vessels ended up as burial offerings. Style was thus active during the life of an individual, and also during his or her death in the mortuary program. Therefore, style is an important element by which to eventually elucidate a sociopolitical organization such as the Moche.

Exploring Similarity and Diversity

In presenting the Moche style in the Santa Valley, it is important to verify the similarity between this specific ceramic production and the original product made in the Moche Valley. This comparison will be of a very general level since the ceramic variability is too great to discuss all categories in a single chapter. In this brief comparative study, the evaluation of similarities and differences are subjective due to the incredible diversity in the ceramic production and the creativity that seems to have characterized the Moche pottery production. In this perspective, the degree of relation between ceramic vessels from the Moche and Santa valleys should be described cautiously. Trade vessels may be identical, whereas vessels made locally in Santa, with molds coming from the Moche Valley, might be considered similar if the potter reproduced with little deviation a well-known style during the last stage of production. Differentiating identical from similar is crucial since Moche production might be identical for the form or shape through the use of molds, and only similar after the potter's finishing touch. Similarity is also very relative since a large spectrum of variation might be involved.

Although potters relied on their skills to model by hand different parts of the ceramics, Moche ceramic production was dominated by the use of molds that would have served to standardize production. Nevertheless, the utility of molds for domestic pots remains unclear. Domestic pottery is rarely decorated, while decorated pottery is regularly well made with a fine-tempered paste, and well fired with a good surface finish and a large diversity of motifs. The decoration can be painted (basically red-on-white or white-on-red), modeled, or both. Ceramic production was not limited to pots but included various categories of objects, including figurines, spoons, spindle whorls, musical instruments, pendants, graters (for maize or yucca), and blow-tubes. The Moche ceramic tradition can be considered standardized in shape and design, but the diversity of themes, subjects, and patterns force us to characterize the ceramics as highly variable. Despite that variability, it is often easy to recognize the Moche style.

One may consider that a normal potter would have taken pride in his trade. He was probably competing with others if working in an independent workshop, or attached to elite for a specific production. Moche potters working in the Santa Valley certainly achieved quality work that readily compares as identical or similar to that of the Moche Valley. Yet variation in local quality can be identified. Low or poor quality production—based on the paste, the firing, the design, the slips, and other characteristics—might be associated with local potters making a bad imitation. These craftsmen may have been of another ethnic group, and it should be difficult to consider them as Moche.

Identical and similar vessels might be explained through the following possibilities expressed by Christopher Donnan (1973:104):

1. The pieces were being made in one area and distributed to the neighboring valleys;
2. The molds were made in one area and distributed to the neighboring valleys where they were used locally to produce vessels;
3. Specimens were made in one center and subsequently distributed to the neighboring areas where they were then used as mold matrices, and the resulting molds where used to produce similar ceramic vessels locally.

Of course, these possibilities could have been occurring at the same time. It is also possible that molds may have been made early or independently by Moche immigrants in the Santa Valley, because the knowledge had been with the potters since they left their homeland. The quality of Moche ceramic production is variable, even at Huacas de Moche. Poor quality vessels have been recovered in the urban sector, whose residents also had access to high quality vessels, which were found on a regular basis inside the residential compounds (Chapdelaine 2001).

Determining the quality of an entire assemblage is very difficult, and prudence is in order. Quantitative data are not available, but the Moche pottery at the capital site can be divided in three quality levels: (1) the very fine vessels with complex design and preference of limited forms, such as stirrup spout vessels and flaring bowls; (2)

good quality vessels with a large diversity in forms and motifs applied on several types of vessels; and (3) low quality vessels with the design poorly rendered, less finely tempered paste, and showing occasional firing defects. The differences between the three levels are suggestive and sometimes difficult to evaluate without a good idea of the whole assemblage. Nevertheless, these variations certainly existed, and not only in the mind of the analyst.

Moche Pottery Types in the Santa Valley

The ceramic diversity is well represented at Moche sites of the lower Santa Valley, but my focus in this study is pottery types. The types will be described first, with the basic goal of assessing the degree of conformity between our sample and the one studied by Donnan (1973). Second, the basic vessel types considered as Moche in the Santa Valley will be compared to the Moche style from the heartland valleys. Before concluding whether a distinctive Santa style evolved from a Moche origin, I first present the pottery types following Christopher Donnan's classification and using two data sets: Donnan's data from his doctoral dissertation (1973), and our recent data from the El Castillo and Guadalupito sites, respectively dated to Moche Phases III and IV.

Very minor differences exist between the two sets (Table 8.3). The PSUM data conform well to Donnan's data; however, vessel diversity and integrity seem to be higher in the older collection. The general resemblance between the two groups also indicates that the ceramic samples taken from the surface collection (usually following the work of looters) are adequately representative of the assemblages that come from excavated contexts. In presenting the pottery types, my objective is to point out the similarities and differences between the two collections and to discuss the chronological implications for stylistic patterns associated with Phases III and IV.

Table 8.3. Pottery Analyzed in Santa by C. Donnan (1973) and C. Chapdelaine (2003)

TYPES	DONNAN 1973		EL CASTILLO 2000–2002		GUADALUPITO GUAD-112[1]	
	F	%	F	%	F	%
DECORATED VESSELS						
Stirrup spouts	196	16.1	99	8.3	48	10.9
Spout and handle bottles	116	9.5	176	14.9		
Fancy Chamber Forms	98	8.1				
Dippers	53	4.4	43	3.6	26	5.9
Neck bowls[2]	51	4.2	115	9.7	39	8.8
Neckless bowls	67	5.5	158	13.3	77	17.5
Thick rim bowls	10	0.8	55	4.6	32	7.3
Flaring bowls	386	31.8	332	28.0	172	39.0
Jars	238	19.6	207	17.5	47	10.6
SUBTOTAL	1,215	100	1185	99.9	441	100
DOMESTIC VESSELS						
Cooking Ollas/Cántaros	?	—	1,352	86.4	450	89.1
Storage Ollas/Tinajas	50	—	212	13.6	55	10.9
SUBTOTAL	> 50	—	1,564	100	505	100

[1]A total of 3,382 ceramic fragments were also collected but they were considered non- analyzable for various reasons although we were able to identify several classes of products such as flaring bowls, stirrup spouts fragments, bases, figurines, etc.
[2]Several neck bowls in the PSUM samples could be considered as thick rim bowls.

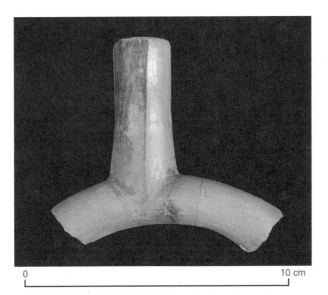

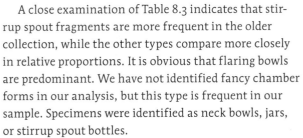

FIGURE 8.7. Moche Phase III stirrup spout. Photograph by author.

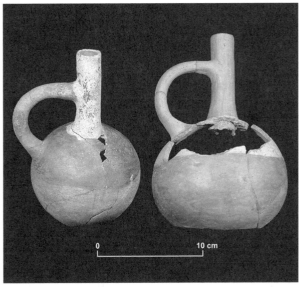

FIGURE 8.8. Diversity of ceramic vessels. Photograph by author.

A close examination of Table 8.3 indicates that stirrup spout fragments are more frequent in the older collection, while the other types compare more closely in relative proportions. It is obvious that flaring bowls are predominant. We have not identified fancy chamber forms in our analysis, but this type is frequent in our sample. Specimens were identified as neck bowls, jars, or stirrup spout bottles.

Stirrup spouts. Most of the spouts in Donnan's collection were classified as Phases III and IV, which is true for our data as well. Yet it should be noticed that we found a transitional type of Moche Phase III stirrup spout bottle at El Castillo. The spout is marked with a little outside bulge of the lip, reminiscent of Moche Phase II (Figure 8.5). This type is not as popular as the classical type of Moche Phase III, but it could be a chronological marker that suggests an early arrival of a Moche group at El Castillo (Figure 8.7). In fact, the stratigraphic positions of several spouts belonging to this early variant support this conclusion. They are mostly found in the lower strata, although a few specimens were found in the upper layers due to intensive looting.

Spout and handle bottles. This form of bottle, with a straight spout and a lateral handle, is more popular during Phase IV at sites such as Guadalupito (Figure 8.8). A

few specimens were found at El Castillo, where evidence of a Moche IV occupation is minimal at best.

Fancy chamber forms. These vessels were not identified as a type in our analysis, but we assume that several of our modeled or molded fragments could be assigned to this category (Figures 8.9, 8.10).

Dippers. Few dippers in our collection are complete; however, most of the rim fragments are large enough to evaluate the original diameter. Several handles have been found, and at least three handles, two feline and one human head found in a Moche Phase III context, support the proposition that the two forms of handle—horn-shaped and modeled heads—are present from the beginning of the Moche presence in the Santa Valley (Figures 8.11, 8.12). Dipper quality varies considerably, but it seems not to be as poor as mentioned by Donnan (1973:64) since the majority of our dippers bear slip painting.

Neck bowls. This category comprises various types with different sizes, including miniature vessels (Figure 8.13). The same diversity is encountered in the two collections, with a variant that seems to characterize a Santa Valley development. The variant consists of decorating domestic ware with the typical motif of neck bowls, which is a geometric design of three or

FIGURE 8.9. Fancy chamber vessel. Photograph by author.

FIGURE 8.10. Fancy chamber vessel. Photograph by author.

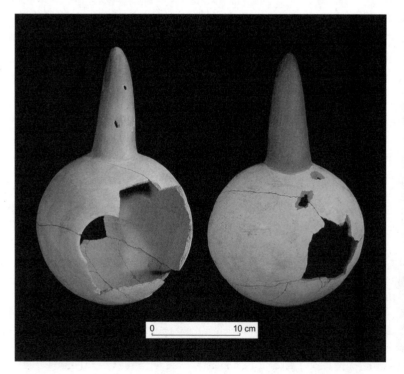

FIGURE 8.11. Dippers. Photograph by author.

FIGURE 8.12. Dipper. Photograph by author.

FIGURE 8.13. Miniature vessels. Photograph by author.

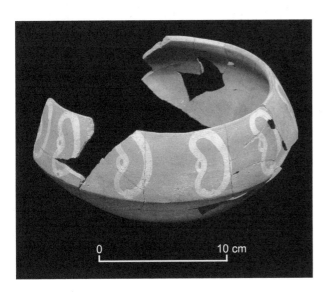

FIGURE 8.14. Neck bowl. Photograph by author.

four vertical lines on the rim's interior and/or exterior (Figure 8.14). This type of decorated neck bowl could also be placed in the thick rim category. Its abundance is clearly a distinctive feature of the Moche style in the Santa Valley. The fine paste type of decorated neck bowls, common at the Huacas of Moche site, is definitely less abundant in the Santa Valley.

Neckless bowls. Donnan identified two variants of neckless bowls (1973:69–74), which we have further identified in our collection. The first variant, characterized by a symmetrical chamber, is spherical and incurving at the top, with small holes for the attachment of a lid (Figure 8.15). Decorated lids with small holes have been found in both collections, and they seem to be very similar, with geometric designs prevailing (Figure 8.16). The second neckless bowl variant, a modeled chamber, could represent human heads, animal forms, and other life forms. We recovered two vessels representing a possible cactus, with an appliqué mouse on one of the ceramics (Figures 8.17, 8.18). We also found a similar

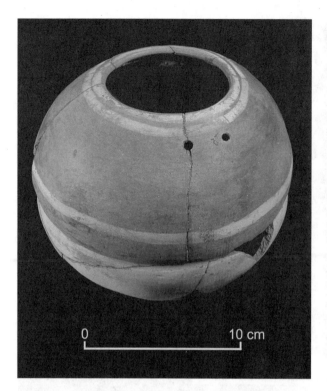

FIGURE 8.15. Neckless bowl. Photograph by author.

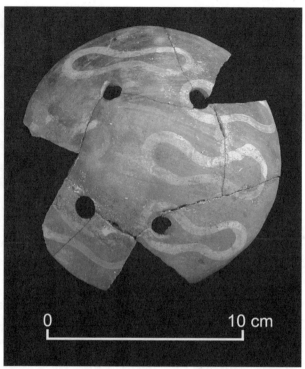

FIGURE 8.16. Lid. Photograph by author.

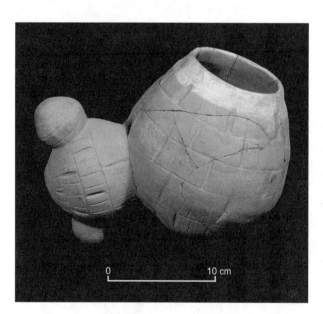

FIGURE 8.17. Vessel with a cactus shape. Photograph by author.

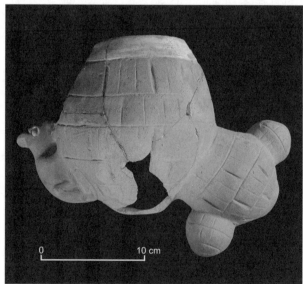

FIGURE 8.18. Vessel with a cactus shape. Photograph by author.

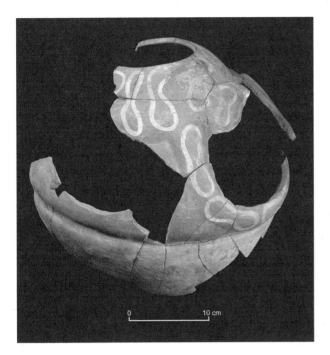

FIGURE 8.19. Vessel with feline motif. Photograph by author.

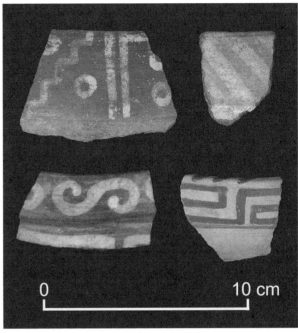

FIGURE 8.20. Thick rim bowls. Photograph by author.

vessel to the one described by Donnan as a modeled exterior with slip representing the skin of a feline (1973: plate 5g). Our specimen is incomplete, but the motif is identical to Donnan's, and a lid decorated with the same motif was found with it (Figure 8.19).

Thick rim bowls. This type of vessel is defined according to paste, finish, and thickness, which are more typical of Moche domestic pottery rather than painted or molded vases (Figure 8.20). The shape could resemble a storage jar (*tinaja*) or a cooking jar (*olla*). Donnan refers here basically to a small storage jar decorated with a geometric design painted on the upper, exterior rim—the design described as the Greek Scalar being the prevailing motif (1973: figs. 255–257). In contrast to Donnan's collection, we have found several examples of this type decorated with organic black pigment (Figure 8.21). Nonetheless, Donnan is correct in saying that the thick rim bowl type ". . . pertains to both phases of the Moche sequence" (1973:74). Our collection complements the older collection, and we think that this type of thick rim bowl constitutes a clear element of what could be called a provincial Moche style in the Santa Valley.

Flaring bowls. The production of flaring bowls was definitely massive since it is the most abundant type of

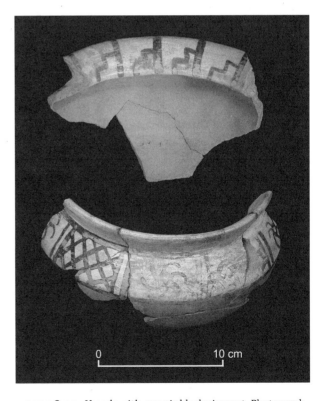

FIGURE 8.21. Vessels with organic black pigment. Photograph by author.

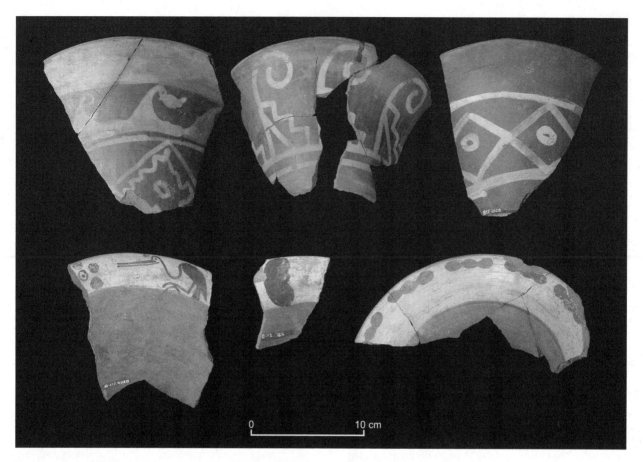

FIGURE 8.22. Flaring bowls. Photograph by author.

decorated pottery in the lower Santa Valley. Based on 257 decorated fragments with a relatively complete design scheme, Christopher Donnan divided his sample into nineteen groups based on the interrelation between the interior and exterior motif (1973:75–79). The classification produced by Donnan should be followed for intra-valley and inter-valley comparisons. After a cursory check of his groups, it is obvious that our collection suffers from bad preservation of the motif, probably related to a poor quality regarding the firing of the slip on the surface. It is also worth signaling that a large portion of Donnan's sample of flaring bowls was characterized by the absence or limited amount of decoration on the interior or exterior surface. Types 8 and 9 are associated with Phase III, while Type 13 is very popular during Phase IV. The fineline drawing of complex motifs on the interior of our flaring bowls assemblage is not frequent, although a high diversity of motifs characterizes this production (Figure 8.22). For example, the 172 flaring bowls analyzed from Guad-112 have several motifs but not a single clear anthropomorphic representation. Of a total of 121 identified motifs, phytomorphic designs account for 11 cases, phytomorphic combined with zoomorphic representations for 4 cases, zoomorphic designs for 34 cases, and geometric patterns for 20 cases. The wave or *"ola"* motif is present on 17 bowls and associated 7 times with the steps motif, the latter of which is further identified 12 times. The fishing net is present in 10 cases, and the nose pendant, or *"nariguera,"* appears on 6 flaring bowls.

Bases of flaring bowls. A large number of bases have been assigned to flaring bowls based on their interior finish. These have been recovered in both collections. Ring bases are the most popular form, followed by rattle bases and flat bases.

Jars. This category is not homogeneous, but its basic

feature is a constricted neck over a chamber that could be symmetrical or modeled. The length of the neck is related to the vessel's size: generally, the bigger the vessel, the longer and wider the neck. This pottery type is very popular at Huacas de Moche, and its presence is also important in the Santa Valley (Figure 8.23). The modeled jars could take human, plant, or animal forms—in particular, owl faces.

Several specimens have a raised ring around the base of the neck, with geometric decoration of white vertical lines combined with hollow circles. These hollow circles, usually white-on-red, are common during Moche Phase III. This simple motif could also be considered an element of the Moche Santa style.

To assess the resemblances and differences between our collection and the one published by Donnan, it is easier to follow Donnan's conclusions (1973:102–105). The improved chronological context will then allow us to comment upon them in relation to the new data.

Among the differences between Moche ceramic vessels in the Santa Valley and Moche ceramics in the Trujillo area recognized by Donnan (1973:103), the most significant are:

1. An almost total lack of reduced fired specimens
2. A scarcity of vessels decorated with fineline drawing
3. A generally cruder surface finish (possibly due in part to a lack of good white slip)
4. The fact that nearly all flaring bowls from Santa have ring bases (which include annular and pedestal forms)

Donnan (1973:103) explains these differences as relating to "... factors such as sampling (all Trujillo specimens are from graves, most of which appear to have been of rather wealthy individuals) and temporal differences. Nevertheless, it would appear that these differences in part reflect a regional variation of Moche style." Donnan also pointed out that new pottery forms developed in the Santa Valley, such as thick rim bowls, figurine jars, neckless bowls, jars with two handles, and a form of spout-and-handle bottle (1973: fig. 88). Except for the figurine jars, the PSUM collection supports these propositions. Nonetheless, the similarities in shapes and designs between the two valleys overshadow these local developments.

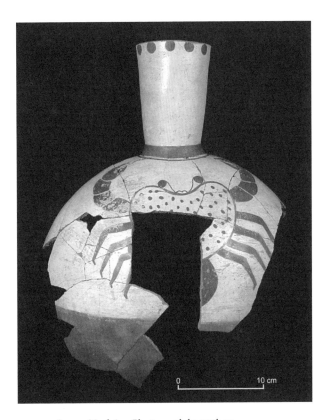

FIGURE 8.23. Neck jar. Photograph by author.

Regarding the chronological implications, the two variants of Moche Phase III stirrup spouts could eventually allow for a more refined sequence for the Southern Moche state. The red-on-white painting of various motifs is definitely more popular during Moche Phase IV, and it could be used as a relative temporal marker, as suggested by Donnan. The rattle base on flaring bowls has been previously assigned to Moche Phase IV. Our data suggest that it was indeed more popular during that time period; however, five flaring bowls with a rattle base have also been recovered from good Moche Phase III contexts at El Castillo. Our Moche Phase III collection allows us to identify several tendencies that might offer clear chronological indicators, such as a flexed interior below the lip, the use of relief decoration, and the application of molded humans or animals on the inside edge of some flaring bowls.

Organic black paint is found on miniature vessels. Donnan is correct when he says that organic black pigment is added for details, particularly for human depictions upon normal size vessels (1973:67). This is true for both phases, although it is almost a trademark during Phase III.

The use of hollow circles made with white slip is not limited to Phase III, as suggested by Donnan. But this distinctive element of the Moche Santa style was less popular during Moche Phase IV. It remains a secondary motif on various pottery types.

Within the diversified neckless bowl category, one form with a gambrel at midpoint and with nearly straight walls was first recognized by Donnan as a new form, and he associated it with Phase IV (1973:71, fig. 88). Our data corroborate the chronological position of this type, which has been found only on Moche IV sites in the lower Santa Valley.

Donnan divided the modeled jars with a human form into three subtypes based on artistic quality, with the idea that "The realistic modeling of the face, and elaboration of the headdress would suggest that this form dates to Phase IV of the Moche sequence. . . ."(1973:87). This proposed stylistic evolution does not hold anymore since several realistic modeled jars derive from good Phase III contexts at El Castillo.

In summary, a rather good general agreement exists between the PSUM collection and the one previously established by Donnan. Minor differences and slight chronological changes are inevitable when comparing two data sets with different backgrounds and collected according to different objectives. Nevertheless, the combined collections should allow us to make a statement on the degree of similarity between the Santa assemblage and the pottery from the homeland, the Moche Valley.

Is There a Santa Style?

The answer to that basic question cannot be definitive for several reasons. First, we are far from being able to compare quantitatively the pottery production of both valleys. Second, the comparisons should take into account the phases, but it is not always possible to distinguish a Moche Phase III from a Moche Phase IV vessel in mixed strata. My conclusions will thus be qualitative, with a bias toward Moche Phase IV, considering the knowledge of this time period at Huacas de Moche. The whole exercise is devoted to evaluate resemblances and differences.

In an initial step to recognize a Moche presence in the Santa Valley, we verified the striking conclusion made earlier by Donnan that all the known pottery types from the Moche capital are regularly encountered at Santa Valley sites. The general resemblance for all categories of decorated vessels is thus a key factor in identifying a physical Moche presence in the Santa Valley. However, the difficulty resides in evaluating this production, which is considered massive and locally produced. The Moche occupation is also part of a longer sequence, at least three centuries. The Santa potters thus had plenty of time to establish themselves and to develop their own style within a highly diversified and dynamic Moche tradition.

Besides the new forms identified by Donnan that are not considered here as major changes (in particular, the thick rim bowls and the neckless bowl with a gambrel at its midpoint), other stylistic differences can be pointed out. The open bowls are more abundant in the Santa Valley, and the potters decided to decorate domestic wares with the same geometric designs normally applied to fine paste neck bowls with thin walls. This behavior conforms well to a provincial attitude to rapidly duplicate a type of bowl that is otherwise not produced in sufficient quantity for the Moche inhabiting the Santa Valley. A similar vessel, but one of crude manufacture, thus replaced the fine paste neck bowls typical of Huacas de Moche. Therefore, it seems that shape and motif prevailed over paste and quality.

Among specific motifs encountered on different types of pottery, hollow white circles were very popular during Phase III but decreased in popularity during Phase IV. Two of the most common designs found on neck jars, flaring bowls, and other pottery types from Huacas de Moche are very rare at Santa Valley Moche sites. The "tie" motif and a fineline "ladder" motif (Figure 8.24) have been encountered at Moche Phase IV sites in limited quantity. These simple motifs, easy to reproduce and considered emblematic to Huacas de Moche, were not popular in the Santa Valley for unknown reasons.

The "bean eye" motif on several modeled vessels is a possible remainder of Gallinazo influence on Moche ceramic production (Figure 8.25), while a neck jar, with its chamber modeled as a human face, represents a figure with some traits leaning toward the highlands (Figure 8.26). This vessel was found in the fill of the

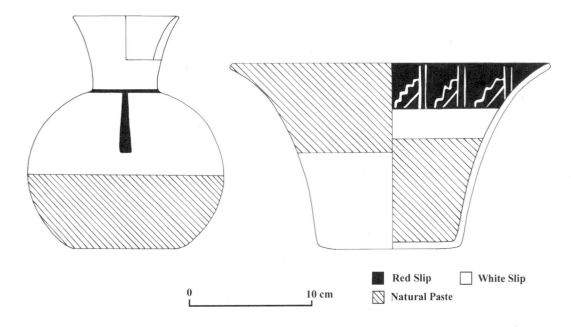

Red Slip   **White Slip**

Natural Paste

0   10 cm

FIGURE 8.24. Neck jar and flaring bowl from Huacas de Moche with tie and step motifs. Drawings by author.

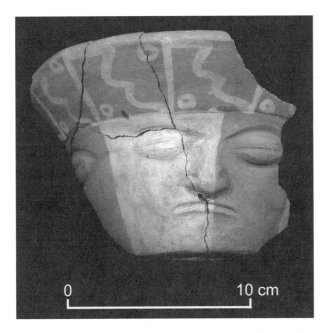

0   10 cm

FIGURE 8.25. Flaring bowl with human face with "bean eye" motif, a possible remainder of Gallinazo influence. Photograph by author.

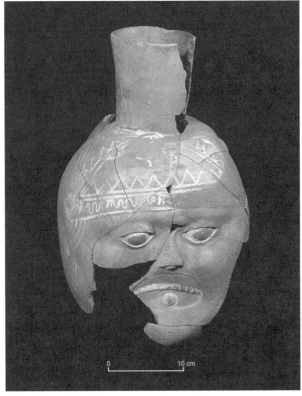

0   10 cm

FIGURE 8.26. Vessel from Guadalupito with human face showing possible highland traits. Photograph by author.

major entrance of Elite Compound 5 at Guadalupito and should date to the latest occupation of the compound, and probably of the site.

Our quest to answer the question regarding the existence of a Santa style should eventually include the other ceramic categories, such as figurines, spindle whorls, and musical instruments, to name a few. The general resemblance is still the basic conclusion. In future research, our spindle whorl collection will allow us to further compare the two Moche stylistic phases with those of a Gallinazo style.

The figurines should be carefully analyzed through this comparative approach. The Santa figurines are of various qualities, with feminine representations prevailing. The hollow figurine type is more frequent in the Santa Valley than in the Moche Valley, and slip painting regularly embellishes it. The comparative analysis of the face elements should shed light on the relations between the two valleys. In this regard, the mouth of the vast majority of hollow figurines and of molded faces on vessels could be typified as a "sad mouth," which I like to refer to as *"la boca Santa"* (Figure 8.27). I do not know if this mouth representation is part of a stylistic canon, but its popularity suggests that it might be another marker of the Santa style.

Not only for provocative purposes, but also to reflect more objectively our knowledge of the PSUM collection and the published data, I favor the idea of a Santa style that is not that different from the style prevailing in the Moche Valley. The evaluation of these differences remains a problem, as well as their relevant consequences and implications at the inter-valley level.

Conclusion

The Moche style in the Santa Valley is easy to recognize from the painted and molded ceramic production. The stylistic variables associated with Phases III and IV have been supported by stratigraphic evidence as well as radiocarbon dates. These same stylistic variables suggest numerous implications regarding the sociopolitical organization within the Santa Valley. The first is a long-term history, at least 300 years or twelve generations, and second, that such history could be divided into two major phases. Third, for each phase, a site stands alone as a strong candidate to be the Moche regional center, the capital of a province. El Castillo is the candidate for

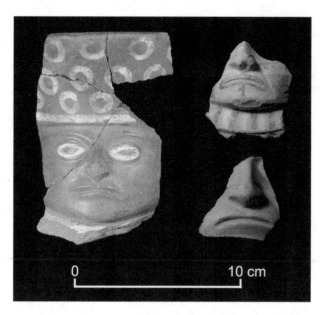

FIGURE 8.27. Vessels and figurines with human face bearing a "sad mouth," or "la boca Santa." Photograph by author.

the earlier phase, and Guadalupito for the later phase. The Moche presence in the Santa Valley thus has a long history, divided into two phases, with a distinct regional capital for each phase.

The Moche occupation does not seem to have been extensive during Phase III, and few sites have been identified to the early arrival and establishment of the Moche. In contrast, more sites display Phase IV occupations. For instance, the size of Guadalupito and the colonization of the Lacramarca sector are good evidence of a stronger and larger Moche population settling in the lower Santa Valley. Nevertheless, the paucity of early Moche sites, or Phase III components, could be explained by their lesser visibility from the surface when these habitation sites were later occupied by Moche Phase IV settlements.

It is not yet possible to conclude that ceramic production in the Moche and Santa valleys during the Moche Phase III was similar. Based on regular contacts between the new settlers and the Moche centers, stylistic differences should not be significant; however, the occupation at El Castillo seems to have lasted more than a century. Therefore, the development of a Santa style is related to the maintenance of a Moche presence in Santa through a second phase associated with more rapid changes.

This second phase is associated with Moche IV style and the new capital at Guadalupito. The consolidation of a power base is illustrated by the construction of two huacas, the larger one being the biggest Moche public monument of the Santa Valley.

The implications of stylistic change in relation to sociopolitical organization of the Moche multi-valley state are speculative at best since we have first to consider the meanings of a possible distinct Moche style in Santa. Stylistic divergence could be interpreted as political autonomy, but how much independence was gained through this ceramic production remains unknown. We do not have sufficient data to suggest that the Santa leaders had enough autonomy to allow them to withdraw from the Southern Moche state in order to start on their own.

In this perspective, it should be interesting to pursue this quest into the Nepeña Valley. Is there a Moche Phase III at Pañamarca or elsewhere in that valley? Was Moche pottery produced locally in Nepeña, or was it obtained through trade with the Moche in Santa? An independent conquest of the Nepeña Valley by the Moche from Santa is not yet testable. I prefer to see the role of the central leaders at Huacas de Moche as being behind the major changes that occurred in the 300 years between AD 400 and 700 in the southern valleys.

The Moche style in Santa puts the analyst at a crossroads since it is possible to argue for stylistic resemblances but also for differences in shape and decoration between ceramics from the Moche and Santa valleys. It is thus hard to give more weight to the differences and to propose a growing stylistic and political autonomy for the Moche of the Santa Valley. From a general comparative perspective, it should be emphasized that the same ceramic categories are found in the Santa and Moche valleys. The large amount of flaring bowls and stirrup spout bottles found on sites of the Santa Valley contrasts markedly with their absence in the Jequetepeque Valley (Castillo 2001, 2003; Castillo and Donnan 1995; Donnan 2003; Donnan and McClelland 1997, 1999). A similar conclusion can be made regarding the famous portrait vessels (see Donnan 2004), although this pottery type is not found in large quantity on Moche sites of the Santa Valley.

Regarding the development of a distinct Moche style in the Santa Valley, the resulting differences could be easily minimized if the time involved in this cultural diversification is taken into account. The Moche immigrants to Santa tried very hard to reconstruct society as established in the Moche and Chicama valleys, and they kept their culture unchanged for several generations. The observed changes could thus be seen as expected variations in the remodeling of a complex society away from the homeland.

Over time, the reproduction of a Moche society in the Santa Valley led to a certain degree of autonomy in ceramic production, a case supported by the identification of at least five centers of production (based on mold discoveries). The exchange of similar ceramic vessels might have been limited, and perhaps only the elite governing the Santa Valley maintained the need or the luxury of importing the newest styles from the homeland. Otherwise, the general resemblance between Moche and Santa ceramics for each category of decorated vessels, as well as the expected changes from Phase III to Phase IV, have more weight than several Santa variants. The development of specific types of vessels and selection of preferred motifs at several ceramic production centers in the Santa Valley are thus considered a first step in studying the emergence of a provincial Moche style. With more data on these variants, it will be possible to argue for a case of political autonomy following the assumptions that decorated vessels express the needs of the local elite, and that the bigger the stylistic differences, the stronger the autonomy of the Santa polity. For the moment, the idea of the Santa polity being "à la mode"—with constant relations between the central power at Huacas de Moche site and the local Moche elite—fits the available data, although the development of a Santa style cannot be denied.

Acknowledgements

I would like to acknowledge the financial support for this project that has been funded by the Social Sciences and Humanities Council of Canada. I would like also to thank all the members of the Université de Montréal Santa Project who have contributed to the success of this project. A special thank-you to Hendrik Van Gijseghem for his comments on an earlier draft and to the editors, Steve Bourget and Kimberly Jones, for their patience and judicious editorial assistance. I am also very grateful to Steve Bourget for inviting me to participate in this Fourth Sibley Family Conference.

Bibliography

Bawden, Garth

1994   La paradoja estructural: La cultura moche como ideología política. In *Moche: Propuestas y perspectivas*, 389–414. Actas del Primer Coloquio sobre la Cultura Moche, Trujillo, 12 a 16 de abril de 1993. Edited by Santiago Uceda and Elías Mujica. Travaux de l'Institut Français d'Études Andines 79. Universidad Nacional de la Libertad, Trujillo, Perú.

1996   *The Moche*. Blackwell, London.

Billman, Brian R.

1996   Prehistoric Political Organization in the Moche Valley, Peru. Unpublished Ph.D. dissertation, Department of Anthropology, University of California at Santa Barbara.

Bonavia, Ducio

1982   *Precerámico peruano: Los gavilanes, mar, desierto y oasis en la historia del hombre.* Corporación de Financiera de Desarallo S.A., COFIDE, Lima, and Instituto Arqueológico Alemán, Perú.

Bourget, Steve

1998   Proyecto Huancaco, investigaciones arqueológicas de la capital moche del valle de Virú, costa norte del Perú. Unpublished report submitted to the Instituto Nacional de la Cultura, Lima.

1999   Proyecto Huancaco, Investigaciones arqueológicas de la capital moche del valle de Virú, costa norte del Perú. Unpublished report submitted to the Instituto Nacional de la Cultura, Lima.

2000   Proyecto Huancaco, Investigaciones arqueológicas de la capital moche del valle de Virú, costa norte del Perú. Unpublished report submitted to the Instituto Nacional de la Cultura, Lima.

2003   Somos diferentes: Dinámica ocupacional del sitio Castillo de Huancaco, valle de Virú. In *Moche: Hacia el Final del Milenio*, Tome II, 245–267. Actas del Segundo Coloquio sobre la Cultura Moche, Trujillo, 1 al 7 de agosto de 1999. Edited by Santiago Uceda and Elías Mujica. Universidad Nacional de Trujillo and Pontificia Universidad Católica del Perú, Lima.

Castillo, Luis Jaime

2001   Last of the Mochicas: A View from the Jequetepeque Valley. In *Moche: Art and Political Representation in Ancient Peru*, 307–322. Edited by Joanne Pillsbury. National Gallery of Art and Yale University Press, Washington, D.C.

2003   Los últimos Mochicas en Jequetepeque. In *Moche: Hacia el Final del Milenio*, Tome I, 65–123. Actas del Segundo Coloquio sobre la Cultura Moche, Trujillo, 1 al 7 de agosto de 1999. Edited by Santiago Uceda and Elías Mujica. Universidad Nacional de Trujillo and Pontificia Universidad Católica del Perú, Lima.

Castillo, Luis Jaime J., and Christopher B. Donnan

1995   Los Mochica del norte y los Mochica del sur. In *Vicús*, 143–176. Edited by Krzysztof Makowski, Christopher B. Donnan, Ivan Amaro Bullon, Luis Jaime Castillo, Magdalena Diez Canseco, Otto Elespuru Revoredo, and Juan Antonio Murro Mena. Banco de Crédito del Perú, Lima.

Chapdelaine, Claude

2000   Struggling for Survival: The Urban Class of the Moche Site, North Coast of Peru. In *Environmental Disaster and the Archaeology of Human Response*, 121–142. Edited by Garth Bawden and Richard M. Reycraft. Anthropological Papers No. 7. Maxwell Museum of Anthropology, Albuquerque, New Mexico.

2001   The Growing Power of a Moche Urban Class. In *Moche: Art and Archaeology in Ancient Peru*, 69–87. Edited by Joanne Pillsbury. National Gallery of Art and Yale University Press, Washington, D.C.

2002   Out in the Streets of Moche: Urbanism and Sociopolitical Organization at a Moche IV Urban Center. In *Advances in Andean Archaeology and Ethnohistory*, 53–88. Edited by William Isbell and Helaine Silverman. Plenum Press, New York.

2003   La ciudad moche: Urbanismo y estado. In *Moche: Hacia el Final del Milenio*, Tome II, 247–285. Actas del Segundo Coloquio sobre la Cultura Moche, Trujillo, 1 al 7 de agosto de 1999. Edited by Santiago Uceda and Elías Mujica. Universidad Nacional de Trujillo and Pontificia Universidad Católica del Perú, Lima.

Chapdelaine, Claude, and Victor Pimentel

2001   Informe del proyecto arqueológico PSUM (Proyecto Santa de la Universidad de Montreal) 2000—La presencia moche en el valle del Santa, costa norte del Perú. Unpublished report submitted to the Instituto Nacional de la Cultura, Lima. (*www.mapageweb.umontreal.ca/chapdelc*)

2002   Informe del proyecto arqueológico PSUM (Proyecto Santa de la Universidad de Montreal) 2001—La presencia moche en el valle del Santa, Costa Norte del Perú. Unpublished report submitted to the Instituto Nacional de la Cultura, Lima. (*www.mapageweb.umontreal.ca/chapdelc*)

Chapdelaine, Claude, Victor Pimentel, and Hélène Bernier

2003   Informe del proyecto arqueológico PSUM (Proyecto

Santa de la Universidad de Montreal) 2002—La presencia moche en el valle del Santa, costa norte del Perú. Unpublished report submitted to the Instituto Nacional de la Cultura, Lima. (*www.mapageweb.umontreal.ca/chapdelc*)

Collier, Donald

1955   *Cultural Chronology and Change as Reflected in the Ceramics of the Virú Valley, Peru*. Fieldiana Anthropology 43. Natural History Museum, Chicago.

Demarrais, Elisabeth, Luis Jaime Castillo, and Timothy Earle

1996   Ideology, Materialization, and Power Strategies. *Current Anthropology* 37:15–31.

Donnan, Christopher B.

1973   *Moche Occupation of the Santa Valley, Peru*. University of California Publications in Anthropology Vol. 8. University of California Press, Berkeley.

1978   *Moche Art of Peru: Pre-Columbian Symbolic Communication*. Fowler Museum of Cultural History, University of California, Los Angeles.

2001   Moche Ceramic Portraits. In *Moche: Art and Archaeology in Ancient Peru*, 127–139. Edited by Joanne Pillsbury. National Gallery of Art and Yale University Press, Washington, D.C.

2003   Tumbas con entierros en miniaturas: Un nuevo tipo funerario moche. In *Moche: Hacia el Final del Milenio*, Tome I, 43–78. Actas del Segundo Coloquio sobre la Cultura Moche, Trujillo, 1 al 7 de agosto de 1999. Edited by Santiago Uceda and Elías Mujica. Universidad Nacional de Trujillo and Pontificia Universidad Católica del Perú, Lima.

2004   *Moche Portraits from Ancient Peru*. University of Texas Press, Austin.

Donnan, Christopher B., and Donna McClelland

1997   Moche Burials at Pacatnamu. In *The Pacatnamu Papers*, Vol. 2: *The Moche Occupation*, 17–187. Edited by Christopher B. Donnan and Guillermo A. Cock. Fowler Museum of Cultural History, University of California, Los Angeles.

1999   *Moche Fineline Painting: Its Evolution and Its Artists*. Fowler Museum of Cultural History, University of California, Los Angeles.

Druc, Isabelle

1998   *Ceramic Production and Distribution in the Chavín Sphere of Influence (North-Central Andes)*. BAR International Series 731. Oxford.

Emberling, Geoff

1997   Ethnicity in Complex Societies: Archaeological Perspectives. *Journal of Archaeological Research* 5 (4):295–344.

Franco, Régulo, César Gálvez, and Segundo Vásquez

1994   Arquitectura y decoración mochica en la Huaca Cao Viejo, Complejo El Brujo: Resultados preliminares. In *Moche: Propuestas y perspectivas*, 147–180. Actas del Primer Coloquio sobre la Cultura Moche, Trujillo, 12 a 16 de abril de 1993. Edited by Santiago Uceda and Elías Mujica. Travaux de l'Institut Français d'Études Andines 79. Universidad Nacional de la Libertad, Trujillo, Perú.

2001   La Huaca Cao Viejo en el Complejo El Brujo. *Arqueológicas* 25:123–171.

2003   Modelos, función y cronología de la Huaca Cao Viejo, Complejo El Brujo. In *Moche: Hacia el Final del Milenio*, Tome I, 125–177. Actas del Segundo Coloquio sobre la Cultura Moche, Trujillo, 1 al 7 de agosto de 1999. Edited by Santiago Uceda and Elías Mujica. Universidad Nacional de Trujillo and Pontificia Universidad Católica del Perú, Lima.

Gálvez, Cesar, and Jesus Briceño

2001   The Moche in the Chicama Valley. In *Moche: Art and Archaeology in Ancient Peru*, 141–158. Edited by Joanne Pillsbury. National Gallery of Art and Yale University Press, Washington, D.C.

Hill, James N.

1985   Style: A Conceptual Evolutionary Framework. In *Decoding Prehistoric Ceramics*, 362–385. Edited by Ben A. Nelson. Southern Illinois University Press, Carbondale.

Millaire, Jean-François

2004   Gallinazo-Moche Interactions at Huaca Santa Clara, Virú Valley, North Coast of Peru. Paper presented at the 69th Annual Meeting of the Society for American Archaeology, Montreal (*www.anthro.umontreal.ca*).

Pozorski, Thomas, and Sheila Pozorski

1996   Cerámica de la cultura moche en el valle de Casma, Perú. *Revista del Museo de Arqueología, Antropología y Historia* 6:103–122.

Proulx, Donald

1968   *An Archaeological Survey in the Nepeña Valley, Peru*. Research Report No. 2. Department of Anthropology, University of Massachusetts, Amherst.

1973   *Archaeological Investigations in the Nepeña Valley, Peru*. Research Report No. 13. Department of Anthropology, University of Massachusetts, Amherst.

Prümers, Heiko

2000   "El Castillo" de Huarmey: Una plataforma funeraria del Horizonte Medio. *Boletín de Arqueología PUCP* 4:289–312.

Quilter, Jeffrey

2002   Moche Politics, Religion, and Warfare. *Journal of World Prehistory* 16 (2):145–195.

Russell, Glenn S., and Margaret A. Jackson

2001   Political Economy and Patronage at Cerro Mayal, Peru. In *Moche: Art and Archaeology in Ancient Peru*, 159–175.

Edited by Joanne Pillsbury. National Gallery of Art and Yale University Press, Washington, D.C.

Russell, Glenn S., Banks L. Leonard, and Jesus Briceño

1994   Cerro Mayal: Nuevos datos sobre la producción cerámica moche en el valle de Chicama. In *Moche: Propuestas y perspectivas*, 181–206. Actas del Primer Coloquio sobre la Cultura Moche, Trujillo, 12 a 16 de abril de 1993. Edited by Santiago Uceda and Elías Mujica. Travaux de l'Institut Français d'Études Andines 79. Universidad Nacional de la Libertad, Trujillo.

1998   The Cerro Mayal Workshop: Addressing Issues of Craft Specialization in Moche Society. In *Andean Ceramics: Technology, Organization, and Approaches*, 63–89. Edited by Izumi Shimada. MASCA Research Papers in Science and Archaeology, Supplement to Volume 15. University of Pennsylvania Museum of Archaeology and Anthropology, Philadelphia.

Strong, William D., and Clifford Evans

1952   *Cultural Stratigraphy in the Virú Valley, Northern Peru:* *The Formative and Florescent Epoch.* Columbia Studies in Archaeology and Ethnology 4. Columbia University Press, New York.

Willey, Gordon R.

1953   *Prehistoric Settlement Patterns in the Virú Valley, Peru.* Bulletin 155. Smithsonian Institution, Bureau of American Ethnology, Washington, D.C.

Wilson, David L.

1988   *Prehispanic Settlement Patterns in the Lower Santa Valley, Peru: A Regional Perspective on the Origins and Development of Complex North Coast Society.* Smithsonian Institution Press, Washington, D.C.

1995   Prehistoric Settlement Patterns in the Casma Valley, North Coast of Peru: Preliminary Results to Date. *Journal of the Steward Anthropological Society* 23 (1–2):189–227.

1999   *Indigenous South Americans of Past and Present: An Ecological Perspective.* Westview Press, Boulder, Colorado.

CHAPTER NINE

The Priests of the Bicephalus Arc

Tombs and Effigies Found in Huaca de la Luna and Their Relation to Moche Rituals

SANTIAGO UCEDA, NATIONAL UNIVERSITY OF TRUJILLO

Abstract

Since 1991, investigations at Huacas de la Luna in the Moche Valley have brought to light a diverse array of archaeological contexts. Recent excavations in Platform I have uncovered certain artifacts resembling objects clearly depicted in the iconography and associated with certain individuals. They correspond to complex scenes of figures chewing coca leaves that are described as rituals associated with rain or agrarian fertility. Through a comprehensive study and interpretation of these and other scenes of both painted and modeled ceramics, I discuss the role of these individuals in Moche human sacrifice. I conclude by examining the possible social structures of the Moche, with special regard to the roles of these individuals in relation to Moche ritual battles.

Moche iconography on ceramics and on some buildings has been one of the fundamental sources for reconstructing part of the mindset of this civilization, which lacked formal writing. From the naturalistic narrative interpretation of these images by Larco Hoyle (2001), to the thematic descriptions by Donnan (1978) and Hocquenghem (1987), and the most recent considerations of the images as mythic and ceremonial narrations, archaeology has not added much to the debate. The discoveries at Sipán by Walter Alva (1994) and at San José de Moro by Christopher Donnan and Luis Jaime Castillo (1992, 1994) were some of the first scientific archaeological discoveries that permitted the successful correlation of archaeological contexts with the iconographic interpretations.

As a result of these findings, a new manner of investigating Moche iconography has been initiated: contrasting Moche iconography with information recovered from archaeological excavations. In this sense, the iconography has come to be used as a toolkit in the same manner that writing or ethnography is used to interpret archaeological data. Yet this manner of using the iconography can go even further, employed as an inspirational source of interpretive models that serve as a base for archaeological excavation projects.

Recent excavations in the complexes of Huaca del Sol and Huaca de la Luna have recovered ritual effigies and emblematic items of figures who appear in one of the complex scenes described as the Coca-Taking Ceremony. The iconographic corpus on this subject is composed of three complex scenes and eleven simpler but isolated examples. The study of this corpus and its correlation with some of the recuperated archaeological contexts in Huaca de la Luna suggests that these scenes and the rituals expressed through them had a distinct or direct relationship with the practice of human sacrifice. In this chapter, I examine the possible Moche social structures that this information brings to light, in particular the roles that certain individuals took on by participating in ritual battles—both as losers and winners.

The Iconographic Register

Moche iconography is quite extensive and varied; however, it may be grouped into a set of diverse themes. For example, Hocquenghem (1987:21) proposes nineteen recognizable themes in Moche iconographic art. One of these themes is known as the "offering and consumption of coca," a title I have retained for this analysis. This theme will serve as the connecting thread through this discussion, offering some explanations for the diverse archaeological contexts recuperated in the last twelve years at Huaca de la Luna.

SCENES OF COCA OFFERING AND CONSUMPTION

From the extensive corpus of Moche visual representations that has been compiled by different scholars, I have selected three main examples (Figures 9.1–9.3). Within these representations, two types of individuals interact. On one side are those figures handsomely dressed in shirts decorated in plates of gold and wearing complex headdresses composed of various elements. The individuals carry bags, or *chuspas*, with lime containers inside. Around their necks hangs an object in the form of an animal skin. In all cases, the figures have their hands

drawn together as if in the act of imploring. The second type of individual is often seated and wears a tunic decorated in geometric designs and a headdress of distinct form, such as a fox head, or with simple diadems. In most cases, these figures carry a lime container in one hand and a spatula in the other. According to Donnan, the spatula would serve to extract the lime from the container and carry it to the mouth to mix with the coca leaves and extract the alkaloids (1978:117). To simplify identification of the figures for the remainder of this analysis, I will call the first set of individuals the Worshippers, and the second set the Coca-Takers.

Notably, the three scenes selected for this discussion are not identical. In the first two scenes, some of the figures are located under a bicephalus arc with large dots

FIGURE 9.1. Ritual activity under bicephalous arc. Linden-Museum, Stuttgart. Drawing by Donna McClelland.

FIGURE 9.2. Ritual activity under bicephalous arc. Museo Arqueológico Rafael Larco Herrera, Lima. Drawing by Donna McClelland.

FIGURE 9.3. Coca-Taking Ceremony. Redrawn from Kutscher 1983, Figure 126. Drawing by author.

represented above them. In Figure 9.1, the Worshipper is found under this arc; in contrast, Figure 9.2 represents the Coca-Takers in this position. Both scenes seem to occur in open spaces. In the third representation (Figure 9.3), one of the seated individuals is masticating and appears to be seated within an architectural structure. I will now examine in detail these two types of individuals in order to identify their emblematic elements.

THE WORSHIPPERS

In addition to the three individuals depicted in Figures 9.1–9.3, I have identified a fourth Worshipper from a vessel in the Rafael Larco Herrera Museum (Figure 9.4A). Generally, two of these worshipping figures (Figure 9.4A, B) are found under the bicephalus arc, which terminates at both ends in fox-serpent heads. This arc has been interpreted by most iconographers as a rainbow or the Milky Way, with the large dots representing rain. Therefore, the scene has often been related to water or an agrarian fertility cult (Bourget 1994b; Hocquenghem 1987). In Figure 9.4B, the principal figure carries the bag with a lime container along with a pendant effigy representing the pelt of an animal, with splayed hind paws and very visible claws. The ears are sometimes round, or they may have holes: the first type is typical of felines, the second of bats. Two more emblematic elements are located in front of the indi-

vidual, as if floating in air. These include another lime container and two more pendant effigies. The person in Figure 9.4A carries the bag with the lime container and the pendant effigy, while behind him are two other lime containers, and in front of him a number of somewhat more enigmatic objects.

In the other two scenes (Figure 9.4C, D), the individuals are no longer under a bicephalus arc. Rather, a group of objects represented in front of them serve to separate the Worshippers from the Coca-Takers. These scenes give the impression that the Worshippers are presenting such objects to the Coca-Takers. In Figure 9.4C, which is a detail from Figure 9.2, the Worshipper carries the bag with the lime container and the effigy. In front of him are three bundles, one of which has three lime containers, some plates, and spatulas in its interior. Above these bundles is a fox effigy headdress; above the headdress is a feather adornment. Two lime containers with spatulas appear in front of the adornment, and above them is an animal pelt pendant effigy (feline or bat). Finally, a club and shield are located between these objects and the supplicating individual. In Figure 9.4D (a detail of Figure 9.3) the Worshipper carries only a very simplified form of an animal pelt effigy over his shoulders. Another pelt effigy rests in front of him along with three *Strombus* shell trumpets. Beyond those are two superimposed bundles and another pelt effigy.

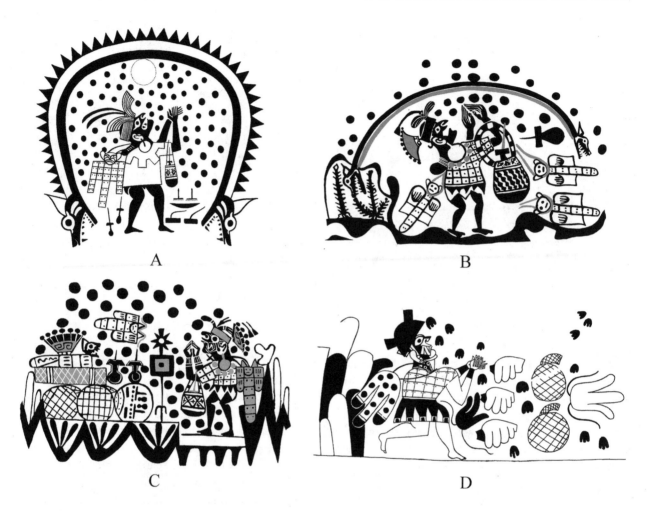

FIGURE 9.4. *A*, ritual activity under bicephalous arc; redrawn from Larco 2001, Figure 368l *B*, ritual activity under bicephalous arc; detail of Figure 9.1; *C*, detail of Figure 9.2; *D*, detail of Figure 9.3. Drawing by author.

The headdresses worn by the Worshippers are of three distinct types. The most complex, and perhaps the most beautiful, is a copper collar upon which are fastened two lateral and two central diadems, as well as a beautiful feather adornment in the back. Two large false earrings are fixed to the sides of the headdress (Figures 9.4B, C). The second type of headdress is similar to the first, lacking only the feather adornment (Figure 9.4A). The third type, however, is quite different. It resembles a semispherical helmet with two divergent rectangular points, and it lacks the attached false earrings (Figure 9.4D). Despite variation in their placement and accoutrements, the Worshippers are all represented with their mouths open. Three of them even have the intercrossed

fangs typical of mythical or divine figures in Moche iconography.

In sum, two actions can be deduced from these scenes of Worshippers. The first is related to a water cult. The second relates to the consecration of ritual objects that form part of these rites or ceremonies, to which I will return below.

THE COCA-TAKERS

The second type of individuals in these scenes wears a large tunic decorated with geometric designs or the heads of serpents or fish. Apart from the three complex scenes addressed above, this same type of coca-taking individual has been identified in three additional exam-

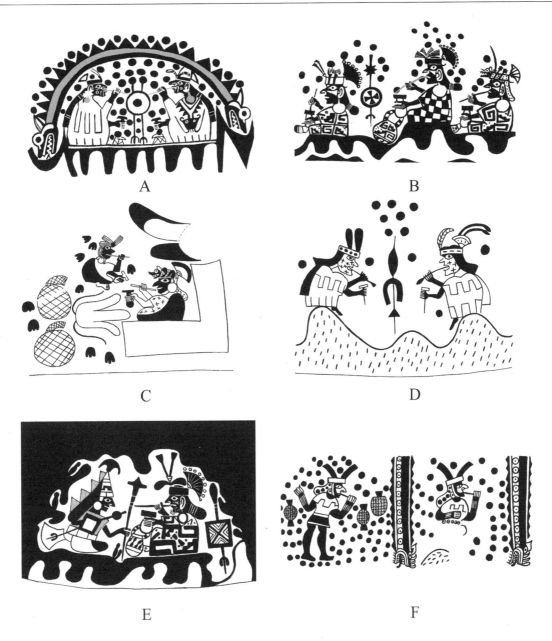

FIGURE 9.5. *A*, detail of Figure 9.2. *B*, detail of Figure 9.1. *C*, detail of Figure 9.3. *D*, redrawn from Kutscher 1983, Figure 131. *E*, redrawn from Kutscher 1983, Figure 129. *F*, redrawn from Kutscher 1983, Figure 131.

ples from the National Museum of Archaeology (Figure 9.5A), the Ethnologisches Museum of Berlin (Figure 9.5B), and the Museum of Archaeology at the Universidad Nacional de Trujillo (Figure 9.5C). In most examples, these individuals occur in pairs. In one scene, however, there are three (Figure 9.5B), and in another the second person appears to be a high-status warrior, given the type of dress and the conical helmet with a half-moon diadem and attached earrings (Figure 9.5E). The Coca-Takers are mostly seated, although in one example the individual's position cannot be determined with certainty because the design has deteriorated (Figure 9.5F).

The action in these scenes occurs under a bicephalus arc (Figures 9.5A, F) or in an enclosed space, possibly a cave (Figure 9.5E). Two scenes depict open, hilly spaces, possibly desert sand dunes, and raindrops falling (Figures 9.5B, D). Interestingly, the lime containers in the two scenes are distinct. In the first group (Figure 9.5B), the Coca-Takers hold oval containers with large, flaring rims. In contrast, the second group (Figure 9.5D) holds apparently distinct lime containers. Another scene (Figure 9.5C) depicts a bench upon which one of the Coca-Takers is seated, with the other appearing next to it (Figures 9.5C).

The Coca-Takers wear two distinct types of headdresses. The dominant form has a neckflap, divergent diadems, a feather adornment, and attached earrings. The other form of headdress has the general form of a headband with a feather adornment, but in two cases the headbands terminate in the front with a fox head (the individuals on the right in Figures 9.5B and 9.5C).

Makowski (1994) has identified such individuals wearing tunics in Moche iconographic art as religious officials, but not priests of high rank. They are generally shown interacting with human figures and are associated with the preparation of sacrificial victims and participation in the sacrifices. In light of this identification, the coca-taking scenes discussed above appear to be comprised of two types of individuals with distinct roles. The first group, the Worshippers, consists of supplicates with divinizing features such as fangs. Their dress associates them with the Moche elite of highest status. They appear to be in charge of consecrating, given certain emblematic elements such as headdresses, lime containers, and pendant effigies used in ritual or ceremonial acts (see also Hocquenghem 1987). Through the remainder of this investigation, I will examine these possible roles further from the perspective of the iconography. The individuals in the second group, the Coca-Takers, appear to be religious officials performing rituals for the divination or invocation of rain. Nevertheless, a detailed analysis of the scenes reveals that these individuals are also associated with weaponry (clubs and shields) and may be high-status warriors.

WORSHIPPERS OF COCA: THE WARRIORS AND THE SACRIFICED

A second set of images relates the Coca-Taking Ceremony to warfare and to sacrificial victims. On one face of a quadrangular bottle is a Coca-Taker with a weapon

bundle behind him; the opposite face depicts a battle between two warriors (Figure 9.6). This relation between the offerings of coca and warriors in battle has already been observed by Makowski (1997).

Figure 9.7 is a scene depicting three individuals. The first wears pendants associated with high status, a headdress with diadems and feather adornments, and a backflap. Over his back is a shawl, which is fastened in the front. In his right hand he carries a bag, and it appears he is signaling to the second individual with his left arm. The second individual, who is naked and has a rope around his neck, drinks from a small container. As a captive, his implements of war are behind him. To the right of the weapon bundle sits a third individual. He holds in one hand a circular shield, and in the other a javelin. He wears a conical helmet that ends in a crescent-shape diadem. The scene thus presents a victorious warrior and the preparation of a captive. Although the individuals in the coca-taking scenes discussed above do not participate in this scene, they relate to the ritual battle and subsequent end of the defeated captive: his sacrifice.

The vessel in Figure 9.8 is also associated with warfare. The individual wears a headdress with a step-and-fret diadem and earrings, and he is carrying a club and a shield (Figure 9.8). He also has a pendant effigy similar to those carried by the Worshippers in the coca-taking scenes. The ornament is on the warrior's back and is fastened with cords at the front of the neck by a simple knot. Another modeled vessel fragment further illustrates this effigy carried by a warrior on foot (Figure 9.9).

The scene depicted in Figure 9.10 shows three warriors and two naked prisoners inside a semicircular net. The captives are easy to identify by the ropes around their necks and their naked appearance. The warrior on the right seems to be of highest rank based on the emblems he wears: a backflap, a headdress with diadems, and feather adornments. He carries the weapons of the captured individuals. The warrior on the left, although elaborately dressed, does not sport a backflap or feather adornments. Over his back, almost at the height of his belt, hangs an element similar to the pendant effigy pictured in the previous scenes. This emblematic element also is present on a third individual who carries only a shield and points toward a plant.

All of these complementary scenes thus provide for

FIGURE 9.6. Coca-Taker and ritual battle on quadrangular stirrup bottle. Staatliche Museen zu Berlin—Preussischer Kulterbesitz, Ethnologisches Museum (VA-18373).

FIGURE 9.7. Warriors, weapons bundles, and sacrificial victim. Ethnologisches Museum, Berlin. Drawing by Donna McClelland.

FIGURE 9.8. Kneeling Warrior with pendant feline effigy on his back. Cleveland Museum of Art, Andrew R. and Martha Holden Jennings Fund (1989.90).

FIGURE 9.9. Warrior with pendant feline effigy on his back. Moche Archive, UCLA. Photograph by Christopher B. Donnan.

FIGURE 9.10. Fineline painting of warriors and sacrificial victims. Redrawn from Kutscher 1983, Figure 131.

the following interpretations or hypotheses, which will be contrasted next with the archaeological evidence:

1. There exists a direct relation between the coca-taking scenes, the battles, the taking of captives, and possibly the sacrifices.
2. The emblematic elements (e.g., the lime containers) could have been used in the rituals of prisoner preparation preceding sacrifice or for propitiatory acts.
3. The pendant effigies were used by warriors who participated in ritual battles. This emblem was perhaps given to and carried by the victors.

The Archaeological Contexts

Three excavated contexts in the Huacas del Sol y de la Luna merit being reviewed and contrasted with the above iconographic analysis. These include Tomb 2, Tomb 18 and its repository, and the sacrificial deposits in Plazas 3a, 3b, and 3c. I will address both funerary contexts and material deposits, focusing most intently on the key emblematic elements.

TOMB 2

Tomb 2 was found at the end of April 1992 when the excavations of wall fill covering the polychrome murals were expanded in Platform I of Huaca de la Luna. The tomb was made in the construction fill that served as the foundation for the final building phase of Huaca de la Luna.[1] A cane coffin had been placed in a funerary chamber measuring 95 by 225 cm. The coffin rested in the southeast part, and eight ceramic offerings (stirrup spout bottles and a pitcher) and gourds containing camelid bones had been placed on the opposite side (Figure 9.11). Four additional stirrup spout bottles rested at the south end of the sarcophagus.

The fill of the tomb consisted of fine sand with some fragments of colored plaster. There were also fragments of simple ceramics, mollusk remains (*Donax* sp., *Tegula* sp., and others), bones (camelid, rodent, and fish vertebrae), and vegetal remains such as peanut shells (*Arachis hipogaea*). The cane coffin is 205 cm long, 50 cm wide, and 25 cm in height.

After the coffin lid was removed, gourds (*Lagenaria* sp.) were encountered face down over the body. The gourds were quite large (30 cm diameter). Although only six gourds remained on the body, there were likely others that had since largely decomposed (Figure 9.12). After removing the layer of gourds, which had adapted to the form of the cadaver, the offerings and implements associated with the individual were then defined (Figure 9.13). The implements directly associated with the person of this tomb, which also ought to form part of his apparel, were disposed of in the following manner in relation to the corpse:

1. Apart from textile fragments, three copper plaques were found over the head. One depicted a feline face, and the other two displayed feline paws (Figure 9.14).
2. To the left of the chest were found discs of gilded copper. Most of these discs had a diameter of 1 cm, but others ranged from 1.5 cm to 2.5 cm. All the discs had a small orifice in the upper part through which a thread would have passed to attach them to the garment.
3. At the level of the dorsal and lumbar vertebrae, and to either side, were found more copper plates. These plates were rectangular, measuring from 4 to 6 cm, with holes around the borders. To the right side rested a elongated copper instrument in the shape of a spatula. One end of the instrument bore a perforation, and the other was filed into the shape of a chisel or spatula.

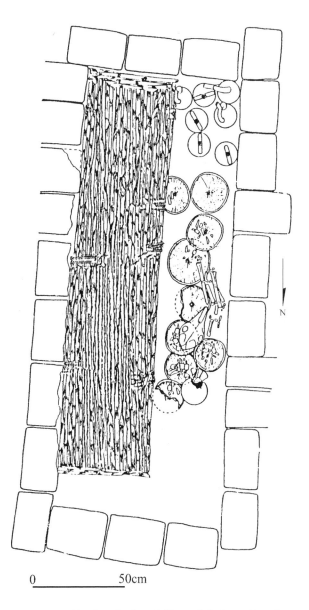

0 _____ 50cm

FIGURE 9.11. Tomb 2, Platform I, Huaca de la Luna. Drawing by author.

4. Over the pelvis was a small gilded copper vessel (Figure 9.15). From its form, it would appear to be a lime container like those depicted in scenes of coca-taking activities. Three types of textiles were used to wrap this object.

5. At the feet and the lower part of the thorax, other copper plaques were found in bad state of conservation or even crumpled.

The skeleton was in a good state of conservation, without notable fractures. It was an adult individual approximately 1.7 m in height. The individual was resting on his back in an extended position with the cra-nium to the south. A gourd had been placed under the cranium, slightly raising the head. The arms extended along the sides of the body, with the hands placed over the pelvis. The extended legs were joined together at the feet. Remains of braided hair were found around the sides of the cranium.

Five vessels had been placed in the coffin, with two stirrup spout bottles resting to either side of the feet. A dipper was located just alongside the right knee. Two other vessels had been placed directly above the legs. One of them was a badly fragmented flaring bowl; the other an exceptional stirrup spout bottle in the form of a war-rior duck holding a shield and a war club (Figure 9.16).

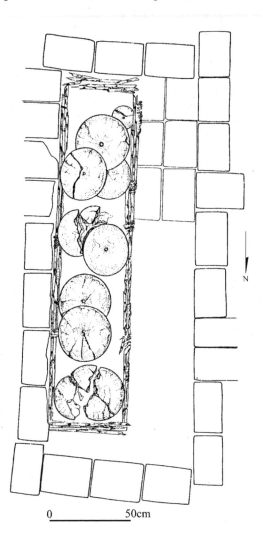

FIGURE 9.12. Tomb 2, Platform I, Huaca de la Luna. Drawing by author.

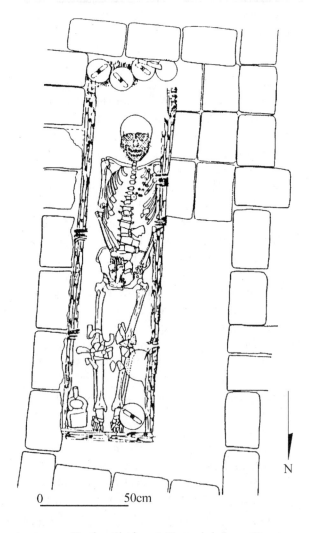

FIGURE 9.13. Tomb 2, Platform I, Huaca de la Luna. Drawing by author.

FIGURE 9.14. Feline effigy found in Tomb 2, Platform I, Huaca de la Luna. Photograph by author.

FIGURE 9.16. Stirrup spout bottle with anthropomorphized duck warrior from Tomb 2, Platform I, Huaca de la Luna. Photograph by author.

FIGURE 9.15. Bottle of gilded copper from Tomb 2, Platform I, Huaca de la Luna. Photograph by Steve Bourget.

FIGURE 9.17. Detail of ritual activity under bicephalus arc, Figure 9.1. Linden-Museum, Stuttgart. Drawing by Donna McClelland.

THE EMBLEMATIC ELEMENTS

Of the offerings associated with Tomb 2, at least three objects figure prominently in the Coca-Taking Ceremony: the lime container (Figures 9.15, 9.17a), the spatula (Figure 9.17b), and the feline effigy (Figures 9.14, 9.17c). Although I previously suggested that the feline effigy was part of a headdress depicted on the Coca-Takers (Uceda 1997), the eventual discovery of a complete and much more elaborate pendant effigy in the same part of Huaca de la Luna has argued otherwise (Figure 9.18).

TOMB 18 AND ITS REPOSITORY

The excavations of the fill covering Building D in Platform I of Huaca de la Luna uncovered two tombs and six elements over and around Tomb 18 (Figures 9.19, 9.20). These elements were most likely intended as a repository for the tomb or as an offering for the interment of Building D (Uceda and Canziani 1998). They consist of a basket made of reeds filled with diverse objects, including a pendant effigy (Figure 9.21).

The recuperation of the Tomb 18 materials was done through layers; however, no order could be observed to indicate that they formed part of a complete deposit or

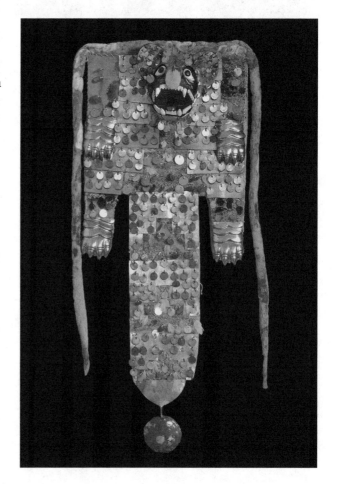

FIGURE 9.18. Feline effigy from Platform I, Huaca de la Luna. Photograph by Steve Bourget.

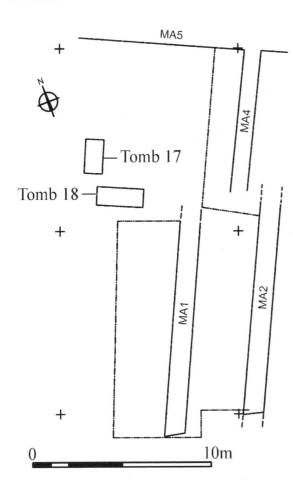

FIGURE 9.19. Plan of Platform I, Huaca de la Luna. Drawing by author.

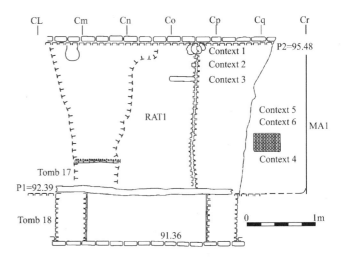

FIGURE 9.20. Cut section of Platform I, Huaca de la Luna. Drawing by author.

FIGURE 9.21. Basket placed in the fill of Building D, Platform I, Huaca de la Luna. Photograph by author.

major elements of one deposit. The only object that was considered complete was the pendant effigy made of a textile covered with applications of laminated gold and other materials (Figure 9.18).

THE FELINE EFFIGY

After conservation efforts on the face, which had been flattened by sediment, it became possible to recognize the structure of this piece. An animal pelt had been cut to give the piece its general shape; however, the back legs and tail exceed normal proportions compared to the size of the body. This skin was then covered with a plain textile, coarse on both sides. Over one face of this support, metal laminates had been attached with seams of cotton thread.

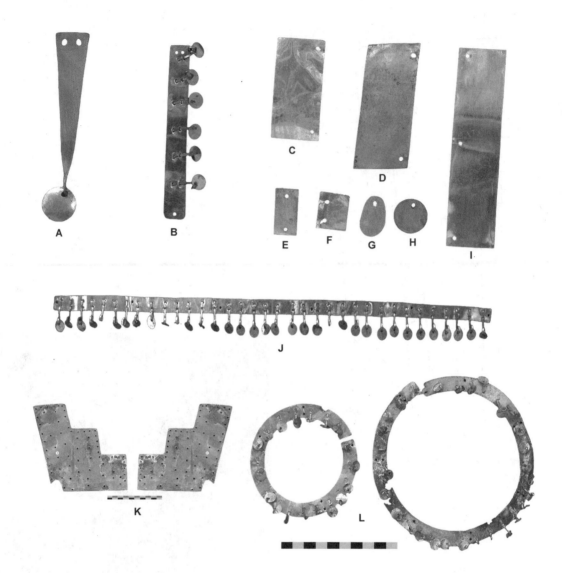

FIGURE 9.22. Offerings placed in the basket. Photograph by author.

On the upper part, in the center, is the sculpted face of a feline made from tree resin. The mouth is open, revealing teeth made from *Conus* shells and a palette and tongue made from one thin piece of copper. The eyes, also made from *Conus* shells, have black stone pupils. A nose ring and a chin guard on the face were made from recut and modeled gold sheet.

Around the head, as if to frame it, were gold plaques with spangles of gold. To either side of and slightly below these plaques, four pressure-modeled plaques composed the feline feet and claws. Two sets of rectangular plaques rested underneath and formed the design of the body.

One pair extended from the extremes to the center, leaving an open space. The second set of much shorter plaques appeared at either extreme, leaving an open space in the shape of a stepped triangle. The plaques possessed spangles of gold fastened with a clasp to the principal plaque. Other gold spangles and yellow feathers further filled the open spaces. At the end of these extremities, some gold plaques were found modeled in the form of plates and claws. Between these and the body were spangles and black feathers.

The tail is composed of three rectangular gold plaques, with a lower part in the form of a stepped pyra-

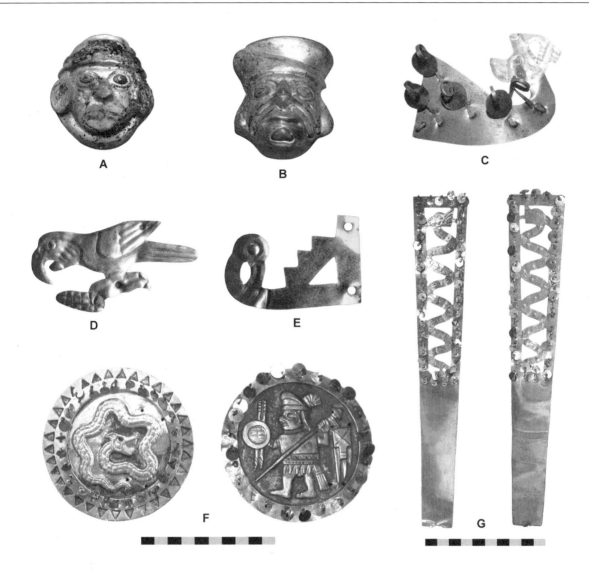

FIGURE 9.23. Offerings placed in the basket. Photograph by author.

mid. It is also decorated with spangles and yellow feathers. The tail ends in a half disc of gold sheet from which hangs a gold disc painted with cinnabar. The entire piece is held at the top by cotton cords, which would have served to attach the pendant effigy around the neck and over the back of the individual wearing it.

THE OTHER OBJECTS
A great variety of materials was recovered from the repository near Tomb 18, including simple rectangular, square, and oval sheets; recut and modeled sheets in the form of parrots, shrimp, small masks, and stairs ending in volutes with bird heads; volutes ending in fox heads; trapezoidal diadems with serpents in step designs; copper plaques in stepped form; and clasps (Figures 9.22–9.24). I have tried to identify these objects in the iconography to determine if they could have been part of other elements depicted in images of the Coca-Takers.

THE EMBLEMATIC ELEMENTS
Without doubt, the ornamental animal pelt effigy found in the cache is similar to the garments adorning the shoulders of the orators and the backs of the warriors (Figures 9.1, 9.8, 9.18). It is the most important emblem-

FIGURE 9.24. These copper shafts that were placed in the basket as offerings may have been used to secure feather ornaments to a headdress. Photograph by author.

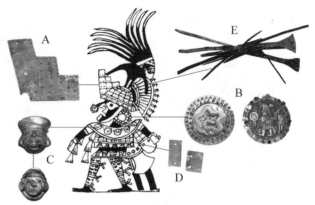

FIGURE 9.25. Correlations between the offerings and the iconography.

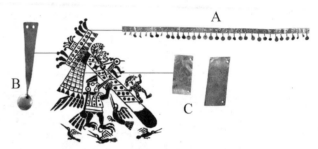

FIGURE 9.26. Correlations between the offerings and the iconography.

FIGURE 9.27. Correlations between the offerings and the iconography.

atic element, not only for its presence in diverse scenes and on diverse individuals, but also for its possible significant connotations.

The other objects—made of copper, gilded copper, and gold—were found relatively dispersed, making it difficult to determine their associations. Nevertheless, I have made an attempt to identify them using images in the iconography. The key pieces are the copper sheets in stepped form and the bundle of punctured articles or articles ending in triangular sheets (Figure 9.22). The first of these, the stepped elements, may have formed part of a headdress (Figure 9.25A). The holes would have served to fasten the gold sheets to some form of background support. The large disks may have been used as ear ornaments, and the beads may have been part of an elaborate necklace (Figure 9.25B, C). The rectangular or square sheets may have been part of a metallic garment (Figure 9.25D), and the copper shafts could have been used to secure feather ornaments to the headdress (Figure 9.25E). These attributions are supported by similar objects found in some of the tombs at Sipán (Alva and Donnan 1993:106).

In Figure 9.26 the band around the crown appears similar to the long strip of metal and spangles found in the repository (Figure 9.26A). The extensions with disks (Figure 9.26B) may have served to decorate the top of the crown, and the rectangular platelets (Figure 9.26C) to

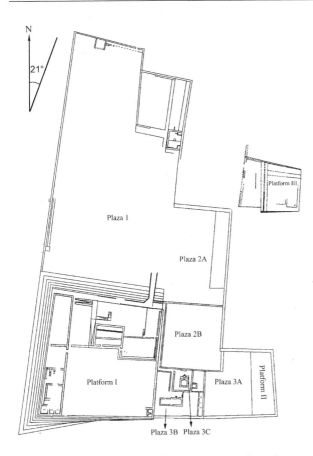

FIGURE 9.28. Plan of Huaca de la Luna. Drawing by author.

decorate the neck coverlet. Two other elements have also been identified. This first element has a long, trapezoidal shape with snakes in it and may have formed part of the front of a Coca-Taker headdress (Figure 9.27A). The second element consists of two disks that may have been false ear ornaments attached to the side of the headdress (Figure 9.27B).

If my analysis is correct, these emblematic elements would correspond to various types of headdresses or shirt adornments, with the diverse types signifying different types of individuals. In the future, it would be interesting to extend such investigations in order to obtain more detailed information about the individuals who used these various elements and thus better define their possible roles.

Human Sacrifices at Huaca de la Luna

The archaeological excavations at Huaca de la Luna have led to the discovery of two sacrificial contexts associated

with two small plazas in the eastern part of the complex. The first context was discovered by Steve Bourget (1997, 1998), and the second by John Verano and Moisés Tufinio (1999, 2000). These areas correspond to two distinct forms of sacrifice, both in their particularities and in their chronology.

The first context, located in Plaza 3a, contained a group of individuals found in three layers of compact sediments. The sedimentation had resulted from the erosion of the plaza walls during strong rains (Figure 9.28), indicating a rather strong El Niño event around AD 600. The bodies were found in articulated positions. Many displayed signs of trauma to the head, quartering of exterior limbs, and cuts to the throat. The individuals were between fifteen and thirty years of age, and many had evidence of previous fractures, suggesting that they were professional warriors. Together with these skeletons, Bourget recuperated thousands of fragments of crude clay sculptures representing captives, many of them decorated with intricate designs.

The second context of sacrificial activities is much older and occupies a smaller space in Plaza 3c (Verano, this volume). Human remains and artifacts were recovered from the floor in layers of clay and sand. The Plaza 3c context had fewer individuals than the one in Plaza 3a. Some had been dismembered, while others were tied with cords around the feet, hands, and neck. Beneath the floor were three clearly distinguished graves of individuals lying in anatomical position, but with signs of cuts to the throat (left or right side at the height of the third or fifth cervical vertebra). The most significant characteristic of this group of skeletons is that all were defleshed but remained articulated by intact joint ligaments.

Plazas 3a and 3c together form part of a larger plaza that occupies the space between Platforms I and II (Figure 9.28). Since 1995, the discovery of various wall structures has obligated us to subdivide Plaza 3 into three smaller spaces (Plazas 3a, 3b, and 3c) (Bourget 1997, 1998; Gamonal 1998; Montoya 1997; Orbegoso 1998).

PLAZA 3C

One approaches Plaza 3c through a corridor that begins at the access ramp of the temple and extends along the length of the east side of Platform I. This plaza was divided into two spaces. One was a small chamber (5.8 m long) in the center of the plaza. Its exterior walls were decorated with three levels of designs. The first two consisted of bands of stylized fish and serpent heads such as those that decorate the facades with the motif of the "Decapitator" on the first floor patio of Platform I (Uceda and Tufinio 2003, Lam. 20.2a). In the third decorative level the motifs change. On the north wall, to either side of the chamber entrance, were two panels with low-reliefs depicting an individual resting on his back and overtaken by a feline (see Figure 11.2). On the other three walls, the same subject is repeated but with only wall paint. Unfortunately, the state of conservation of these paintings is poor. A low-lying lintel over the doorway provided restricted access into a small interior space. A bench or low wall that once rested in front of this access may have been intended to impede vision of the chamber interior.

The second space in Plaza 3c, to the east of the first, was smaller (7.5 by 14 m) and had white-painted interior walls. It was accessed at the extreme north end of the corridor. At one time this space had a second access in the south wall, which was later sealed. Another small passageway (2.4 by 2.8 m) was found near the west wall; however, it was partially destroyed, so it could not be determined whether it originally provided access. In the chamber's southeast corner, the floor had been torn open and a large hole filled with sacrificed human remains (Figure 9.29). As mentioned above, these skeletons had been defleshed, but the tendons and ligaments were left intact, maintaining their articulation (Verano 1998).

The second space had also been impacted by natural phenomena such as El Niño events that occurred following the deposition of the sacrificed bodies, similar to

FIGURE 9.29. Human remains in Plaza 3c. Photograph by John Verano.

those recorded by Bourget in Plaza 3a (1997, 1998). The layers consisted of sand deposits, rain sediment layers, and new sand deposits. In the middle and northern parts of the space, at least two sand sedimentation levels contained skeletal remains with evidence of throat cuts at the second and third cervical vertebrae. Some skeletons showed traces of having been defleshed. Their flexed positions, along with other features, suggest that this group differed from the group placed in the floor pit, relating instead, to some degree, to the group in Plaza 3a. All of Plaza 3c had been refilled with sand and covered by an adobe floor, which formed the platform level that provided access to Plaza 3a and Platform I when the construction of Building A began.

PLAZA 3B

Plaza 3b appears to have been in the form of an L. It was reached through the same corridor described for Plaza 3c. To the west of the corridor was a space whose western wall adjoined the eastern wall of Building C. The exterior of this wall was plastered and painted white. Later, a wall was added along with a tall bench in the manner of a step, corresponding to the construction of Buildings A and B. It is during this time that the facade was decorated with polychrome murals.

The most significant architectural elements of Plaza 3b are two chambers (Figure 9.28). Chamber I, on the west side of the plaza, measures approximately 7.3 by 3.8 m. Only its west wall and the corners of the north and south walls remain, so it is unclear whether the east wall shared with that of Chamber II. The west wall of Chamber I is 60 cm wide and stands up to 2 m above the latest floor level. The walls were redressed with a coarse layer of clay.

Chamber II, measuring 6.5 by 4 m, is composed of four massive walls up to 1 m thick. The interior and exterior wall faces were all coated in a fine white plaster, which evinces layers of redressing. An 80 cm wide access was located in the north. Behind the access were a series of benches and low walls; however, destruction by looter trenches unfortunately impedes the reconstruction of these elements. One thin wall form, which projects from the northeast corner of the chamber, closes the passage up to the east part of the plaza. The only access to this space, then, was by a small corridor (1.10 m wide) between the west side of Chamber II and Platform I.

Based on the architectural sequence, the construction of Chamber II and the first architectural floor appear to correspond with Building C and Platform I. The second floor and construction of Chamber I, along with the arrangement of elements behind Chamber II, are associated with Buildings A or B (Gamonal 1998:80). A thick layer of sediment, again suggesting the occurrence of strong rains, is associated with the presence of crude, broken sculptured effigies representing prisoners (Uceda and Tufinio 2003: fig. 20.11). These sculptures are similar to those described by Bourget for Plaza 3a (Bourget 1998).

PLAZA 3A

Plaza 3a is to the east of Plazas 3b and 3c, and forms the southern extreme of Plaza 2. It was initially an L-shaped room whose south wall corresponded with that of Plaza 3b and measured 54 m in length. From this wall, another wall projected eastward up to 48 m. The north wall measured 33 m and united with the east wall of Plaza 2. The space that remained between the east wall of Plaza 2 and the north wall of Plaza 3a could well have corresponded to the access to Plaza 3a during the construction of Building C of Platform I. It seems that Platform II was constructed along with new adjacent, internal walls only after the sealing of Plaza 3c and the south part of Plaza 2. The new access could have been affected by the west wall and by a new floor addition. The peculiar element of this plaza is the presence of a rocky outcrop that forms part of the architectural space and may have been perceived as a sort of "captured mountain" (Figure 9.30). The presence of natural formations within the architecture of later cultures such as the Inca is well known, and usually is associated with sacred functions and ritual activities.

The excavations of Plaza 3a were directed by Steve Bourget (1997, 1998). The central objective of the excavations was to examine a possible functional and ritual relation between the huaca and Cerro Blanco. The presence of the rocky outcrop was hypothesized to be a replica of Cerro Blanco used for the execution of ceremonies and rituals of great importance for Moche society. The results of these excavations supported this hypothesis and brought to light the first arena of Moche human sacrifices.

Following the excavations in 1995 and 1996, it was

FIGURE 9.30. View of Plaza 3a. Photograph by author.

possible to establish a sequence of natural events from the sediments of clay and sand, as well as cultural events from the skeletal and material remains. The stratigraphic sequence was composed of eleven layers of alternating sedimentation and accumulation of fine sand. The cultural events associated with these natural layers were recorded by Bourget (1998:49–52).

Evidence of the first cultural event was found in the Sand 4 layer. It consisted of the burial of three children and an adult male, apparently all of whom were wrapped in textiles. A layer of thick sand followed, which was later covered by a layer of sediment (Sediment 4) resulting from an episode of fierce rains. No cultural remains were recorded for the Sediment 4 layer; however, according to Bourget (1998), the distinction between Sediment 4 and Sand 3 was not completely clear. The next layer of sedimentation (Sediment 3) contained evidence of sacrifices related to El Niño events.

Following the events associated with the Sediment 3 layer, the Moche excavated part of this arena and the west wall to form a pit. This action appears to have been contemporaneous with the sacrifices found in Sand 2, based on the presence and distribution of crude ceramic statuettes. Much later, a new sediment layer (Sediment 2) was produced by the erosion of the surrounding adobe walls during another major rain event. Sediment 2 was associated with another layer of sacrifices connected to the natural phenomenon (Figure 9.31). A final sacrificial event took place in the uppermost layer of aeolian sand deposition (Sand 1). With this event, the occupation of Plaza 3a ended, marking the abandonment of this monumental sector.

Discussion

From the archaeological contexts in Plazas 3a, 3b, and 3c at Huaca de la Luna, I have identified a series of emblematic elements that appear in complex scenes of Moche iconography. First I identified a scene that presents two central types of figures, which I have labeled Worshippers and Coca-Takers. One particular ornament appears as part of some warriors' attire in both sculpted and painted representations (Figures 9.8, 9.9). These same warrior figures wore other objects that have been identified as garments or headdresses worn by diverse individuals in scenes related both to the Worshippers and Coca-Takers, as well as to human sacrifice.

Based on this information, I will focus the remaining discussion on three central objectives. The first is to identify the individuals and their roles in Moche society. The second is to understand the Moche ceremonies in which these individuals interacted. The final objective is to explore how their participation in the ceremonies might have permitted social mobility, which may have addressed the social conflicts of the time.

IDENTIFICATION OF THE INDIVIDUALS AND THEIR ROLES IN MOCHE SOCIETY

So far, I have offered only broad interpretations of the coca-taking scenes without noting the formal differ-

ences between the represented individuals. Nevertheless, I have demonstrated that the individuals have distinct characteristics not only in their dress, but also in their actions. For example, the Worshippers never ingest the contents of the small containers, and the Coca-Takers never adopt the supplicating pose of the Worshippers. From this perspective, I propose that the two types of individuals had different statuses and social roles. Given their type of dress and adornments, the Worshippers were Moche elite. The feline pendant that they carry or sport hanging from the shoulder does not constitute an element of dress. From their association with other emblematic elements in the scene, these individuals appear to have had the role of carrying the emblematic elements for their consecration, to be used in particular rituals or ceremonies.

The Coca-Takers are the individuals depicted using

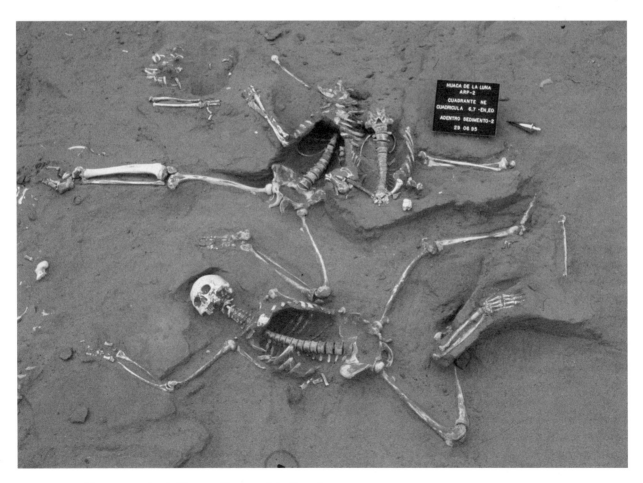

FIGURE 9.31. Human remains in Plaza 3a. Photograph by Steve Bourget.

the containers, which may have held lime used to extract the alkaloids of the coca leaf, as Donnan maintains (1978:117), or a mixture of datura (*Datura stramonium*), as Bourget maintains (1994a:73). Regardless, ingesting such substances remains an element of the curing and divination practices of shamans on the north coast. The actions of the represented individuals suggest that they participated in a ritual similar to those performed by modern shamans. They, too, may have ingested halluci-nogenic substances to allow them to enter a trance, to have visions, or to see another world.

What, then, is the role of the bicephalus arc in these scenes? Diverse interpretations have been given to its form and meaning. Nevertheless, these do not pres-ent conflicts in understanding since it is very probable that, for the Moche, the bicephalus arc was polysemic, occurring in diverse contexts and with differing actors. In one scene, the actors reside below the bicephalus arc, while in another they appear outside of it (Figures 9.1, 9.2). In the first scene, if the Worshippers are members of the elite, their relation with the world of the ances-tors and the celestial bodies would explain their pres-ence in the interior of the bicephalus arc. In this case, the world of the divine is represented; the shamans and officials (Coca-Takers) would be preparing for a moment of ecstasy that will take them to the world of the ancestors. In the second case, the presence of the Coca-Takers within the bicephalus arc suggests that after they ingested the hallucinogenic substances, they became part of the celestial world.

The so-called lime containers and spatulas are associ-ated only with the individuals dressed in large tunics. These same individuals are associated with scenes of prisoners, where they appear to be instructing or prepar-ing the captives (Kutscher 1983: figs. 120, 123). They are also associated with ritual acts and are never depicted in scenes with individuals of high-status dress. If these tunicked figures were in charge of the rituals, they may be initiated subjects who possess the power to be in two cosmic planes or to enter into contact with them.

The headdresses, clothing, ornaments, and feline effigy constitute the dress of other diverse individuals, both elite individuals and warriors. Such items suggest that these emblematic elements were socially significant in various ways. First, they may have signified the role and function that these individuals acquired through

blood. The individuals may have carried the emblems publicly to display their rank, and upon their death, the objects accompanied them in burial.

On the other hand, the objects may not have been acquired through sacrificial rites. Rather, they may have been used by members of the elite to interact in specific ceremonies intended to legitimize their authority. In that case, the emblems would have been placed in burial contexts to establish the individuals' rank and function in the world of the ancestors. A combination of these two hypotheses, however, may be justified. In other words, certain individuals may have used such emblems to express their social rank (such as the Lord of Sipán). When the objects were carried by simple warriors, however, they may have signified the status acquired by fulfilling this special role within the community. In other words, the emblems signified a form of social recognition. Could such recognition have some larger significance?

THE MOCHE CEREMONIES AND SOCIAL MOBILITY

Moisés Tufinio and I have previously attempted to reconstruct some of the ceremonies that could have occurred in Huaca de la Luna, based on the recovered archaeological contexts (Uceda 1997; Uceda and Tufinio 2003). Our intention was to corroborate whether or not form and function were intimately related across the different spaces. The ideology and authority of Moche society and elites were founded on a system of ceremonies and rituals. Understanding this system and its mechanics thus provides a better understanding of how the Moche articulated and constructed authority. In other words, how did the Moche social and economic structures function?

Therefore, I will conclude by reconstructing once again the possible ceremonies and rituals that occurred in Huaca de la Luna—their actors, forms, and func-tions. I will work from the archaeological contexts, for example, to offer an explanation for the functions of the grand passageways while cross-comparing the contexts with the iconographic data. In previous works, I inter-preted the scene of coca-offering as a propitiatory act that could have served as an initiation to or a termi-nation of the ritual of human sacrifice. The evidence presented here, however, indicates that the coca-offering ceremony was composed of various rituals. It would be initiated by supplication and the presentation of the emblematic offerings, which were used in the remaining acts of the ceremony. The ritual of sacrifice would then take place at the end of the ritual process.

I would argue that this concluding ritual included two different types, which other studies have distinguished: sacrifices to the gods of offerings presented as the best of the society, and sacrifices of the punished (Hocquenghem 1987). The Plaza 3a remains correspond to what Anne Marie Hocquenghem has denoted as the punished (skeletons with evidence of torture, dismemberment of arms and legs, decapitation, lapidation, and so on) (Hocquenghem 1987, this volume). In contrast, the skeletal remains of Plaza 3c are complete, with evidence that the individuals had their throats cut and were intentionally defleshed. In a previous work (Uceda and Paredes 1994), I suggested that the grand decorated patio of the lower level of the platform could have been the scene of throat-cutting rituals. This patio and sacrificial act may have been reserved for one of the most important rituals represented in Moche iconography: the presentation of sacrificed blood before the gods (Donnan 1978).

It is necessary here to present a sequential order for one of the documented ceremonies in archaeological contexts, one associated with the cult of fertility. Much of the structure and ideology of Moche rulership is based on the cult of fertility in its two modalities: (1) agrarian fertility, to guarantee the economic development of the society; and (2) social fertility, to guarantee the reproduction of leaders. These modalities correspond with research presented by other scholars who propose that Moche iconography represents a series of related ceremonies and rituals (Hocquenghem 1987; Bourget 1994a). In this sense I intend to give a select group of iconographic scenes an order of succession based on a logical sequence of events evinced by the archaeological contexts. Although I shall reference a limited number of scenes, it remains possible that others not considered here also form part of this ceremony.

The actions would proceed as follows:

1. The battle (ritual or conquest) with the intent to capture the defeated.
2. The procession of naked captives before the huaca, the gods, and the priests.
3. The preparation or delivery of offerings.
4. The sacrifice (extraction of blood).
5. The presentation of blood and the act of fertilization.

Many scenes in Moche iconography represent the capture of defeated warriors in battle, yet debate surrounds whether or not the captured warriors derived from an expansionistic military battle or from a Moche ritual battle (Quilter, this volume). I would argue that, based on the role of the captive warriors as eventual sacrificial offerings, and the results of recent mtDNA testing of sacrificial remains (Shimada et al. 2005; Shimada, this volume), it is more plausible that the captured warriors were taken during a ritual battle between groups of the same society. Ethnographic examples of such battles exist in the southern sierra of Peru. Based on the iconography, these battles took place outside of the huacas, most likely on the desert plains. The defeated were then stripped of their warrior garb, bound with ropes, and escorted by the victors back to the huaca.

Several painted scenes illustrate the procession of the conquerors and the conquered. This scene is also represented on the frontispiece of Huaca Cao Viejo in the Chicama Valley (Franco, Gálvez, and Vásquez 1994). Such a position suggests that the plaza in front of the huaca was the final destination of this procession. It further assumes that the remainder of the ceremony developed within the building, where the prisoners would have been directed to specific rooms, such as those in the interior of Plaza 3b.

The preparation and indoctrination of the sacrificial victims likely occurred in specific localities, probably near the sacrificial arena. I propose that this location may have been the corner room of the patio with reliefs, on the principal platform of Huaca de la Luna. The preparation was likely handled by a priest through the use of hallucinogens and other psychotropic elements, which would have predisposed the sacrificial victims to their immolation. The sacrifices related to the cult of fertility would be those of Plaza 3c, found within the excavated floor pit. The skeletal remains of Plaza 3a correspond to a different ceremony; many of these individuals passed through varying lengths of captivity before being sacrificed, and some individuals show healing fractures that indicate a passage of more than two weeks (Verano

1998). The different characteristics of the sacrifices have various implications. First, it differentiates the rituals in Plaza 3a from those of the throat-cutting found in Plaza 3c. Second, it may suggest an unequal treatment of captured victims from different ethnic backgrounds. Further detailed studies are needed before exploring this line of inquiry.

Throat-cutting was the penultimate act, and one probably less public if it occurred in the patio with reliefs. The dimensions of this patio, although large, are considerably smaller than those of Plaza 1. The aim of this ritual was to extract blood from the victim for collection in a cup. The iconographic scenes clearly represent this act, with priest figures and zoo-anthropo-morphic individuals always in direct association.

Finally, the cup of the sacrificial victim's blood was carried by the Priestess and presented before a person of high rank. Alva and Donnan (1993) identify this figure as having status equal to that of the Lord of Sipán. This individual would drink the blood, or possibly offer it to the sea or earth, as in later Inca ritual, completing the cycle of this ceremony. This final act likely took place on the upper terrace of Huaca de la Luna, overlooking Plaza 1 (Uceda 2001). By completing the ritual, both agrarian and social fertility would have been guaranteed.

I would like to conclude, however, with one last observation and proposition. The warriors who carry the pendant effigies were treated with particular significance. If the individuals participating in ritual battle were professional Moche warriors, and of a lower status than the Moche elite, it would appear that some social groups had distinctly differentiated access to the fruits of labor. Following this premise, it would appear that the pendant effigy worn by the victorious warrior may have conferred upon him a series of privileges, as occurs in other societies under similar conditions. Victory in battle may have served as a format permitting social mobility, prizing those members of society who participated in sacrificial acts. It may have further provided a way to reduce the stress created by different social classes, while also encouraging the cohesion of Moche society as a whole.

The information and theories presented in this analysis are in need of continued critique. Nevertheless, they offer possibilities for future analyses and discussion, regarding not only the significance of the iconography, but also the tools used for examining and approaching archaeological contexts.

Note

1. To date, six successive architectural projects have been identified on the Huaca de la Luna main platform (Platform I). Each of these projects, overlapping the previous one, would have functioned as a ritual system of interment of the previous building in order to renovate it and symbolically reproduce the authority of the rulers (Uceda and Canziani 1998).

Bibliography

Alva, Walter
1994   *Sipán*. Colección Culturas y Artes del Perú, Lima.

Alva, Walter, and Christopher B. Donnan
1993   *Royal Tombs of Sipán*. Fowler Museum of Cultural History, University of California, Los Angeles.

Benson, Elizabeth P.
1987   Bats in South American Iconography. *Andean Past* 1:165–190.

Bourget, Steve
1994a   Bestaire sacre et flore magique: Ecologie rituelle de l'iconographie de la culture Mochica, côte nord du Perou. Ph.D. dissertation, Department of Anthropology, University of Montreal.

1994b   Los sacerdotes a la sombra del Cerro Blanco y del arco bicéfalo. *Revista del Museo de Arqueología, Antropología e Historia* 5:81–125. Universidad Nacional de Trujillo, Perú.

1997   Las excavaciones en la Plaza 3a. In *Investigaciones en la Huaca de la Luna 1995*, 51–59. Edited by Santiago Uceda, Elías Mujica, and Ricardo Morales. Universidad Nacional de Trujillo, Perú.

1998   Excavaciones en la Plaza 3a y en la Plataforma II de la Huaca de la Luna durante 1996. In *Investigaciones en la Huaca de la Luna 1996*, 43–64. Edited by Santiago Uceda, Elías Mujica, and Ricardo Morales. Universidad Nacional de Trujillo, Perú.

Castillo, Luis Jaime
1991   Narrations in Moche Art. Master's thesis, Department of Archaeology, University of California, Los Angeles.

Castillo, Luis Jaime, and Christopher B. Donnan
1994   La ocupación Moche de San José de Moro, Jequetepeque. In *Moche: Propuestas y perspectivas*, 93–146. Actas del Primer Coloquio sobre la Cultura Moche, Trujillo, 12 a 16 de abril de 1993. Edited by Santiago Uceda and Elías

Mujica. Travaux de l'Institut Français d'Études Andines 79. Universidad Nacional de la Libertad, Trujillo, Perú.

Donnan, Christopher B.

1978.   *Moche Art of Peru: Pre-Columbian Symbolic Communication*. Museum of Cultural History, University of California, Los Angeles.

Donnan, Christopher B., and Luis Jaime Castillo

1992   Finding the Tomb of a Moche Priestess. *Archaeology* 45 (6):38–42.

1994   Excavaciones de tumbas de sacerdotisas moche en San José de Moro, Jequetepeque. In *Moche: Propuestas y perspectivas*, 415–425. Actas del Primer Coloquio sobre la Cultura Moche, Trujillo, 12 a 16 de abril de 1993. Edited by Santiago Uceda and Elías Mujica. Travaux de l'Institut Français d'Études Andines 79. Universidad Nacional de la Libertad, Trujillo, Perú.

Donnan, Christopher B., and Donna McClelland

1999   *Moche Fineline Painting: Its Evolution and Its Artists*. Fowler Museum of Cultural History, University of California, Los Angeles.

Franco, Régulo, César Gálvez, and Segundo Vásquez

1994   Arquitectura y decoración mochica en la Huaca Cao Viejo, Complejo El Brujo: Resultados preliminares. In *Moche: Propuestas y perspectivas*, 147–180. Actas del Primer Coloquio sobre la Cultura Moche, Trujillo, 12 a 16 de abril de 1993. Edited by Santiago Uceda and Elías Mujica. Travaux de l'Institut Français d'Études Andines 79. Universidad Nacional de la Libertad, Trujillo, Perú.

Gamonal, Antonio

1998   Excavación en el sector suroeste de la Plaza 3b de la Huaca de la Luna durante 1996. In *Investigaciones en la Huaca de la Luna 1996*, 75–81. Edited by Santiago Uceda, Elías Mujica, and Ricardo Morales. Universidad Nacional de Trujillo, Perú.

Hocquenghem, Anne Marie

1987   *Iconografía mochica*. Fondo Editorial de la Pontificia Universidad Católica del Perú, Lima.

Kutscher, Gerdt

1983   *Nordperuanische Gefässmalereien des Moche-Stils*. Verlag C. H. Beck, Munich.

Larco Hoyle, Rafael

2001   *Los Mochicas*. Museo Arqueológico Rafael Larco Herrera, Lima.

Lavallée, Danielle

1970   *Les represéntationes animales dans la céramique mochica*. Memoirs de l'Institut d'Ethnologie IV. Université de Paris.

Makowski, Krzysztof

1994   La figura del «oficiante» en la iconografía mochica:

¿Shaman o sacerdote? In *En el nombre del señor: Shamanes, demonios, y curanderos del norte del Perú*, 52–101. Edited by Luis Millones and Moisés Lemlij. Seminario Interdisciplinario de Estudios Andino, Lima.

1997   La guerra ritual. *Perú El Dorado* 9:62–71. PromPerú, Lima.

Montoya, María

1997   Excavaciones en la Plaza 3B. In *Investigaciones en la Huaca de la Luna 1995*, 61–66. Edited by Santiago Uceda, Elías Mujica, and Ricardo Morales. Universidad Nacional de Trujillo, Perú.

Orbegoso, Clorinda

1998   Excavaciones en el sector sureste de la Plaza 3c de la Huaca de la Luna durante 1996. In *Investigaciones en la Huaca de la Luna 1995*, 67–73. Edited by Santiago Uceda, Elías Mujica, and Ricardo Morales. Universidad Nacional de Trujillo, Perú.

Shimada, I., K. Shinoda, S. Bourget, W. Alva, and S. Uceda

2005   MtDNA Analysis of Mochica and Sicán Populations of Pre-Hispanic Peru. In *Biomolecular Archaeology: Genetic Approaches to the Past*. Edited by David Reed. Center for Archaeological Investigations, Southern Illinois University, Carbondale.

Uceda Castillo, Santiago

1997   El poder y la muerte en la sociedad moche. In *Investigaciones en la Huaca de la Luna 1995*, 177–188. Edited by Santiago Uceda, Elías Mujica, and Ricardo Morales. Universidad Nacional de Trujillo, Perú.

2001   El nivel alto de la Plataforma I de Huaca de la Luna: Un espacio multifuncional. *Arkinka, Revista de Arquitectura, Diseño y Construcción* 67:90–95.

Uceda, Santiago, and José Canziani

1998   Análisis de la sequencia arquitectónica y nuevas perspectivas de investigación en Huaca de la Luna. In *Investigaciones en la Huaca de la Luna 1996*, 139–158. Edited by Santiago Uceda, Elías Mujica, and Ricardo Morales. Universidad Nacional de Trujillo, Perú.

Uceda Castillo, Santiago, and Arturo Paredes

1994   Arquitectura y función de la Huaca de la Luna. *Masa* 6 (7):42–46. Instituto Nor Peruano de Desarollo Economico y Social (INDES), Trujillo, Perú.

Uceda, Santiago, and Moisés Tufinio

2003   El complejo arquitectónico religioso moche de Huaca de la Luna: Una aproximación a su dinámica ocupacional. In *Moche: Hacia el Final del Milenio*, Tome II, 179–228. Actas del Segundo Coloquio sobre la Cultura Moche, Trujillo, 1 al 7 de agosto de 1999. Edited by Santiago Uceda and Elías Mujica. Universidad Nacional de Trujillo and Pontificia Universidad Católica del Perú, Lima.

Verano, John W.

1998   Sacrificios humanos, desmembramientos y modificaciones culturales en restos osteológicos: Evidencias de las temporadas de investigación 1995–96 en la Huaca de la Luna. In *Investigaciones en la Huaca de la Luna 1996,* 159–171. Edited by Santiago Uceda, Elías Mujica, and Ricardo Morales. Universidad Nacional de Trujillo, Perú.

Verano, John W., and Moisés Tufinio

2003   Plaza 3c. In *Investigaciones en la Huaca de la Luna 2000.* Edited by Santiago Uceda, Elías Mujica, and Ricardo Morales. Universidad Nacional de Trujillo, Perú.

CHAPTER TEN

The Moche People
Genetic Perspective on Their Sociopolitical Composition and Organization

IZUMI SHIMADA, UNIVERSITY OF SOUTHERN ILLINOIS

KEN-ICHI SHINODA, NATIONAL SCIENCE MUSEUM, TOKYO

WALTER ALVA, MUSEO TUMBAS REALES DE SIPÁN

STEVE BOURGET, UNIVERSITY OF TEXAS AT AUSTIN

CLAUDE CHAPDELAINE, UNIVERSITY OF MONTREAL

SANTIAGO UCEDA, NATIONAL UNIVERSITY OF TRUJILLO

Abstract

Recent excavations of well-preserved Mochica sacrificial victims and burials have provided us with a unique opportunity to shed light on some outstanding demographic, social, and political issues of Mochica archaeology through mtDNA analysis. This chapter presents salient findings of a large-scale mtDNA study of Prehispanic populations that was initiated in 1999. Maternal kinship relationships, as well as haplotype composition and distribution, defined by mtDNA analysis both support and question the existing views concerning Mochica societies. Our study also illustrates the importance of sampling well-defined populations and situating mtDNA analysis within broader archaeological research for meaningful interpretations of the resulting genetic information.

One of the most persistent and distinguishing features of Moche archaeology has been its preoccupation with elite funerary practice and associated goods, rituals, and ideology, resulting in excavation of a relatively large number of well-preserved burials from various sites on the north coast. This chapter reports results of our ongoing, long-term mitochondrial DNA analysis of many of these burials. Together with archaeological evidence, the study aims to elucidate genetic and sociopolitical relationships predominantly among members of social elite of major Moche sites in the Lambayeque, Chicama, Moche, and Santa valleys. Although our north coast individuals are relatively homogenous compared to the genetic variability documented so far for the entire Andean area, we nonetheless see differences suggesting that elites in different valleys of the Moche domain pertained to discrete lineages. This chapter explores the implications of this and other findings in regard to archaeological conceptions of Moche sociopolitical organization and territorial expansion, sacrificial activities, and other issues.

Research Setting, Issues, and Aims

In this chapter, we discuss some of the salient findings of our ongoing archaeogenetic research of Prehispanic populations predominantly of coastal Peru. Archaeogenetic archaeology is a relatively new and rapidly growing field that uses analysis of ancient DNA extracted from excavated human remains to explore past kinship structures, relationships among diverse social and cultural groups, and population movements—areas that often elude traditional archaeological approaches (e.g., Renfrew and Boyle 2000:xix; Schurr 2000).

The project reported here grew out of a fruitful collaboration between Ken-ichi Shinoda, a physical anthropologist at the National Science Museum in Tokyo specializing in ancient DNA study, and Izumi Shimada, who explored kinship relationships among twenty-four individuals found in a 1,000-year-old Middle Sicán (a.k.a. Classic Lambayeque) elite shaft tomb at Huaca Loro in the mid La Leche Valley (Figure 10.1; Corruccini, Shimada, and Shinoda 2002; Shimada et al. 2004; Shimada et al. 2005). Underlying our decision to undertake a long-term multicultural study was a recognition that (1) since the mid-1980s, many well-preserved burials and sacrificial victims of diverse social positions and roles, time periods, and cultures have been excavated on the Peruvian coast, particularly the north coast; and (2) no systematic ancient DNA study of Prehispanic burials in Peru had yet been conducted (Shimada et al. 2005). In other words, we felt that there was a large untapped information source that could be exploited by ancient DNA analysis and thus sought collaboration of archaeologists who have excavated burials with well-defined contexts. We believe that, in spite of various serious drawbacks (to be discussed later), this analytical method holds considerable potential for shedding light on various unresolved demographic, social, and political issues in Andean archaeology.

We began our project with a number of specific research issues and objectives, and proceeded to collect samples from appropriate burials. In addition to establishing an ancient DNA data bank on major Prehispanic north coast populations, we aimed to (1) test the evolutionary model of Moche sociopolitical organization, which postulates the coexistence of competing polities that shared basic religious beliefs, an art style, and a changing geopolitical situation (Shimada 1994a, 1994b), and (2) to elucidate the nature of the relationship (including biological) between the Gallinazo and Moche populations that coexisted for centuries over much of the north coast. Subsumed within these objectives is our concern with identifying the groups depicted in Moche art who are represented in paired combat.

The Moche sociopolitical organization has received much attention, at least from the days of Larco (1938) and Kutscher (1955), without any clear resolution (see, e.g., Bawden 1989; Canziani 2003; Chapdelaine 2003; Quilter 2002; Shimada 1994a, 1994b). Quilter (2002) characterizes the pertinent literature in terms of three basic positions: the single expansive state centered at the site of Moche in the Moche Valley, northern and southern Moche polities, and individual valley-wide autonomous polities. These models, however, should not be seen as mutually exclusive; any one of them may be nested within another or represent a phase of the long and dynamic Moche political history. We do concur with Quilter in noting that none of these models has been adequately tested. We believe our ancient DNA study can offer valuable data in testing these models. For example, in the case of the valley-level, autonomous polities, we would expect to find a relatively high internal genetic homogeneity among elite members of each valley polity that was concerned with the establishment and

maintenance of its identity and legitimacy. That same situation should also result in notable genetic differences among contemporaneous elite groups of different valleys. A significant genetic overlap, on the other hand, might reflect frequent marriage exchange and alliance, or the same lineage in possession of political leadership in a number of valleys. Analysis of ancient DNA can also test the presence of external administrators in provinces—as hypothesized by the single, expansive state model—because such administrators would be expected to differ at the haplotype level from local elites (see below). In tandem, strontium isotope ($87Sr/86Sr$) analysis of bone samples and trace element characterization of associated grave goods could differentiate where the deceased grew up and artifacts were made, respectively.

What about the Gallinazo-Moche relationship? This is a topic that has received only sporadic attention since the days of Bennett (1939, 1950) and Larco (1945; e.g., Fogel 1993; Shimada and Maguiña 1994; Ubbelohde-Doering 1983; Wilson 1988), again without any clear answers. But the coexistence of the Gallinazo and Moche in time and space, spanning the entire period of the Moche political life and domain, from the Piura to the Casma Valley, seems relatively well established. It is in regard to their sociopolitical relationship that we witness divergent opinions, from a Moche military conquest and political subjugation of the Gallinazo people in the Virú and Santa valleys (e.g. Collier 1955; Wilson 1988), to their tense coexistence to share limited resources (Proulx 1982). Shimada has suggested that—at least in the Lambayeque region—the Moche and Gallinazo constituted two competing, asymmetrical moieties, with the latter being socially and politically subordinate to the former, at least during the Moche V phase (Shimada 1994a; Shimada and Maguiña 1994). Thus, the regional Gallinazo population is seen to have been relocated to the urban settlement of Pampa Grande to serve as a major labor force. Despite the persistent use of the term Gallinazo, the nagging question that Ubbelohde-Doering (1949, 1957, 1967, 1983) posed and struggled to answer remains: Was the population represented by the Gallinazo style biologically or ethnically distinct from the Moche, or were these two populations two different sociopolitical divisions of a single pan-north coast population? Ancient DNA analysis can contribute to the resolution of this persistent question.

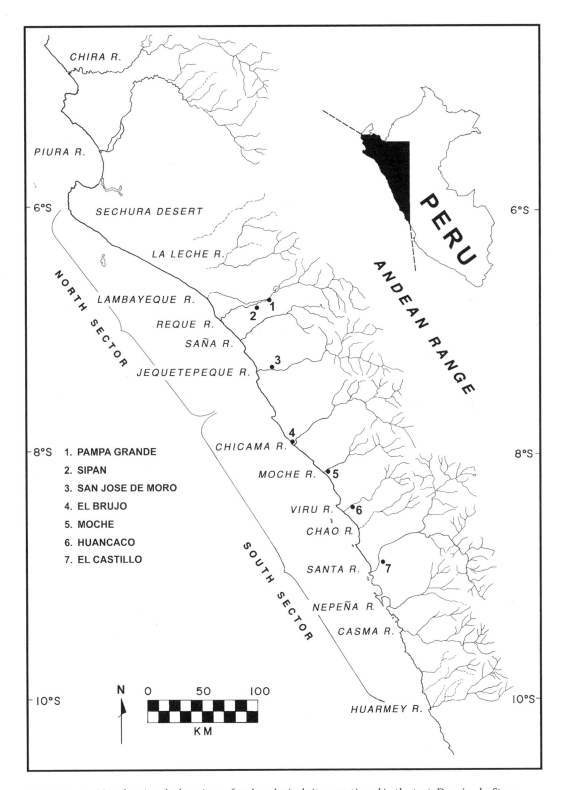

FIGURE 10.1. Map showing the locations of archaeological sites mentioned in the text. Drawing by Steve Mueller and Izumi Shimada.

MtDNA Analysis

Ancient DNA analysis is only one of various methods available for exploring genetic relationships among excavated human remains. Its rising popularity owes largely to its superior discriminatory power over other methods, such as those based on blood groups and other genetically determined markers derived from living populations (Renfrew 2000).

The specific laboratory protocol used by Shinoda is described elsewhere (Shimada et al. 2005). For a general characterization of the technical details of ancient DNA analysis, the reader is referred to various publications cited here (e.g., Kaestle and Horsburgh 2002; O'Rourke, Hayes, and Carlyle 2000; Pääbo 1999; Stone 2000; Sykes and Renfrew 2000). Our discussion of this analytical method will be limited to its underlying principles, pertinent concepts, and potential limitations to be kept in mind as we consider the cultural significance of their results.

Deoxyribonucleic acid, or DNA, is the double-stranded molecule that encodes genetic information for all life. Weak bonds between base pairs of nucleotides hold it together. The four nucleotides in DNA contain the bases adenine, cytosine, guanine, and thymine, denoted by the letters A, C, G, and T, respectively. Most ancient DNA studies focus on DNA found in mitochondria (Figures 10.2–10.4), called mitochondrial DNA or mtDNA for short. Human mtDNA is a small particle in the cell cytoplasm. It is a circular body consisting of only about 16,500 base pairs (Figures 10.3, 10.4). This com-

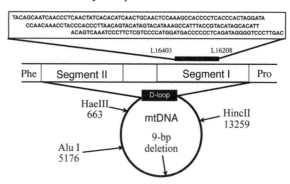

FIGURE 10.3. Schematic drawing showing the D-loop, the highly variable segment of mtDNA that is the focus of mtDNA analysis. Prepared by Ken-ichi Shinoda.

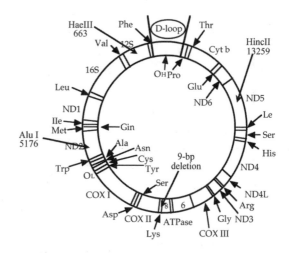

FIGURE 10.4. Schematic drawing showing the human mtDNA genome, with the approximate locations of the four mtDNA markers and D-loop region. Prepared by Ken-ichi Shinoda.

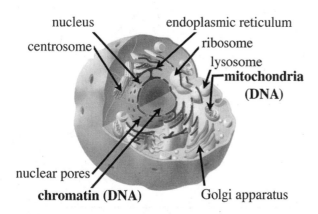

FIGURE 10.2. Schematic drawing of a human cell showing the location of mitochondria. Drawing by Ken-ichi Shinoda.

pares with the some three billion base pairs contained in nuclear DNA (nDNA).

There are various good reasons why archaeogenetic studies have focused on mtDNA. For one, nDNA degrades quite readily, and thus its analysis generally cannot be applied to skeletons that have been buried for a substantial period of time, perhaps over 100 years or so (e.g., Brown and Brown 1992). Furthermore, while nDNA occurs only twice per cell, mtDNA is present in many copies, up to perhaps a thousand per cell. Those two factors translate into a much greater chance of recovering mtDNA than nDNA. Another key feature is that mtDNA does not undergo genetic recombination, the process by which chromosomes shuffle their genes every generation to produce potentially advantageous new combinations. Recombination, which complicates the task of tracing kinship relationships, does not occur with mtDNA (Sykes and Renfrew 2000:14). Yet another important feature is the relatively high frequency at which mutations occur in mtDNA. Genetic variation due to mutation is critical for differentiating individuals and tracing their kinship ties. Without such variation, the task is very difficult. It is estimated that the rate of mutation in mtDNA is "perhaps 20 times faster than in nuclear DNA" (Sykes and Renfrew 2000:10). The "D-loop" or the "control region" (Figures 10.3, 10.4), with some 1,000 base pairs, is the fastest-changing segment of mtDNA, making it "by far the most variable stretch of DNA" (ibid.); therefore, mtDNA analysis focuses on defining the sequence of this highly variable segment.

A key fact to remember in assessing the results of any mtDNA study is that mtDNA is maternally inherited. An individual inherits all of his or her mtDNA from his or her mother, who in turn has inherited it from her mother, and so on. Paternal linkage remains undefined in mtDNA studies. Y chromosomes may be studied toward this end if nDNA can be successfully recovered (e.g., Dudar, Waye, and Saunders 2003). As noted above, however, nDNA does not preserve well, limiting the general applicability of Y chromosome analysis.

There are other limitations and difficulties involved in mtDNA analysis (e.g., Brown and Brown 1992; Kaestle and Horsburgh 2002; O'Rourke, Hayes, and Carlyle 2000; Renfrew 1998). For example, it requires costly specialized equipment and a strictly sterile laboratory facility, as well as much rigor and time, largely due to the less

than ideal condition of the samples, minute quantities of surviving genetic material, and potential contamination in field and laboratory settings.

Challenges posed by degradation and contamination of genetic material cannot be overstated. DNA in living tissues such as bone and hair degrades after death with the passage of time. Thus, DNA extracted from ancient materials is considered to be in low concentration and degraded condition. We must keep in mind the possibility that the original sequences may even have changed due to the aging of the DNA. At the same time, often a sufficient amount of mtDNA can be extracted from a single tooth, an important consideration given the destructive nature of ancient DNA analysis.

Contamination from modern DNA, including those involved in excavation or laboratory work, is a serious and pervasive problem. Ideally, two or more independent laboratories analyze the same sample and compare their results for greater reliability (Kaestle and Horsburgh 2002). Shinoda has established such an arrangement with Noboru Adachi of the Graduate School of Medicine of Tohoku University in Sendai, Japan, and Sloan Williams at the University of Illinois at Chicago. In our study, we have adopted a conservative strategy of excluding any suspected false positive results stemming from contamination with contemporary DNA (Lawlor et al. 1991), as well as other questionable data (e.g., Kolman and Tuross 2000). For our mtDNA study, a well-preserved tooth was extracted and used from each individual since teeth are relatively abundant, easy to sample, and form an effective natural barrier to external DNA contamination, among other reasons (Figures 10.5–10.7) (Shimada et al. 2004:378; Shimada et al. 2005).

Thus far, we have sampled 16 individuals from Sipán in the Lambayeque Valley, 73 from the sacrificial setting of Plaza 3a and other locations atop the Huaca de la Luna mound and the nearby Urban Zone at the site of Moche, 15 from the Huaca Cao Viejo mound and its vicinity (El Brujo) in the Chicama Valley, 9 from Huancaco in the Virú Valley, and, most recently, 11 from El Castillo in the Santa Valley. This is a total of 124 Moche burials from five sites in five different valleys within the Moche domain.

Our intent has been to sample as many as possible well-preserved burials with good contextual data that represent different time periods, geographical areas,

Step 1

The maxillar and mandibular teeth were examined and a single well-preserved tooth was extracted from each individual. The samples were ground to a fine powder in a press machine.

Step 2

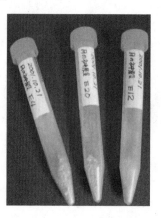

DNA was extracted under sterile conditions using disposable and ultraviolet irradiated instruments.

FIGURE 10.5. Summary graphic presentation of our mtDNA analytical procedure, Steps 1 and 2. Prepared by Ken-ichi Shinoda.

Step 3

PCR was performed in 25μl reaction volumes containing 1.5 units Taq polymerase, 200 μM of each deoxynucleoside triphosphate, 20 pM of each primer, 160 μg/ml of bovine serum albumin (BSA) as stabilizers, buffer supplied by the manufacturer and 5 μl of recovered DNA.

Typically 40 cycles of amplification were carried out, with each cycle consisting of denaturation at 96°C for 1 minute, annealing at 56°C for 1 minute, and extension at 72°C for 1 minute. Amplifications of region V were annealed at 59°C.

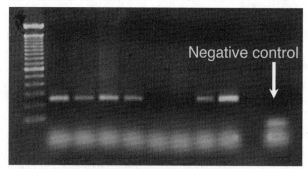

Gel electrophoretic analysis of PCR products

FIGURE 10.6. Summary graphic presentation of our mtDNA analytical procedure, Step 3. Prepared by Ken-ichi Shinoda.

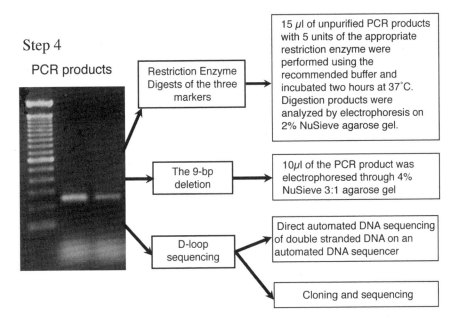

FIGURE 10.7. Summary graphic presentation of our mtDNA analytical procedure, Step 4. Prepared by Ken-ichi Shinoda.

genders, ages, and social positions. We have been reasonably successful in this regard, though social elites remain overrepresented in our sample. But due to the modern contamination and degradation of genetic materials that we described earlier, sampling, however carefully designed, does not assure good results. The rate of successful recovery and determination of mtDNA sequence varies a good deal from one site to the next, or even within one site. For example, of the 53 individuals from Huaca de la Luna we sampled in 1999 (predominantly sacrificial victims in Plaza 3a; Bourget 2001), 45 yielded sufficient DNA, of which 43 were successfully typed, translating into unusually high DNA recovery and sequencing rates of 84.9 percent and 81.1 percent, respectively. In contrast, of the 13 individuals from the Urban Zone sampled in 2002, only 7, or 53.8 percent, were successfully sequenced. Furthermore, not surprisingly, of the 17 poorly preserved individuals from Plaza 3c, presumably sacrificial victims excavated by John Verano and his team, only 2 (16.8 percent rate) yielded sufficient DNA (Verano, this volume). These 2 individuals were typed, but we remain skeptical of their authenticity. None of the nine samples from Huancaco yielded a reliable sequence. Even good preservation does not

assure a higher rate of successful mtDNA sequencing if samples have been contaminated. Overall, even after carefully selecting for well-preserved teeth, our sequencing rate thus far is only about 50 percent.

Results and Implications of the MtDNA Analysis

With the above caveats and background knowledge, let us turn our attention to the available analytical results. For the site of Sipán, mtDNA sequences were established for ten of the sixteen individuals we sampled, including the Lord of Sipán (Tomb 1), the Old Lord of Sipán (Tomb 3), and the Priest (Tomb 2), already described by Alva (2001; Alva and Donnan 1993). These individuals can be classified into seven haplotypes according to their sequences. The largest haplotype group is composed of four individuals, while one individual each represents the remaining six haplotypes. The haplotype is not an easy concept to define, but for our purpose it can be simply thought of as a distinct DNA sequence defined in the D-loop of mtDNA. By definition, each haplotype has a unique series of base pairs. It can also be thought of as a set of genes that tend to be inherited as a group. A haplogroup corresponds to a major lineage cluster of similar haplotypes. It is generally agreed that most of the mtDNA from modern Amerindians can be traced to one of four maternal lineages (designated as A, B, C, and D) that have been well documented thus far among the ancient founders of New World populations (Schurr 2000; Schurr et al. 1990). Haplogroup X, which exists in North America, has not been documented in South America. Recent research, including our own, indicates that in Prehispanic times there were haplotypes that are different from those known among modern Amerindians (e.g., Easton et al. 1996; Ribeiro-Dos-Santos et al. 1996) and that additional haplogroups other than the four currently known were once present in South America (Shimada et al. 2004:378, 396).

The fact that four individuals at Sipán shared the same haplotype indicates that they were maternally related to each other. They are the Lord, the Old Lord, a young woman, and a young man who accompanied the Priest. This evidence serves as strong independent support for the view that Mound I at Sipán was a mausoleum for members of a regional elite family and close associates. A logical interpretation of the relationship between the Old Lord and the Lord would be that they were either two brothers, or cousins, or an uncle and a nephew. Given the significant stratigraphic difference between their tombs, they seem more likely to have been an uncle-nephew pair several generations removed.

Late Prehispanic myths of the central and north coast explain that male elites (i.e., *curacas* or *señores*), female elites, and commoners were derived from distinct stars or eggs (gold, silver, and copper; Calancha 1976 [1638]; Rostworowski 2001; Rowe 1948), implying the institutionalization of marked social differentiation. If this is any reflection of the earlier Moche social reality, then endogamy or even sibling or cousin marriage among Northern Moche elites in Lambayeque remains a strong possibility. Something akin to the differentiated access to metal that has been documented for the Middle Sicán culture (AD 900–1100; e.g., Shimada 1994c)—high karat gold, tumbaga (low karat gold-silver-copper alloys), and arsenical copper serving as the material symbols of high ranking elites, low ranking elites, and commoners—is already recognizable among the Sipán burials (Shimada 1999).

Endogamy is a custom that confined the choice of a mate to someone within one's social group. In this regard, it is notable that we did not find in the sampled

Sipán burials any linkage along the maternal line between individuals of the highest social "rank" and their associates, on the one hand, and those of the second "rank" and their inferred "retainers," on the other.

Two distinct generations of male rulers who are maternally related could come about in a number of ways. For example, ethnohistorical documents pertaining to the north coast (Rostworowski 1961, 2000:178; cf. Netherly 1990; Zevallos 1989) speak of the prevalent rule of succession "in which it was the brother of the deceased rather than his son who assumed power," and that this "process continued through to the last brother of that generation, before passing to the generation below" (Rostworowski 2000:178). Though the scenario is suggestive, it should be kept in mind that any attempt to equate this or any other theoretical rules with actual succession is difficult since the latter could have significantly diverged from the former for political, health, or other reasons.

MtDNA sequences of fifty-four and five Moche burials were determined from the sites of Moche and El Brujo, respectively. For the latter, only three determinations can be considered reliable. The situation at Huaca de la Luna (the site of Moche) is in a number of ways exceptional and requires scrutiny. As previously mentioned, not only do we have an unusually high rate of successful mtDNA typing, but more importantly, other than six individuals whose haplotype determinations may have been compromised by either DNA contamination or degradation, all the others (48: 19 sacrificial victims and 29 burials) have similar haplotypes that pertain to a single haplogroup, A. Because of this surprising result, Shinoda experimented with 16 randomly selected samples from the 48 that had already been typed once. He obtained very similar results, with 15 out of 16 pertaining to Haplogroup A and one to "Others."

How can we interpret this genetic homogeneity? Before we consider this question, we should clearly recognize the fact that our sample crosscut time and space; that is, it included burials in the Urban Zone that were clearly stratified and associated with ceramics spanning Moche III to Late Moche IV (estimated AD 450–700), as well as burials and sacrificial victims at and around Plaza 3a atop the Huaca de la Luna mound (e.g., Chapdelaine 2001, 2003; Tello, Armas, and Chapdelaine 2003). In terms of the associated grave goods and their iconographic imageries, one burial near Plaza 3a is thought to have been the sacrificer (Bourget and Newman 1998; Shimada et al. 2005).

One possible explanation of the aforementioned genetic homogeneity is that the local population(s) experienced a genetic bottleneck—a drastic reduction in number perhaps due to prolonged warfare, famine, or epidemics in the recent past. Yet there is no evidence that clearly supports these catastrophic possibilities. Perhaps the most elegant explanation for the observed genetic situation is that the sampled individuals (essentially social elite) from Huaca de la Luna and the Urban Zone come from a relatively closed (in the genetic sense) local population that practiced endogamy for at least several generations. That is to say, given that mtDNA is maternally inherited, its variability diminishes rapidly over time unless there is a considerable, and more or less regular, influx of genes from outside groups, such as the case of women coming in as marriage partners and perhaps establishing or reinforcing political alliances. Theoretically, an endogamous society could attain the observed level of haplogroup homogeneity in about four generations, or a span of 100 or fewer years. The inclusion of burials from different time periods in our study suggests that the inferred endogamy may have had a considerable time depth.

Our study raises a distinct possibility that, concurrent with the territorial expansion and political centralization of the Southern Moche polity at the site of Moche starting sometime during Moche II, the succession of power and marriage practices may have become increasingly formalized and centered on an ever narrowing circle of individuals who shared real or mythical descent. Concurrently, social mobility may have become increasingly limited over time. In addition to an increasing degree of genetic homogeneity, we would expect funerary treatment and goods to exhibit greater formalization and differentiation.

The identity of the Moche warriors and their captives or sacrificial victims has been long debated (e.g., Hocquenghem 1978; Quilter 2002; Shimada 1994a, 1994b). In this regard, Verano (2001a:116) summarized three plausible possibilities: (1) The ruling groups of different valleys of the north coast "may have competed against one another to obtain captives for their respective temples"; (2) "combat may have been arranged between different centers within a single valley or perhaps between different warrior societies at a single ceremonial/population center"; or (3) sacrificial victims may have been captured through combat with neighboring non-Mochica population(s).

Our mtDNA data also suggest that the sampled sacrificial victims pertained to the same closed population as the sacrificers and urban residents, or to a nearby population that shared the same founders or maintained regular bride exchange. The possibility that the sacrificial victims pertained to contemporaneous Cajamarca and Recuay societies centered in the adjacent upper valleys and highlands seems remote. Other lines of evidence in support of our view are presented elsewhere (Shimada et al. 2005). Here we emphasize that the Plaza 3a sacrificial victims were a very select group of warriors engaged in ritual battles (Bourget 2001; Verano 2001a, 2001b), and that there is a close relationship between the sacrificial site at Huaca de la Luna, on one hand, and ritual battles and sacrifices represented in Moche iconography, on the other. Donnan's 2001 study of Moche "portrait vessels" suggests that the sacrificed individuals were selected from within Moche society and that their lives were honored, if not celebrated, by the Moche themselves. In contrast to the widespread belief that ritual combat took place in a desert setting, it is hypothesized here that the ritual battles took place in Plaza 1, just on the north side of Platform I, with its surrounding murals of warriors, captured victims, and various supernatural (zoomorphic and anthropomorphic) "decapitators" (Shimada et al. 2005). In other words, the whole process of sacrificial rituals, including combat, was not only performed locally, but also with the close involvement of the local community.

The unique haplogroup composition of the sample from the site of Moche, taken together with that of Sipán, El Brujo, and El Castillo, suggests that elite members at these sites belonged to distinct lineages. For example, though only five of the fifteen sampled Moche burials from the Huaca Cao Viejo mound at El Brujo were successfully sequenced, we find that the three haplogroups A, B, and D are equally represented by one individual each. Two individuals pertain to "Others." On the other hand, Haplogroup D predominates (60 percent, six out of ten) among the Sipán individuals, with A, B, C, and "Others" occurring at 10 percent (*n*

= 1) each. Finally, of the ten Moche burials excavated at the site of El Castillo that we sampled, seven yielded DNA and sequenced with Haplogroups A and D, represented by one individual each, with five pertaining to "Others." Comparison of specific haplotypes identified within the samples from Moche and El Castillo shows that, although both contain haplotypes that pertain to Haplogroup A, they are nonetheless distinct from one another.

As a whole, the ancient DNA data that we have collected thus far lends support to the view that during much of Moche III and IV, what we collectively call Northern and Southern Moche polities were each in reality an aggregation of local polities that held control of one or a few contiguous valleys (Castillo and Donnan 1994; Shimada 1994a, 1994b, 1999) and that elites in the mid Lambayeque, lower Chicama, and lower Moche valleys are likely to have represented distinct lineages.

These working hypotheses regarding Moche sociopolitical organization and sacrificial rituals are based largely on the available mtDNA data. While the reliability of our mtDNA data has been tested through the repeated experiments described earlier, it sheds light only on maternal linkage among sampled individuals. Statistical analysis of the inherited dental traits of excavated individuals at the site of Moche by Sutter and Cortez (2005) suggests that the sacrificed individuals in Plaza 3a were derived from a group that is genetically distinct from that of burials excavated in the vicinity of Plaza 3a and in the Urban Zone. This discrepancy is not surprising given that we are comparing (1) nominal and ordinal data, and (2) unilaterally (maternal) and bilaterally (both maternal and paternal) determined features. Our previous comparison of mtDNA and dental trait data showed only limited agreement (Coruccini, Shimada, and Shinoda 2002; Williams, Chagnon, and Spielman 2002). One explanation that may account for both the mtDNA and dental trait data would be that the sacrificial victims represented a group that had splintered relatively recently from, or maintained bride exchange with, the population at the site of Moche.

In our effort to shed light on the Gallinazo-Moche relationship, fourteen Gallinazo and eleven Moche burials—excavated by the University of Montreal Santa Project directed by Claude Chapdelaine at the site of El Castillo in the Santa Valley—were sampled in the sum-

mer of 2003. Identification of their "cultural affiliation" was based on the style of associated ceramics. Noboru Adachi of the Tohoku University in the city of Sendai, Japan, successfully established the DNA sequence for four Moche burials, with three pertaining to Haplogroup A and one to Haplogroup D. Though DNA amplification was achieved for three additional Moche burials, their sequences suggest exogenous contamination and are thus excluded here. Among Gallinazo burials that were successfully sequenced, three belong to Haplogroup A, and one each to Haplogroups C and D.

Though the Huaca de la Luna and three of the El Castillo Moche samples pertain to Haplogroup A, these two groups differ at the more specific haplotype level, suggesting that they pertain to two different biological populations. At the same time, our knowledge of genetic variability for each group is still too limited to make any definitive judgments regarding the validity of the hypothesis that the sampled Moche population was composed of migrants from the site of Moche (Chapdelaine 2004). Our sample of the Moche population in the Santa Valley needs to be significantly increased. Furthermore, we cannot discount the possibility of Moche men interbreeding with local Gallinazo women. Given the relative preponderance of Haplogroup A among the sampled Gallinazo burials (whose sample size is again quite small) and the maternal inheritance indicated by mtDNA analysis, this possibility cannot be dismissed.

Generally speaking, our mtDNA data indicate that the sampled Moche and Gallinazo individuals were genetically quite similar to each other, raising the possibility that they were two different sociopolitical groups that belonged to a single biological population, or that they were two distinct ethnic groups that interbred with some regularity. Among the Gallinazo burials that pertain to Haplogroup A, one individual (Burial 159-3) had a haplotype identical to that of the Moche burials from El Castillo (Burials 43-1, 141-3, 211-8), and another (Burial 213-13) shares the haplotype that dominated the Huaca de la Luna sacrificed victims. One Gallinazo burial (213-14) had a unique haplotype that has not been found thus far among the Moche burials analyzed from various sites. In essence, our best chance of genetically differentiating Gallinazo and Moche individuals lies in haplotype comparison.

When viewed from a much broader perspective, both

the sampled Gallinazo and Moche individuals, with their predominance of Haplogroup A, resemble various modern lower Central American and North Andean populations that have been tested thus far. At the same time, the conspicuous absence of Haplogroup D clearly distinguishes the Gallinazo and Moche samples from the late Prehispanic and modern populations in the southern highlands of Peru and the South Andes (Figure 10.8; Shinoda et al. 2006; Bert et al. 2001; Merriwether, Rothhammer, and Ferrell 1994; Rodriguez-Delfin, Rubin-de-Celis, and Zago 1999).

We end with a note of caution. The small sample size (i.e., inadequate understanding of intra-population genetic variability) and the possibility of interbreeding mentioned earlier should be kept in mind in comparing the Moche and Gallinazo data for the Santa Valley.

Conclusions

The research issues that guided our ongoing mtDNA study of Prehispanic north coast populations—the nature of the Gallinazo-Moche relationship and Moche sociopolitical organization—call for long-term, problem-oriented research employing multiple analytical perspectives. In this chapter, we made a case for the relevance of ancient DNA study in this respect. This study has perhaps more than its share of limitations and

pitfalls, including those related to degradation of ancient DNA and its contamination with modern DNA, the difficulty of securing nDNA including Y-chromosome DNA (yDNA), and high analytical costs. At the same time, with judicious sample selection, this method can identify maternal kinship as demonstrated by the sample from Sipán. Systematic sampling of human remains from various contexts in time and space at Moche has resulted in the documentation of a genetically and perhaps socially closed elite community at this site. Given that the site of Moche often serves as the comparative basis for analysis and interpretation of the Moche culture as a whole, it behooves us all to keep in mind what appears to be the unique genetic and social composition (i.e., a relatively high proportion of social elite) and dynamics that our study documented.

In regard to the nature of the Moche sociopolitical organization, the available mtDNA data are still too limited to draw any definitive conclusions. We need many more samples, not only from the sites considered thus far, but also from sites at local and regional levels, so that we have a grasp of intra- and inter-population variability. Then we will be able to test the applicability of the ethnic, political, and territorial divisions between the north and south banks of north coastal valleys that ethnohistorical sources indicate for late Prehispanic

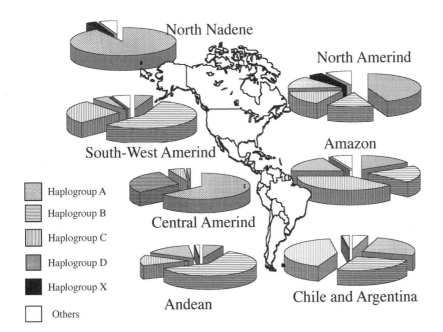

FIGURE 10.8. Frequencies of mtDNA haplogroups in Native American populations. Note the marked difference in the frequencies of Haplogroups A and D in the lower Central American and southern Andean highlands. Prepared by Ken-ichi Shinoda based on Schurr 2000, page 250, Figure 4.

times (Netherly 1984). We also need to be assured that the samples are comparable in regard to time period and social status. These considerations are particularly important to test the hypothesis that the establishment of the Moche hegemony in the Santa Valley was accompanied by a migration of Moche population from the site of Moche (Chapdelaine 2004). Given the basic genetic similarity of the Gallinazo and Moche populations in the valley that our study indicates, we need to consider the distinct possibility of some interbreeding between them, with the men of the politically dominant Moche taking local Gallinazo women as their consorts.

We are also making an assumption that the burials and sacrificial victims were not brought in from distant areas. With the accumulating evidence that points to a widespread and persistent practice of pre-interment curation and secondary burial in north coast prehistory (e.g., Franco, Gálvez, and Vásquez 1998; Hecker and Hecker 1992; Klaus 2003; Millaire 2002; Shimada et al. 2004), we cannot readily assume the validity of this assumption. Burial treatment and context must be scrutinized before we can consider the broader implications of mtDNA and other genetic data.

We end this chapter with the affirmation that ancient DNA study has much to contribute to illuminating the genetic, social, and political character of the Moche people vis-à-vis various synchronous populations on different parts of the north coast. The quality of the resultant knowledge, however, depends on the quality of our samples, and we take this opportunity to request the continuing collaboration of fellow Moche specialists in making well-preserved samples with good contextual data available for what is clearly a long-term and worthwhile research endeavor.

Acknowledgments

We are grateful to members of the Brüning Regional Archaeological Museum, El Brujo Complex Archaeological Project, Huaca de la Luna Project, and Yutaka Yoshii for their assistance in collection of the tooth samples used in the mtDNA analysis. We are indebted to Noboru Adachi, Associate Professor in the Department of Anatomy and Anthropology, Graduate School of Medicine, of Tohoku University in Sendai, Japan, for his analysis of the samples from El Castillo. Research by Shinoda was supported by a Grant-in Aid (No. 13575017) for Scientific Research from the Ministry of Education, Science, Sports and Culture, Japan. Richard Sutter generously shared with us unpublished findings from his dental trait analysis of human remains from the site of Moche.

Bibliography

Alva, Walter
2001   The Royal Tombs of Sipán: Art and Power in Moche Society. In *Moche: Art and Archaeology in Ancient Peru*, 222–245. Edited by Joanne Pillsbury. National Gallery of Art and Yale University Press, Washington, D.C.

Alva, Walter, and Christopher B. Donnan
1993   *Royal Tombs of Sipán*. Fowler Museum of Cultural History, University of California, Los Angeles.

Anderson, S., A. T. Bankier, B. G. Barrell, A. R. Coulson, J. Drouin, I. C. Eperon, D. P. Nierlich, B. A. Roe, F. Sanger, P. H. Schreir, A. J. Smith, R. Staden, and I. G. Young
1981   Sequence and Organization of the Human Mitochondrial Genome. *Nature* 290:457–465.

Bawden, Garth
1989   Andean State as a State of Mind. *Journal of Anthropological Research* 45:327–333.

Bennett, Wendell C.
1939   *The Archaeology of the North Coast of Peru*. Anthropological Papers 37, Part 1. American Museum of Natural History, New York.
1950   *The Gallinazo Group, Virú Valley, Peru*. Publications in Anthropology 43. Yale University, New Haven.

Bert, Francesc, Alfons Corella, Manel Gené, Alejandro Pérez-Pérez, and Daniel Turbón Borrega
2001   Major Mitochondrial DNA Haplotype Heterogeneity in Highland and Lowland Amerindian Population from Bolivia. *Human Biology* 73 (1):1–16.

Bourget, Steve
2001   Rituals of Sacrifice: Its Practice at Huaca de la Luna and Its Representation in Moche Iconography. In *Moche: Art and Archaeology in Ancient Peru*, 89–109. Edited by Joanne Pillsbury. National Gallery of Art and Yale University Press, Washington, D.C.

Bourget, Steve, and Margaret E. Newman
1998   A Toast to the Ancestors: Ritual Warfare and Sacrificial Blood in Moche Culture. *Baessler-Archiv*, Neue Folge, 46:85–106. Berlin.

Brown, Terence A., and Keri A. Brown
1992   Ancient DNA and the Archaeologist. *Antiquity* 66:10–23.

Calancha, Antonio de
[1638] 1976   *Corónica moralizada del orden de San Agustín en el*

Perú con sucesos egemplares vistos en esta monarquía. P. Lacavallería, Barcelona.

Canziani, José

2003   Estado y ciudad: Revisión de la teoría sobre la sociedad moche. In *Moche: Hacia el Final del Milenio*, Tome II, 287–311. Actas del Segundo Coloquio sobre la Cultura Moche, Trujillo, 1 al 7 de agosto de 1999. Edited by Santiago Uceda and Elías Mujica. Universidad Nacional de Trujillo and Pontificia Universidad Católica del Perú, Lima.

Castillo, Luis Jaime, and Christopher B. Donnan

1994   Los Mochica del norte y los Mochica del sur. in *Vicús*, by Krzystof Makowski, Christopher B. Donnan, Iván Amaro Bullón, Luis Jaime Castillo, Magdalena Diez Canseco, Otto Eléspuru Revoredo, and Juan Antonio Murro Mena, 143–181. Colleción Arte y Tesoros del Perú, Lima.

Chapdelaine, Claude

2001   The Growing Power of a Moche Urban Class. In *Moche: Art and Archaeology in Ancient Peru*, 68–87. Edited by Joanne Pillsbury. National Gallery of Art and Yale University Press, Washington, D.C.

2003   La ciudad de Moche: Urbanismo y estado. In *Moche: Hacia el Final del Milenio*, Tome II, 247–285. Actas del Segundo Coloquio sobre la Cultura Moche, Trujillo, 1 al 7 de agosto de 1999. Edited by Santiago Uceda and Elías Mujica. Universidad Nacional de Trujillo and Pontificia Universidad Católica del Perú, Lima.

2004   The Moche Occupation of the Lower Santa Valley and the Nature of the Southern Moche State. Paper presented at the 69th Annual Meeting of the Society for American Archaeology, March 31–April 4, Montreal.

Collier, Donald

1955   *Cultural Chronology and Change as Reflected in the Ceramics of the Virú Valley, Peru*. Fieldiana: Anthropology 4. Field Museum of Natural History, Chicago.

Corruccini, Robert S., Izumi Shimada, and Ken-ichi Shinoda

2002   Dental and mtDNA Relatedness among Thousand Year Old Remains from Huaca Loro, Peru. *Dental Anthropology* 16 (1):9–14.

Donnan, Christopher B.

2001   Moche Portrait Vases. In *Moche Art and Archaeology in Ancient Peru*, 126–139. Edited by Joanne Pillsbury. National Gallery of Art and Yale University Press, Washington, D.C.

Dudar, J. C., J. S. Waye, and S. R. Saunders

2003   Determination of a Kinship System Using Ancient DNA, Mortuary Practice, and Historic Records in an Upper Canadian Pioneer Cemetery. *International Journal of Osteoarchaeology* 13:232–246.

Easton, R. D., A. D. Merriwether, D. E. Crew, and R. E. Ferrell

1996   MtDNA Variation in the Yanomami: Evidence for Additional New World Founding Lineages. *American Journal of Human Genetics* 59:213–225.

Fogel, Heidy P.

1993   Settlements in Time: A Study of Social and Political Development during the Gallinazo Occupation of the North Coast of Peru. Ph.D. dissertation, Department of Anthropology, Yale University, New Haven.

Franco Jordán, Régulo, César Gálvez Mora, and Segundo Vásquez Sánchez

1998   Desentierro ritual de una tumba moche: Huaca Cao Viejo. *Sian* 3 (6):9–18.

Hecker, Gisela, and Wolfgang Hecker

1992   Huesos humanos como ofrendas mortuarias y uso repetidas de vasijas. *Baessler-Archiv* n.s. XL (1):171–195.

Hocquenghem, Anne Marie

1978   Les combats mochicas: Essai d'interprétation d'un matériel archéologique a l'aide de l'iconologie, de l'ethnohistoire et de l'ethnologie. *Baessler-Archiv* 26:127–157.

Kaestle, F. A., and K. A. Horsburgh

2002   Ancient DNA in Anthropology: Methods, Applications, and Ethics. *Yearbook of Physical Anthropology* 45:92–130.

Klaus, Haagen

2003   Life and Death at Huaca Sialupe: The Mortuary Archaeology of a Middle Sicán Community, North Coast of Peru. Master's thesis, Department of Anthropology, Southern Illinois University, Carbondale.

Kolman, Connie J., and Noreen Tuross

2000   Ancient DNA Analysis of Human Populations. *American Journal of Physical Anthropology* 111 (1):5–23.

Kutscher, Gerdt

1955   *Ancient Art of the Peruvian North Coast*. Gebauer Mann, Berlin.

Larco, Rafael

1938   *Los Mochicas*. Tomo 2. Empresa Editorial "Rimac," Lima.

1945   *La cultura Virú*. Sociedad Geográfica Americana, Buenos Aires.

Lawlor, D. A., C. D. Dickel, W. W. Hauswirth, and P. Parham

1991   Ancient HLA Genes from 7,500-Year-Old Archaeological Remains. *Nature* 349:785–788.

Merriwether, D. A., F. Rothhammer, and R. E. Ferrell

1994   Genetic Variation in the New World: Ancient Teeth, Bone, and Tissues as Sources of DNA. *Experientia* 50:592–601.

Millaire, Jean-François

2002   *Moche Burial Patterns: An Investigation into Prehispanic Social Structure*. BAR International Series 1066. Oxford.

Netherly, Patricia J.

1984   The Management of Late Andean Irrigation Systems on the North Coast of Peru. *American Antiquity* 49:227–254.

1990   Out of Many, One: The Organization of Rule in the North Coast Polities. In *The Northern Dynasties: Kingship and Statecraft in Chimor*, 461–487. Edited by Michael E. Moseley and Alana Cordy-Collins. Dumbarton Oaks, Washington, D.C.

O'Rourke, Dennis H., M. Geoffrey Hayes, and Shawn W. Carlyle

2000   Ancient DNA Studies in Physical Anthropology. *Annual Review of Anthropology* 29:217–242.

Päabo, Svante

1999.   Ancient DNA. In *The Human Inheritance*, 119–134. Edited by Bryan Sykes. Oxford University Press, Oxford.

Proulx, Donald A.

1982   Territoriality in the Early Intermediate Period: The Case of Moche and Recuay. *Ñawpa Pacha* 20:83–96.

Quilter, Jeffrey

2002   Moche Politics, Religion and Warfare. *Journal of World Prehistory* 16:145–195.

Renfrew, Colin

1998   Applications of DNA in Archaeology: A Review of the DNA Studies of the Ancient Biomolecules Initiatives. *Ancient Biomolecules* 2:107–116.

2000   Archaeogenetics: Towards a Population Prehistory of Europe. In *Archaeogenetics: DNA and the Population Prehistory of Europe*, 3–12. Edited by Colin Renfrew and Katie Boyle. McDonald Institute for Archaeological Research, Cambridge.

Renfrew, Colin, and Katie Boyle

2000   Introduction. In *Archaeogenetics: DNA and the Population Prehistory of Europe*, 1–3. Edited by Colin Renfrew and Katie Boyle. McDonald Institute for Archaeological Research, Cambridge.

Ribeiro-Dos-Santos, A. K. C., S. E. B. Santos, A. L. Machado, V. Guapindaia, and M. A. Zago

1996   Heterogeneity of Mitochondrial DNA Haplotypes in Pre-Columbian Natives of the Amazon Region. *American Journal of Physical Anthropology* 101:29–37.

Rodriguez-Delfin, Luis A., Verónica E. Rubin-de-Celis, and Marco A. Zago

1999   Genetic Diversity in an Andean Population from Peru and Regional Migration Patterns of Amerindians in South America: Data from Y Chromosome and Mitochondrial DNA. *Human Heredity* 51:97–106.

Rostworowski, María

1961   *Curacas y sucesiones: Costa norte*. Imprenta Minerva, Lima.

2000   The Incas. In *The Inca World: The Development of Pre-Columbian Peru, A.D. 1000-1534*, 143–188. Edited by Laura Laurencich Minelli. University of Oklahoma Press, Norman.

2001   La religiosidad andina. In *Los dioses del antiguo Perú*, 185–221. Colección Arte y Tesoro del Perú. Banco de Crédito del Perú, Lima.

Rowe, John H.

1948   The Kingdom of Chimor. *Acta Americana* 6:26–59.

Schurr, Theodore G.

2000   Mitochondrial DNA and the Peopling of the New World. *American Scientist* 88:246–253.

Schurr, T. G., S. W. Ballinger, Y. Y. Gan, J. A. Hodge, D. A. Merriwether, D. N. Lawrence, W. C. Knowler, K. M. Weiss, and D. C. Wallace

1990   Amerindian Mitochondrial DNAs Have Rare Asian Mutations at High Frequencies Suggesting a Limited Number of Founders. *American Journal of Human Genetics* 46:613–623.

Shimada, Izumi

1994a   *Pampa Grande and the Mochica Culture*. University of Texas Press, Austin.

1994b   Los modelos de la organización sociopolítica de la cultura moche: Nuevos datos y perspectiva. In *Moche: Propuestas y perspectivas*, 359–387. Actas del Primer Coloquio sobre la Cultura Moche, Trujillo, 12 a 16 de abril de 1993. Edited by Santiago Uceda and Elías Mujica. Travaux de l'Institut Français d'Études Andines 79. Universidad Nacional de la Libertad, Trujillo, Perú.

1994c   The Role of Metals in Middle Sicán Society. In *The Illustrated Encyclopedia of Humankind*, Vol. 4: *New World and Pacific Civilizations*, 94–95. Edited by Göran Burenhult. University of Queensland Press, Australia.

1999   The Evolution of Andean Diversity: Regional Formations, ca. 500 B.C.–A.D. 600. In *Cambridge History of Native Peoples of the Americas*, 350–517. Edited by Frank Salomon and Stuart Schwartz. Cambridge University Press, Cambridge.

Shimada, Izumi, and Adriana Maguiña

1994   Una nueva visión sobre la cultura gallinazo y su relación con la cultura moche. In *Moche: Propuestas y perspectivas*, 31–58. Actas del Primer Coloquio sobre la Cultura Moche, Trujillo, 12 a 16 de abril de 1993. Edited by Santiago Uceda and Elías Mujica. Travaux de l'Institut Français d'Études Andines 79. Universidad Nacional de la Libertad, Trujillo, Perú.

Shimada, I., K. Shinoda, S. Bourget, W. Alva, and S. Uceda

2005   MtDNA Analysis of Mochica and Sicán Populations of Pre-Hispanic Peru. *Biomolecular Archaeology: Genetic Approaches to the Past* 32:61–92.

Shimada, Izumi, Ken-ichi Shinoda, Julie Farnum, Robert Corruccini, and Hirokatsu Watanabe

2004   An Integrated Analysis of Pre-Hispanic Mortuary Practices: A Middle Sicán Case Study. *Current Anthropology* 45 (3):369–402.

Shinoda, Ken-ichi, Noboru Adachi, Sonia Guillen, and Izumi Shimada

2006   Mitochondrial DNA Analysis of Ancient Peruvian Highlanders. *American Journal of Physical Anthropology* 131 (1):98–107.

Stone, Anne C.

2000   Ancient DNA from Skeletal Remains. In *Biological Anthropology of the Human Skeleton*, 351–372. Edited by M. Anne Katzenberg and Shelley. R. Saunders. Wiley-Liss, New York.

Sutter, Richard C., and Rosa Cortez

2005   The Nature of Moche Human Sacrifice: A Bio-Archaeological Perspective. *Current Anthropology* 46 (4):521–549.

Sykes, Bryan, and Colin Renfrew

2000   Concepts in Molecular Genetics. In *Archaeogenetics: DNA and the Population Prehistory of Europe*, 3–12. Edited by Colin Renfrew and Katie Boyle. McDonald Institute for Archaeological Research, Cambridge.

Tello, Ricardo, José Armas, and Claude Chapdelaine

2003   Prácticas funerarias moche en el complejo arqueológico Huacas del Sol y de la Luna. In *Moche: Hacia el Final del Milenio*, Tome II, 247–285. Actas del Segundo Coloquio sobre la Cultura Moche, Trujillo, 1 al 7 de agosto de 1999. Edited by Santiago Uceda and Elías Mujica. Universidad Nacional de Trujillo and Pontificia Universidad Católica del Perú, Lima.

Ubbelohde-Doering, Heinrich

1949   *Ceramic Comparisons of Two North Coast Peruvian Valleys*. Proceedings of the 29th International Congress of Americanists, New York, 5–12 September, 1:224–231.

1957   Der Gallinazo-Stil und die Chronologie der altperuanischen Fruhkulturen. Bayerischen Akademie der Wissenschaften, Philosophisch-Historische Klasse, *Sitzungsberichte* 9:1–8.

1967   *On the Royal Highways of the Inca*. Thames and Hudson, London.

1983   Vorspanische Gräber von Pacatnamú, Nordperu. *Materialien zur Allgemeinen und Vergleichenden Archäologie*, Band 26. Verlag C. H. Beck, München.

Verano, John W.

2001a   War and Death in the Moche World: Osteological Evidence and Visual Discourse. In *Moche: Art and Archaeology in Ancient Peru*, 111–126. Edited by Joanne Pillsbury. National Gallery of Art and Yale University Press, Washington, D.C.

2001b   The Physical Evidence of Human Sacrifice in Ancient Peru. In *Ritual Sacrifice in Ancient Peru*, 165–184. Edited by Elizabeth P. Benson and Anita G. Cook. University of Texas Press, Austin.

Williams, Sloan R., Napoleon A. Chagnon, and Richard S. Spielman

2002   Nuclear and Mitochondrial Genetic Variation in the Yanomamö: A Test Case for Ancient DNA Studies of Prehistoric Populations. *American Journal of Physical Anthropology* 117:246–259.

Wilson, David L.

1988   *Prehispanic Settlement Patterns in the Lower Santa Valley, Peru: A Regional Perspective on the Origins and Development of Complex North Coast Society*. Smithsonian Institution Press, Washington, D.C.

Zevallos, Jorge

1989   *Los cacicazgos de Lambayeque*. Consejo Nacional de Ciencia y Tecnología, Trujillo, Perú.

CHAPTER ELEVEN

Communality and Diversity in Moche Human Sacrifice

JOHN W. VERANO, TULANE UNIVERSITY

Abstract

The nature of human sacrifice has become a topic of ever-increasing debate in Moche studies, especially since the discovery of two particular contexts (Plazas 3a and 3c) at the Huacas de Moche site in the Moche Valley. In this chapter, I will first review important shared features seen in Plazas 3a and 3c that provide evidence of a particular form of Moche human sacrifice: the ritual killing of captives. I will then explore differences between Plazas 3a and 3c that reveal a greater complexity in Moche sacrificial practices than has been previously recognized.

Depictions of armed combat and of the capture and sacrifice of prisoners are well-known in Moche iconography. Since 1995, the iconographic record has been joined by archaeological evidence of the sacrificial practices themselves. The most dramatic discoveries have been made at Huaca de la Luna in the Moche Valley, in two small courtyards (Plazas 3a and 3c) located adjacent to Platform I. Excavations conducted in these plazas between 1995 and 2001 have recovered evidence of sacrificial rituals spanning multiple centuries. Although these deposits share many common features, they also demonstrate a number of important differences.

Place and Context

Plazas 3a and 3c are not the only areas where remains of sacrificial victims have been found at the Pyramids of Moche, but no other excavations have produced such a concentration of skeletal remains. Sacrificed retainers have been found associated with some tombs in the Urban Zone, and three skeletons found lying face down at the base of the west facade of the Huaca de la Luna appear to be sacrifices (Delabarde n.d.). No direct skeletal evidence of violent death was found in any of these cases; however, the context and body positions of these

remains suggest that they were offerings. Two modified human skulls found in a niche in Sector 8 of the Urban Zone also appear to have come from sacrificial victims (Verano et al. 1999), and it is likely that other modified human bones remain to be found at the site.

Plazas 3a and 3c are exceptional in that they appear to represent locations specifically dedicated to human sacrificial activities—and on a relatively large scale. From the available archaeological evidence, it cannot be determined whether these plazas were the actual locations where victims were killed, or whether they served primarily as repositories for the remains of victims sacrificed in some other location. The latter seems likely for Plaza 3c, as will be argued below; Plaza 3a, with its natural rock outcrop as a central focus, seems a more likely candidate for a primary sacrificial site.

Commonalities

Plazas 3a and 3c, and the archaeological materials found within them, show many similarities. These include the general location of the sacrificial areas, the demographic profile of the victims, manner of sacrifice, and objects found associated with the skeletal remains. Other similarities include the presence of associated tombs, as well as ceremonial architecture or geological features of apparent ritual significance.

Location of Deposits

Plazas 3a and 3c are located southeast of the principal construction of the Huaca de la Luna, Platform I (Figure 11.1). They form part of a series of courtyards, small enclosures, and corridors that lie between Platform I and the west flank of Cerro Blanco (Tufinio n.d.; Uceda and Tufinio 2003). A small adobe platform (Platform II) forms the eastern wall of Plaza 3a and bisects a natural rock outcrop that constitutes the ceremonial focus of the plaza (Bourget and Millaire 2000). Plaza 3c has no associated rock outcrop or platform, but the plaza walls enclose a room (Recinto I) decorated on the exterior with polychrome friezes (Figure 11.2). At the entrance is a small raised platform and an altar. The eastern half of Plaza 3c is separated from the western half by a wall and contains a smaller enclosure, Recinto II (Figure 11.3). The remains of sacrificial victims and fragments of ceramic prisoner vessels were found exclusively in this eastern part, which seems to have functioned as a repository for these materials (Tufinio n.d.). Plazas 3a and 3c were linked to Platform I by narrow corridors that provided only limited access and would not have been visible either from the north courtyard (Plaza 1) of the Huaca or from the urban sector. Their limited access and visibility suggest that the plazas were not designed for public traffic or for large audiences. Nevertheless, anyone passing downwind (to the north/northeast) of these areas during periods of active deposition of bodies would have been struck by the odor of decomposition, and would have gained a visceral impression of the activities that went on in these courtyards even if they could not directly observe them. The archaeological evidence suggests that the bodies of most or all of the sacrificial victims in Plaza 3a, and some in Plaza 3c, were left to decompose on the surface rather than being promptly buried.

Other than isolated puncture marks on a few of the thousands of bones recovered from Plazas 3a and 3c (Verano 2001a; Hamilton 2005), there is no evidence of carnivore damage, indicating that mammalian scavengers such as dogs or foxes did not have access to the remains. Yet numerous pupa cases found in association with skeletons in both Plazas 3a and 3c indicate that

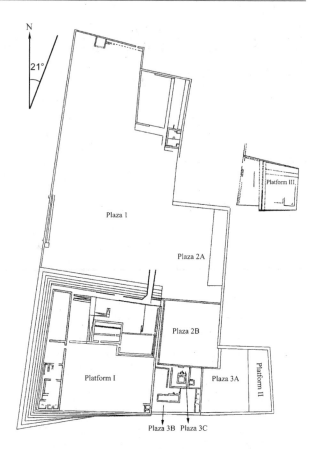

FIGURE 11.1. Map of Huaca de la Luna, showing the location of Plazas 3a and 3c. Courtesy of the Huaca de la Luna Archaeological Project.

FIGURE 11.2. External view of the north side and doorway of Recinto I, Plaza 3c, showing friezes depicting felines on top of human figures. Photograph by author.

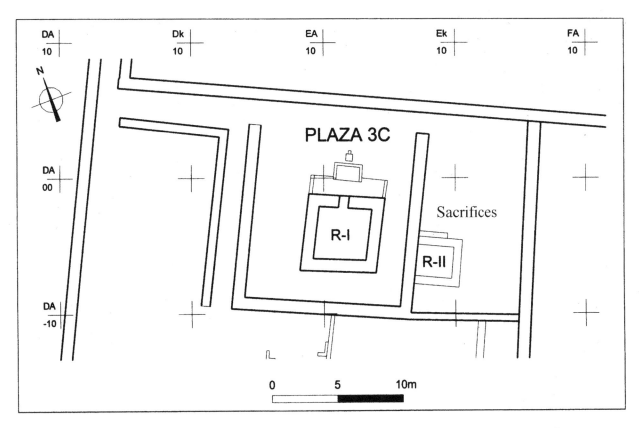

FIGURE 11.3. Map of Plaza 3c showing Recinto I (R-I) with a small platform and altar at its north entrance, the smaller Recinto II (R-II), and the area where human remains were found. Courtesy of the Huaca de la Luna Archaeological Project.

flies visited and laid eggs on the decomposing bodies (Bourget 2001b; Verano n.d.). It is possible that vultures fed upon them as well. Black vultures are commonly shown in Moche art in association with scenes of punishment and human sacrifice (Donnan 1978; Rea 1986), and some of the disarticulation and scattering of skeletal elements seen in Plaza 3a would be consistent with vulture scavenging. Steve Bourget, however, has identified a number of cases in Plaza 3a where bodies and skeletal elements appear to have been intentionally manipulated by humans as part of the sacrificial rituals (Bourget 1998). The final disposition of human skeletal remains in Plaza 3a probably reflects a complex interaction of human and nonhuman actors, as well as natural taphonomic processes as the bodies decomposed. As will be described later in this chapter, the human remains in Plaza 3c appear to present a different scenario since most of them show evidence of having been defleshed prior to their deposition in the plaza.

Demographic Profile and Life History of the Victims

Both the demographic profile and evidence of skeletal trauma seen in the sacrificial victims in Plazas 3a and 3c support the hypothesis that these were captives taken in armed conflict. All appear to be healthy males between the ages of approximately fifteen to forty years, and many show old injuries—including healed fractures of the ribs, skull, and mandible, and several cases of "parry" fractures (fractures incurred while blocking a blow) of the forearms—suggesting a prior history of interpersonal conflict. In addition, some individuals in both Plazas 3a and 3c show fractures of the arm, ribs, or shoulder blade that were in the early stages of healing at the time of death (Verano 1998, 2001a). These healing injuries appear to mark wounds received in combat or following capture. They are consistent with Moche depictions of armed combat, where the primary objective seems to have been to disable and capture rather

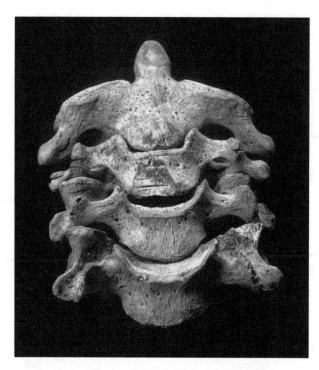

FIGURE 11.4. Multiple cut marks across the body and transverse processes of the third and fourth cervical vertebrae, Individual E2, Plaza 3c. Photograph by author.

FIGURE 11.5. Skull with three articulated cervical vertebrae and feet, Plaza 3c, H33. Photograph by author.

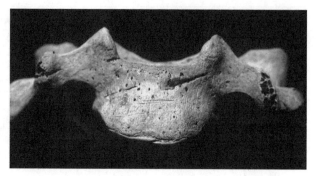

FIGURE 11.6. Anterior view of the third cervical vertebra of P3c H33, showing fine horizontal cuts across the body, and deeper and broader cuts made at a distinct angle, apparently when decapitating the victim. Photograph by author.

than kill one's opponent (Alva and Donnan 1993; Donnan 1997:52). These healing fractures are also important in indicating that some time (at least several weeks, perhaps more) elapsed between the moment of capture and death (Verano 2001b).

Manner of Sacrifice

Moche artistic depictions of prisoner sacrifice show victims having their throats slit and their blood collected for presentation to an elaborately dressed figure (Alva and Donnan 1993). Skeletal evidence from Plazas 3a and 3c is consistent with the art: the most common perimortem injury (occurring around the time of death [Sauer 1998]) seen in these skeletons is cut marks across the bodies and transverse processes of the cervical vertebrae (Figure 11.4). The location of the cut marks (limited in most cases to the anterior surfaces of the vertebrae) indicates that the objective was to slit the throat, not decapitate the victim. Although many isolated skulls and headless trunks have been found in Plazas 3a and 3c, only a small number of unequivocal cases of decapitation can be confirmed on the basis of cut mark location and patterning. One example (P3c-H33) is a skull found with three articulated cervical vertebrae and a pair of feet. These were buried together in a small pit beneath the floor of Plaza 3c (Figure 11.5). The cervical vertebrae exhibit two distinct forms of cut marks: fine cuts horizontally across the body of the third cervical vertebra, typical of throat slitting, and a set of deeper, angled cuts and fracturing of the spinous and transverse processes of C3 that occurred with forced separation of the third and fourth cervical vertebrae during decapitation (Figures 11.6, 11.7). Another example is a partial skeleton (P3c-H36) that shows deep cut marks on the posterior surface of the second cervical vertebra's odontoid process (Figure 11.8). These marks apparently were made when the neck was cut repeatedly from behind to remove the head.

Recently, a detailed study by Laurel Hamilton of cut marks on the entire Plaza 3a skeletal sample (including all isolated bones as well as complete and partial skeletons) has identified ten additional cases of vertebrae with cut marks suggesting decapitation (Hamilton 2005). But in skeletal remains lacking cut marks indicating intentional decapitation, other mechanisms must be considered to explain the isolated skulls and clusters of skulls that were found in Plazas 3a and 3c. Skulls may have been moved intentionally following decomposition of the body (Bourget 1998), dislodged by vultures, or separated from the neck vertebrae during decomposition. Skulls have a natural tendency to disarticulate from the neck and roll, as has been observed frequently in modern forensic cases (Ubelaker and Scammell 1992).

The Moche are known to have decapitated victims in some circumstances, as is documented by the discovery of eighteen severed heads at Dos Cabezas in the Jequetepeque Valley (Cordy-Collins 2001), and of two modified human skulls from the urban sector at Moche (Verano et al. 1999). Trophy heads are also shown in Moche art, as are supernaturals holding *tumi* knives and severed heads (Cordy-Collins 2001). Why some Moche sacrificial victims were decapitated and others not is unknown, but the osteological evidence from Plazas 3a and 3c indicates that both slitting of the throat and decapitation of captives occurred at Huaca de la Luna.

SKULL FRACTURES

Skull fractures are also seen in the Plaza 3a and 3c victims, although in a relatively small number of cases. Eight individuals from Plaza 3a and one from Plaza 3c have skull fractures that occurred at or around the time of death. Some of these are massive and presumably were caused by blows with a large club or rock (Figure 11.9). Steve Bourget hypothesizes that some of them may have been produced with a wooden club of a distinctive form that appears in Moche scenes of sea lion and deer hunts

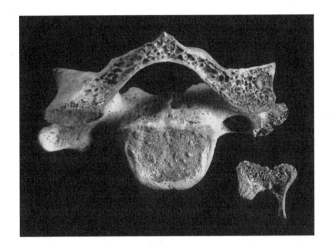

FIGURE 11.7. Inferior view of the third cervical vertebra of P3c H33, showing sectioning and fracture of the transverse and spinous processes caused by decapitation. Photograph by author.

FIGURE 11.8. Cut marks on the posterior surface of the odontoid process of the second cervical vertebra associated with decapitation, Plaza 3c, H36. Photograph by author.

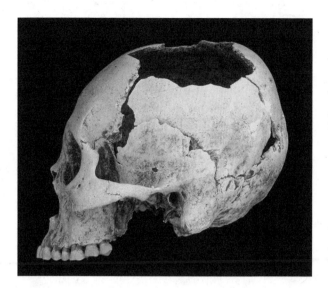

FIGURE 11.9. Cranium with massive blunt force trauma, Plaza 3a, Skull XI. Photograph by author.

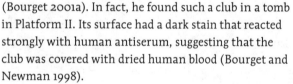

FIGURE 11.10. Skull fragment with rectangular impact scar (lower margin), Plaza 3a. Photograph by author.

(Bourget 2001a). In fact, he found such a club in a tomb in Platform II. Its surface had a dark stain that reacted strongly with human antiserum, suggesting that the club was covered with dried human blood (Bourget and Newman 1998).

Two other skull fractures in Plaza 3a were produced with a different type of weapon, as can be seen from impact scars along the broken margins (Figures 11.10, 11.11). The scars are small, and their shapes indicate that an object with multiple protuberances struck the skull. The object was likely a star-headed mace: a short, single-handed weapon carried by some Moche warriors (Donnan 1978: figs. 110, 111; Donnan and McClelland 1999: figs. 4.19, 4.25). These clubs have copper or stone heads with multiple protuberances that are circular or quadrangular in cross-section. One of the fractured skulls from Plaza 3a (Figure 11.10) shows small rectangular impact scars; the other (Figure 11.11) shows semicircular fractures produced by a mace head with rounded points.[1]

Only one case of perimortem skull fracture was found in Plaza 3c. An isolated skull vault (H41) has multiple radiating fractures from an oval-shaped impact in the forehead area. Like the majority of the Plaza 3a cases, the fractures appear to have resulted from a blow from a large club.

It is unclear why some victims in Plazas 3a and 3c were struck with clubs. In Moche art, warriors some-

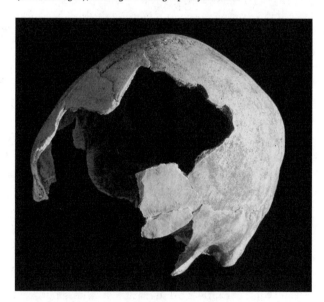

FIGURE 11.11. Partial cranium with semicircular impact fractures, Plaza 3c. Photograph by author.

times are shown hitting captives in the nose to induce a nosebleed, but I am not aware of any scenes where captives are clubbed to death. Moreover, five of the seven individuals with skull fractures whose cervical vertebrae could be examined also show cut marks, indicating that their throats were slit in the standard fashion. Thus, it appears that clubbing was not an alternative method of execution in these cases, but perhaps an embellishment

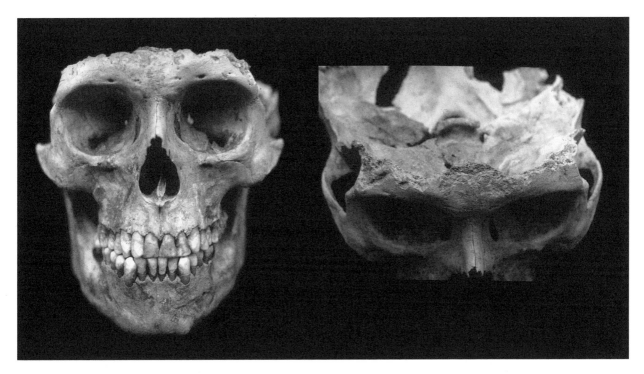

FIGURE 11.12. Skull with upper portion of braincase broken and missing, Plaza 3c, HG99-5, and detail showing impact scars around broken margin. Also visible are cut marks on the nasal bones, suggesting flaying of the face. Photograph by author.

reserved for a select few. In support of this, Bourget noted that three of the individuals with skull fractures lay in close proximity to one another in Sediment 2 (Bourget 1998).

An unusual case of multiple skull fractures was found in a single individual (HG99-5) in Plaza 3c. It is distinct from the fractures described above because it represents intentional postmortem modification. This skull, which was found still articulated to a nearly complete skeleton, was missing the entire upper portion of the braincase (Figure 11.12). Small fractures around the broken margins mark where the upper portion was broken away by a series of percussion blows. Presumably, the skull was fractured to gain access to the brain.

PENETRATING WOUNDS

Two individuals, one in Plaza 3a and one in Plaza 3c, have penetrating wounds produced by a sharply pointed weapon. An isolated sternum found in Plaza 3a has a single wound with an entrance on the anterior surface, and an exit with radiating fractures on the posterior surface (Figure 11.13).[2] The wound is very similar to

those found in a Late Intermediate period mass burial of sacrificed individuals at Pacatnamú (Figure 11.14; Verano 1986). A skeleton in Plaza 3c (HG99-3), excavated by Moises Tufinio during the 1999 field season (Tufinio n.d.), shows punched-in lesions on multiple bones of the lower neck and thoracic cage (right fourth rib, vertebrae C7, T1, T4, and T9), also similar to those seen in the Pacatnamú skeletons (Figure 11.15). Two pointed bone fragments were found in lower levels of the Plaza 3c sacrificial area. Each is a long bone shaft fragment with one end that terminates in a sharp point. One of them is slightly over 7 cm long, and the pointed end shows obvious polishing (Figure 11.16). The second is about 5 cm long and also terminates in a point, although it does not show polishing. These fragments are similar in size and shape to bone points found in the Pacatnamú mass burial and may represent the tips of atlatl darts. In Moche iconography, atlatls are the weapon of choice in deer hunting but are rarely shown being used against human targets in combat scenes (Bourget 2001a; Donnan 1997; Verano 2001b). Atlatl darts (often with barbed points), however, are frequently depicted as a component

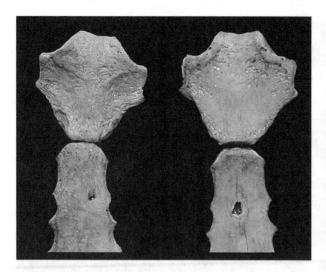

FIGURE 11.13. Penetrating wound on an isolated sternum from Plaza 3a. Entrance is on the ventral side, exit on the dorsal side. Photograph by author.

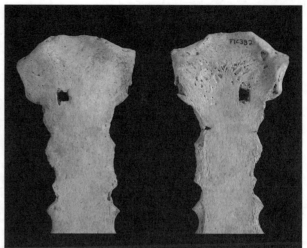

FIGURE 11.14. Sternum from Pacatnamú mass burial with a penetrating wound similar in form to that seen in Figure 11.13. Photograph by author.

of weapons bundles and as isolated elements in combat scenes (Donnan and McClelland 1999), suggesting that they were used in some combat situations. It is possible that the Plaza 3a sternum represents a nonlethal combat wound (depending on how far the point penetrated beyond the sternum), but the multiple wounds deep within the thoracic cavity of HG99-3 would undoubtedly have been fatal. Consistent with this, HG99-3 shows no cut marks on his cervical vertebrae.

Associated Artifacts

The most common artifacts associated with the sacrificial victims in Plazas 3a and 3c were fragments of ceramic vessels. Other cultural materials—including textile fragments; small, perforated, gilded copper plates of the type sewn on elaborate garments; and food remains—also were found.[3] Included in the ceramic assemblages from Plazas 3a and 3c are numerous examples of prisoner figures. In the case of Plaza 3a, these are large, unfired clay effigy figures in the form of seated nude males with ropes around their necks (Bourget 2001a, 2001b). In Plaza 3c, we found fragments of smaller, fired vessels in the form of seated prisoners with ropes around their necks and hands bound behind the back (Figure 11.17). All vessels from Plaza 3c were fragmentary, but two were complete enough to allow reconstruction of their original form (Figures 11.18, 11.19). The prisoner vessel

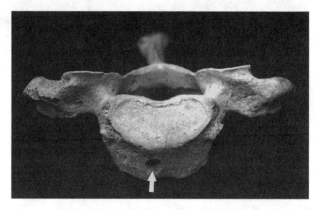

FIGURE 11.15. Seventh cervical vertebra with a penetrating wound on the anterior surface of the vertebral body, Plaza 3c, HG99-3. Photograph by author.

FIGURE 11.16. Bone fragment with a polished end, possibly a dart (atlatl) tip, from Plaza 3c. Scale is 5 cm. Photograph by author.

FIGURE 11.17. Fragments of prisoner figures from Plaza 3c sub-floor. Photograph by author.

FIGURE 11.18. Reconstructed prisoner vessels found above the floor of Plaza 3c. Drawings by José Armas.

FIGURE 11.19. Reconstructed prisoner vessels found above the floor of Plaza 3c. Drawings by José Armas.

fragments from Plaza 3c are similar in size and decoration to complete examples found as funerary offerings in a number of tombs at the site of Moche, including three vessels found in Tomb 2 of Platform II (Bourget 2001b).

Given their direct association with the skeletal remains of sacrificial victims, the unfired and fired vessels found in Plazas 3a and 3c clearly played some role in the sacrificial rituals, and their intentional breakage seems to have been an integral part of the process. In Plaza 3a, the effigy figures appear to have been placed with the victims and broken in situ (Bourget 2001b). In contrast, in Plaza 3c the distribution of vessel fragments indicates that they were broken prior to being deposited. All vessels are incomplete, and in several cases we found matching fragments of a single vessel scattered widely across the plaza.

Also found in Plaza 3c was one complete example and sixteen fragments of undecorated ceramic discs. The discs are circular, with a diameter of approximately 9 cm. José Armas, who analyzed the ceramics from Plaza 3c, believes these discs may have been used to carry the blood-filled goblets in prisoner sacrifices. In support of this hypothesis, he notes that the Priestess in the sacrifice ceremony carries a goblet in one hand and a disc-shaped object in the other (Armas n.d.).

Association with Tombs

Moche tombs were found in indirect association with both Plazas 3a and 3c. In the case of Plaza 3a, these were chamber tombs placed in Platform II during or shortly after its construction. Although disturbed by early looting, they still preserved an abundance of ceramic and other funerary offerings (Bourget 1998, 2001b; Bourget and Millaire 2000). In the case of Plaza 3c, several tombs were found under the plaza floor in close proximity to the sacrificial victims. Two of these were simple interments, but one was a larger tomb (Tomb 2) whose chamber had been created by removing a rectangular block of adobes from the plaza construction fill (Figure 11.20). The principal occupant of the tomb was an adult male, accompanied by a bundle containing the remains of

three infants. Fifteen ceramic vessels were found in wall niches and on the tomb floor (Verano and Tufinio n.d.).

The close proximity of tombs and sacrificial victims in Plazas 3a and 3c might at first appear incongruous. Based on his analysis of the funerary goods associated with the Platform II tombs, Bourget concluded that their occupants may have been directly involved with the sacrifice of victims in Plaza 3a (Bourget 1998; Bourget and Millaire 2000). A similar argument can be made for the principal burial in Tomb 2 in Plaza 3c. While no clubs or weapons other than a fragment of a chisel-like knife were found in the tomb, ceramic offerings included representations of a warrior, two captives (one associated with a detail of a deer hunting scene), and a portrait head vessel (Figures 11.21–11.24). The portrait

FIGURE 11.20. View of Plaza 3c excavation, showing an exploratory trench through the plaza floor and the location of Tomb 2 (*A*). Photograph by author.

FIGURE 11.21. Stirrup spout vessel with modeled warrior and war club in clay slip from Tomb 2. Photograph by author.

FIGURE 11.22. Stirrup spout vessel from Tomb 2 depicting a seated prisoner, identifiable by the rope around his neck and exposed genitalia. Photograph by author.

FIGURE 11.23. *Canchero* with handle from Tomb 2 that terminates in a modeled human head with a rope around the neck. On the inferior surface of the chamber is a deer pierced by darts. Photograph by author.

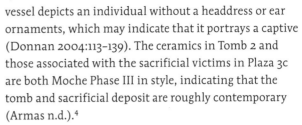

FIGURE 11.24. Portrait head vessel from Tomb 2. Photograph by author.

vessel depicts an individual without a headdress or ear ornaments, which may indicate that it portrays a captive (Donnan 2004:113–139). The ceramics in Tomb 2 and those associated with the sacrificial victims in Plaza 3c are both Moche Phase III in style, indicating that the tomb and sacrificial deposit are roughly contemporary (Armas n.d.).[4]

Diversity

As discussed above, the sacrificial sites of Plazas 3a and 3c share many similarities. Yet there are some differences between the two that are important for understanding the activities that went on at these two locations. These differences include the dates of construction and use of the two plazas, the distinctive way in which bodies in Plaza 3c were manipulated postmortem, and the possible motivations for sacrificial rituals.

Chronology

The first distinction is chronological: there is now good evidence that Plazas 3a and 3c were not in use at the same time, but date to different construction phases of Huaca de la Luna. Excavations during the 1999 field season revealed that Plaza 3c was buried by windblown sand and sealed with adobes prior to the construction of Plaza 3a (Tufinio n.d.). Attempts to radiocarbon date the skeletal remains from Plaza 3a were unsuccessful due to poor collagen preservation. But construction of Plaza 3a corresponds to one of the latest phases at the Huaca de la Luna (Edificio A), and an algorrobo log sample from the roof of a Platform II tomb yielded a calibrated date (2 sigmas) of AD 425–690 (Uceda et al. n.d.).

Four radiocarbon dates were obtained from materials in Plaza 3c: two from materials above the plaza floor and two from below it. Three utilized samples of rope recovered from around the ankles and wrists of skeletons or isolated limbs; the fourth was done from a sample of fly and beetle remains collected from within the skull of H33. Because of the small size of the samples, all were analyzed by accelerator mass spectrometry (AMS). Since skeletal remains were found in two stratigraphically distinct contexts—above and below the floor of Plaza 3c—we expected some differences in dates. Laboratory results confirmed these expectations.

The first above-floor sample, collected from Skeleton E5, produced a conventional radiocarbon age of 1560 +/- 40 BP (Beta-146464), with a 2 sigma calibrated result (95 percent probability) of Cal AD 410–600, and an intercept of the radiocarbon age with the calibration curve of Cal AD 530. Rope from around an isolated foot (H2), produced a conventional radiocarbon age of 1570 +/- 40 BP (Beta-146465), with a 2 sigma calibrated result (95 percent probability) of Cal AD 460–480 and Cal AD 520–650, and an intercept of the radiocarbon age with the calibration curve of Cal AD 580.

The two radiocarbon determinations made from materials below the floor of Plaza 3c yielded substantially earlier dates. A rope fragment from Skeleton E16 produced a conventional radiocarbon age of 1880 +/- 40 BP (Beta-158974), with a 2 sigma calibrated result (95 percent probability) of Cal AD 50–230, and an intercept of the radiocarbon age with the calibration curve at Cal AD 120. The insect sample collected from the skull of H33 produced a conventional radiocarbon age of 1810 +/- 40 BP

FIGURE 11.25. Sacrificial victims below the floor of Plaza 3c, incorporated into construction fill used to raise the level of the plaza. Photograph by author.

(Beta-158975), with a 2 sigma calibrated result (95 percent probability) of Cal AD 110–330, and an intercept of the radiocarbon age with the calibration curve of Cal AD 230.

The four radiocarbon dates from Plaza 3c are consistent with its stratigraphy and construction sequence, and the above-floor dates correspond well with the established building chronology of Huaca de la Luna. The dates for the sub-floor sacrificial remains, however, are surprisingly early, representing some of the earliest radiocarbon dates to be reported from the site of Moche (Uceda et al. n.d.). If the two sub-floor dates are not anomalous, they indicate that remains of sacrificial victims were deposited in Plaza 3c over many centuries, beginning with some of the earliest construction phases of the Huaca de la Luna.

Stratigraphic Context

The construction sequence of Plaza 3a and deposition of bodies appear to be quite distinct from that of Plaza 3c. From his excavation data, Bourget concludes that Plaza 3a and Platform II were constructed rapidly during one of the final construction phases of the Huaca de la Luna, and that Plaza 3a and Platform II may have been built specifically as a response to an impending El Niño event. A series of sacrifices were then made both during and following episodes of heavy rainfall, as evidenced by skeletons found in alternating layers of hardened mud and windblown sand.

The stratigraphic data and radiocarbon dates for Plaza 3c, in contrast, appear to document a slow, accretional deposit of victims over multiple centuries. The sub-floor remains were incorporated in the sand and adobe fill that was used to raise the level of the plaza during its construction (Figure 11.25). The above-floor remains, in contrast, were covered with adobe fragments or simply left to be buried by accumulating windblown sand (Figure 11.26). Evidence of occasional rainfall was found in the form of thin layers of hardened silt alternating with windblown sand, and water streaks on the painted surface of the east wall of the plaza. No evidence of torrential rains, however, was found in Plaza 3c, nor was any correlation found between episodes of light rainfall and the deposition of sacrificial victims.

Postmortem Treatment of Sacrificial Victims

Although complete, articulated skeletons were found in both Plazas 3a and 3c, partial skeletons—as well as isolated limbs, hands, feet, and scattered bones—were more common. Upon seeing the degree of disarticulation in the Plaza 3a skeletal material, our initial hypothesis was that the victims were intentionally disarticulated as part of the sacrificial ritual. But extensive examination of the Plaza 3a sample has revealed only a handful of bones with cut marks consistent with dismemberment or defleshing (Bracamonte 1998; Hamilton 2005). If fresh bodies had been dismembered with a sharp tool, we would expect to see numerous cut marks, particularly around the joint surfaces. Such marks are absent in all but a few bones in Plaza 3a. Manipulation and dismemberment of decomposing bodies may have occurred, however, and this could explain the high degree of disarticulation in Plaza 3a, as well as the apparent grouping of mandibles, skulls, and limbs seen there (Bourget 1997, 1998, 2001b).

In contrast, the human remains in Plaza 3c show abundant evidence of complex postmortem treatment and manipulation. Laboratory examination revealed cut marks on nearly all skeletons and partial remains

FIGURE 11.26. Sacrificial victim (E8) above the floor of Plaza 3c, buried in a deposit of windblown sand and scattered adobes. Photograph by author.

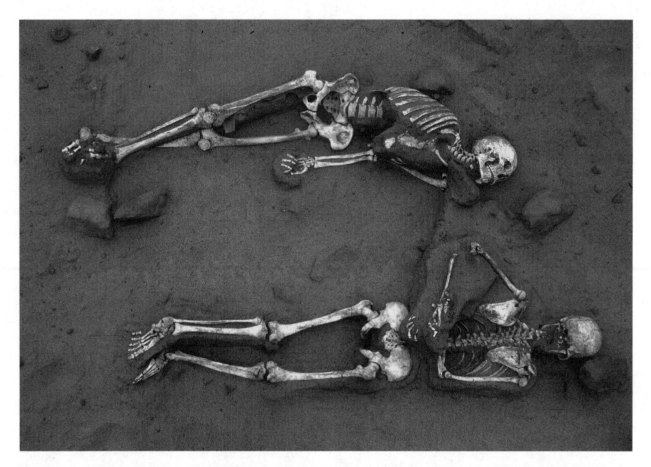

FIGURE 11.27. Skeletons E4 and E5, Plaza 3c, above-floor deposit. Cut marks on Skeleton E4 are diagrammed in Figure 11.28. Photograph by author.

in Plaza 3c. Interestingly, the cuts are most common in areas of muscle attachment rather than on or around the joint surfaces of bones (Figures 11.27, 11.28), suggesting that the objective was to deflesh rather than disarticulate the victims. This is supported by the fact that many skeletons were found largely articulated, despite having cut marks on all major bones. While the specific motive for the defleshing is unknown, the victims' bodies in Plaza 3c were not systematically dismembered, as is typical in butchering of large food animals such as deer and camelids. Furthermore, there is no evidence of burning or fracturing of bones to extract marrow. Apparently the Moche were not cannibalizing the bodies of their victims, but seem to have been more interested in the skeletons themselves—using them, or parts of them, for display or some other ritual purpose. An example is E6, a partial set of remains found in sand

above the floor of Plaza 3c, covered by adobe fragments (Figure 11.29). It consists of the crossed bones of the upper and lower limbs, with all elements (including the shoulder blades) still articulated, suggesting that the bones were still held together by soft tissue at the time they were buried. All of the bones show cut marks on their external surfaces, including the small bones of the hands and feet (Figure 11.30). These marks indicate that the skin and muscles were cut from them, apparently leaving only ligaments to hold the bones together. The extensive and time-consuming defleshing of these bones, while carefully maintaining their articulations, suggests intentional preparation for some purpose rather than simple butchery and consumption. Unfortunately, no evidence remains of what was done with the flesh removed from E6 and other skeletons in Plaza 3c. We thus cannot exclude the possibility that the flesh

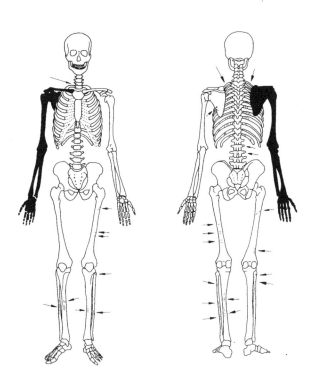

FIGURE 11.28. Location of cut marks on Skeleton E4, Plaza 3c. Darkened areas indicate missing bones. Drawings by author.

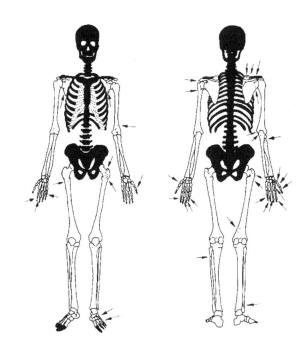

FIGURE 11.29. Skeleton E6, Plaza 3c, above-floor deposit. Photograph by author.

of captives, as well as their blood, was consumed in Moche sacrificial rituals.

Also found in Plaza 3c were remains of rope around the wrists and ankles of isolated limbs and around the necks of defleshed skeletons. These ropes suggest that articulated arms and legs, and in some cases whole skeletons, may have been suspended and displayed in some location at the Huaca de la Luna. Depictions of amputated limbs with ropes tied around them are known from Moche art, although in all cases they are fleshed, not skeletal limbs (Donnan 1978; Donnan and McClelland 1999; Hill 2000; Hocquenghem 1987). Animated skeletons engaged in various activities are also known in Moche art, but I am not aware of any depictions of suspended skeletons.

The extensive postmortem processing of the Plaza 3c remains, along with evidence that they represent a gradual accretional deposit over an extended period of time, suggests that the small rectangular area was dedicated to the final deposition of sacrificial victims following extensive postmortem preparation and ritual use.

FIGURE 11.30. Location of cut marks on Skeleton E6. Darkened areas indicate missing bones. Drawings by author.

In contrast, Plaza 3a appears to be a primary sacrificial site, where bodies were cast (or placed) around the rocky outcrop following their death. Plazas 3a and 3c thus may have functioned in very different ways, despite the fact that both served as places where the remains of sacrificial victims were deposited.

Motivation for Sacrificial Practices

The specific motivation behind the sacrifice of captives by the Moche remains a subject of significant interest among Moche specialists. Steve Bourget concludes that prisoner sacrifices in Plaza 3a were performed in times of crisis associated with torrential El Niño rains, since some of the sacrificial victims appear to have been killed during periods of heavy rainfall (Bourget 1997, 1998; Bourget and Millaire 2000). In Plaza 3c, we also found evidence of occasional rainfall that deposited thin layers of silt over the plaza; however, none of the skeletons were directly associated with these layers. Therefore, we could not find evidence to support a direct relationship between El Niño rains and human sacrifice in Plaza 3c. Given the three temporally distinct deposits of sacrificial victims at the Huaca de la Luna (Plaza 3c sub-floor; Plaza 3c above-floor; Plaza 3a), it is now evident that sacrifices were made over a period of centuries. Sacrifice of captives was clearly a long-standing cultural tradition that played an important role in ritual activities at the Huaca de la Luna, and not exclusively a response to episodic environmental crises such as the El Niño phenomenon. While sacrifices in Plaza 3a may have been made for different reasons than those in Plaza 3c (Uceda and Tufinio 2003), the type of victims chosen and the way in which they were killed are very similar.

As I have argued elsewhere, the sacrifice of captives, whether from ritual combat among the Moche or from more secular battles with non-Moche polities, likely functioned to affirm the religious and political power of major centers like the Pyramids at Moche, the El Brujo complex, San José de Moro, Sipán, and others (Verano 2001b). To what degree Moche combat was ritual or secular continues to be a subject of debate among Moche scholars (Alva and Donnan 1993; Castillo 2000; Donnan 1997; Topic and Topic 1997). Unfortunately, most of this debate centers on interpretations of Moche iconography. In my opinion, Moche iconography alone cannot tell us whether combat was ritual or secular since Moche art is highly formalized and must be interpreted with caution (Verano 2001b). Some new attempts to identify the genetic characteristics and population affiliation of the Plaza 3a and 3c victims using mitochondrial DNA (Shinoda et al. 2002; Shimada et al. 2005; Shimada et al., this volume) and dental morphological traits (Sutter and Cortez 2005) may shed new light on the issue. Unfortunately, the results of these preliminary studies are not in agreement. While Shimada finds the Plaza 3a sample internally homogeneous and similar to a comparative sample of mtDNA from burials at the Huaca de la Luna, Sutter and Cortez find them quite distinctive, supporting the hypothesis that they were captives brought from another location. Attempts to extract and amplify mtDNA from Plaza 3c skeletons have been unsuccessful, but analysis of dental morphological traits is in progress.

Regardless of the debate over the nature of Moche combat and the identity of its participants, it is now clear that the capture and sacrifice of prisoners was a significant and deeply rooted focus of ritual activities at the Huaca de la Luna. It remains to be seen whether the sacrifice of captives played an equally important role in ritual activities at other Moche ceremonial complexes such as El Brujo, San José de Moro, or Sipán. Further excavation at these sites will be needed to answer this question.

Acknowledgments

I would like to thank the directors of the Huaca de la Luna Project, Santiago Uceda and Ricardo Morales, and my field co-director, Moises Tufinio, who made the Plaza 3c excavations possible. Thanks also to a dedicated team of graduate and undergraduate students from Tulane University who participated in the excavation of Plaza 3c and analysis of material during the 2000 and 2001 field seasons: Laurel Hamilton, Cathy Gaither, Lori Jahnke, Anne Titelbaum, Ginesse Listi, Stan Serafin, Mary Sawyer, and Teresa Gotay. I am also grateful to Florencia Bracamonte and Moises Rivero of the Universidad Nacional de Trujillo, Mellisa Lund of the Universidad Nacional Mayor de San Marcos, and Melissa Murphy of the University of Pennsylvania for their participation in excavation and laboratory analysis. Thanks also to Tulane anthropology students Heather Backo, Julia

Drapkin, Helen Rich, and Kris Krowicki, who assisted with excavation and analysis of skeletons during the 1999 excavations of Plaza 3c under the direction of Moises Tufinio. Special thanks to my friend and colleague Steve Bourget, who first invited me to study the osteological material from Plaza 3a in 1995.

Funding for the 2000–2001 Plaza 3c excavations was provided by grants 6784-0 and 7024-01 from the National Geographic Society's Committee for Research, and from the Huaca de la Luna Project. The Roger Thayer Stone Center for Latin American Studies at Tulane University kindly provided summer research grants for graduate student travel. Julia Drapkin and Teresa Gotay received travel funding from the Kenneth J. Opat Fund, Department of Anthropology, Tulane University.

Notes

1. Steve Bourget found a circular stone mace head at the foot of the stone outcrop in Plaza 3a, but in a disturbed context (Bourget 1997:57)

2. This wound was identified by Laurel Hamilton in her inventory of the Plaza 3a skeletal remains, conducted as part of her dissertation research (Hamilton 2005).

3. Food remains found in Plaza 3c included nonhuman bone (probably camelid), marine and terrestrial gastropod shells, and carbonized maize cobs. These items were scattered through the plaza fill along with over 1,300 nondiagnostic ceramic sherds. It is unclear whether these food remains and ceramic fragments were associated with sacrificial activities or were simply occupational refuse included in construction fill (see note 4 below).

4. Fragments of Gallinazo style ceramics were also found in the sub-floor strata of Plaza 3c (Armas n.d.).

Bibliography

Alva, Walter, and Christopher B. Donnan

1993   *Royal Tombs of Sipán*. Fowler Museum of Cultural History, University of California, Los Angeles.

Armas, José

n.d.   Análisis del material ceramográfico de la Plaza 3c. In *Investigaciones en la Huaca de la Luna 2001*, 179–198. Edited by Santiago Uceda and Ricardo Morales. Universidad Nacional de Trujillo, Perú.

Bourget, Steve

1997   Las excavaciones en la Plaza 3a. In *Investigaciones en la Huaca de la Luna 1995*, 51–59. Edited by Santiago Uceda, Elías Mujica, and Ricardo Morales. Universidad Nacional de Trujillo, Perú.

1998   Excavaciones en la Plaza 3a y en la Plataforma II de la Huaca de la Luna durante 1996. In *Investigaciones en la Huaca de la Luna 1996*, 43–64. Edited by Santiago Uceda, Elías Mujica, and Ricardo Morales. Universidad Nacional de Trujillo, Perú.

2001a   Children and Ancestors: Ritual Practices at the Moche Site of Huaca de la Luna, North Coast of Peru. In *Ritual Sacrifice in Ancient Peru*, 93–118. Edited by Elizabeth P. Benson and Anita G. Cook. University of Texas Press, Austin.

2001b   Rituals of Sacrifice: Its Practice at Huaca de la Luna and Its Representation in Moche Iconography. In *Moche Art and Archaeology in Ancient Peru*, 88–109. Edited by Joanne Pillsbury. National Gallery of Art and Yale University Press, Washington, D.C.

Bourget, Steve, and Jean-François Millaire

2000   Excavaciones en la Plaza 3a y Plataforma II de la Huaca de la Luna. In *Investigaciones en la Huaca de la Luna 1997*, 47–60. Edited by Santiago Uceda, Elías Mujica, and Ricardo Morales. Universidad Nacional de Trujillo, Perú.

Bourget, Steve, and Margaret E. Newman

1998   A Toast to the Ancestors: Ritual Warfare and Sacrificial Blood in Moche Culture. *Baessler-Archiv*, Neue Folge, 46:85–106. Berlin.

Bracamonte, G. Florencia

1998   Los sacrificios humanos en la Plaza 3a afloramiento rocoso Plataforma II Huaca de la Luna: La evidencia de cultos de crisis. Master's thesis, Universidad Nacional de Trujillo, Perú.

Castillo, Luis Jaime

2000   La ceremonia del sacrificio: Batallas y muerte en el arte mochica. In *La ceremonia del sacrificio: Batallas y muerte en el arte mochica* (exhibition catalog), 14–29. Museo Arqueológico Rafael Larco Herrera, Lima.

Cordy-Collins, Alana

2001   Decapitation in Cupisnique and Early Moche Societies. In *Ritual Sacrifice in Ancient Peru*, 21–33. Edited by Elizabeth P. Benson and Anita G. Cook. University of Texas Press, Austin.

Delabarde, T.

n.d.   Análisis de los restos humanos de la Plataforma Uhle. In *Investigaciones en la Huaca de la Luna 2000*, 209–216. Edited by Santiago Uceda, Elías Mujica, and Ricardo Morales. Universidad Nacional de Trujillo, Perú.

Donnan, Christopher B.

1978   *Moche Art of Peru: Pre-Columbian Symbolic Commu-*

nication. Museum of Cultural History, University of California, Los Angeles.

1997   Deer Hunting and Combat: Parallel Activities in the Moche World. In *The Spirit of Ancient Peru: Treasures from the Museo Arqueológico Rafael Larco Herrera* (exhibition catalog), 51–59. Edited by Kathleen Berrin. Fine Arts Museum of San Francisco, Thames and Hudson, New York.

2004   *Moche Portraits from Ancient Peru.* University of Texas Press, Austin.

Donnan, Christopher B., and Donna McClelland

1979   *The Burial Theme in Moche Iconography.* Dumbarton Oaks, Washington, D.C.

1999   *Moche Fineline Painting: Its Evolution and Its Artists.* Fowler Museum of Cultural History, University of California, Los Angeles.

Hamilton, Laurel A.

2005   Cutmarks as Evidence of Precolumbian Human Sacrifice and Postmortem Bone Modification on the North Coast of Peru. Unpublished Ph.D. dissertation, Department of Anthropology, Tulane University, New Orleans.

Hill, Erica

2000   The Embodied Sacrifice. *Cambridge Archaeological Journal* 10 (2):317–326.

Hocquenghem, Anne Marie

1987   *Iconografía mochica.* Fondo Editorial de la Pontificia Universidad Católica del Perú, Lima.

Rea, Amadeo M.

1986   Black Vultures and Human Victims: Archaeological Evidence from Pacatnamu. In *The Pacatnamu Papers,* 1:139–144. Edited by Christopher B. Donnan and Guillermo A. Cock. Museum of Cultural History, Los Angeles.

Sauer, N. J.

1998   The Timing of Injuries and Manner of Death: Distinguishing Among Antemortem, Perimortem and Postmortem Trauma. In *Forensic Osteology: Advances in the Identification of Human Remains,* 321–332. Edited by Kathleen J. Reichs. Charles C. Thomas, Springfield, Illinois.

Shinoda, Ken-Ichi, Izumi Shimada, Walter Alva, and Santiago Uceda

2002   DNA Analysis of Moche and Sicán Populations: Results and Implications. Paper presented at the 67th Annual Meeting of the Society for American Archaeology, Denver, March 21. *http://gross.anatomy.sagamed.ac.jp/ shinoda/SAA/poster.html.*

Shimada, Izumi, Kazuo Shinoda, Steve Bourget, Walter Alva, and Santiago Uceda

2005   MtDNA Analysis of Mochica and Sicán Populations of Pre-Hispanic Peru. *Biomolecular Archaeology: Genetic Approaches to the Past* 32:61–92.

Sutter, Richard C. and Rosa Cortez

2005   The Nature of Moche Human Sacrifice: A Bio-Archaeological Perspective. *Current Anthropology* 46 (4):521–549.

Topic, John R., and Teresa L. Topic

1997   La guerra mochica. *Revista Arqueológica SIAN* 4:10–12. Universidad Nacional de Trujillo, Perú.

Tufinio, Moises

n.d.   Plaza 3c. In *Investigaciones en la Huaca de la Luna 2001.* Edited by Santiago Uceda, Elías Mujica, and Ricardo Morales. Universidad Nacional de Trujillo, Perú.

Ubelaker, Douglas H., and Henry Scammell

1992   *Bones: A Forensic Detective's Casebook.* 1st ed. Edward Burlingame Books, New York.

Uceda, Santiago, Claude Chapdelaine, Claude Chauchat, and John W. Verano

n.d.   Fechas radiocarbónicas para el complejo arqueológico Huacas del Sol y la Luna: Una primera cronología del sitio. In *Investigaciones en la Huaca de la Luna 2001.* Edited by Santiago Uceda, Ricardo Morales, and Elías Mujica Universidad Nacional de Trujillo, Perú.

Uceda, Santiago, and Moises Tufinio

2003   El complejo architectónico religioso moche de Huaca de la Luna: Una aproximación a su dinámica ocupacional. In *Moche: Hacia el Final del Milenio,* Tome II, 179–228. Actas del Segundo Coloquio sobre la Cultura Moche, Trujillo, 1 al 7 de agosto de 1999. Edited by Santiago Uceda and Elías Mujica. Universidad Nacional de Trujillo and Pontificia Universidad Católica del Perú, Lima.

Verano, John W.

1986   A Mass Burial of Mutilated Individuals at Pacatnamu. In *The Pacatnamu Papers,* 1:117–138. Edited by Christopher B. Donnan and Guillermo A. Cock. Museum of Cultural History, Los Angeles.

1995   Where Do They Rest? The Treatment of Human Offerings and Trophies in Ancient Peru. In *Tombs for the Living: Andean Mortuary Practices,* 189–227. Edited by Tom D. Dillehay. Dumbarton Oaks, Washington, D.C.

1998   Sacrificios humanos, desmembramientos y modificaciones culturales en restos osteológicos: Evidencias de las temporadas de investigación 1995–96 en la Huaca de la Luna. In *Investigaciones en la Huaca de la Luna 1996,* 159–171. Edited by Santiago Uceda, Elías Mujica, and Ricardo Morales. Universidad Nacional de Trujillo, Perú.

2001a   Paleopathological Analysis of Sacrificial Victims at the Pyramid of the Moon, Moche River Valley, Northern Peru. *Revista de Antropología Chilena* 32 (1):61–70.

2001b   War and Death in the Moche World: Osteological Evidence and Visual Discourse. In *Moche Art and Archaeology in Ancient Peru*, 111–125. Edited by Joanne Pillsbury. National Gallery of Art and Yale University Press, Washington, D.C.

n.d.   Esqueletos humanos de la Plaza 3c. In *Investigaciones en la Huaca de la Luna 2001*. Edited by Santiago Uceda,

Ricardo Morales, and Elías Mujica. Universidad Nacional de Trujillo, Perú.

Verano, John W., and Moises Tufinio

n.d.   Plaza 3c. In *Investigaciones en la Huaca de la Luna 2000*. Edited by Santiago Uceda, Elías Mujica and Ricardo Morales. Universidad Nacional de Trujillo, Perú.

Verano, John W., Santiago Uceda, Claude Chapdelaine, Ricardo Tello, María I. Paredes, and Victor Pimentel

1999   Modified Human Skulls from the Urban Sector of the Pyramids of Moche, Northern Peru. *Latin American Antiquity* 10 (1):59–70.

CHAPTER TWELVE

Art and Moche Martial Arts

JEFFREY QUILTER, PEABODY MUSEUM OF ARCHAEOLOGY AND ETHNOLOGY,
HARVARD UNIVERSITY

Abstract

Much of Moche art, especially in its later phases, celebrates warfare and sacrifice. Scholars have used these images to infer the nature of conflict and ritual as well as their social contexts. Some interpretations view Moche warfare as highly ritualized, while Moche sacrifices, at the same time, were performed as the final act of military campaigns. This chapter examines the issues surrounding warfare as ritual and ritual as warfare, the problems faced in this apparently close relationship, and their implications for understanding larger issues of Moche politics and society.

To judge by their art, the Moche were a warlike people. From early modeled warriors to late painted battle scenes, their ceramics celebrate the martial arts. The famous marching prisoner frieze at Huaca Cao Viejo (Figure 12.1) and a similar depiction recently discovered at Huaca de La Luna testify to the celebration of victorious battles, whether or not a specific battle is indicated in such scenes. Humans fight and so do gods, and mythical heroes or demigods are frequently shown in combat (Figure 12.2). By Late Moche times, the club-and-shield and a more elaborate trophy display appear to become iconic, summarizing symbols of a militaristically oriented Moche ideology (Quilter 1990). Although interpretations differ widely concerning the nature of Moche political organization, economics, and religion, there is unanimity among Moche specialists that the themes of warfare, of one kind or another, played a central role in human affairs on the north coast of Peru during the first several centuries of the Common Era.

Representations of warriors, warfare, and other forms of combat provide the opportunity to explore several different types of issues concerning the Moche. We can identify weapons and thereby infer military tactics and even strategy. From these we may make inferences

or at least speculate on some of the social conditions to which Moche militarism was tied. In doing this, however, we must take into account the fact that depictions of armed conflict were selectively chosen by ancient artists and their patrons, and rendered in specific ways to convey distinct messages about social relations. In short, we can only interpret Moche combat art in relation to larger cultural considerations. What the Moche chose to show on their pots, walls, and in other media may only partly reflect Moche warfare. In considering what the Moche did not show, we may also raise questions about the nature of Moche society and the role of both warfare and art within it.

In the following section, I review previous discussions of Moche military issues and add some of my own observations. I will then suggest an interpretation of Moche combat drawn from the corpus of Moche art and archaeology. The chapter concludes with some comments on the implications of my analysis of combat and art.

Previous Studies

Although all Moche scholars have acknowledged the ubiquity of militaristic themes, there have been surprisingly few systematic studies of Moche warriors

FIGURE 12.1. Marching prisoner frieze at Huaca Cao Viejo, led by a warrior, poorly preserved. Fragments of a second group also are present in a wall section to the right of this one, suggesting that prisoners were marched in groups of ten.

FIGURE 12.2. God or mythical hero battling an anthropomorphic bird as depicted on a Moche pottery vessel. The figure at left holds a dart in a spear-thrower, while that on the right holds a small club. Both figures hold enigmatic objects in their other hands. Redrawn from Kutscher 1954, Figure 56A.

or warfare. This is curious given the fact that, lately, warfare has received a considerable amount of attention, especially among North American prehistorians (Haas 1999; Lambert 2002; LeBlanc 1999, 2001; Milner 1999), Mesoamericanists (Flannery and Marcus 2003; Hassig 1988; Trejo 2000; Webster 1999, 2000), and European prehistorians (Thorpe 2003; Vencl 1999). Most discussions of Moche militarism are expressed in general terms referring to the "manpower to overrun southern valleys" and expansion through "conquest and coercion," as Michael Moseley phrases his proposal of the establishment of a single Moche state throughout the north coast (1992:183). Otherwise, fineline representations of combat and the presence of numerous fortified sites are offered as evidence of warfare (Moseley 1992: figs. 72, 82).

In discussing Tomb 1 at Sipán, Alva and Donnan (1993) suggest (1) that depictions of processions of warriors may indicate that they marched to battle, and (2) that the hills and plants depicted in some battle scenes imply that battlefields were at some distance from Moche population centers. They also note a lack of scenes of warriors attacking fortifications and an absence of depictions of aggression towards noncombatants. They state:

> Moreover, there is no evidence that the Moche employed any equipment or tactics that involved teams of warriors acting in close coordination. We see no regular formations of troops like Greek phalanxes, or siege instruments whose operation consisted of trained squads of individuals. (Alva and Donnan 1993:129)

Alva and Donnan posit that while some depictions show two warriors attacking a single opponent, the "essence" of Moche warfare was one-on-one combat (ibid.). The depiction of a death in combat is rare, whereas the defeat of an enemy by a blow to the head or upper torso is more commonly shown. Once defeated, the prisoner was bound for the sacrifice ceremony. Alva and Donnan never explicitly state that Moche warfare was carried out for the purpose of providing sacrificial victims. Nevertheless, the implication is in the structure of their argument, and many other scholars have interpreted Moche warfare as in the service of a cult of sacrifice.

Indeed, today there are two schools of thought on representations of Moche combat. Some scholars believe that warfare was primarily ritual, for the purpose of fulfilling religious obligations to sacrifice war captives. Others see depictions of combat as representing military engagements for political purposes.

The school of thought supporting the idea of warfare as primarily motivated by religious and ritual reasons includes a great number of scholars and is pervasive in Andean studies well beyond the investigation of the Moche. Although ritual motivations have been questioned (Kellner 2001), the model of contemporary ritual battles with low casualty rates, known as *tinkuy*, informs a host of studies (Browne, Silverman, and Garcia 1993; Carmichael 1992; Castillo 2000; Donnan 1997; Hocquenghem 1978; Topic and Topic 1997).

The only scholar to systematically review Moche militarism was the founder of modern Moche studies, Rafael Larco Hoyle (2001:199–229). Larco mostly concentrates on military costumes and weaponry, but his thoughts on other matters are sometimes implied or referenced in his discussion. Perhaps his most salient point in this regard is his reference to "common" warriors (*guerreros communes*) and elites (*grandes jefes*), who, he notes, were at the same time political leaders (*gobernantes*). Both higher- and lower-ranking warriors wore the same basic outfit and carried similar arms. The differences were mostly in the degree of costume elaboration.

Warrior Clothing and Armaments

Basic warrior clothing consisted of a long shirt-like garment (sometimes shown with short sleeves), a tunic that reached mid-thigh and was secured at the waist by a belt. A conical helmet completed the basic costume. The conical helmet design was well chosen to deflect blows to the head. Helmets often are shown adorned with crests and feathers. The basic conical helmet also was sometimes wrapped with a thick band around its lower part and with ear spool–like ornaments. Chin straps are occasionally shown, and almost every helmet appears to have been bound with cloth, which included a loose section that covered the back of the neck, like a stereotypical French Foreign Legionnaire.

Many fineline paintings depict the components of a warrior's costume as separate items (Figure 12.3). Among these is commonly included a trapezoidal object

FIGURE 12.3. Fineline painting from a Moche vessel depicting weaponry and warriors. Redrawn from Larco 2001, Figure 255.

that appears to be fabric shown flat, judging by the loose cords on each side of its upper part. These garments also are frequently shown bicolored and with small circles on their lower edge, which may represent metal disks, bells, or similar objects. The shape and other aspects of this item suggest that it is either a cape for the upper body or a skirt. If it is a skirt, then this suggests that Moche warrior garb consisted of two pieces, an upper shirt and a lower skirt. Alternatively, this skirt may have been an extra layer of clothing worn over the lower section of the shirt, below the belt.

The final item of dress for many warriors was the backflap. Larco refers to these items as "knives" (*cuchillos*), pointing out their resemblance to knives shown in combat and sacrifice scenes, and suggesting that the form of these ornamental clothing elements derived from them (2001:215). The five examples in the Larco Museum range in size from 15.5 cm to 32 cm in

length (Larco 2001:215). In painted representations, backflaps are shown at a much larger scale in relation to the height of the individuals wearing them. Presumably, real backflaps would have been worn flat, hanging from the belt of a warrior over his backside. In painted renditions, however, these items are shown as if twisted from the position in which they would normally be viewed, signaling their importance and the desire of the artist to make sure that the viewer recognizes that the warriors in question wore backflaps. The same distortion was done for helmet crests.

Not all warriors depicted in the art wear backflaps. Some appear to have trapezoidal cloths or similar objects descending from higher on the back than the belt, although these may represent two smaller backflaps. Some warriors with or without backflaps also are shown with what appears to be a rope-like loop of fabric or other material, often with a serrated edge, extending from their upper back. The quadrangular objects appear to be connected to this loop, while the backflaps are attached to the belt below it.

In addition to costume, many warriors sported dark face paint. Some are shown with dark colored wrists, suggesting either paint or, perhaps more likely, wristlets. Almost all warriors are shown with paint covering their toes and shins, with a separate thin line encircling the leg slightly higher. Some warriors also have knee caps covered in circles of paint with a surrounding, thin concentric ring. No footwear is shown for any warriors. Either artistic conventions did not include the showing of sandals or similar gear, or Moche warriors did not wear them.

The Moche weapons and related equipment listed by Larco (2001:207–216) include maces (*mazas* or *poras*), spear-throwers (*estólicas*), spear-thrower darts, lances, slings, bags for slingshots, shields, and helmets. Larco's catalog of armaments is drawn from representations in art as well as actual examples (see Figure 12.3). For the lances, he presents information on four in the collection, all of them over 2 m long (Larco 2001:213). He distinguishes these *lanzas* from spear-thrower darts (*dardos para la estólica*), of which he had no examples in his collection, so he did not confuse the categories as some might do. Still, the absence of darts in the collection is of concern. Perhaps darts were made of lighter materials and have not preserved as well as lances. Because darts are always shown as compound weapons consisting of a long point and a thicker shaft, the difference between lances and darts appears to be genuine; however, true lances or long spears are rarely, if ever, shown in Moche art, suggesting that they may have had limited use in space and time. In the same section in which he discusses lances, Larco also discusses large copper points (50.2, 41.7, 45, and 24.5 cm in length [Larco 2001:214]) and suggests that these are the working ends of lances.

The copper points that Larco illustrates may have been used for lances, but given the fact that lances are rarely shown in Moche art, these copper spikes may have been dart tips. If they were used for spear-thrower darts, a great amount of counter weight would have had to be added to the lower shaft in order for the weapon to balance properly when held in the spear-thrower, making the weapon heavy. The advantage of a metal-pointed dart may have been less important than lighter darts that could be thrown more rapidly. It also seems rather unlikely that a spear-thrower dart would be tipped with a copper point close to half a meter in length. I would also question whether Moche industry could have produced sufficient quantities for spear-thrower darts, which would have had high rates of loss when thrown at the enemy.

Many depictions of darts show a variety of points, including barbs. To my knowledge, no barbed copper weapons have been found to date, perhaps suggesting that barbed dart points were made of wood rather than metal. Until darts with metal tips are discovered, the question of whether the Moche spear-thrower and dart weaponry was light or heavy artillery, or a combination of both, will remain unanswered.

I believe that the long copper points were not used on projectiles but served as spikes on the bottom ends of large, two-handed clubs, a category of weapon I propose calling the Moche war club. Archaeological examples do not reveal such a basal spike, but frequently, in artistic renditions, the lower section of the typical Moche war club is long and thin and colored differently than the main shaft of the weapon (Figure 12.4). In some renditions, the lower part of the weapon bulges slightly, suggesting that the end of the club's wooden shaft was inserted into a socket in the metal spike rather than the metal being inserted into the wood. In other examples,

FIGURE 12.4. Two examples of weapons bundles from Moche ceramics. The example on the left shows a club with possible basal spike and two possible spear-thrower darts. The example on the right may also show darts and a club. Note the ring near the base of the club. The dotted circles indicate where the stirrup spout connected to the body of the vessel. After Kutscher 1954, Figure 16F (*left*) and A (*right*).

the bottom point of the weapon is not colored differently but has a ridge or ring running around the bottom of the shaft, just above the section where the taper begins. Perhaps such a ring was made on clubs, which had sharpened ends rather than copper stilettos. This device likely would have served to prevent the pointed end of the club from penetrating too deeply into an enemy's body, making it difficult to withdraw and endangering the attacker. It might be expected that during the Moche era there were variations in the use of the pointed base of a war club or a spike added to it. At least one fineline painting seems to clearly show the spike in use (Figure 12.5). Perhaps only elite warriors, or a certain group at a particular time and place, used clubs with basal spikes. In close hand-to-hand fighting they would have provided a significant, deadly advantage to any warriors equipped with them.

Larco (2001: fig. 236) illustrates a large, likely two-handed mace and a shorter example; both exhibit the distinct biconical distal end with a ridge separating the two sections, typical of the Moche war club so frequently depicted in art. No examples of the larger varieties exhibit basal spikes. If clubs were inserted into a socket in the spike, however, the metal could have been removed and recycled, even in prehistory. Close inspection of some of the extant clubs might reveal wear patterns that would indicate the former presence of basal spikes. Larco (2001: fig. 240) also illustrates smaller clubs, none of which show the distinctive biconical head and which range to sizes so small that they are difficult to consider as clubs for serious use as weapons at all.

Moche Combat and Tactics

Although hand-to-hand combat and its weapons are frequently depicted in Moche art, especially fineline painting, the presence of distance weapons such as slings, spear-throwers, and darts is testimony to a different type of combat (Figures 12.2, 12.3, 12.6). In all warfare, ancient or modern, artillery or its equivalent is used to "soften up" an enemy force before hand-to-hand fighting occurs. Of course, these weapons may be used against individual enemies in much the same way that an anti-tank missile can be used against an infantryman, but it is not for such purposes that missile weapons are designed.

A dart fired from a spear-thrower would have been useful against an individual enemy in the rush of lines as warriors were about to engage in hand-to-hand combat. Otherwise, darts and sling stones are best employed either in ambushes or by massed attackers against massed defenders, when it is less easy for those being attacked to side-step missiles as they are faced not with a single projectile, but rather an oncoming rain of stones or darts. One way to determine how Moche slings and spear-throwers were employed would be to study collections of available weapons and to conduct experimental studies using replicas. The lengths of slings could serve as indications of the distances covered by the missiles thrown by various slings. Spear-throwers induce trajectories that range from flat for relatively short distances, to arcs for longer ones. Experiments with replicas should help to determine the ranges of Moche spear-throwers and their darts, as well as the kinds of combats in which they were employed.

FIGURE 12.5. Detail of a Moche battle scene. The left-hand figure in the central pair of combatants appears to be using the basal spike as his preferred armament in combat. The second figure from the right may also be using his spike. After Kutscher 1954, Figure 21.

FIGURE 12.6. Vessel depiction of a battle in hills or mountains. Figure 1 holds darts behind a shield as well as a club. Two warriors (2 and 5) may wear wooden slat armor. After Kutscher 1954, Figure 20A.

Once hand-to-hand combat began, it appears that the two-handed club with a biconical, ribbed head and, occasionally, a basal spike was the preferred weapon. It is interesting to consider that while single-handed clubs are shown in Moche art, they are less common in later fineline painting. Stone mace heads are hallmarks of the earlier Salinar culture (Burger 1996), and it may be that they decreased in use, perhaps remaining as a kind of "side arm" or sign of rank but diminishing over time as a primary weapon of war for the Moche. Some of the small clubs presented by Larco and discussed above may have served as such emblems of rank or authority more than as actual weapons.

The distinctive two-handed club may, in fact, be the innovation that resulted in Moche military superiority over their neighbors. In hand-to-hand combat, a greater reach is a critical advantage, just as broad swords became the weapon of choice as Antiquity gave way to the Middle Ages. The Moche war club would have delivered a powerful blow, and if the basal spike were employed, it would have been doubly lethal. The power of such weapons may have been so great as to render shields effectively useless, perhaps resulting in their diminished size over time, becoming more useful as arm guards or to ward off the occasional sling stone or dart than as true shields for body protection. If the size of Moche shields, usually circular but sometimes square, were roughly at the scale depicted in most art, they would have been most useful to protect the head or a vital body part from

such missile attacks, but insufficiently strong enough to withstand blows in hand-to-hand combat with clubs.

If held with the hands close together at the lower end of the shaft, elasticity in the wood of the Moche war club would have added a whip-like force to a blow; experiments, again, could examine this issue. Delivering such a blow, however, endangers the attacker if he misses his target as the likelihood of losing balance is great with so much concentration of force invested in it.

Moche warriors are frequently shown holding their long clubs with their hands spaced widely on the shafts. This may be an "at ready" position, but it may also be the stance of actual combat, especially if clubs were armed with basal spikes. The mode of combat with these weapons may have favored using them much as staves were employed in contemporary Europe (as in Friar Tuck and Robin Hood) rather than strictly as striking weapons. In this form of combat, the warrior needs both hands free to be able to shift them for blocking an opponent's blow and also to reposition them to employ the weapon's two ends in an attack and, when advantageous, strike a powerful blow with hands close together near the base of the shaft.

This proposed method of using Moche war clubs may have encouraged the reduction of shield size in order to free hands to wield the weapon in various positions. This point, combined with the apparent lack of defense against missiles, suggests that Moche tactics emphasized aggression much more than defense. Moche armies probably attempted to engage the enemy in hand-to-hand combat as quickly as possible. Tactics likely would have varied, however, depending on whom the Moche were fighting. If they confronted armies with different weapons than their own, we would expect that they would have adjusted their tactics accordingly.

Moche Military Organization and Warfare

Alva and Donnan (1993:129) note that there are no depictions in art of teams of warriors acting in close coordination, no regular formations of troops, and no siege weapons. These points are raised in defense of the proposition that the warfare depicted in art was ritual, not for seizing territory or other political purposes. They also offer support for their argument of ritual warfare by noting that battles appear to occur away from population centers (Figure 12.6). Engagements are never shown near towns or ritual centers, and occasionally small desert plants are depicted, as if the warriors are fighting outside of river valleys, in the wastelands that separate them. These proposals may be countered by considering other possibilities, both in terms of what we may deduce about Moche tactics, and how art may or may not depict warfare.

As noted above, the two-handed war club may have been the critical weapon that gave Moche armies advantages in the field. Nevertheless, slings and spear-throwers do appear in art. Both of these weapons are ancient and may have arrived with the first human inhabitants of the New World. What is more certain is that both weapons served not only military purposes but subsistence ones as well. Slings are the traditional weapons of pastoralists to defend their herds and can also be used for hunting. The spear-thrower and its darts also are used for hunting and are shown wielded by warriors in deer hunting scenes. Deer are often depicted by the Moche as bound prisoners, and it appears that deer hunting was seen as analogous to, perhaps even symbolic of, human combat (Donnan 1997), in much the same way as similar analogies were made by the Maya.

In the simplest agrarian and pastoral nonindustrial societies, there is little distinction between tools and weapons. Sharp-edged tools or bludgeons, which serve purposes of providing food, are pressed into service to do violence to enemies who threaten life and livelihood. As sectors of society begin to specialize as warriors, how-

ever, specialized weapons also emerge. Cadres of elite warriors often spurn the use of anything other than arms that distinguish them apart from the common folk using older tool-weapons. Spear-throwers and slings do occasionally appear in Moche art, however (Figures 12.6, 12.7), and elite warriors may have used them. The poorest combatants probably used farm implements, such as digging sticks, and perhaps slings and spear-throwers retained their role as weapons appropriate for elites.

A thorough study of representations of slings and spear-throwers in Moche art would help to explicate the degree of weaponry specialization in relation to warrior status. Slings appear to be shown the least often, while spear-throwers are shown more frequently but far less often than clubs, especially the Moche war club. Perhaps there was increasing specialization through time. The projectile weapons may have been more common earlier, with the war club coming to dominate warrior representations later, or, alternatively, some kind of regional variation may have been in operation. This is but another example of our need to gain better temporal and spatial control over data. Even if there was some variation, however, the Moche war club appears to be the preeminent weapon of choice of Moche warriors as depicted in the art and, particularly, later in prehistory.

Elite warrior groups not only use their own armaments but also try to dictate the way in which warfare is conducted. They will often persist in ineffective practices because of the social implications of change. Japanese samurai realized that their social supremacy would be undermined if peasant armies were equipped with firearms, which were first introduced in 1543. Within five years the peasant armies were winning major battles, and by the end of the century, Japan had more firearms than Europe. By the early 1600s, however, gun use diminished as elites realized that their positions were being undermined on the battlefield and in society. Guns virtually disappeared until the arrival of Commodore Perry in 1855, which accelerated their reintroduction into arsenals (Perrin 1980).

In a similar vein, one of the most effective strategies for killing great numbers of the enemy in preindustrial warfare was massed volleys of arrows, as French mounted knights learned to their sorrow against English archers in the Hundred Years War. In the absence of arrows, sling stones and darts could have the same

FIGURE 12.7. A battle scene in which use of a sling is shown. Drawing by Donna McClelland.

effect. Against such an onslaught, the defender must either get out of the range of the oncoming volley (not always possible) or have sufficient defensive weaponry to withstand the attack. The strongest defenses are either strong, large shields or armor. Although there are suggestions that some Moche warriors wore slat wood armor (Figures 12.5, 12.6, 12.7), no large shields are depicted. It may be safe to say that warrior codes worldwide emphasize attackers, not defenders, and that hiding behind a shield is not the kind of military activity that tends to be celebrated in art.

It is quite likely that all, or at least most, of the warriors shown in Moche art were elites. Their costumes are elaborate, sporting many decorations and devices analogous to heraldic designs. These include helmet crests and other adornments, as noted above, as well as markings on helmets, tunics, and shields; however, there are no clear patterns that can be easily used to segregate warriors into recognizable grades or ranks. This likely is due to four possible reasons: (1) there were no warrior ranks; (2) warrior ranks were not marked in the art; (3) means of distinguishing ranks consisted of criteria not observable in art; and (4) incomplete evidence, partly due to the collapsing of temporal and spatial dimensions of analysis, makes any patterns that might be apparent with more evidence inchoate.

Following my earlier discussion, it seems very likely that warrior ranks did exist. Such ranks certainly appear to be manifest in the art, given the various crests and other markings noted above. It also is unlikely that rank was denoted by nonvisual means that would not have carried over to artistic depictions. Elite warriors, even in relatively egalitarian societies (such as the Cheyenne Dog Soldiers), always visually signal their rank in order to gain social capital with their bravery in their own society, to serve as rallying points or examples in the heat of battle, and for many other reasons.

Therefore, Moche art may have depicted only elite warriors, even though lower ranks existed. The depiction of common foot soldiers is relatively rare in the history of art. Elite warriors are more likely to be favored subjects, even if consumers of the art include common people, because of cultural values fostering hero worship of knights, commanders, generals, and the like. The choice of subject depicted in military art has less to do with the relative importance of high- or low-ranking warriors in campaigns and battles than who commissions the art when the battles are over.

The different costumes seen on warriors in Moche art may all be indicators of elite status. In other words, the variations observable are within a general class of dress and weaponry that was only available to elite warriors. Common warriors likely were much more simply dressed and not shown in the art at all, or so rarely that we cannot easily recognize such figures. Artists (or their patrons) may have insisted on twisting helmet crests and backflaps, violating the relative verisimilitude of representation in their art, because these two costume elements were part of sumptuary privileges reserved for elite warriors; common soldiers would have had no helmet crests and no backflaps. Moche common soldiers may appear in the art as individuals without these traits. It is also possible that, for most of the Moche era, it was a warrior's prerogative to dress as he chose or according to standards that were linked to personal, lineage, or clan affiliations rather than to ranks per se.

Classical Greek warfare and art are analogous to those of the Moche in that warfare was preindustrial and that Attic vases served as vehicles for depicting a wide range of human activities, including warfare. On such vases the emphasis tends to be on one-on-one combat of ancient heroes, such as Achilles and Hector, or Ajax's suicide, rather than on showing coordinated fighting by teams. Moche art is not Athenian art, but craftsmen in both societies were faced with issues of how to portray combat in the limited, curving space of pottery vessels. Given those limitations, as well as the social realities of societies that glorified the achievements of famous warriors, it is reasonable to propose that similar factors led to common foot soldiers not being included in art. Even in relatively recent times, when generals are rarely portrayed but foot soldiers are, the great number of behind-the-lines providers of weaponry, food, and supplies rarely are memorialized, even though they are as vital to successful military endeavors as combat soldiers.

The Beazley Archive (2005) is a large collection of documents on Classical Greek pottery, gems, and sculpture. The Web site of the archive provides a means to search 250,000 black-and-white images of pottery vessels. I conducted a search of this Web archive in early 2005 with the search fields of "Athenian," "vases," "black figure," and "warriors" and called for only those records in the archives for which pictures were available. The result was 3,034 records in which 908 vases were represented. Other categories included sherds of other vessel types, as well as line drawings of vessel profiles and the like. I reviewed the first 400 images in the list

of results. I picked 400 in an effort to approximate a 10 percent sample of the total collection, since some of the images are profile line drawings of vessels and do not depict imagery.

Of the 400 images, only two might be interpreted as representing Athenian warriors of the Classical Age in ranks. Even in these cases, their formation is uncertain and not much different than groups of warriors shown on some Moche vessels. Most of the images show groups of armed fighters preparing for battle, in scenes that may represent periods before or after engagements, and fights themselves. The ways in which battles are depicted are not that different from Moche fineline painting save for the fact that the Athenian artists overlapped figures to give a sense of depth, whereas Moche artists tended to picture individuals in sequence around a vessel. Occasionally, however, figures are depicted in higher or lower positions in the plane of representation to indicate an action not within the main field of events and to add depth to the imagery.

The most likely explanation of why Moche art portrays only elite warriors is because the society in which militarism played so great a role was highly ranked or stratified. As in the case of Athenian warfare, armies likely clashed with common soldiers, with elites quickly joining in hand-to-hand combat. But it was the exploits of heroes who faced each other by circumstance or challenge that became the stuff of legend and of art. After the sling stones were hurled and the darts flicked from spear-throwers, the heavy infantry likely made the difference in battle. The bronze-tipped spears of the Achaeans and Trojans rang off of the shields of enemies into legends and into the songs of Homer. So too, the heavy clubs of great Moche warriors pounded their ways into oral tales and fineline paintings.

Figure 12.6 depicts an engagement of three pairs of combatants. The stippled mounds below the feet of the warriors suggest that the fight took place in the hills. Small plants, some of which may be cacti, fill in some of the spaces between the figures. It is tempting to interpret the dark band running through the hills as a river, but this is speculative. Two warriors (1 and 2) are about to engage in hand-to-hand combat, while two others (3 and 5) appear to be defeating their opponents (4 and 6), judging by the loss of their helmets and body positions. Warriors 2 and 5 are dressed in similar battle dress, which may include the slat wood armor occasionally seen in other depictions, as in Figure 12.5.

Two similarly dressed warriors (2 and 5) in Figure 12.6 might lead us to interpret them as members of the same side in the battle, but we cannot know this for certain. Perhaps the sides are to be read by the direction in which they are moving, from left to right, for one side, and right to left for the other. If the directional reading is followed, we might interpret the warriors in the proposed slat armor as of higher rank than the others, but on opposing sides. It is interesting to note, however, that Warriors 5 and 6 share the same interlocking spiral motif on their tunics. These clearly are opponents, and yet they share the same motif on their clothes. Warriors 2, 3, and 4 all exhibit circles on their tunics, and yet again, two (3 and 4) are clearly opponents and share the closest pattern of circles on the chest areas of their tunics although other sections of their costumes differ.

Another interesting detail of this combat scene is Warrior 1. In his right hand he holds a large club, and in his left hand he holds a circular shield with three darts behind it. No spear-thrower is depicted, but perhaps it is clasped in the hand holding the shield and thus out of view. Nevertheless, it is interesting to consider that this warrior is using both the Moche war club and projectiles. Apparently, at least at some times and places, elite warriors used spear-throwers and darts.

The fact that some of these warriors wear similar clothing with similar designs could be interpreted as evidence that Moche warfare was ritual, occurring within the same community and for the sake of religion. But the argument could just as easily be made that the similarity in costume can be attributed to artistic license, or because elements of elite warrior dress and design elements cross-cut the social units that fought each other. The latter explanation certainly was true for medieval knights. Indeed, in many places and times, the most common enemies are closely related: the fleur-de-lis was on the coats of arms of both the English and French in the Hundred Years War because the former claimed territory in France through rights of kingly inheritance.

No cities or temple mounds are shown in Moche battle scenes. For societies such as the Moche's, the defense of a city would have been a last, desperate measure, only occurring when military strategy called for total destruction of the enemy, as was the case among the ancient Maya and Aztecs (Hassig 1988; Webster 2000). Such extreme measures only occurred when larger economic and political forces were unraveling whole societies. Warfare can be serious and deadly without having the final outcome of conflict as its goal—as in, for example, the playing out of status rivalries (Webster 1999).

The most critical resource to defend for agrarian societies are agricultural fields and grain storage facilities; for those who depended on irrigation, canals and water would have been equally vital, if not more critical, to defend. Defensive strategy for the Moche would have compelled them to try to stop an enemy force before it reached the defender's home territory—the river valley, canals, and agricultural fields—since their vulnerability was so high. The place to stop advancing forces would have been the No Man's Land of the desert between river valleys.

Concluding Remarks

The points raised above are offered as considerations as to why it cannot simply be assumed that Moche art can be read straightforwardly as presenting a complete picture of Moche warfare; clearly the lack of certain features in the art necessitates that we consider it as representing ritual warfare. Archaeologists are uncomfortable with negative evidence, but art cannot be simply accepted at face value, and my case for Moche warfare is not based solely on negative evidence. Slings, spear-throwers, and darts are shown in the art, just not very frequently in use. But someone did use them, and when used, they clearly would have been potentially lethal when employed effectively. Nevertheless, these weapons are not frequently shown in depictions of human combat, and when they are, they are not shown in use, as in the case of the combatant in Figure 12.6. It is reasonable to assume, therefore, that many aspects of Moche warfare were not depicted in their art. I believe that the reason for this is simply because there were conventions of artistic taste and style that privileged hand-to-hand combat by elites, as has been the case in many times and places throughout history.

It is no minor point that Moche culture lasted for about 700 years, and that during that time, society and warfare likely changed considerably. It is quite possible that at different times in those many centuries, war took on more formal, regulated, and symbolic aspects, while at others, rules of engagement broke down and Moche lords did whatever they could to conquer their enemies.

Warfare always has a ritual component and more so, perhaps, when elites are directly involved in combat. The founder of the Teotihuacan-related dynasty at Copán, Yax K'uk Mo', yielded a skeleton to forensic studies that revealed he had been well-muscled in life and quite likely had suffered wounds in combat (Nystrom, Braunstein, and Buikstra et al. 2004). The skeleton of the Lord of Sipán was not as well preserved as that of his near-contemporary in Honduras. Alva and Donnan, reporting John Verano's study of the remains of Tomb 1, note that the male individual was between thirty-five and forty-five years old at his death, relatively tall (166 cm) but with "fairly delicate" bones and no "signs of heavy muscle development" (1993:104–105). The issue of Moche lords as war leaders may need further samples and forensic studies. More generally, the fact that Moche lords were commonly depicted as warriors suggests that they probably were, indeed, actively engaged in warfare.

Many monarchs assume warrior garb without necessarily taking the field themselves, and this may have been the case for the Moche. This seems unlikely, however. Future analyses of human remains will surely clarify this issue. The impression I have from current iconographic and archaeological remains, however, is (1) that Moche lords were combatants or, at least, actively involved in warfare during their youth, and (2) that through such activities they gained and maintained power, probably coupled with inherited status as the result of birth in leading families. If this is the case, Moche political organization may have been much more centered on family and lineage, as in the case of the Maya, than on an elaborate state bureaucratic apparatus. The fact that Moche lords may have served the ritual role of the "Warrior Priest" (formerly, the "Rayed Being") suggests that the lines between political and religious offices themselves were blurred or, at least, linked in the supreme leader. I offer this less as a certainty than as a hypothesis for future study.

Returning to the issue of the nature of Moche warfare, I believe that the simplest interpretation of the iconography and archaeology is that the illustrations of military activities mostly represent martial strife in the service of political ends—not rituals. Taking into account my caveat that seven centuries of art surely cover a range of activities, it nonetheless seems self-evident to me that the Moche were a warlike people. I have previously made arguments in favor of this interpretation (Quilter 2002), and here I have added some further points.

It is universally agreed that actual combat is evanescent in the archaeological record. The dead are buried or otherwise disposed of by humans, or feed scavengers, and the material residues of strife are collected, reused, and recycled. Except for occasional memorials and monuments, even Industrial Age battles, such as the American Civil War, leave little residue; only with a massive scale of destruction and numerous unexploded shells do battlefields remain as prominent (and dangerous) cultural features on the landscape (Saunders 2004).

Although field campaigns are difficult to find archaeologically, warfare is shown in great detail in Moche iconography. Of course, many societies may be aggressive but not show it in their art: the Inca were bellicose, and yet their art shows few overt military themes (Cummins 2002). Still, it is difficult to accept the idea that a society that depicts warriors and conflict to a comparatively great degree was not militaristic and that, instead, all of such representations are merely the expression of a religious cult. It is ironic that archaeologists search with great difficulty to find material traces of warfare, while at the same time many of them dismiss, as in the case of the Moche, its representation in art by the people who were warriors.

The Aztec Flower War was merely one aspect of a wide range of a belligerent Aztec strategy of conquest (Hassig 1988); it was not an isolated ritual activity. Even if some Moche art does represent highly ritualized battles designed to provide sacrificial victims (Bourget 2001), it seems reasonable to consider that this was part of a much larger array of militaristic activities that included real warfare for high stakes of conquest and defense.

It might be argued that real Moche warfare evolved into ritual combat. Former aggressions may have been channeled into ritual as an expanding Moche state consolidated its hold over local principalities. This is a hypothesis worthy of investigation. At present, however, there is insufficient evidence to support it. We would need to know when the cult of sacrifice shown in art became popular. Current evidence suggests that sacrificial practices were fairly long-lasting, judging from the evidence at Huaca de La Luna. Furthermore, the proposal that Moche was a single conquest state has been undermined of late rather than supported. Moche society appears to have been more unstable and disintegrating late in its prehistory, when fineline art depicting many military themes appears to increase. Archaeological evidence at sites such as Huaca Cao Viejo suggest that these sites were deliberately destroyed or "decommissioned" and that such acts, whether done by the occupants or rivals, included episodes of burning, tearing down of walls, and other activities that appear to have been done with malice. While it is possible that these were acts of desanctification carried out by the people who had previously used and maintained the huacas, the most economical interpretation of these events is that they were the final phases of aggression.

Flannery and Marcus (2003) utilize an evolutionary model and cross-cultural comparison in discussing early warfare in Oaxaca. Within this model, inter-village raiding begins with the establishment of segmentary societies and then escalates into chiefly rivalry with the increasing investment in agriculture and greater demographic pressures on resources (Kelly 2000). Chief rivalry emerges as warfare intensifies. Flannery and Marcus (2003:11802) note that the first hieroglyphic writing (ca. 2540+/- 90 BP or 590 BC) emerged in this context: a carved stone depicts a naked corpse of a captive whose heart had been torn out, and an inscribed hieroglyph, presumably with his name. They also cite a study of Maori warfare in which it was stated:

> No matter how great the casualty list after an engagement, if there were no chiefs killed, there was nothing much to talk about. If there was no chiefly name to connect the engagement with a tribal genealogy, the battle was without a name. (Buck 1949:400; cited in Flannery and Marcus 2003:11802)

This quote is important in its recognition that low-ranking men were involved in warfare, but that ideological constructs and the social system were such that the emphasis was on chiefs. Such a perspective and attitude are common in the warrior ethos of many preindustrial societies, and it is likely to have been true among the Moche. Approaching Moche sociopolitical organization as likely a segmentary one also makes sense, although the topic is complex and requires a separate treatise.

Certainly, in future studies, much more will be learned regarding Moche militarism, the societies that engaged in it, and the art that depicted it. This chapter has offered several ideas to suggest that much of the depicted combat represented in the iconography was closely tied to some form of warfare or rituals that were an expression of a greater culture of military aggression.

Acknowledgments

Thanks to Steve Bourget for inviting me to the conference from which this chapter was born. Thanks to various commentators on the conference paper. Thanks also to Kristy Wolford, assistant to the director of Pre-Columbian Studies, for help in preparing the manuscript.

Bibliography

Alva, Walter, and Christopher B. Donnan
1993   *Royal Tombs of Sipán*. Fowler Museum of Cultural History, University of California, Los Angeles.

Beazley Archive
2005   http://www.beazley.ox.ac.uk/BeazleyAdmin/Script2/default.htm. Faculty of Classics, Oxford University, England.

Bourget, Steve
2001   Rituals of Sacrifice: Its Practice at Huaca de la Luna and Its Representation in Moche Iconography. In *Moche Art and Archaeology in Ancient Peru*, 89–110. Edited by Joanne Pillsbury. National Gallery of Art and Yale University Press, Washington, D.C.

Browne, David, Helaine Silverman, and Raul Garcia
1993   A Cache of 48 Nasca Trophy Heads from Cerro Carapo, Peru. *Latin American Antiquity* 4:274–294.

Buck, Peter Henry
1949   *The Coming of the Maori*. Whitcombe and Tombs, New Zealand.

Burger, Richard L.
1996   Mace Head. In *Andean Art at Dumbarton Oaks* 1:84–86. Edited by Elizabeth H. Boone. Dumbarton Oaks, Washington, D.C.

Carmichael, Patrick H.
1992   Interpreting Nasca Iconography. In *Ancient Images, Ancient Thought: The Archaeology of Ideology*, 187–197. Edited by A. S. Goldsmith, S. Garvie, D. Selin, and J. Smith. Department of Archaeology, University of Calgary.

Castillo, Luis Jaime
2000   *La ceremonia del sacrificio: Batallas y muerte en el arte*

mochica. Museo Arqueológico Larco Rafael Herrera, Lima, Perú.

Cummins, Tom B. F.

2002   *Toasts with the Inca: Andean Abstractions and Colonial Images on Quero Vessels*. University of Michigan Press, Ann Arbor.

Donnan, Christopher B.

1997   Deer Hunting and Combat: Parallel Activities in the Moche World. In *The Spirit of Ancient Peru: Treasures from the Museo Arqueológico Rafael Larco Herrera* (exhibition catalog), 51–59. Edited by Kathleen Berrin. Fine Arts Museum of San Francisco, Thames and Hudson, New York.

Flannery, Kent V., and Joyce Marcus

2003   The Origin of War: New 14C Dates from Ancient Mexico. *PNAS* 100 (20):11801–11805. www.pnas.org/cgi/doi/10.1073/pnas.195344526100

Haas, Jonathan

1999   The Origins of War and Ethnic Violence. In *Ancient Warfare: Archaeological Perspectives*, 11–24. Edited by John Carman and Anthony Harding. Sutton Publishing, Ltd., Phoenix Mill.

2001   Warfare and the Evolution of Culture. In *Archaeology at the Millennium*, 329–350. Edited by Gary M. Feinman and T. Douglas Price. Kluwer Academic Publishers, New York.

Hassig, Ross

1988   *Aztec Warfare: Imperial Expansion and Political Control*. University of Oklahoma Press, Norman.

Hocquenghem, Anne Marie

1978   Les combats mochicas: Essai d'interpretation d'un material archeologique a l'aide de l'iconologie, de l'ethno-histoire, et de l'ethnologie. *Basessler-Archiv* 26:126–157.

Kellner, C. M.

2001   Ritual or Just Plain Warfare? Trophy Heads of the Julio C. Tello Collection, Nasca, Peru. *American Journal of Physical Anthropology*, Suppl. 32:89.

Kelly, Raymond C.

2000   *Warless Societies and the Origin of War*. University of Michigan Press, Ann Arbor.

Kutscher, Gerdt

1954   *Monumenta Americana I: Nordperuanische Keramik* (Cerámica del Perú septentrional). Verlag Gebr. Mann, Berlin.

Lambert, Patricia M.

2002   The Archaeology of War: A North American Perspective. *Journal of Archaeological Research* 10 (3):207–401.

Larco Hoyle, Rafael

2001   *Los Mochicas*. Tomos I–II. Museo Arqueológico Rafael Larco Herrera, Lima.

LeBlanc, Steven A.

1999   *Prehistoric Warfare in the American Southwest*. University of Utah Press, Salt Lake City.

2001   *Deadly Landscapes: Case Studies in Prehistoric Southwestern Warfare*. University of Utah Press, Salt Lake City.

Milner, George R.

1999   Warfare in Prehistoric and Early Historic Eastern North America. *Journal of Archaeological Research* 7 (2):105–151.

Moseley, Michael E.

1992   *The Incas and Their Ancestors: The Archaeology of Peru*. Thames and Hudson, London.

Nystrom, K. C., E. M. Braunstein, and J. E. Buikstra

2004   Field Paleoradiography of Skeletal Material from the Early Classic Period of Copán, Honduras. *Canadian Association of Radiologists* 55 (4):246–253.

Perrin, Noel

1980   *Giving up the Gun: Japan's Reversion to the Sword, 1543–1879*. D. R. Godine, Boston.

Quilter, Jeffrey

1990   The Moche Revolt of the Objects. *Latin American Antiquity* 1:42–65.

2002   Moche Politics, Religion, and Warfare. *Journal of World Prehistory* 16 (2):145–195.

Saunders, Nicholas J., ed.

2004   *Matters of Conflict: Material Culture, Memory and the First World War*. Routledge, New York.

Thorpe, Ian J.

2003   Anthropology, Archaeology, and the Origin of Warfare. *World Archaeology* 35:145–165.

Topic, John R., and Teresa L. Topic

1997   Hacia una compresión conceptual de la guerra andina. In *Arqueología, antropología, e historia en los Andes: Homenaje a María Rostworowski*, 567–590. Edited by Rafael Varón Gabai and Javier Flores Espinoza. Instituto de Estudios Peruanos, Lima.

Trejo, Silvia, ed.

2000   *La guerra entre los antiguos mayas: Memoria de la Primera Mesa Redonda de Palenque, México*. Instituto Nacional de Antropología e Historia, México, D.F.

Vencl, S.

1999   Stone Age Warfare. In *Ancient Warfare: Archaeological Perspectives*, 57–72. Edited by John Carman and Anthony Harding. Sutton Publishing Ltd., Phoenix Mill.

Webster, David

1999   Warfare and Status Rivalry: Lowland Maya and Polynesian Comparisons. In *Archaic States*, 464–470. Edited by Gary M. Feinman and Joyce Marcus. School of American Research Press, New Mexico.

2000   The Not So Peaceful Civilization: A Review of Maya War. *Journal of World Prehistory* 14 (1):65–119.

CHAPTER THIRTEEN

Moche Textile Production on the Peruvian North Coast

A Contextual Analysis

JEAN-FRANÇOIS MILLAIRE, UNIVERSITY OF WESTERN ONTARIO

Abstract

This chapter explores the potential of and limits to using the Moche system of representation to document specific aspects of ancient Peruvian technology. Because of the verisimilitude within Moche iconography, many specialists simply use complex scenes to illustrate their arguments. Scholars have used one such complex scene, which occurs on a florero in the British Museum Collection and depicts weavers, to exemplify Moche work organization and social structure. The only way to understand this particular scene, however, is to undertake a contextual analysis of Moche hand spinning and weaving technologies based on available data. In this chapter, I compare Moche iconography to the archaeological record, and evaluate the nature of the representations against other categories of information. This approach aims to contribute to the general theme of the volume by exploring the very thin but extremely fascinating interface between iconographical and archaeological information about Moche societies.

Moche iconography is to South America what Attic Red Figure painting is to the Mediterranean Basin: a rich corpus of representational art providing modern viewers with insights into actions that were deemed worth exhibition. Moche art was unique in the Ancient Andes for its emphasis on narrative and its tendency towards verisimilitude—having the appearance of depicting true or real subject matters. Following a long artistic tradition, Moche artisans introduced new conventions that led to development of an art form that appears to be more accessible to the viewer than earlier art styles (Quilter 2001:21).

From the vast corpus of representations, the scenes most frequently reproduced seem to celebrate warfare, victory in battle, and human sacrifice (Benson 1972; Bourget 2001; Donnan 1978; Donnan and McClelland 1999). These scenes are sometimes presented as proof of a Moche conquest over populations of the coastal region (Wilson 1988:338) or to argue for the existence of battles, ritual or otherwise, between high-ranking Moche individuals (Verano 2001). When used in this manner, Moche iconography is confronted by the archaeological record, and the nature of the representations is evaluated against other categories of information. Our under-

standing of specific scenes is refined by research carried out in the archaeological field and vice versa. Unfortunately, because of the verisimilitude of Moche iconography, scholars have often been tempted to use complex scenes simply to *illustrate* their argument. Employed in this manner, Moche art becomes a corpus of illustrations from which archaeologists and art historians pick what best demonstrates their hypotheses. This is done at the detriment of more holistic investigations of Moche art in search of the underlying logic of this complex system of representation.

This approach has also been the case with a widely reproduced representation, painted on the rim of a flaring bowl, that appears to be representing a weaving workshop supervised by high-status individuals (Figures 13.1, 13.2). The model of work organization depicted on this vessel has been used to substantiate claims that Moche society had developed a mode of work organization characterized by the large-scale production of textiles within specialized workshops (Bawden 1996; Campana 1994; Shimada 1994, 2001). Used in this manner, Moche iconography acts as a privileged source of knowledge that carries a certain sense of authenticity. In the context of this analysis, I would suggest that

FIGURE 13.1. Flaring bowl depicting a complex weaving activity. By kind permission of the Trustees of the British Museum, London (1913-10.25).

this scene does not illustrate a common practice but a specific kind of weaving that most commoners probably never experienced.

The only way to understand this scene is to undertake a contextual analysis of Moche hand spinning and weaving technologies based on available data. The contextual approach is based on the conviction that all possible aspects of an archaeological culture need to be examined in order to understand the significance of each of its parts (Hodder 1987, 1991; Trigger

1989:348–350). In this chapter, Moche iconography will be compared to the archaeological record, and the nature of the representations will be evaluated against other categories of information; my intention is that these analyses will help to document Moche society's mode of production. If these independently constituted lines of evidence converge, it will provide a compelling support for the model. Should they diverge, however, new lines of interpretation will need to be explored (Wylie 2002). I will begin with an overview of Moche political organization and craft production. The Weavers' Scene, currently held at the British Museum, will then be described in some detail. Finally, a contextual analysis of Moche textile production—complemented by information from ethnographic research carried out along the north coast—will be used to assess the nature of the information conveyed by the Weavers' Scene and to argue for an alternative reading of the artist's work.

Craft Production in Moche Society

Faced with an ever-growing body of data on the Moche occupation of the Peruvian north coast, archaeologists have expressed a renewed interest in this society's social structure and political organization. Moche society is generally described as a stratified social formation, ruled by local lords who were overseen by an elite composed of administrative and religious authorities (Bawden 2001; Chapdelaine 2001; Uceda 2001). The nature of Moche political organization and the extent to which it varied in time and space, however, is still a matter of debate. In this regard, Richard Schaedel (1972, 1985) and Izumi Shimada (1994:110–111) have argued that Moche society represented a multi-valley chiefdom, at least until the end of the Middle Moche period. Anthropologically, chiefdoms are usually defined as a complex form of sociopolitical organization in which social relations are mainly based on kinship, marriage, age, and gender, and in which chiefs and their close relatives control the administration of the people and the land.

Several north coast specialists, however, have argued that the Moche had political and economic institutions of such complexity that the Moche polity can no longer be defined as a chiefdom. While doing so, the tendency has been to draw up lists of the characteristics of early states from other cultural areas, and subsequently assess the closeness of fit between the model and the

FIGURE 13.2. Fineline painting of the weaving activity on the flaring bowl (Figure 13.1). By kind permission of the Trustees of the British Museum, London. Drawing by Donna McClelland.

archaeological record. Definitions of states differ from one author to another, but they are usually described as political entities characterized by territorial sovereignty and the use of force by recognized authorities.

To assess the nature of Moche political organization, scholars have undertaken settlement pattern analyses (Billman 1996, 1999; Chapdelaine, this volume; Dillehay 2001; Donnan 1973; Gálvez and Briceño 2001; Proulx 1985; Willey 1953; Wilson 1988)—an approach that provides a privileged point of view on elements of political centralization and site hierarchy. Other studies have focused on urbanism (Chapdelaine 2001; Shimada 1994) or burial patterns (Donnan 1995; Millaire 2002). But one of the most stimulating approaches to Moche political organization and social control involves studying the work of full-time craft specialists inside state-sponsored workshops.

Among early state formations around the world (city-states), full-time craft workers usually acquired the raw materials that they needed from trade and then manufactured products that they sold or exchanged at local markets without the direct control of the ruling elite. However, among territorial states and hegemonic city-states, elite goods were generally produced by full-time craft workers who were employed by the state and worked in state-sponsored workshops (Trigger 2003). As Bruce Trigger points out, "in this manner the central government created a monopoly of high-quality goods that reinforced its political control" (Trigger 2003:370). In this context, the archaeologist's assessment of the control exerted by the elite on craft specialists becomes a measure of the state's monopoly over trade, production, and utilization of resources. While demonstrating the political achievement of Moche society, it has thus become common practice to look for evidences of craft specialization, with the degree of specialization becoming a measure of the state's political success.

Crafts, including ceramic production, metallurgy, ornament making, and the manufacture of clothes, have all been studied in those terms. For example, the work of ceramists and their position in the Moche state has been documented through the excavation of workshops at Huacas de Moche in the Moche Valley (Armas 1996; Chapdelaine, Millaire, and Kennedy 2001; Uceda and Armas 1998) and Cerro Mayal in the Chicama Valley (Russell and Jackson 2001; Russell, Leonard, and Briceño

1994, 1998). The work of Early Intermediate Period metallurgy specialists has also been studied (Lechtman 1976; Shimada 1998; Shimada, Epstein, and Craig 1983; Shimada and Merkel 1991), as well as the manufacture of ornaments at Huacas de Moche (Bernier 1999) and Pampa Grande (Shimada 1994). More recently, Shimada has thoroughly documented the nature of elite control over multi-craft production at Pampa Grande, illustrating the level involved in the manufacture of prestige goods such as ceramic vessels inlaid with shells or stones (Shimada 2001).

Results from these studies have generally supported the state model of political organization for Moche society. For example, they have largely confirmed claims that the Moche had a complex system of elite goods production on which the state exerted either direct or indirect control. This line of argument has recently led Shimada to argue that, during the Late Moche period, the production of textiles was carried out inside workshops where commuting artisans wove under the supervision of high-status officials (Shimada 2001). Part of Shimada's argument was based on a comparison of data he gathered at Pampa Grande and his reading of a complex scene painted on the rim of a Middle Moche flaring bowl.

According to my research, however, the manufacture of clothes in Moche society was a domestic activity carried out by women in the vicinity of their homes, not inside specialized workshops. In other words, I not only question Shimada's interpretation of the archaeological record, but also his reading of the Weavers' Scene and his use of Moche iconography as a direct source of information. I therefore intend to demonstrate that far from being trivial, this problem is a clear illustration of the present debate on the nature of Moche art and the way archaeologists can profit from careful use of this rich corpus of visual information.

The Moche Weavers' Scene

Painted on the inner rim of a flaring bowl (Figures 13.1, 13.2), the Weavers' Scene illustrates an activity central to Andean people, past and present: weaving.[1] The flaring bowl, part of the British Museum collection, probably came from a burial excavated in the Chicama Valley at the turn of the last century (*Illustrated London News* 1909; de Bock 1999). The painting on the bowl is exceptional in being the only example of a weaving scene, and one of the few representations apparently showing an everyday activity. Indeed, in the corpus of Moche art, very few scenes depict secular themes. Another famous scene represents the annealing process involved in the fabrication of metal implements (Donnan 1978: fig. 15; Shimada 1994:272n, 127), and a well-known vessel shows the preparation of a substance thought to be maize beer (Donnan 1978: fig. 105).

The Weavers' Scene was laid out by the artist in such a way as to suggest a central court surrounded by side benches shaded by cane roofs (Campana 1994). Seated on these benches are eight individuals weaving fabric on backstrap looms attached to roof posts. On the basis of this representation alone, it is difficult to say whether the artist meant to represent women or men, and whether the weavers were young or elderly. At their sides, spindles full of yarn are ready to be used in the production of elaborate fabrics. The weavers are apparently producing two types of garments: shirts with sleeves, and headdresses. Considering how elaborate the woven designs are and the number of colors used (as indicated by the number of spindles employed), it appears that the artist meant to show that the textiles being produced were of high quality (possibly tapestry works).[2] Elaborately dressed individuals are represented at the ends of each bench. From their position, the way they are dressed, their overall attitude, and their relative size, at least three of them seem to be supervising the work of the artisans. Finally, two more persons appear to be visiting the workshop. One is standing in front of a seated individual holding a bowl; in another section of the scene, a person is seated in front of a dignified individual. Around the weavers and the other characters, ritual ceramic vessels such as stirrup spout and spout-and-handle bottles, jars with fastened covers, flaring bowls, and stacked containers are represented. Incidentally, all of these containers are traditionally found as offerings inside Moche graves and are often represented in other complex scenes from the Moche corpus, in particular burial-related scenes (Donnan and McClelland 1979).

From this representation, it appears that weaving occurred as a formally organized activity in Moche society, and that the work was done inside workshops under the supervision of high-status individuals. The depiction also indicates that such workshops produced high-quality garments decorated with elaborate designs. Therefore, this scene seems to represent a solid piece of information about Moche work organization, suggesting the existence of a class of full-time craft workers employed by the upper class to create elite goods in sponsored workshops—a model of craft organization common to most territorial states and hegemonic city-states (Trigger 2003:370). On the basis of the present evidence, however, it is not possible to say how many weavers in Moche society performed their art under the supervision of members of the elite. This problem can be summarized by one simple question: Is this the illustration of the daily production of cloth inside Moche state workshops, or the representation of a special kind of weaving carried out in a special context?

I would argue that this scene evokes a highly specialized workshop dedicated to the production of exceptional clothes and garments that were probably designed for formal occasions. The fact that several ritual containers are painted inside the workshop, and that the scene itself adorns a ceremonial vessel, all suggest a close relationship with ceremonial activities. Following Elizabeth Benson (1972:106), I would even argue that it celebrates the creation of funerary clothes for important members of Moche society by specially trained weavers working under the close supervision of ritual specialists.

But how should we decide between these two interpretations of the Weavers' Scene? Is it an illustration of the general mode of production, or the representation of a workshop dedicated to the manufacture of special fabrics? Apparently, the only way to understand the nature of this representation is to undertake a contextual analysis of Moche spinning and weaving activities. Such an analysis requires examining all evidence of Moche textile production in the archaeological record and taking advantage of rich ethnographical information available on the use of cotton on the Peruvian north coast.

Textile Production in Moche Society

The Moche inherited a long tradition of weaving going back to the Preceramic period. Because of natural conditions, relatively few Moche textiles have survived; however, excavations in exceptionally dry contexts have revealed the technological and artistic skills of Moche weavers, who produced some of the most sophisticated textiles in the Andean region. When textiles were decorated, the designs were often created using woollen yarns (dyed in bright colors) that were woven into tapestries or double cloths (Conklin 1979; Prümers 1995). But archaeological research has revealed that the vast majority of Moche fabrics were undecorated plain weave made of cotton fibers, taking advantage of the natural shades of creams, browns, and grays of the locally grown *Gossipium barbodensas* (Bird 1979; Donnan and Donnan 1997; Vreeland 1986).

The production of clothes can be roughly divided into three stages: procurement of the raw material, processing of the fibers leading to the fabrication of the yarns, and weaving. Little or nothing is known of Moche cotton cultivation techniques, and there are as yet no data available on the economic mechanisms involved in the acquisition of fiber by noncultivators. To my knowledge, it is therefore still impossible to answer the following question: How did cotton fiber reach artisans in large urban agglomerations such as Huacas de Moche and Pampa Grande?

More information is available on cotton processing. In the 1970s, James Vreeland studied the use of cotton in the Lambayeque region and produced a detailed description of traditional processing methods (Vreeland 1986). From his study we learn that, once harvested, cotton fibers need to be cleaned of their seeds before they can be used. But since cotton loses some of its conservation properties through this process, artisans usually prepare only the quantity they need, keeping unprocessed fibers inside domestic jars or other containers (Vreeland 1986:367). The antiquity of this and other stages of the manufacture of clothes has been proven by recent archaeological investigations along the Peruvian north coast.

For example, Shimada found archaeological evidence of fiber storage at the Late Moche site of Pampa Grande. Inside Compound 16, seed cotton was uncovered immediately outside of a broken ceramic container, and two constricted jars at the top of a small platform overlooking Sector H contained cottonseeds mixed with beans (Shimada 1994:208). Each jar would have accommodated relatively small quantities of fibers, suggesting that they served as storage facilities for individual artisans, not for large workshops. Similarly, at Huacas de Moche, burnt cottonseeds were found inside a kitchen hearth in Compound 9. These seeds manifestly came from the fiber cleaning process and had been tossed into the fire

by local residents, indicating that this stage of production was performed inside Moche residential complexes.

According to Shimada, large-scale processing of fibers did take place at Pampa Grande. At least one structure could have functioned as a processing workshop under the control of local officials (Shimada 1994:206–210, 2001:184–187). On the basis of archaeological evidence, Shimada argued that a relatively large room, known as Deer House, had served for the processing of bundles of raw cotton brought there as tribute. A fire had razed the structure, preserving charred cotton on the floor. Shimada interpreted the remains as evidence that large quantities of cotton had been unloaded inside this room. As a measure of the scale of the work performed, Kent Day argued that carriers had used a small ramp as a dock for unloading the bundles of fibers (Shimada 1994:272n, 129).

Taking into account Vreeland's ethnographic work, Shimada proposed that this room was also used for the beating of deseeded cotton. Indeed, according to Vreeland, before spinning cotton, artisans beat the fibers using wooden switches (Vreeland 1986:367). Today, artisans beat natural cotton inside courtyards, creating thin *tortas* of fibers that are left to dry for some time before they are ready to use. Shimada found support for his argument in the presence of burnt cotton fibers on the room floor, and in the discovery of several ceramic drum frames. The drums, Shimada argued, could have been used to "create a solemn or, conversely festive atmosphere for the delivery and processing of cotton" (Shimada 1994:208).

Examining this evidence, I have to disagree about the scale of work apparently carried out inside Deer House. First, there is no archaeological, historical, or ethnographic evidence that drums were ever beaten to maintain the artisans' cadence. Second, a close look at the excavation plan reveals that the cotton remains were concentrated into two patches, each measuring no more than 2 m² (Shimada 1994: fig. 8.23). These cotton patches are similar to the ones created by artisans when beating cotton (Vreeland 1986: fig. 4). Taking into account both archaeological and ethnographical data, I would therefore suggest that Deer House provides a clear example of a small-scale, nonindustrial cotton processing area where *tortas* of beaten fibers had been left to dry. Although there may have been specialized work-

FIGURE 13.3. Woman spinning according to the Bororó technique. After a drawing from the Museo Brüning, Lambayeque, Peru.

shops employing large numbers of people for processing cotton fibers during Moche times, I believe that tangible evidence is still missing from the archaeological record.

Once cotton fibers were beaten and dried, they were ready to be transformed into yarns. Until recently, two hand-spinning traditions have existed side by side in the Andean area: the "Bakaïrí" and "Bororó" techniques (Frödin and Nordenskiöld 1918; Nordenskiöld 1919, 1924). The Bakaïrí technique is a highland technology focusing on camelid fibers and using the drop spindle method. While a shaft holds the fibers, the artisan uses a vertical spindle, which hangs in the air. Spindles are generally longer and thicker than those found on coastal sites (Nordenskiöld 1919). The yarn is produced at the proximal end of the spindle (nearest the artisan's hand) and is invariably Z spun (counter-clockwise). The Bororó technique, on the other hand, is a lowland technology focusing on cotton (Figure 13.3). Artisans usually sit on the ground near a post or a tripod to which cotton fibers have been tied (Vreeland 1986:367). The fingers of the left hand are used to draw the fibers (and control the evenness of the yarn being produced), while the right hand holds the spindle horizontally. Bororó spindles are usually shorter and more slender than those used by their highland neighbors. In this case the yarn, which is produced at the distal end of the spindle, is invariably

S spun (clockwise). In other words, as Vreeland notes, "the motion of the fingers in both the North Highland Z and the North Coast S-spinning format is essentially the same" (Vreeland 1986:370); only the position of the spindle in relation to the fibers differs, hence the opposite twists.

To facilitate the spinning process, whorls were generally mounted on the distal end of the spindle (Figure 13.4). These weights function as flywheels, maintaining the movement of the spindle once it is set in motion. In practice, anything from a folded leaf to a corncob section can be used as a whorl. Nevertheless, among the Moche, artisans used specially made whorls of relatively small size. Some were made of stone or copper, but most were ceramic (Figure 13.5). Their shape varied from conical to biconvex. Some were round, and others were even made to resemble small domestic jars.

Between 1995 and 1998, I studied a collection of 255 whorls recovered from the excavations of residential and corporate architecture at the site of Huacas de Moche. A number of conclusions could be drawn from the analysis of the shape, weight, and dimensions of these artifacts (Millaire 1997). First, all the whorls exhibited a small perforation, indicating that they had been used in conjunction with a slender spindle. Second, they were all designed to produce a small moment of inertia, suggesting that they were not meant to spin coarse fibers but rather softer material such as cotton. Therefore, I concluded that these instruments were used to spin soft fibers in the Bororó spinning tradition (Millaire 1997).

A contextual analysis of Moche spinning implements brought interesting results. At Huacas de Moche, 167 whorls were found in the residential sector excavated by Claude Chapdelaine. These tools were found inside thirty-seven rooms or patios located in fifteen distinct architectural compounds scattered on the urban plain. They were found either pressed in the clay floor or inside the fill between the floors, suggesting that the whorls had been lost by their owners. More importantly, the distribution of the whorls also indicates that the spinning of cotton fibers was not confined within specialized workshops in the capital city of the Moche state, but carried out everywhere inside the residential sector.[3] In fact, none of the rooms where spinning implements were found showed evidence of large-scale production, as would have been expected if this stage of cloth pro-

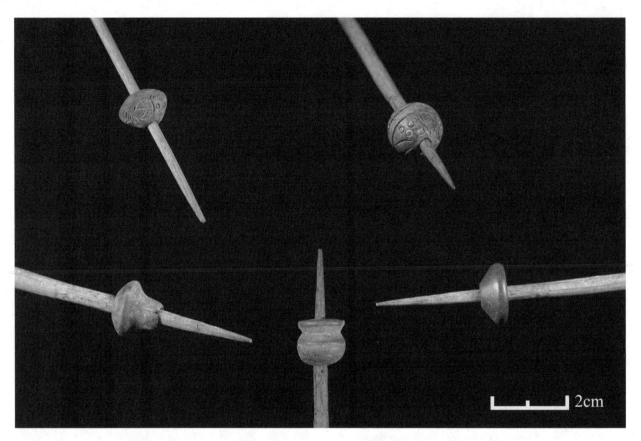

FIGURE 13.4. Moche spindle whorls from the residential sector at Huacas de Moche. Photograph by author.

duction had been carried out inside specialized work-shops. Rather, from one to eleven whorls were uncovered inside habitation rooms, suggesting that cotton yarns were produced in every household at Huacas de Moche. In Compound 12, an architectural complex at the core of the Moche capital (Chapdelaine 2001), archaeologists uncovered seven whorls inside a small domestic jar set in the floor of a small patio. This jar may have been used as a container to store an artisan's tool kit—a practice that was also documented at Castillo de Tomaval in Virú (Strong and Evans 1952:121).

Similar conclusions can be drawn from the distribu-tion of spinning implements at the Late Moche settle-ments of Galindo and Pampa Grande. At Galindo, Garth Bawden (1996:81, 85) noted that spinning, weav-ing, and sewing implements were found clustered on the floors of the *salas,* the typical living area of Late Moche residential structures. A similar pattern was found at Pampa Grande, where fifteen whorls were discovered in

Sector D (Shimada 2001:185), an area where residential units with *salas* were also identified (Shimada 1994:169). At Galindo, the discovery of food remains revealed that meals were periodically taken inside these rooms (Bawden 1996:81), reinforcing the view that cotton processing never left the domestic sphere. On the basis of the present evidence, I would therefore argue that the spinning of cotton yarn took place within individual Moche households, not inside specialized workshops controlled by state officials, and that this pattern was not altered by the political transformations that marked the passage from the Middle to the Late Moche period.[4]

The contextual information on weaving also seems to point towards the domestic nature of this produc-tion stage. Very little information is yet available on the Moche weaving process. There seems to be little doubt that artisans used the backstrap loom to manufacture fabrics, but the fact that these looms were made of per-ishable materials makes their conservation unlikely at

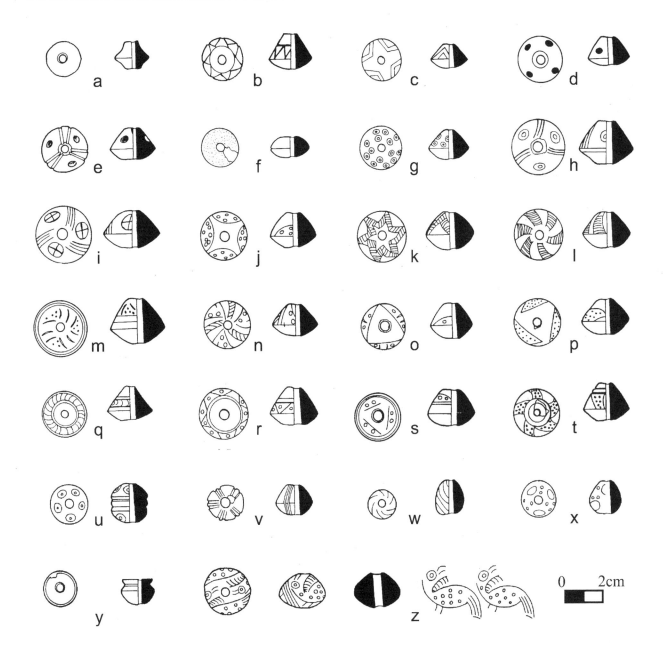

FIGURE 13.5. Sample of Moche spindle whorls from the residential sector at Huacas de Moche: copper (*a*), stone (*b–e*), and ceramic (*f–z*). Drawing by Magali Morlion.

most Moche settlements. In fact, a single direct weaving implement has not yet been identified. At Pampa Grande, Shimada reported the discovery of a batten on the floor of a room from Sector H. A batten is an instrument used to open sheds to facilitate the weaving process. Room ARm 78 was unusual in that it featured ten unaligned postholes (Shimada 1994:209). Inside this room, a drum frame, a macaw burial, and a flaring bowl were also found (Shimada 2001:186). Guided by the Weavers' Scene (Figures 13.1, 13.2), Shimada argued that these posts could have been used to support the looms of several weavers. This possibility, coupled with the presence of a single weaving implement, led Shimada to conclude that the room once stood as an important workshop where weaving took place under the close supervision of high-status individuals. Here again, a drum would have provided rhythmic beats to pace the weavers' work (Shimada 1994:209). Considering the nonresidential character of this area of the site, Shimada further surmised that this workshop was manned by commuting artisans (Shimada 2001:187).

Based on present evidence, I would argue that there is not sufficient data to comment on the nature or scale of the work carried out inside this room. If anything, the presence of a batten indicates that an artisan used to weave inside or in the vicinity of this room during the Late Moche period. In fact, until large numbers of backstrap looms (or textile miniatures used as patterns) are found inside a specific structure, the identification of Moche weaving workshops will remain a hazardous matter.

More information on the context of cloth manufacture can be drawn from the distribution of sewing implements on Moche sites. Much of the clothing was composed of several panels of fabric (Donnan and Donnan 1997) that were sewn together using needles or awls made of copper or bone. Since copper needles are often found during excavations, their distribution on archaeological sites should shed some light on the context in which the manufacture (or mending) of clothes took place. Interestingly, at Huacas de Moche the distribution of needles closely resembled that of spinning tools. In the residential area, needles were found on the floor or in the fill of several rooms inside most architectural compounds. A similar pattern was found at the sites of Galindo and Pampa Grande, where sewing imple-

ments were also found in residential sectors, and where no unusual concentrations were reported (Bawden 1996:85; Shimada 2001:185). The distribution of needles on Moche sites therefore indicates that the manufacture and mending of clothes, like the spinning of yarn, took place within individual households.

Incidentally, these results are in agreement with the distribution of textile-related tools in Moche burials. While studying Moche funerary practices, I collected information on spinning and weaving implements for all burials available for study (Millaire 2002). Restricting analyses to burials for which sex had been independently established by a physical anthropologist, I looked at the distribution of whorls and needles. Thirty individuals were buried with textile-related implements, all of whom had been identified as females except one. This was an elderly man buried at Huacas de Moche with a spindle whorl and a copper needle (Donnan and Mackey 1978:102). It is significant that these burials were not clustered in specific areas but came from residential structures, cemeteries, and corporate architecture at the sites of Pacatnamú, El Brujo, Huanchaco, Huacas de Moche, and Huaca de la Cruz (Millaire 2002). It is also worth noting that these implements were found inside graves showing all degrees of elaboration, indicating that textile manufacture was not associated with a specific group in Moche society.

Evidence suggesting that hand-spinning and weaving activities were not restricted to commoners comes from Huaca Cao Viejo, in the Chicama Valley. Found inside this platform mound was the burial of an elderly female of very high status (Franco, Gálvez, and Vásquez 1999:9–15). An analysis of her finger bones suggested to physical anthropologists John Verano and Guido Lombardi that during her life she had frequently used her hands to perform the kind of work required by weaving (Verano and Lombardi 1999:50). Incidentally, this member of the local elite had three metal spindle whorls buried with her (Franco, Gálvez, and Vásquez:13, 43–44).[5]

In summary, the evidence available on the manufacture of clothes seems to converge on the domestic rather than the public sphere. Nothing found by the contextual analysis presented here suggests that the production of textiles was conducted in specialized workshops at Moche settlements. In fact, from the evidence available, it seems that in most Moche households, women prepared, spun, sewed, and possibly wove cotton fiber, creating their own fabrics without direct supervision. The fact that the manufacture of clothes remained a domestic activity in a state-organized society is not necessarily surprising. The Moche could have maintained a traditional mode of production that worked perfectly well without direct control. The authorities may have exacted part of each household's production through a *mit'a*-like system, but if so, the evidence suggests that it was done according to a traditional mode of production, not inside state-sponsored workshops. This characteristic should therefore be taken into consideration when discussing Moche statecraft.

A Contextual Reading of the Weavers' Scene

If the manufacture of clothes was not restricted to supervised workshops during Moche times, one wonders why an artist felt that it was appropriate to represent this mode of production on a ritual vessel. A possible explanation is that the painter wanted to immortalize a form of weaving that was extraordinary—possibly carried out by a special category of artisans. This special and unusual scene appears to have celebrated not the everyday technical achievements of Moche society, but the manufacture of exceptional goods created for extraordinary occasions.

Traditionally, farmers and their families around the world produce everyday goods during their spare time. When individuals concentrate on producing a single type of product, they are able to perfect their skills while producing goods of higher quality. In this context, the growth of a class of part-time specialists usually necessitates the development of a wider economic network, with exchanges occurring at markets located in villages or towns. Full-time specialists produce even better quality goods, which other people cannot manufacture because they lack the specific equipment, access to the raw material, or the necessary technological knowledge or craftsmanship. Higher up in the hierarchy are artisans specialized in the production of elite goods of exceptional quality for the state and the upper class (Trigger 2003:358).

Artisans producing the highest-quality goods specifically serve the interests of the ruling elite by fashioning objects that are imbued with symbolism and ideology.

As Bawden (1996:92) has pointed out, through their work the artisans proclaimed "the principal tenets of an ideology that supported Moche leadership and the political system through which it exercised power." In Moche society, full-time craft workers often produced goods from imported raw materials that were either bought or provided by their patrons (Shimada 2001; Russell and Jackson 2001). Among early civilizations, elite craft workers sometimes sold their production through local markets, while others combined independent production with work carried out under the auspices of a patron (Trigger 2003:358). For example, in Aztec society, while most artisans worked in their homes and sold their production in local markets, some were invited to palace workshops to produce goods for the king, who rewarded them for their work (Brumfiel 1987).[6] But early state formations also usually employed full-time craft specialists who worked for the government, for specific temples, or for wealthy members of the upper class. As Trigger has pointed out, "though treated with considerable respect, [these artisans] were bound to their employers in much the same manner as were less skilled craft workers or household servants" (Trigger 2003:358).[7]

Taking into account the contextual information available on the manufacture of textiles in Moche society, I would argue that the painter of the Weavers' Scene intended to represent the work of a group of elite craft workers dedicated to producing goods for the Moche elite. Indeed, the workers are shown weaving elaborate clothes that were probably worn during specific ceremonies. Although it is difficult to be categorical on the function of these textiles, the fact that several funerary vessels surround the weavers leads me to believe that they are somehow related to the ritual domain—an association that is even stronger if we consider that this flaring bowl was once part of a funerary lot.

In his study of Moche art, Christopher Donnan pointed out that the artisans from the Weavers' Scene are making headdresses and shirts to be worn in nonsecular occasions (Donnan 1978:175). As mentioned earlier, Benson (1972:106) offered a similar interpretation, arguing that the scene was set inside a building under the supervision of religious authorities. According to her, this scene probably represents a workshop under religious jurisdiction that specialized in manufacturing burial clothes for important members of Moche society.[8]

FIGURE 13.6. Figure holding a tunic. Museo Nacional de Antropología, Arqueología e Historia, Lima (C-00641).

FIGURE 13.7. Figure holding a tunic. Museo Nacional de Antropología, Arqueología e Historia, Lima (C-61527).

In this context, it is worth remembering that the artist took great care to indicate that the weavers were not manufacturing plain weaves, but rather elaborate tapestry works, as indicated by the number of spindles being used and the textile patterns they are replicating. Clearly, these artisans were weaving clothes of exceptional quality, probably for exceptional individuals. This line of interpretation is stimulating, as it explains why an activity such as weaving was deemed worth representation by a Moche ceramist whose art was otherwise essentially focused on a complex system of symbolic representation.

Understood in those terms, the Weavers' Scene sheds new light on a series of fascinating sculpted vessels from the vast corpus of Moche art. These bottles follow a unique pattern: an individual, with a special hairstyle

and eyes wide open, stretches open a finely decorated shirt, showing the fine design woven onto its surface (Figures 13.6, 13.7). Taken alone, the meaning of these vessels is hard to interpret, but when examined in conjunction with the Weavers' Scene, they both seem to be part of what Donnan defines as a "basic theme" (Donnan 1978:158). Indeed, these bottles and the Weavers' flaring bowl appear to illustrate the production of sophisticated textiles and the "presentation" of the completed clothes.

The correspondence between the woven textiles represented on the *florero* and those displayed on the sculpted vessels becomes clearer when we take a closer look at the design found on a vessel from the National Museum of the American Indian (Figure 13.8) and the motif executed by a weaver on a shirt with sleeves

FIGURE 13.8. Figure holding a tunic. Courtesy of the National Museum of the American Indian. Photograph by Christopher B. Donnan.

(Figure 13.9). Although not exactly alike, both tunics are decorated with a bird and a stepped design. Is this the representation of a male weaver presenting the fruit of his work? Or is this the representation of a kind of supervisor in charge of overseeing the work of the artisans?[9] The range of activities performed by these individuals could be the key to understanding their function in the iconography. All of these vessels may in fact be part of a wider iconographic theme that celebrated the production of all categories of ceremonial goods. In arguing for the nonsecular nature of Moche art, Donnan noted a correspondence between the Weavers' Scene and a unique vessel showing four artisans in the process of manufacturing headdress ornaments near a furnace (Donnan 1978: fig. 15). This vessel, like the one illustrating the preparation of *chicha* or another substance by two individuals (Donnan 1978: fig. 105), may also have been produced to celebrate the work of those involved in the preparation of ceremonial paraphernalia of all kinds. This would not be surprising in the context of Moche art, whose nonsecular character has long been documented.

Conclusion

The scene painted on the *florero* held at the British Museum is of utmost importance as it seemingly offers privileged information concerning the work of artisans inside supervised workshops. As such, it is an important building block in any discussion of the nature of Moche

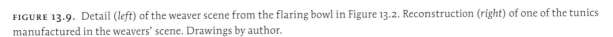

FIGURE 13.9. Detail (*left*) of the weaver scene from the flaring bowl in Figure 13.2. Reconstruction (*right*) of one of the tunics manufactured in the weavers' scene. Drawings by author.

statecraft. Considering the evidence on textile production presented here, however, its use to illustrate the general mode of production among Moche society must be questioned.

From this vessel, we learn that Moche leaders relied at least to a certain degree on a group of elite weavers whose work was performed under the control of political or religious officials. Metallurgists, and at least certain master ceramists, may also have been part of this group of elite artisans, charged with the task of manufacturing special clothes, ornaments, and ritual paraphernalia for their leaders—still alive or recently deceased. In this context, the celebration of their art on Moche ritual vessels would simply mark the importance of their work from a religious point of view.

Since it represents a specific and even ritual kind of weaving that commoners probably never experienced nor witnessed, the Weavers' Scene simply cannot be used to illustrate the general nature of textile production in Moche society. Specialized workshops possibly existed, and the state probably sponsored the production of certain goods of exceptional quality. But it should be clear from this analysis that Moche textile production never totally left the domestic sphere. As seen here, all the evidence suggests that the manufacture of clothes was done by women in the vicinity of their homes, not by artisans in state-supervised workshops. Thus, as for every other scene from the rich corpus of Moche art, this *florero* needs to be interpreted by taking into account all of the available information on the actions being represented. Only then will its complex meaning begin to be revealed.

Acknowledgments

This research was supported through postdoctoral fellowships by Quebec's Fonds pour la Recherche sur la Société et la Culture and by Canada's Social Sciences and Humanities Research Council. The final editing process was conducted as part of a Fellowship in Pre-Columbian Studies at Dumbarton Oaks. I would like to thank the following people for commenting on previous versions of this chapter: Steve Bourget, Kimberly Jones, Magali Morlion, and Bruce G. Trigger.

Notes

1. Areas of the Weavers' Scene where the painting was missing were completed by Donna McClelland.

2. Each weaver is apparently replicating a distinct pattern. Patterns that may have been used in this manner were identified at Pacatnamú (Bruce 1986).

3. The only identified concentration of spinning implements came from the ceramic workshop excavated by José Armas (Armas 1996). Most of the thirty-five whorls uncovered were of poor quality, however, suggesting that they were production rejects.

4. Marilyn Beaudry-Corbett and Sharisse McCafferty recently analyzed the distribution of spindle whorls inside household contexts at the Maya site of Joya del Ceren in El Salvador. Interestingly, they found that local woman were responsible "not only for household provisioning but also for products that moved beyond the household" (2002:65).

5. Archaeologists originally identified these artifacts as beads, but their size, shape, and design all suggest that these are spindle whorls (cf. Franco, Gálvez, and Vásquez 1999:13).

6. A similar pattern was found among Yoruba craft workers in West Africa (Trigger 2003).

7. Incidentally, the Incas employed labor of both kinds (Murra 1980). Indeed, some young males (*yanakuna*) were taken from their families to become lifelong servants, craftsmen, or farmers for the king or other members of the nobility, whereas others worked only occasionally for the Inca through the *mit'a* corvée system.

8. In the Old Kingdom, the Egyptian state had workshops called *w'bt* (pure place) where elite goods were manufactured for royal and upper class burials. A parallel institution may have existed in Moche society (Trigger 2003:369).

9. See also Daniel Arsenault's (1993) analysis of Moche stewards, characterized by one or two missing feet.

Bibliography

Armas, José

1996   Los talleres alfareros. In *Informe Técnico Financiero 1995*, 98–113. Edited by Santiago Uceda and Ricardo Morales. Manuscript on file. Proyecto Arqueológico Huaca de la Luna. Facultad de Ciencias Sociales, Universidad Nacional de La Libertad, Trujillo.

Arsenault, Daniel

1993   El personaje del pie amputado en la cultura Mochica del Perú: Un ensayo sobre la arqueología del poder. *Latin American Antiquity* 4 (3):225–245.

Bawden, Garth

1996   *The Moche*. Blackwell, Oxford.

2001   The Symbols of Late Moche Social Transformation. In
        Moche: Art and Archaeology in Ancient Peru, 285–305.
        Edited by Joanne Pillsbury. National Gallery of Art and
        Yale University Press, Washington, D.C.

Beaudry-Corbett, Marilyn, and Sharisse McCafferty

2002   Spindle Whorls: Household Specialization at Ceren. In
        Ancient Maya Women, 52–67. Edited by Traci Ardren.
        AltaMira Press, Walnut Creek, California.

Benson, Elizabeth P.

1972   *The Mochica: A Culture of Peru*. Praeger, London.

Bernier, Hélène

1999   L'usage de la parure corporelle dans la culture Moche
        du Pérou précolombien et le cas du site Moche, capitale
        urbaine. Master of Science thesis, Université de Mon-
        tréal.

Billman, Brian R.

1996   The Evolution of Prehistoric Political Organizations in
        the Moche Valley, Peru. Ph.D. dissertation, University
        of California, Santa Barbara.

1999   Reconstructing Prehistoric Political Economies and
        Cycles of Political Power in the Moche Valley, Peru. In
        *Settlement Pattern Studies in the Americas: Fifty Years
        Since Virú*, 131–159. Edited by Brian R. Billman and Gary
        M. Feinman. Smithsonian Institution Press, Washing-
        ton, D.C.

Bird, Junius B.

1979   Fiber and Spinning Procedure in the Andean Area. In
        *The Junius B. Bird Pre-Columbian Textile Conference, May
        19th and 20th, 1973*, 13–17. Edited by Ann Pollard Rowe,
        Elizabeth P. Benson, and Anne-Louise Schaffer. The
        Textile Museum, Washington, D.C.

de Bock, Edward K.

1999   Appendix B: The Van den Bergh Collection. In *Moche
        Fineline Painting: Its Evolution and Its Artists*, 301–303. By
        Christopher B. Donnan and Donna McClelland. Fowler
        Museum of Cultural History, University of California,
        Los Angeles.

Bourget, Steve

2001   Rituals of Sacrifice: Its Practice at Huaca de la Luna and
        Its Representation in Moche Iconography. In *Moche:
        Art and Archaeology in Ancient Peru*, 89–109. Edited by
        Joanne Pillsbury. National Gallery of Art and Yale Uni-
        versity Press, Washington, D.C.

Bruce, Susan L.

1986   Textile Miniatures from Pacatnamu, Peru. In *The Junius
        B. Bird Conference on Andean Textiles, April 7th and
        8th, 1984*, 183–204. Edited by Ann P. Rowe. The Textile
        Museum, Washington, D.C.

Brumfiel, Elizabeth M.

1987   Elite and Utilitarian Crafts in the Aztec State. In

        Specialization, Exchange, and Complex Societies, 102–118.
        Edited by Elizabeth M. Brumfiel and Timothy K. Earle.
        Cambridge University Press, Cambridge.

Campana, Cristóbal

1994   El entorno cultural en un dibujo mochica. In *Moche:
        Propuestas y perspectivas*, 449–473. Actas del Primer
        Coloquio sobre la Cultura Moche, Trujillo, 12 a 16
        de abril de 1993. Edited by Santiago Uceda and Elías
        Mujica. Travaux de l'Institut Français d'Études Andines
        79. Universidad Nacional de la Libertad, Trujillo, Perú.

Chapdelaine, Claude

2001   The Growing Power of a Moche Urban Class. In *Moche:
        Art and Archaeology in Ancient Peru*, 69–87. Edited by
        Joanne Pillsbury. National Gallery of Art and Yale Uni-
        versity Press, Washington, D.C.

**Chapdelaine, Claude, Jean-François Millaire, and Greg
Kennedy**

2001   Compositional Analysis and Provenance Study of
        Spindle Whorls from the Moche Site, North Coast of
        Peru. *Journal of Archaeological Science* 28 (8):795–806.

Conklin, William J.

1979   Moche Textile Structures. In *The Junius B. Bird Pre-
        Columbian Textile Conference, May 19th and 20th, 1973*,
        165–184. Edited by Ann Pollard Rowe, Elizabeth P. Ben-
        son, and Anne-Louise Schaffer. The Textile Museum,
        Washington, D.C.

Dillehay, Tom D.

2001   Town and Country in Late Moche Times: A View from
        Two Northern Valleys. In *Moche: Art and Archaeology
        in Ancient Peru*, 259–283. Edited by Joanne Pillsbury.
        National Gallery of Art and Yale University Press,
        Washington, D.C.

Donnan, Christopher B.

1973   *Moche Occupation of the Santa Valley, Peru*. University of
        California Publications in Anthropology 8. University
        of California Press, Berkeley and Los Angeles.

1978   *Moche Art of Peru: Pre-Columbian Symbolic Commu-
        nication*. Museum of Cultural History, University of
        California, Los Angeles.

1995   Moche Funerary Practice. In *Tombs for the Living:
        Andean Mortuary Practices*, 111–159. Edited by Tom D.
        Dillehay. Dumbarton Oaks Research Library and Col-
        lection, Washington, D.C.

Donnan, Christopher B., and Sharon G. Donnan

1997   Moche Textiles from Pacatnamu. In *The Pacatnamu
        Papers, Vol. 2: The Moche Occupation*, 215–242. Edited by
        Christopher B. Donnan and Guillermo A. Cock. Fowler
        Museum of Cultural History, University of California,
        Los Angeles.

Donnan, Christopher B., and Carol J. Mackey

1978   *Ancient Burial Patterns of the Moche Valley, Peru*. University of Texas Press, Austin.

Donnan, Christopher B., and Donna McClelland

1979   *The Burial Theme in Moche Iconography*. Studies in Pre-Columbian Art and Archaeology 21. Dumbarton Oaks Research Library and Collection, Washington, D.C.

1999   *Moche Fineline Painting: Its Evolution and Its Artists*. Fowler Museum of Cultural History, University of California, Los Angeles.

Franco, Régulo, César Gálvez, and Segundo Vásquez

1999   *Tumbas de cámara moche en la plataforma superior de la Huaca Cao Viejo, Complejo El Brujo*. Programa Arqueológico "El Brujo." Boletín No. 1 (July).

Frödin, Otto, and Erland Nordenskiöld

1918   Über Zwirnen und Spinnen bei den Indianern Südamerikas. W. Zachrissons, Göteborg.

Gálvez, César, and Jesús Briceño

2001   The Moche in the Chicama Valley. In *Moche: Art and Archaeology in Ancient Peru*, 141–157. Edited by Joanne Pillsbury. National Gallery of Art and Yale University Press, Washington, D.C.

Hodder, Ian

1987   The Contextual Analysis of Symbolic Meanings. In *The Archaeology of Contextual Meanings*, 1–10. Edited by Ian Hodder. Cambridge University Press, Cambridge.

1991   *Reading the Past: Current Approaches to Interpretation in Archaeology*. Cambridge University Press, Cambridge.

Illustrated London News

1909   A Wonderful Civilisation of 7000 Years Ago. Report of archaeological excavations by T. Hewitt Myring in the Chicama Valley, Peru, 803–806. December 4.

Larco Hoyle, Rafael

2001   *Los Mochicas*. Museo Arqueológico Rafael Larco Herrera, Lima.

Lechtman, Heather N.

1976   A Metallurgical Site Survey in the Peruvian Andes. *Journal of Field Archaeology* 3:1–42.

Millaire, Jean-François

1997   La technologie de la filature manuelle sur le site Moche de la côte nord du Pérou précolombien. M.Sc. thesis, Université de Montréal.

2002   *Moche Burial Patterns: An Investigation into Prehispanic Social Structure*. BAR International Series 1066. Oxford.

Murra, John V.

1980   The Economic Organization of the Inka State. JAI Press, Greenwich, Connecticut.

Nordenskiöld, Erland

1919   *An Ethno-Geographical Analysis of the Material Culture of Two Indian Tribes in the Gran Chaco*. Comparative Ethnographical Studies 1. AMS Press, New York.

1924   *The Ethnography of South America Seen from Mojos in Bolivia*. Comparative Ethnographical Studies 3. AMS Press, New York.

Proulx, Donald A.

1985   *An Analysis of the Early Cultural Sequence in the Nepeña Valley, Peru*. Research Report 25. Department of Anthropology, University of Massachusetts, Amherst.

Prümers, Heiko

1995   Un tejido moche excepcional de la tumba del "Señor de Sipán" (valle de Lambayeque, Perú). *Beiträge zur allgemeinen und vergleichenden Archäologie* 15:338–369.

Quilter, Jeffrey

2001   Moche Mimesis: Continuity and Change in Public Art in Early Peru. In *Moche: Art and Archaeology in Ancient Peru*, 21–45. Edited by Joanne Pillsbury. National Gallery of Art and Yale University Press, Washington, D.C.

Russell, Glenn S., and Margaret A. Jackson

2001   Political Economy and Patronage at Cerro Mayal, Peru. In *Moche: Art and Archaeology in Ancient Peru*, 159–175. Edited by Joanne Pillsbury. National Gallery of Art and Yale University Press, Washington, D.C.

Russell, Glenn S., Banks L. Leonard, and Jesús Briceño

1994   Cerro Mayal: Nuevos datos sobre la producción de cerámica moche en el valle de Chicama. In *Moche: Propuestas y perspectivas*, 181–206. Actas del Primer Coloquio sobre la Cultura Moche, Trujillo, 12 a 16 de abril de 1993. Edited by Santiago Uceda and Elías Mujica. Travaux de l'Institut Français d'Études Andines 79. Universidad Nacional de la Libertad, Trujillo, Perú.

1998   The Cerro Mayal Workshop: Addressing Issues of Craft Specialization in Moche Society. In *Andean Ceramics: Technology, Organization and Approaches*, 63–89. Edited by Izumi Shimada. Supplement to MASCA Research Papers 15. The University Museum of Archaeology and Anthropology, University of Pennsylvania, Philadelphia.

Schaedel, Richard P.

1972   The City and the Origin of the State in America. In *Proceedings of the 39th International Congress of Americanists*, Vol. 2:15–33.

1985   The Transition from Chiefdom to State in Northern Peru. In *Development and Decline: The Evolution of Sociopolitical Organization*, 156–169. Edited by Henri J. M. Claessen, Pieter van de Velde, and M. Estellie Smith. Bergin and Garvey, South Hadley, Massachusetts.

Shimada, Izumi

1994   *Pampa Grande and the Mochica Culture*. University of Texas Press, Austin.

1998   Sicán Metallurgy and Its Cross-Craft Relationships. *Boletín Museo del Oro* 41:26–61. Bogota.

2001   Late Moche Urban Craft Production: A First Approximation. In *Moche: Art and Archaeology in Ancient Peru*, 177–205. Edited by Joanne Pillsbury. National Gallery of Art and Yale University Press, Washington, D.C.

Shimada, Izumi, Stephen M. Epstein, and Alan K. Craig

1983   The Metallurgical Process in Ancient North Peru. *Archaeology* 36 (5):38–45.

Shimada, Izumi, and John F. Merkel

1991   Copper-Alloy Metallurgy in Ancient Peru. *Scientific American* 256 (1):80–86.

Strong, William D., and Clifford Evans

1952   *Cultural Stratigraphy in the Virú Valley, Northern Peru: The Formative and Florescent Epochs.* Columbia Studies in Archaeology and Ethnology IV. Columbia University Press, New York.

Trigger, Bruce G.

1989   *A History of Archaeological Thought.* Cambridge University Press, Cambridge.

2003   *Understanding Early Civilizations: A Comparative Study.* Cambridge University Press, Cambridge.

Uceda, Santiago

2001   Investigations at Huaca de la Luna, Moche Valley: An Example of Moche Religious Architecture. In *Moche: Art and Archaeology in Ancient Peru*, 47–67. Edited by Joanne Pillsbury. National Gallery of Art and Yale University Press, Washington, D.C.

Uceda, Santiago, and José Armas

1998   An Urban Pottery Workshop at the Site of Moche, North Coast of Peru. In *Andean Ceramics: Technology, Organization, and Approaches*, 91–110. Edited by Izumi Shimada. MASCA Research Papers in Science and Archaeology, Supplement to Volume 15. Museum Applied Science Center for Archaeology, University of Pennsylvania Museum of Archaeology and Anthropology, Philadelphia.

Verano, John

2001   War and Death in the Moche World: Osteological Evidence and Visual Discourse. In *Moche: Art and Archaeology in Ancient Peru*, 111–125. Edited by Joanne Pillsbury. National Gallery of Art and Yale University Press, Washington, D.C.

Verano, John W., and Guido P. Lombardi

1999   Apéndice 3: Análisis del material oseo. In *Tumbas de cámara moche en la plataforma superior de la Huaca Cao Viejo, Complejo El Brujo*, 48–51. Edited by Régulo Franco, César Gálvez, and Segundo Vásquez. Programa Arqueológico "El Brujo." Boletín No. 1 (July).

Vreeland, James M.

1986   Cotton Spinning and Processing on the Peruvian North Coast. In *The Junius B. Bird Conference on Andean Textiles, April 7th and 8th, 1984*, 363–383. Edited by Ann P. Rowe. The Textile Museum, Washington, D.C.

Willey, Gordon R.

1953   *Prehistoric Settlement Patterns in the Virú Valley, Peru.* Bulletin 155. Bureau of American Ethnology, Washington, D.C.

Wilson, David J.

1988   *Prehispanic Settlement Patterns in the Lower Santa Valley, Peru: A Regional Perspective on the Origins and Development of Complex North Coast Society.* Smithsonian Institution Press, Washington, D.C.

Wylie, Alison

2002   *Thinking from Things: Essays in the Philosophy of Archaeology.* University of California Press, Berkeley.

CHAPTER FOURTEEN

Spiders and Spider Decapitators in Moche Iconography

Identification from the Contexts of Sipán, Antecedents and Symbolism

NÉSTOR IGNACIO ALVA MENESES, MUSEO TUMBAS REALES DE SIPÁN

Abstract

The Tombs of Sipán in northern Peru provided some of the first contextualized Moche metallic objects depicting anthropomorphized spider beings with decapitated heads and tumi knives in their hands, as well as more naturalized spider representations. I begin this chapter by tracing the visual theme of such naturalized spider and anthropomorphized Spider Decapitator images from the preceding Formative period Cupisnique culture through the Moche system of representation, as found at other sites such as Loma Negra and Huaca Cao Viejo. I draw extensively on the work of Burger and Salazar-Burger, as well as Alana Cordy-Collins. From the numerous and varied representations in the tombs at Sipán, I identify the spider according to species, arguing that it represents a common north coast orb-weaving spider, Argiope argentata. The chapter concludes with a broad discussion of the symbolic qualities of A. argentata that the Moche perhaps recognized and referenced in their incorporation of the species into the material goods of such high-status elite burials as the Tombs of Sipán.

Following the discovery of Tombs 1 and 2, in 1987 the excavations at Sipán unearthed the elaborate funerary remains of a third high-ranking individual known as the Old Lord of Sipán. This Tomb 3 individual had been buried with an extensive assortment of metal, shell, ceramic, and feather objects (Figure 14.1). Many of the objects featured stylized zoomorphic images modeled into ornaments and effigies. One of the most elaborate and significant burial ornaments was a pectoral of ten gold, biconvex beads. Each piece of the necklace bore the representation of a spider suspended in the center of its web with its abdomen transformed into a human head (Figure 14.2). The reverse side features a low-relief spiral comprised of three serpentine birds (Figure 14.3).

From a detailed analysis of these particular components of Tomb 3 at Sipán, I have determined that these objects were meant to represent a particular species of spider, *Argiope argentata* (Figure 14.4). Based on its particular characteristics, I would argue that this spider species was modeled in both natural and figural manner on the ceramic and metal objects from Sipán, as well as on objects from other Moche sites. Such spiders further appear upon the facades of Moche ceremonial centers.

Not surprisingly, the species *A. argentata* also likely provided the natural model for one set of spider representations in the preceding Cupisnique tradition.

In order to understand the basis for this spider identification, and its meaning for the context of the Old Lord, I will first assess the iconographic data of Cupisnique and Moche spider representations. I will then examine the natural characteristics of *A. argentata* in greater detail in order to evince the correspondences between the iconographic forms and natural models. Such analyses should provide for a better understanding of the greater symbolic significance of the spider representations in Moche iconography, most notably those associated with the funerary assemblages at Sipán. Along with other natural models, the spider *A. argentata* references a fundamental system of duality and serves as a symbol of fecundity and cyclic regeneration. Through its representation, the Moche further recall concepts of the center, of inversion, and of symbolic dualities. Thus, I will conclude with a more in-depth assessment of each of these qualities and visual metaphors provided by the spider, which actively participated in the symbolic universe of the Early Moche culture.

FIGURE 14.1. View of Tomb 3 during excavation, Sipán. Photograph by Walter Alva.

FIGURE 14.2. Spider beads in gold from Tomb 3, Sipán.
Photograph by Christopher B. Donnan and Donna McClelland.

FIGURE 14.3. Back view of a spider bead, Tomb 3, Sipán.
Photograph by Christopher B. Donnan and Donna McClelland.

FIGURE 14.4. Spider *Argiope argentata*. Photograph by Sean M. McCann.

FIGURE 14.5. Spider being, North Wall, Huaca de la Luna. Photograph by author.

The Iconographic Record

In the iconography of the Cupisnique and Moche cultures, spider and Spider Decapitator images appear on objects associated with elite funerary contexts at sites such as Limoncarro, Sipán, and Loma Negra. They further occur on the facades of important monuments such as Garagay, Huaca de la Luna (Figure 14.5), and Huaca Cao Viejo. These icons attest to the fundamental role of spiders in the religious systems of the north coast, constituting one of the links between the Formative period tradition and the Moche style of the Early Intermediate period.

In contrast to the earlier Cupisnique forms, the naturalistic tendency of Early Moche art likely benefited from the perfecting of ceramic and metalworking techniques. The Moche visual system thus seemingly reorganized the previous north coast iconological system through an increased emphasis on specific zoological models, structuring a greater empirical system or cosmological discourse based on tangible forms in nature. To understand better, within this discourse, the represented spider forms in Early Moche visual culture and their associated meanings in the funerary assemblage of

the Old Lord of Sipán, I begin with the known Formative period Cupisnique examples.

Cupisnique Spiders

In 1982, Lucy Salazar-Burger and Richard Burger undertook a study of arachnid figures in north coast Formative period iconography. The objects consisted of a series of six stone receptacles that were decorated in low relief with a similar theme of natural and anthropomorphized arachnids (Salazar-Burger and Burger 1982:213). By remaining largely absent from the highland Chavín system of representation, these arachnid figures provided a significant model by which to demarcate a more localized north coast visual repertoire, termed *Cupisnique* by Larco Hoyle. Yet as Salazar-Burger and Burger note, the spider images themselves present stylistic correspondences with Chavín de Huántar that are notable and suggest a mutual contemporaneity (ibid.).

According to the investigators, the Spider Decapitator in particular "symbolizes one of the deities of the Cupisnique ideological system, whose role we believe would have been to mediate in the ritual activities of the fertility and fecundity of the earth" (ibid:238).[1] In a more recent publication, Salazar-Burger and Burger (2000) propose that the Spider Decapitator may even represent the principal deity of a Cupisnique pantheon. As such, "this figure does not appear in the friezes uncovered at Huaca de los Reyes, perhaps because the access was limited to mythical stories and mysteries, and thereby the principal deities were not represented on the facades, as we see in the case of Chavín de Huantar" (2000:37).[2]

In their analysis, Salazar-Burger and Burger organized the Cupisnique images into the two distinct groups— spiders and Spider Decapitators—depicted on numerous stone objects. For example, the spider figures appear on the Larco Plate and the Dumbarton Oaks Vase (Figures 14.6, 14.7); the Spider Decapitator images appear on the Dumbarton Oaks Plate and the Brooklyn Museum Plate (Figures 14.8, 14.9). Salazar-Burger and Burger (1982) also make reference to monumental images such as the petroglyph at Alto de las Guitarras and the Middle Temple Frieze 3 at Garagay (see also Ravines 1984). In these two cases, the features are arachnid and anthropomorphic, respectively. I would add to this corpus two Cupisnique ceramics, one reported by Walter Alva (1986:110, fig. 61) and the other by Alana Cordy-Collins (2001:27, fig. 2.5).

FIGURE 14.6. Spider with two heads etched on a stone bowl. Museo Arqueológico Rafael Larco Herrera, Lima. Redrawn from Salazar-Burger and Burger 1982, Figure 2.

FIGURE 14.7. Spiders with two heads etched on a stone bowl. Dumbarton Oaks Research Library and Collections, Washington, D.C. Redrawn from Salazar-Burger and Burger 1982, Figure 4.

FIGURE 14.8. Anthropomorphic spider holding a human head. Dumbarton Oaks Research Library and Collections, Washington, D.C. Redrawn from Salazar-Burger and Burger 1982, Figure 8.

FIGURE 14.9. Anthropomorphic spider. The Brooklyn Museum. Redrawn from Salazar-Burger and Burger 1982, Figure 11.

The spider images modeled upon the two stone receptacles display a bisymmetrical design achieved by adding a second head to the opposing end (Figure 14.6, 14.7). This tripartite representation alters the anatomy of the arachnid (cephalothorax, abdomen) to that similar to an insect (head, thorax, and abdomen). The intention was likely to establish the image's signified "center." This relates in intent to the four-part crosses incised on the Cupisnique bottle reported by Walter Alva (1986:110, fig. 61), which also correspond to the concept of the "center."

In contrast, the Spider Decapitator images on these stone containers exhibit a diagonal or vertical contraposition of human and animal attributes (Salazar-Burger and Burger 1982). The human side is depicted in profile, while the animal is seen as if from above (Figure 14.8). On the Dumbarton Oaks Plate, the "net full of heads" element constitutes the center of the figure (Figure 14.8). The dual organization of the spider and Spider Decapitator images thus appears to have been well-defined within the north coast Cupisnique tradition, and it continues into the Early Moche style.

Salazar-Burger and Burger (1982) address studies of Moche representations performed by Lavallée (1970) and Larco Hoyle (1938) that identify such spider representations as *Mygalia* sp., or tarantulas based largely on the placement of the chelicera and the species' large size and great speed. Yet the researchers also turned to ethnohistoric data provided by Polo de Ondegardo, Pablo José de Arriaga, and Vega Bazán, who describe the use of large web-building spiders in Andean divinatory rites. Based on such accounts and those of Cayón (1971), Salazar-Burger and Burger (1982) aptly associated the appearance of spiders with rain.

From a subsequent visual analysis of the images, I further support their assertion regarding the masculine nature of the Spider Decapitator. This masculine nature may be defined by the relationship of the spider with *Strombus* and serpent images, as observable upon the Brooklyn Museum Plate (Figure 14.9). From their placement within the main arachnid figure, such images suggest phallic and seminal symbols. The web-semen-rain metaphor then acquires meaning in the context of agrarian fecundity, which the spider images reference.

Given the very determined stylization of the spider images, I would suggest that the Cupisnique system already sought to represent a particular species of spider

FIGURE 14.10. Spider *Argiope trifasciata*. Photograph by Lynette Schimming.

in the monumental and portable visual programs. Without venturing greater analysis here upon these early Cupisnique representations, I would argue that the Larco Plate and Dumbarton Oaks Vase display images of the spider *Argiope trifasciata* (Figures 14.6, 14.7, 14.10), although the agnathic face that composes the inferior part of the Dumbarton Oaks Plate figure is notably similar in form and design to the abdomen of *Argiope argentata* (Figure 14.4). Furthermore, the geometric border in the form of a Z recalls the webs made by spiders of the genus *Argiope* (Figure 14.8), to which I will return below.

This diversity in species selection and representation in Cupisnique iconography suggests the existence of an early system of classification of a depth still unknown to modern scholarship. As a result, I will not propose a direct one-to-one correspondence between these Cupisnique forms and the succeeding Moche spider images. Nevertheless, as I will demonstrate, the structure of dual representation and the shared visual features remain significant, and the Moche undoubtedly referenced this earlier tradition in manifesting their new visual and symbolic system.

Moche Ceramics

Various Early and Middle Moche ceramics represent idealized spiders in a manner similar to those images of the preceding Cupisnique style, with a third body part often

added to give the spider an unreal or fantastic appearance. One false-necked, incised vessel shows an idealized spider with a divine face in the abdomen (Figure 14.11). Resembling the gold-beaded pectoral from Sipán, I would suggest that this spider image depicts the species *Argiope argentata*, or possibly *Gasteracantha*, based on the facial representation within the abdomen. Only one sculpted ceramic bottle of Early Moche style actually represents *Argiope argentata* in naturalistic form (Figure 14.12). In later phases of Moche ceramics, the representations of spiders are less frequent and appear associated with mythic scenes or as marginal motifs on certain vessel necks (Figure 14.13).

FIGURE 14.11. Spider with a fanged being depicted on its back. Redrawn from Kutscher 1983, Figure 148.

FIGURE 14.12. Spider modeled on a stirrup spout bottle. Museo del Banco Central de Reserva del Perú, Lima (ACE-593). Photograph by author.

Various Early Moche globular bottles display a painted frontal image of the Spider Decapitator. For example, a very elaborate, early sculpted bottle from Vicús represents this spider deity. Although the arms are now missing, the spider figure likely once held a knife and decapitated head in either hand (Figure 14.14). Another stirrup spout bottle looted from the area of Sipán illustrates the spider deity in profile. The figure carries a knife and decapitated head in its hands and has arachnid legs extending to the sides. Under the belt appears a rattle, or bell, an object which may bear close analogy with the multisectioned abdomen of *A. argen-*

tata, based on the Tomb 3 and Tomb 1 examples of rattles and backflaps from Sipán (Figure 14.15). In Late Moche fineline ceramics, the Spider Decapitator participates in complex scenes of combat and possibly defeat before the anthropomorphic deity Wrinkle Face. Yet another ceramic vessel depicts at least five individuals with spider characteristics accompanying the Rayed Deity as he ascends a ladder between two levels (Figure 14.13).

Moche Monumental Facades

Spider images have also been recorded on the facades of some of most significant excavated Moche buildings.

FIGURE 14.13. Fineline painting of the Presentation Theme individuals. Drawing by Donna McClelland.

FIGURE 14.14. Bottle in the form of a Wrinkle Face with spider attributes and an octopus headdress. Museo del Banco Central de Reserva del Perú, Lima (ACE-507). Photograph by author.

FIGURE 14.15. Gold backflap with turquoise inlay from Tomb 3, Sipán. Photograph by Christopher B. Donnan and Donna McClelland.

For example, the third level of the Huaca de la Luna platform complex presents polychrome reliefs of stylized spiders, likely Spider Decapitators. Each spider figure is composed of a central body with two schematized heads to either end, each head distinct from the other. The heads that face toward the west possess eyes, chelicerae, and antennae. The opposing heads to the east have only two pairs of chelicerae. The legs are distributed in four groups above and below, totaling fourteen in all. On the inferior part, certain legs are replaced by hands that carry a knife and an undefined object, possibly a head (Figure 14.5).

A largely destroyed mural relief, similar to that described above and in a relative location with respect to the architectural layout, was uncovered at Huaca Cao Viejo (Franco, Gálvez, and Vásquez 2001). The spiders that appear on this structure have four pairs of extended legs and zigzag bands across the abdomen (Figure 14.16). As such, they closely recall the species *Argiope trifasciata*

(Figure 14.10). Images of the Spider Decapitator also appear on the mural reliefs at Huaca Cao Viejo. The northern mural of the ceremonial chamber located on the upper platform is divided into two panels that depict figures with bilobed ears, half-moon crowns, and four groups of three spider legs. In their right hands, the figures carry a staff ending in the head of a condor while in the left hand they hold a decapitated head. The colors are distinct on each figure (Figure 14.17).

Metal Objects

Metallic ornaments from the site of Loma Negra in Piura represent spider figures in a rather realistic manner. An earplug of silver and gold features a spider on its web, and a rectangular gold-and-silver nose pendant was decorated with six spiders of a similarly represented species (Jones 2001:212, fig. 2). Some perforated plates display three-dimensional, bound metal spiders and probably were part of a royal standard or adornment. These

FIGURE 14.16. Mural of a spider being holding a sacrificial knife, Huaca Cao Viejo. Photograph by author.

FIGURE 14.17. Mural of a spider being holding a sacrificial knife and a human head, Huaca Cao Viejo. Photograph by author.

same spiders appear on similar pieces made of copper. In all such examples from Loma Negra, the number of abdominal sections varies and does not necessarily correspond to the natural number in a zoological species. Nevertheless, these objects of relatively similar provenance evidently represent *Argiope argentata* based on their form and dual composition in gold and silver.

Other objects from Loma Negra, such as nose pendants and discs, represent the Spider Decapitator in a manner similar to those from Sipán. A half-moon copper crown depicts a divine head in the center with two Spider Decapitators in profile to either side. This image recalls that of the backflaps and bells at Sipán, described below.

Sipán

The funerary context of the Old Lord of Sipán in Tomb 3 offers the most singular and clear examples of spider representations on the ornaments of elite personages of Moche society (Alva 1994; Alva and Donnan 1993). These include the pectoral of ten biconvex pieces of gold, mentioned above. Each piece of the necklace displays a

spider figure centered on its web, and each spider exhibits the image of a human head on its abdomen (Figure 14.2). Each human head is adorned with a collar of nine beads, which coincide with the number of body segments of the spider *A. argentata*. The web is composed of seven concentric circles and twenty crossing strands. The reverse side displays a spiral of six interlinked spokes. Three of the spokes resemble serpent-birds with serrated backs, while the other three are plain bands. The interior space between the two halves contains three bells, which could represent spider eggs but also serve as rattles (Figure 14.3).

There are no other recorded representations of such spiders within the other burial contexts of the funerary platform at Sipán. Nevertheless, there are images of the so-called Spider Decapitator. In the funerary context of the Old Lord, for example, the excavators recuperated two groups of ten gold and silver bells, along with a backflap made of gold, all depicting a similar figure (Figure 14.18). The figure illustrated has bilobed ears and a ferocious face displaying fangs. In one hand he holds a knife, while in the other he carries a decapitated

FIGURE 14.18. Silver bell from Tomb 3, Sipán. Photograph by Christopher B. Donnan and Donna McClelland.

head. This individual is further adorned by a semicircular headdress with the face of an owl in the center, a crenulated belt, and a shirt of longitudinal bands. From the shoulders and belt emerge four diagonal pairs of spider legs (Cordy-Collins 1992). Careful observation suggests that the X form and transverse segments of these defined extremities resemble those characteristic of the spider *A. argentata*. Additionally, there exists a close similarity between the shape of these bells and backflaps—a semicircular design lined with spheres—and the broad, flaring, multilobed abdomen of the spider *Argiope argentata* (Figure 14.4).

In the other funerary contexts at Sipán, elite individuals possessed bells and backflaps similar to the images from the tomb of the Old Lord. One looted funerary context recovered at the beginning of the project contained gold and copper bells of an undefined number, along with a large gold backflap, some of which clearly featured the Spider Decapitator (Alva and Donnan 1993). In a similar manner, this spider deity was depicted in the well-known funerary context of the Lord of Sipán on two gold bells, two backflaps (gold and silver), and a small, half-moon crown of gold. A context of lesser rank, Tomb 7, excavated in the same funerary platform, pertained to a pair of adolescents. It contained, among other offerings, a stirrup spout bottle with a high-relief decoration of an anthropomorphic being in profile holding a knife in one hand and a captured bird in the other—clearly a decapitator. The figure also carries a bell with an inscribed face and exhibits appendages in the form of spider legs.

The funerary contexts at Sipán thus actively reinforce certain conceptions regarding the symbolic significance of certain spider species, most notably *Argiope argentata*. The dual representation of spiders in Moche iconography as naturalistic and anthropomorphic beings remains consistent from the Cupisnique tradition. Yet it is the manner of representation in the funerary assemblage of the Old Lord that provides the most concrete information for identifying this particular species of spider. It visually demonstrates the correspondence between the natural model and the symbolic role that the spider assumes in Moche culture.

In Book 4 of *Historia de nuevo mundo* ([1653] 1956), Father Cobo observed that the spiders in the Andean world differ in size, color, and shape, and that certain medium-sized spiders appear to represent the shape of a human face on their abdomen, though varying in design. Although brief, this statement indicates the attention that certain spider species received in the greater Andean region based on their resemblance to the human face. This feature most certainly identifies spiders of the genus *Argiope*. Indeed, it seems that Father Cobo described the same image that the Moche expressed in the pectoral beads associated with the Old Lord of Sipán.

Entomological Information

Spiders are arthropods, meaning they possess eight legs, and their bodies are clearly divided into two parts, cephalothorax and abdomen. They possess a pair of pedipalps near the mouth, and two chelicerae that serve to inject venom. On the inferior part of the abdomen are the spinnerets that produce the silk with which they create their webs, which permit the spiders to hunt prey, store food, and wrap eggs.

Although vagrant spiders that live in semisubterranean burrows and capture victims by ambush do exist, sedentary spiders live on woven webs suspended above the ground. These spiders create such webs first by stringing a line between two objects and then by creating a star with lines running around the edges and uniting at the center. The spiders then trace over the exterior edges and radiating lines, completing the design with an adhesive spiral running from the outer edge toward the center of the web.

In addition to capturing insects, the spider web serves to condense water in the form of drops. Using this trait to their advantage, spiders may lay dozens of eggs wrapped in sacks of thread, which further resemble the water drops. In a few days, hundreds of small spiders disperse through the air, suspended from and floating away on their individual threads. These floating spiders can cover large distances and will establish themselves in a new place and produce new webs.

The venom of spiders generally kills its prey. Indeed, the venom literally dissolves the insides of the captured prey so that the spider can directly ingest the liquefied food source. This natural act may have been considered a powerful metaphor for ritual sacrifice in the north coast agrarian societies—and a symbolic factor in Moche spider representations (Cordy-Collins 1992). Certainly, the venomous and predatory character of such spiders was an important component in Moche ideology. Such spiders, however, also provide a positive, natural control on insect populations, in particular those destructive to crops. This aspect of agricultural protector presumably further defines their symbolic role in Moche culture, reflecting the spider's dual role in the natural world as both sacrificers and protectors.

Toward an Identification

The spider *Argiope argentata* is a common species across nearly all of the Americas and is found regularly along the coast of Peru. Other species of *Argiope*, such as *A. trifasciata,* occur at higher altitudes. Similar to other populations of spiders on the north coast of Peru, the populations of *Argiope argentata* rise notably during the recurring climatological phenomenon of El Niño/Southern Oscillation (ENSO) (see Polis et al. 1997). During such times, the spiders proliferate in the lower valleys, where their populations are usually scarce.

Not only is the species *A. argentata* common to the north coast, with its presence corresponding significantly to the dramatic effect of the El Niño phenomenon, but the physical appearance of *A. argentata* is also very striking. The spider's coloration literally defines its two halves: the thorax and upper half of the abdomen shimmer, while the lower half of the abdomen bears points and lines of yellow, black, and silver. The predominant color on the ventral side is black, with a transverse band of yellow across the abdomen. The spider's abdomen is multisectional, with nine conical protuberances. This combination of colors and sections on the abdomen often resembles a face (Figure 14.4). The extremities are yellow, with occasional dark transverse zones. When resting on its web during the day, the spider positions its legs in two opposing pairs to form an X (Figure 14.4). In this position, the spider's head always faces downward. Finally, *Argiope* species weave elaborate webs with stabilimenta, which are portions of the web redressed in zigzag lines in a manner like lace. These zigzagging stabilimenta may be circular or take a radial form in the shape of an X. Either way, they present identifiable and significant visual designs.

Another genus of spider that also possesses a multilobed abdomen resembling the design of a human face is *Gasterocantha*. Its voluminous abdomen nearly hides its small legs and head, and its web is often symmetrical and lacking zigzagging stabilimenta. Therefore, it seems that despite the visual resemblance to a human face, *Gasterocantha* are less likely to be the spiders drawn upon in Moche iconography. Rather, the Moche appear to have referenced quite exclusively the species *Argiope argentata* for very particular reasons.

The notable characteristics of *Argiope argentata*—its coloration, form, and ecology—permit the creation of certain complex metaphors of cosmological and cosmogenic principles in Moche culture. Unlike any other natural model, this spider provides multiple symbolic concepts of relevant use for the complex Moche visual system of representation. As noted by Father Cobo, these principles remain accessible to modern scholars based on the continued presence and observable nature of the actual species on the north coast of Peru. By highlighting the significant natural qualities of *Argiope argentata*, I will thus pursue the symbolic nature of their representation in Moche iconography.

The Concept of the Center

On the Cupisnique stone receptacles, such as the Larco Plate and the Dumbarton Oaks Vase, the spider image is conceived as a central, circular body with symmetrical heads and feet to the sides and ends (Figures 14.6, 14.7). In the Spider Decapitator images, such as that on the Dumbarton Oaks Plate, the centers indicated by the nets over their backs (Figure 14.8). As such, the spiders, spider webs, and spider deities in Cupisnique iconography are symbolic as "centers."

On the pectoral beads from the assemblage of the Old Lord of Sipán, the spider at the center of the web suggests the same concept. The association of the spider to the spiral likely refers to the dynamics of these centers as generators of the universe (Figure 14.2). The spiral suggests kinetic energy, as visible in a whirlwind of air, whirlpools of water, and snail shells (Harth-Terre 1976). Sometimes the spiral is stylized with fish or bird combinations (Figure 14.3), signifying through these joined elements the dynamic interdependency of the worlds above and below.

The spider *A. argentata* refers to this same principle through the spiral shape of its web, which unites the worlds at its center. The center is visually reinforced by the zigzag stabilimenta in the form of an X. Indeed, the web designs of *A. argentata* are very complex, emanating from the spider's body like a primordial substance. The spider rests during the day in the center of this web, suspended between the earth and sky. Its four pairs of legs form another cross or X shape, defining the concept of an "axis mundi." As such, the spider is the mediating nexus between two worlds.

Furthermore, if the identification of *A. argentata* for the Spider Decapitator in Moche iconography is valid, then the symbolism of the center transfers from the animal to the divine figure and to the carriers of these images. These individuals thus reflect the "center" of the social organization. It is for this reason that the bells and backflaps, which recall the multilobed abdomen of *A. argentata,* appear in the funerary contexts of the highest-ranking individuals at Sipán.

Concepts of Duality and Inversion

The coloration of *A. argentata* and its positions on the web, with the silver half of its body toward the earth and the yellow half toward the sky, present another clear visual metaphor connecting the binary roles of earth and sky. Also, the colors silver and yellow closely relate to the duality of gold and silver expressed in the funerary complex of the Old Lord of Sipán. In Tomb 3, the Spider Decapitator appears on bells and backflaps of both gold and silver, situated one above the other. However, despite this display of metalwork proficiency, as well as the naturalism of Moche art, no object displays a spider modeled half in silver and half in gold. There always thus remains one feature to distinguish a spider image from the natural model, such as a lesser number of protruding elements.

In addition, in the natural world *A. argentata* rests at the center of its web and faces downward. Yet on the pectoral beads of the Old Lord of Sipán, the spider figure is depicted with its head facing upward (Figure 14.2). The spider assumes this same position on the nose guard from Loma Negra. I would argue that this upward-facing direction was perhaps intended to express an inversion of the natural model. Other contexts and motifs support this concept. For example, in Early Moche tombs at the site of Dos Cabezas in the Jequetepeque Valley, Donnan and Cock recovered two associated vessels that represent the Andean condor and vulture, respectively (Donnan 2003). The colors of each piece are contrary to the natural model, constituting an opposition (*Vultur gryphus* has coloration that is the inverse of *Sarcorhamphus papa*). The duality of the natural model is thus reinforced by the inversion of these colors in the visual representation.

Concepts of Regeneration and Fertility

Various species of spider, especially *Argiope argentata*, proliferate during the climatic phenomenon known as El Niño/Southern Oscillation (ENSO), spreading from the *lomas* to the lower valleys (Polis et al. 1997). The notorious presence of these spiders at these times directly relates them to the universal cycle of regeneration. During an El Niño event, the landscape of the north coast returns to one of overabundance: pasture land grows in the desert, streams run through normally dry quebradas, and lakes and marshes are reborn. The event thus defines a grand cycle of regeneration. Notably, according to Meneses and Chero (Alva 1994, 1998), the impact of El Niño events on the architectural structure at Sipán determined the sequence of construction phases on the funerary platform.

The newborn spiders—transported by the wind while suspended from their threads—would have further constituted a clear metaphor of the cycle of rains and dispersal of life (Cayón 1971:137). These floating spiders appear in spectacular quantities during El Niño events, as they do during the annual humid season. Hundreds of newborn spiders emerge from eggs resembling water droplets. They are then elevated into the air in the manner of clouds, only to later fall back to the earth like rain. The spiders are thus not only prognosticators of rain by their actions, analogous to the fluvial cycle, but their proliferation during the annual rainy season also relates them to the seasonal cycles of fecundity and fertility. I recall here the research by Cayón (1971), in which he demonstrates that in some Andean communities the spiders are announcers of the coming rains.

The Cupisnique images, such as upon the Dumbarton Oaks Plate, also relate to agricultural fecundity, representing vegetal elements in association with the Spider Decapitator (Salazar-Burger and Burger 1982). The fanged mouths to the sides of the central figure could be maize kernels (Figure 14.8). If one considers that maize possesses hair-like fibers that cover teeth-like seeds, then the vegetal and human "hairs" and "heads" are located at the "center" of the spider deity. Decapitation then

FIGURE 14.19. Feline head beads, gold with shell inlay, from Tomb 3, Sipán. Photograph by Christopher B. Donnan and Donna McClelland.

takes on an agricultural connotation: the heads within the nets and hands of the Spider Decapitator symbolize at the same time seeds, harvested fruits, sacrificed heads, and spider eggs within the web (Cordy-Collins 1992). All present metaphors that interweave life with death, nature with society, and planting with harvesting in a ritual agrarian context.

Cosmological Parallels

In the context of the Old Lord of Sipán, there exists a relation between the necklace of the spiders and a necklace of a similar type that represents feline heads (Figure 14.19). The feline faces are modeled on the front of ten spherical beads that host spirals of serpents on the reverse sides. The beads of these two pectorals thus agree

in the number of pieces, material, and the symbol of a spiral on their reverse sides. In the funerary assemblage, the necklace of spiders was located over the bundle, whereas the collar of felines was placed over the individual's chest. I would argue that the represented feline is an ocelot (*Leopardus pardalis*), given that the species possesses colors and pelage designs similar to *A. argentata*. Their symbolic association would thus refer to the analogies of color and form between these two species. The abdomen of the spider may even resemble the head of the feline.

Considering that the feline in Andean myths is often related to rain, lightning, and earthquakes, its association with the spider confirms the parallels between these two species, which define cosmological levels related to fecundity and the power over life. In this light, the feline features of the Spider Decapitator ought to be reconsidered.

Finally, the position of the pectoral of spider beads over the bundle of the Old Lord returns us to the funerary context of Tomb 3 (Figure 14.1). The spider beads rest over the complete funerary bundle. Through such placement, the bundle wrapped in a shroud of threads may serve as an apt metaphor for the captured prey of the spider, wrapped in silk. The spiders—as regenerators, protectors, and destroyers—thus conduct the cycle of life and death. The symbol of the spider in this discussion then terminates where it began, with the burial assemblage of the Old Lord of Sipán.

Notes

1. Translation by Kimberly L. Jones.
2. Translation by Kimberly L. Jones.

Bibliography

Alva, Walter
1986   Cerámica temprana en el valle de Jequetepeque, norte del Perú. *Materialien zur Allgemeinen und Vergleichenden Archäologie*, Band 32, München.
1994   *Sipán*. Colección Cultura y Artes del Perú, Lima.
1998   *Sipán: Descubrimiento e investigación*, Lima.
Alva, Walter, and Christopher B. Donnan
1993   *Royal Tombs of Sipán*. Fowler Museum of Cultural History, University of California, Los Angeles.
Cayón Armelia, Edgardo
1971   El hombre y los animales en la cultura Quechua. *Allpanchis Phuturinqa* 3:135–162.
Cobo, Bernabé
[1653] 1956   *Historia de nuevo mundo*. Lib. IV. Biblioteca de Autores Españoles, Madrid.
Cordy-Collins, Alana
1992   Archaism or Tradition? The Decapitation Theme in Cupisnique and Moche Iconography. *Latin American Antiquity* 3 (3):207–219.
2001   Decapitation in Cupisnique and Early Moche Societies. In *Ritual Sacrifice in Ancient Peru*, 21–34. Edited by Elizabeth P. Benson and Anita G. Cook. University of Texas Press, Austin.

Donnan, Christopher B.
2003   Tumbas con entierros en miniatura: Un nuevo tipo funerario moche. In *Moche: Hacia el Final del Milenio*, Tome I, 43–78. Actas del Segundo Coloquio sobre la Cultura Moche, Trujillo, 1 al 7 de agosto de 1999. Edited by Santiago Uceda and Elías Mujica. Universidad Nacional de Trujillo and Pontificia Universidad Católica del Perú, Lima.
Franco Jordán, Régulo, César Gálvez Mora, and Segundo Vásquez
2001   La Huaca Cao Viejo en el complejo El Brujo: Una contribución al estudio de los Mochicas en el Valle de Chicama. *Arqueológicas* 25:55–59.
Harth-Terre, Emilio
1976   *El vocabulario estético de los Mochicas: Una lengua muerta que vive en su arte*. J. Mejia Baca, Lima.
Jones, Julie
2001   Innovation and Resplendence: Metalwork for Moche Lords. In *Moche Art and Archaeology of Ancient Peru*, 207–222. Edited by Joanne Pillsbury. National Gallery of Art and Yale University Press, Washington, D.C.
Kutscher, Gerdt
1983   *Nordperuanische Gefässmalereien des Moche-Stils*. Verlag C. H. Beck, Munich.
Larco Hoyle, Rafael
1938   *Los Mochicas*. Tomo I. Casa Editora, S.A. Limitada, Lima.
Lavallée, Daniélle
1970   *Les représentations animals dans la céramique mochica*. Université de Paris, Mémoires de l'Institute d'Ethnologie-IV, Paris.
Polis, Gary A., Stephen D. Hurd, C. Todd Jackson, and Francisco Sanchez Piñero
1997   Multifactor Population Limitation: Variable Spatial and Temporal Control of Spiders on Gulf of California Islands. *Ecology* 79 (2):490–502.
Ravines, Roger
1984   Sobre la formación de Chavín: Imágenes y símbolos. *Boletín de Lima* 35:27–45.
Salazar, Lucy C., and Richard L. Burger
2000   Los divinidades del universo religioso Cupisnique y Chavín. In *Los dioses del antiguo Perú*, 1–28. Banco de Crédito del Perú, Colección Arte y Tesoros del Perú, Lima.
Salazar-Burger, Lucy, and Richard L. Burger
1982   La araña en la iconografía del horizonte temprano en la costa norte del Perú. *Beitrage zur Allgemeinen und Vergleichenden Archaologie*, Band 4:213–253. Munich.

CHAPTER FIFTEEN

The Third Man

Identity and Rulership in Moche Archaeology and Visual Culture

STEVE BOURGET, UNIVERSITY OF TEXAS AT AUSTIN

Abstract

To date, the ritual and social identity of the person resting in the third burial at Sipán has remained an enigma. In contrast to the first two burials, which were successfully identified by Alva and Donnan (1993), this male individual was buried alone in a simple pit. Nonetheless, the quality and diversity of the ritual paraphernalia and regalia placed with him indicate his rank and symbolic importance. An identity is thus suggested through a detailed analysis of these objects in Moche visual culture and archaeology.

This chapter is an exploration into the identity of a male individual buried in Tomb 3 at Sipán, and into the nature of rulership in Moche society. Commonly known as the Old Lord of Sipán, he was between 45 and 55 years of age (Alva and Donnan 1993). He had been buried in the first construction phase of the funerary platform, making him the most ancient high-ranking individual found at the site so far. Before being deposited in a simple chamber, a woman and a llama were placed at the head of the burial perpendicular to the body of the main occupant. Although the deceased man had been denied a plank coffin like those of his successors in Tombs 1 and 2, and had been simply encased in reed mats and textiles, he was covered from head to toe with an impressive array of objects made of precious materials such as gold, silver, semiprecious stones, and exotic seashells. In fact, many of the most elaborate artifacts located at Sipán so far have come from the context of Tomb 3.

The social identity of this person, though, remains elusive. Numerous objects in the burial—such as scepters, backflaps, and crescent-shaped bells—were nearly identical to those found with the main individuals in Tombs 1 and 2, which have already successfully been related to the iconography by Alva and Donnan. Yet the scholars could not offer identification for this individual: "On the basis of tomb contents, it is not possible to identify the principal figure in Tomb 3 as one of the participants in the Sacrifice Ceremony" (Alva and Donnan 1993:215). They suggested that a possible reason for this failure is that, because of the early date of this burial, which is located in the first construction phase of the platform, the distinctive features of a "Warrior-Priest" of the Sacrifice Ceremony may not have been fully developed, making a positive identification difficult (Alva and Donnan 1993:217). This might be possible, but the quality of the objects associated with the deceased, and the fact that many of them were nearly identical to those found in the later contexts, suggest otherwise. In other words, if the regalia buried with this Moche dignitary are fully consistent with the other contexts that led to a positive identification, it would be likely that this individual's social position, or ritual persona, was also clearly delineated but had escaped the scrutiny of the investigators. As a research hypothesis, I thus propose that the ritual roles or social persona of the individual in Tomb 3 were already firmly established and formed part of the same symbolic structure displayed in the succeeding burials as well. I believe that a slightly more complex reading of both the artifacts present in the tomb and in the iconography might tease out this information and lead to a positive identification of this individual.

In the first part of this chapter, I review the principal identifications made over the last sixty years concerning a number of individuals found at Sipán and other Moche sites. This will permit identification of the main elements used in the recognition of these subjects. Second, some of the implications of these identifications will be explored to clarify both the iconography and the political and ideological positions of these subjects. Finally, I offer some ideas on the symbolic nature of rulership in an early archaic state such as that of the Moche. By using models developed elsewhere, especially in the Polynesian region, I intend to show that disparate religious, ritual, and political systems may yet draw upon similar structures for justification of the appearance of social inequality and the concentration of power within the hands of an early form of rulership.

IDENTITIES

During the last sixty years or so, a series of propositions have been made concerning the identity of a number of individuals buried in elaborate Moche tombs. The propositions have concerned the possibility that these individuals could have been the real-life counterparts of some of the most prominent subjects depicted in the iconography. The fact is that the majority of burials containing what appeared to be high-ranking individuals, usually surrounded by a retinue of people, have already been linked to the iconography. To date, this exercise has been attempted with varying degrees of success at four Moche sites: Huaca de la Cruz (Virú Valley), Huacas de Moche (Moche Valley), San José de Moro (Jequetepeque Valley), and Sipán (Lambayeque Valley). I will proceed chronologically and describe succinctly each of the attributions that derived from the latter locations.

In 1946, during their last day of fieldwork at Huaca de la Cruz, Duncan Strong and Clifford Evans stumbled upon one of the most complex Moche burials ever found archaeologically (Strong 1947; Strong and Evans 1952:14)—that is, before the discovery of the Sipán mausoleum some forty years later (Alva and Donnan 1993). This large burial, known as the Warrior-Priest tomb, held the remains of five individuals along with a large number of offerings, including ceramic vessels, headdresses, reed boxes, gourd plates, and three finely carved wooden staffs. The contents of the tomb were remarkably well preserved. On the basis of numerous similarities noted between the artifacts and the main individual in the tomb, Strong and Evans surmised that the old male individual might well have been the living representative of the fanged deity so prominently displayed in the iconography.

The two archaeologists established an especially convincing correlation between the staff, depicting on its upper section a being with fangs and a snake belt with a child standing on its left side, with physical remains found in the burial. They suggested that the same position between the being with fangs and the child (who also displayed prominent canines) had been intentionally re-created in the burial by the placement of an adolescent boy on the proper right side of the old man resting on his back. The main individual was wearing an elaborate headdress made of textile and of the fur and cranial bones of a desert fox (*Lycalopex sechurae*). Adorned with sheet metal fashioned into paws, ears, and nose, the zoomorphic headdress recalled the headgear worn by the "fanged deity" depicted on the staff, and consistently depicted with this individual in other representations of the iconography (Figure 15.1). These elements supported the very first identification of a Moche high-ranking individual:

> Thus, from these major artifacts alone, it can be concluded that the old man buried beneath these offerings not only represented in his own person the great tusked deity of the Mochica but that in this incarnation he had to assume the economic roles of an agricultural deity, a priest, a war leader, and a councillor as well. . . . However, to find direct evidence of a human being who, in his own lifetime, appears to have assumed these roles in the eyes of his people, makes the record written in ceramics and other portrayals even more vivid. (Strong and Evans 1952:199)

Unfortunately, this proposition linking iconic representations with buried individuals was largely ignored, possibly due to a lack of archaeological research with such a problematic in mind. It would take another twenty-five

FIGURE 15.1. Wooden club with a sculpture of a being with fangs and a child. Museo Nacional de Antropología, Arqueología e Historia, Lima. Photograph by author.

years before another serious attempt was undertaken to establish a bridge between Moche archaeology and iconography. In July 1972, in the context of the Chan Chan–Moche Valley Project, nine burials excavated from a mud-brick platform located on the eastern side of the Huaca del Sol contained the remains of possibly another group of significant iconographic subjects:

> The burials are all high status adult males, many of whom have large copper disc headdresses like those worn by certain individuals shown in Moche art. The concentration of these burials on the mud-brick platform suggests that this was a cemetery reserved exclusively for high status adult males who apparently shared an affiliation to a specific Moche ceremony. (Donnan and Mackey 1978:208)

One of these burials, that of a male individual in his late forties, was particularly noteworthy. He had been laid to rest with a few fine vessels, one of which, a stirrup spout bottle, was decorated with a fineline painting depicting anthropo-zoomorphic ritual runners. Placed directly across his body was a set of unusual metallic objects: a round copper sheath and two copper crosspieces. The relative position of these objects in the burial suggests that they were originally attached to a long pole or wooden shaft (Donnan and Mackey 1978:154).

This possibility was also noted by the investigators. Some time later, in 1985, Christopher Donnan suggested that this wooden object fitted with metallic crosspieces may have been used by the deceased in a ritual game inappropriately named "Ceremonial Badminton" by Kutscher (1958). Donnan argues that "Perhaps this very individual participated in the ceremony, casting the staff with crosspieces skyward from the summit of the Pyramid of the Sun, and then watching the string unwind and float slowly downward over the very spot where he was eventually buried" (1985:375). The presence of this burial in the same mud-brick platform containing adult males with copper disc headdresses and the presence of a stirrup spout bottle depicting ritual runners with supernatural attributes would tend to indicate that ritual running and this ceremony were related activities performed by the same individuals. They could have formed part of a group of males fulfilling specific ritual functions. Another fifteen years would go by

FIGURE 15.2. Fineline painting of the Sacrifice Ceremony. Staatliches Museum für Völkerkunde, Munich. Drawing by Donna McClelland.

before other startling correlations were made between the real world and Moche visual culture.

In 1987, the seizure of magnificent artifacts looted from the site of Sipán led to the discovery of the most stunning Moche burials ever found (Alva and Donnan 1993). Over a period of about twelve years, Walter Alva, Susanna Meneses, Luis Chero, and their crew unearthed in a special platform alongside the two main huacas the tombs of at least ten high-ranking individuals buried with attendants and hundreds of ceremonial artifacts. Several lesser tombs seemingly related to the broad concept of warfare were also found. On the basis of the corresponding objects located in the major contexts—including headdresses, bells, golden backflaps, and scepters—two male individuals were eventually identified by Alva and Donnan as the main subjects of the Sacrifice Ceremony (Figure 15.2A and B) (Alva and Donnan 1993). This theme is the most prominent one of Moche iconography, and consequently, it probably depicts the most important subjects as well (Donnan 1975).

Perhaps the clearest identification for the person in Tomb 1, an adult male aged thirty-five to forty-five years, is Individual A. He was found with a golden crescent headdress, circular earspools, and numerous crescent-shaped backflaps similar to those shown in the fineline paintings. The size of the objects found in the burial even matched those depicted on the individual in the

representation of the Sacrifice Ceremony (Figure 15.2). For example, a metallic rattle terminating in a sharp chisel and lying in his right hand possesses the same shape as the object located just underneath the dog in the lower register of the scene; the item is just above the litter and seems to be attached to a cup or a bowl placed on the back of a feline (Figure 15.3).

The identification of the second subject in Tomb 2 as Individual B (Figure 15.2) is a little bit more hazardous as it is largely based on the presence of an elaborate owl headdress and a copper cup by his right hand. The headdress led the investigators to refer to this man as the bird impersonator. The man was about the same age as the first individual in Tomb 1. If we include Strong and Evans' identification of the Huaca de la Cruz burial mentioned earlier, this was the second time that a positive identification was established between a real person and a subject possessing zoomorphic attributes, such as the bird impersonator.

Another important aspect is that the funerary platform studied at Sipán and the one located alongside the Huaca del Sol at the Huacas de Moche site seem to have been dedicated only to certain types of individuals. The people buried in each of these platforms would have pertained to the same ritual class. At Sipán, those identified so far belonged to participants in the Sacrifice Ceremony and their retainers. Those encountered in the Huaca del

FIGURE 15.3. Rattle-chisel from Tomb 1, Sipán. Photograph by Christopher B. Donnan.

FIGURE 15.4. Ceremonial goblet decorated with a painting depicting anthropomorphized war implement holding cups. Proyecto Arqueológico San José de Moro. Photograph by Christopher B. Donnan.

Sol platform were part of the Ritual Runner and Badminton Player contingent.

In the 1990s, at San José de Moro in the Jequetepeque Valley, Christopher Donnan and Luis Jaime Castillo excavated the complex burials of two women who were eventually linked to the Sacrifice Ceremony as well. They became identified as representatives of Individual C (Figure 15.2; Donnan and Castillo 1992, 1994). Their

coffins were rectangular boxes constructed with six cane panels tied together. The caskets had been anthropomorphized with the addition of legs, arms, and a large mask, all made of a silver copper alloy (Donnan, this volume). Two long tassels of the same metal were placed on each side of the mask, probably on top of the coffin, to mimic the serrated-edge extensions or plumes worn by Individual C of the Sacrifice Ceremony scene (Figure 15.2). Reinforcing the identification, ceremonial goblets very similar to the one being exchanged between Individuals A and B were also found (Figure 15.4).

During this same period, two individuals found in the Huaca de la Luna main platform were quickly identified as subjects depicted in the Coca-Taking Ceremony (Bourget 1994; Uceda, this volume). Each of these individuals had been buried with a metallic bottle virtually

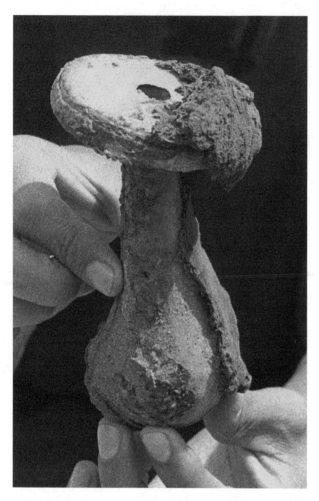

identical to those depicted in the iconography (Figures 15.5, 15.6).

Finally, one of the last subjects was identified in 1994 when the reanalysis of a tomb (Burial 10) excavated in 1946 by Strong and Evans at the site of Huaca de la Cruz in the Virú Valley led to the recognition of a fourth subject of the Sacrifice Ceremony. A wooden staff buried with a woman led Daniel Arsenault to identify her as Individual E; she is the figure performing a human sacrifice on the lower register of the scene, immediately underneath Individual D (Figure 15.2) (Arsenault 1994). The staff measures 71 cm in length, and carved in its upper section is a woman sitting on a raised dais (Figure 15.7). Her back is placed against the base of the four prongs, and two smaller human figures are seated in front of her. In the Sacrifice Ceremony, Individual E appears as an anthropomorphized staff collecting blood from a captive male. The four prongs form part of her headdress, and the extremity of the staff is clearly visible as a sharp point appearing between her legs. I have not been able to clearly ascertain the exact function of this object, but it reappears in another Sacrifice Ceremony scene (Figure 15.8). Two of these staffs are located on each side of the sacrificial activity depicted at the left of the scene. This staff is also prominent in certain scenes of ritual warfare and thus carries a symbolic charge directly associated with these interrelated ritual activities.

Although the zoomorphic counterpart of the staff-woman, the feline conducting the second sacrifice to her left (Figure 15.2) has not yet been identified in a

FIGURE 15.5. Bottle of gilded copper from Tomb 2, Platform I, Huaca de la Luna. Proyecto Arqueológico Huacas del Sol y de la Luna, Trujillo. Photograph by author.

FIGURE 15.6. Ritual activity under bicephalous arc. Linden-Museum, Stuttgart. Drawing by Donna McClelland.

burial. This feline subject has been found represented on a mural at Huaca de la Luna. This mural is located on the wall of a small building that may have been used for some of the sacrifices performed at the site. The mural represents a feline overpowering a sacrificial victim, a theme associated with dismemberment and bloodletting (Figure 15.9).

These short descriptions indicate that the identification of these individuals with the iconography has consistently been made with a series of specific objects: headdresses, staffs, scepters, backflaps, and cups. Also, in at least two cases, purposely built mud-brick platforms have been created to house the burials, and it would appear that these structures were dedicated to specific types of social personae. The platform near the Huaca del Sol contained Ritual Runners and Badminton Players, activities performed by the same type of individuals in the iconography. In similar fashion, the two individuals identified in the Sipán platform pertain to the Sacrifice Ceremony.

This propensity of locating certain types of ritual practitioners in specific structures may have also been extended to the temples. At Huaca de la Luna, the main platform was also the sole resting place of coca-taking individuals found thus far (Uceda, this volume). At San José de Moro, the tombs of the two Priestesses, identified as Individual C of the Sacrifice Ceremony (Figure 15.2), have also been found in the same general area, some 20 m apart, underneath a large plaza near the access ramp of Huaca la Capilla (Donnan and Castillo 1994). A third funerary chamber, that of a child, was located

FIGURE 15.7. Wooden club with a sculpture of a woman sitting in front of two smaller figures. Museo Nacional de Antropología, Arqueología e Historia, Lima (MO-0879).

FIGURE 15.8. Sacrifice Ceremony. Museo Nacional de Antropología, Arqueología e Historia, Lima. Drawing by Donna McClelland.

FIGURE 15.9. External view of the north side and doorway of Recinto I, Plaza 3c, showing sacrificial victims overtaken by felines. Photograph by John Verano.

between those of the Priestesses. Although the evidence is not as clear as those found with the adults, this person might also have been associated with the same type of individual. The child had been buried in an elaborate funerary chamber, somewhat similar to those of the adult females, surrounded by numerous offerings, with two adults placed at her feet. Four other children had also been buried in the shaft. Thus, if this child was a priestess-to-be, then such status can be assumed to have been acquired at birth. These contexts may indicate that this section of the plaza, near the main huaca, may have constituted a burial ground dedicated to this type of individual.

The Third Man

So who was the Third Man at Sipán—that is, the man found in Tomb 3 (Figure 15.10)? The information provided by the contents of the tombs already identified at

Sipán and at San José de Moro suggests that the role of a high-ranking Moche individual was hereditary and may have been already fixed at the moment of birth. In fact, ancient mitochondrial DNA studies recently carried out on the Sipán burials have indicated that a number of buried persons were maternally related and that the structure was probably a mausoleum for members of a regional elite lineage and close associates (Shimada et al. 2005:78). Furthermore, the genetic proximity between the Old Lord in Tomb 3 and the Lord in Tomb 1 suggests that they may have been an uncle and a nephew distant by several generations (Shimada et al., this volume). Thus, if most of the individuals buried in the platform were genetically related, and if their status was acquired at birth, then all the highest-ranking individuals found in the platform would necessarily have been linked to the Sacrifice Ceremony pageantry. This hypothesis is also supported by the fact that individuals performing

FIGURE 15.10. View of Tomb 3 during excavation, Sipán. Photograph by Guillermo Cock.

similar religious and political roles are usually buried at the same place.

As a research hypothesis, I would suggest that Tomb 3, the burial of a man aged between thirty-five and forty-five, like the Lord in Tomb 1, was also related to the Sacrifice Ceremony and was the living embodiment of Individual D. In Figure 15.2, he stands to the right of the exchange ceremony. In order to establish his identity, I will first adopt the approach used by other investigators, which consists of establishing a positive link between objects and contexts found in the burials with their counterparts in Moche visual culture. Second, I will explore in more detail the "iconographical persona" of this individual.

Perhaps the most diagnostic element establishing a positive link between the archaeological context and Individual D is the object depicted just behind him in the Sacrifice Ceremony (Figure 15.2b). This anthropo-morphized object is clutching a cup in its right hand and a large disc against its chest (Figure 15.11). Because of the pointy end of the anthropomorphized object, it could itself depict an animated club. Both possibilities are not mutually exclusive, as the real object—a gold rattle found in the right hand of the Old Lord—may also have been meant to represent a diminutive war club (Figure 15.12). The main difference is that the ritual war clubs consistently depicted in the iconography possess triangular heads, even in their animated state (Figures 15.13, 15.14). These objects accurately correspond to real wooden clubs, such as those found at Huaca Cao Viejo (Figure 15.15).

The object associated with Individual D in the Sacrifice Ceremony (Figure 15.2), however, is different. It is rounder and decorated with a series of vertical lines (Figure 15.11) that appear to imitate almost exactly the vertical lobes of the rattle (Figure 15.12). Defining these

FIGURE 15.11. Detail of anthropomorphized rattle-chisel in Figure 15.2b. Staatliches Museum für Völkerkunde, Munich. Drawing by Donna McClelland.

objects as scepters may not be completely appropriate as these are more than mere emblems of power and authority: these are bloodletting tools. Indeed, the lower extremities of these objects take the form of a long and narrow rectangular blade.

The fact that the animated object in the Sacrifice Ceremony might be a cross between a war club and a chisel should not be too surprising. Both tools are closely associated with human sacrifice. A bottle from the Rafael Larco Museum depicts a seated individual holding an object identical to the one encountered in Tomb 3 (Figure 15.16). The chisel is held against a bowl resting on a small textile. In all likelihood, the chisel, with its narrow and sharp blade, would have been used to cut the jugular vein of a sacrificial victim. The bowl would have served to collect the blood gushing from the neck wound, and the textile may have served to carefully cover the bowl with its precious red liquid. A second chisel had also been placed in Tomb 3. The upper part of this object, made of silver, depicts a warrior with two human heads hanging above him in a special rack (Figure 15.17). After the collection of the blood, then, some of the victims may have been decapitated.

In addition to the golden chisel-rattle, which led to a positive identification of the main person in the tomb as Individual A (Figure 15.2), a second chisel of solid silver had been placed in his left hand. These two objects were also closely related to the concepts of ritual warfare and sacrifice. The first depicts on the five sides of the rattle an elaborate warrior, with wrinkles on his face, clubbing

FIGURE 15.12. Rattle-chisel from Tomb 3, Sipán. Photograph by Christopher B. Donnan and Donald McClelland.

FIGURE 15.13. Fineline painting of a warrior. Drawing by Donna McClelland.

FIGURE 15.14. Fineline painting of a weapons bundle. Museo Amano, Lima. Drawing by Donna McClelland.

FIGURE 15.15. Wooden club found at the base of Huaca Cao Viejo, Chicama Valley. Photograph by author.

a prisoner seated in front of him (Figure 15.3). On the handle, just above the blade of the chisel, is an elaborate display of military implements: war clubs, spear-throwers and darts, a shield, a backflap, a tunic, and a conical helmet decorated with the diagnostic crescent shape ornament (Alva and Donnan 1993:98–99). The second chisel has in its extremity a small sculpture of a sacrificial victim facing another Wrinkle Face figure holding a war club and a square shield (Alva and Donnan 1993:100–101).

It is thus interesting to note that both male individuals associated with the upper register of the Sacrifice Ceremony would have been buried with two pairs of scepter-chisels constituting not only a symbol of their offices but also very effective tools for human sacrifice. In each case, one of the implements is a golden chisel with a rattling function, whereas the second one is solid silver and solely constitutes a chisel. The blades of these chisels are considerably more narrow than those of the usual crescent-blade knifes, suggesting that they may

FIGURE 15.16. Seated individual holding a chisel over a bowl. Museo Larco, Lima. Photograph by author.

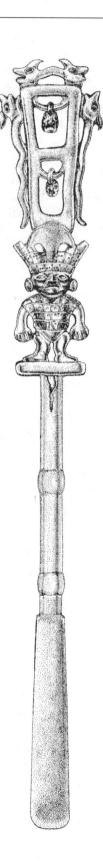

FIGURE 15.17. Chisel from Tomb 3, Sipán. Drawing by Alberto Gutiérrez.

have been employed during specialized sacrificial activities such as the collection of human blood.

The hypothesis that these chisels may have been used for blood collecting is consistent with two types of representations and one archaeological context. The first type of representation is the Sacrifice Ceremony itself, which has been widely recognized as a ritual involving the presentation of human blood taken from human captives (Alva and Donnan 1993; Bourget and Newman 1998; Donnan 1978). The second type belongs to a whole genre of stirrup spout bottles that depict a seated individual holding a spatula-like implement over a bowl usually resting on a rectangular piece of textile (Figure 15.16). In some cases, such as an example located in the tomb of a Huaca de la Luna individual (Figure 15.18), it could depict a zoo-anthropomorphic subject such as a fox-being. It is interesting to note that this bottle was found in the tomb of an individual buried in a mud-brick platform (Platform II) directly associated with Plaza 3a, the largest sacrificial area found at the site. This led me to suggest that this individual may have been one of the sacrificers at Huaca de la Luna (Bourget 2001). Unfortunately, this tomb was severely looted during colonial times, and all the metallic objects except for a small disc had probably been removed.

Human sacrifice is perhaps the most complex and symbolically charged of all ritual activities. Thus, it is not surprising that different aspects of the ceremony may have required different tools such as clubs, chisels, and knives. The crescent-blade knife, commonly known as a *tumi*, is a rather crude implement that may have been used more extensively for decapitation and dismemberment. A sort of butcher's tool, it was used for dismemberment, decapitation, and various activities necessitating blunt force. The chisel, in contrast, is a surgeon's implement dedicated to finer interventions, such as the cutting of arterial veins.

Having thus linked some of the objects of Tomb 3 with iconographical items of Individual D, I shall now delve deeper into a survey of his role in the Sacrifice Ceremony—the second step in establishing the religious and political identity of the Third Man. This process will permit me to map the range of attributes and activities associated with this subject. The third step is to compare these attributes with those depicted on the objects found in Tomb 3.

FIGURE 15.18. Anthropomorphized fox, seated and holding a chisel over a bowl, Tomb 2, Platform II, Huaca de la Luna. Proyecto Arqueológico Huacas del Sol y de la Luna, Trujillo. Photograph by author.

FIGURE 15.19. Fineline painting of the Sacrifice Ceremony. Museo Arqueológico Rafael Larco Herrera, Lima. Drawing by Donna McClelland.

Sacrifice Ceremony Scenes

To my knowledge, there are at least seven distinct fine-line paintings related to the Sacrifice Ceremony, five of which are discussed here. The second one of this group (Figure 15.19) is almost identical to the first (Figure 15.2) and may have been produced in the same workshop. It depicts an identical group of individuals in a similar position and surrounded by the same objects. In fact, the only object missing is the rattle-chisel behind Individual D in Figure. 15.2, which we associated with the rattle-chisel found in Tomb 3.

The third example of the Sacrifice Ceremony shows a slightly different lineup (Figure 15.20). On the upper register, Individual A receives a cup from what appears to be the bird impersonator, Individual B. In this scene, however, the subject wears the semicircular headdress and rectangular train usually assigned to Individual D, who in this case is not in the scene. The feline collecting blood from a victim is now located immediately above Individual C, and the lower register is filled with a battle scene. Have the identifying attributes for one individual been transferred to another personage? Or has Individual D taken the form of a bird? These questions are, at present, impossible to answer and warrant a new investigation. Nevertheless, it appears a certain degree of fluidity may have existed between these different scenes, especially regarding the zoomorphic attributes of these individuals. Furthermore, certain types of headdresses

may not be the avatar of only one specific individual; for example, at the site of Dos Cabezas, twelve headdresses were found covering the body of a single individual (Donnan 2003:55). It is not clear if some of these attributes were interchangeable and could be adopted by different individuals. Another aspect worth considering is the relationship that may have existed between certain representations and historical figures. Did a given representation belong to a specific person? Was it created for the commemoration of a specific event? Unfortunately, a depiction of the Sacrifice Ceremony has yet to be found in a secure archaeological context.

In the fourth Sacrifice Ceremony, the order has been inverted, and Individual A is now looking in the other direction (Figure 15.21). He is no longer being offered a cup from the bird impersonator, but instead receives a bleeding warrior from an anthropomorphized feline. He acknowledges the reception of the sacrificial blood by extending his right hand toward the face of the captive. To the left of this threesome stands a bird being holding a war club. This bird is not a raptor but rather a marine bird, probably a cormorant, wearing a semicircular headdress with a human face in its center. This headdress effigy is terminated by octopus tentacles. The captive and both animal beings wear rectangular trains. In the lower register, two warriors with their eyes missing (blind?) accompany what appears to be a captured anthropomorphized fox.

FIGURE 15.20. Fineline painting of the Sacrifice Ceremony. Museo Nacional de Antropología, Arqueología e Historia, Lima, Drawing by Donna McClelland.

FIGURE 15.21. Fineline painting of the Sacrifice Ceremony. Drawing by Donna McClelland.

The fifth Sacrifice Ceremony scene (Figure 15.8), discussed above, lacks the two registers of the other examples. It depicts a group of five individuals in a single line separated into two main activities. The first activity, to the left, consists of the sacrifice of a captive by a warrior in the guise of a vampire bat (based on the wing design) who collects the blood of the victim into a cup. In the second activity, immediately to the right, Individual C is presenting a cup to Individual D, who is seated on a sort of dais. The three-pronged staffs and the cups placed above the sacrificer and between the two

activities would suggest certain continuity between the actions, and that the cup being exchanged is effectively the same one being filled by the bat impersonator. These staffs would thus stand for Individual E and relate to ritual warfare and sacrificial blood.

In summary, if we regroup the different representations of Individual D in the iconography (Figure 15.22), it is apparent that this subject is connected to a number of maritime subjects, including the cormorant being with the octopus headdress in Figure 15.21. He generally has a train, which I associate with fishing net, and a pair of

FIGURE 15.22. Depictions of Individual D from Sacrifice Ceremony scenes. Drawings by Donna McClelland.

FIGURE 15.23. Fineline painting of Individual D in the form of an anthropomorphized crayfish. Redrawn from Kutscher 1983, Figure 243.

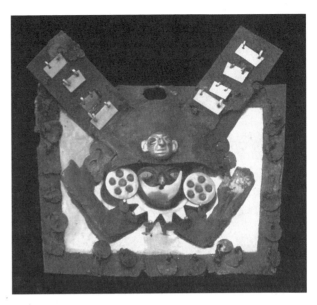

FIGURE 15.24. Nose ornament from Tomb 3, Sipán. Photograph by Christopher B. Donnan and Donald McClelland.

FIGURE 15.25. Metallic pectoral in the form of octopus tentacles, Tomb 3, Sipán. Painting by Alberto Gutiérrez.

appendages under the chin (Figure 15.22). These appendages and the headdress usually associated with this individual are also depicted on an anthropomorphized crayfish (Figure 15.23), additional evidence that the most significant elements forming the ritual persona of this subject originated from the sea or a marine context: crayfish, octopus, cormorant, and fishing net. Furthermore, a nose ornament from Tomb 3 depicts an individual wearing the same type of headdress (Figure 15.24).

Among the numerous artifacts uncovered in Tomb 3—headdresses, earspools, nose ornaments, necklaces, pectorals, and effigies—an impressive array of objects bear depictions of this maritime association such as sea lions, sea birds, catfish, borracho fish, stingrays, and crabs. But they also, to a lesser extent, indicate a terrestrial connection through the presence of owls, spiders, foxes, felines, condors, and vampire bats. It is not pertinent here to follow all the iconographical ramifications of these marine and terrestrial subjects. Instead, I will concentrate on only the most important objects that may have constituted the expression of the ritual and social persona of the Old Lord.

The first object is an impressive pectoral in the form of eight octopus tentacles (Figure 15.25). Measuring 90 cm in width, it would have covered the whole chest of this individual, transforming him into an authentic octopus being.

The second object is a magnificent necklace made of ten large beads in the form of a spider resting on his web (Figure 15.26). Each of these intricate objects is made of gold and contains small pellets that would have pro-

duced a rattling sound. The presence of a human head forming the body of the spider recalls the Cupisnique tradition, in which the spider constitutes a central element. The body of the spider is also depicted with a number of human heads. On the back of the spider bead there is a finely incised motif of spirals terminated by seabird heads.

The third subject is an effigy in the guise of a crab being (Figure 15.27). Although it is difficult to assess the exact species represented, a study I recently conducted on this subject suggests that it may have personified a

FIGURE 15.26. Gold spider beads from Tomb 3, Sipán. Photograph by Christopher B. Donnan and Donald McClelland.

swimming crab. In the iconography, this species can easily be identified by the fifth pair of legs, which are flattened into paddles for swimming. On one nose ornament (Figure 15.28) the species represented is the blue crab (*Callinectes arcuatus*). These large crabs normally live in great numbers in Ecuador and Colombia. During severe El Niño events, most of the local species of crabs are severely hit, and their carcasses cover the beaches in thick layers. In fact, two other species mentioned above—the octopus and spider—are also greatly affected by these conditions. Instead of facing annihilation, though, the octopuses multiply in water warmed by El Niño events, perhaps because of an augmentation of food sources and decreased competition with other

predators (Arntz and Fahrbach 1996:134). Numerous species of spiders also multiply in great numbers during these conditions due to a beneficial increase in humidity and insect populations (Alva, this volume).

The trilogy of the spider, crab, and octopus further shares a certain form of consubstantiality and as such are often represented together in the iconography. The Moche may have associated these species together on the basis of a series of ecological and morphological similarities. First, the three species possess or, in the case of the crab, seem to possess, eight extremities. They are highly sensitive to changes in climatic conditions, especially in relation to El Niño events. Furthermore, the spider and crab may be placed in a position of symbolic duality with regard to the octopus. The spider and crab have exo-skeletons, whereas the octopus has no bone structure. The sculpture in Figure 15.29, a Wrinkle Face bottle, is a good example of this morphological interrelation-ship. It portrays a being with fangs wearing an octopus headdress with twelve tentacles and the effigy of an owl in its center. The rectangular elements emanating from each side of its body are pairs of spider legs (Cordy-Collins 1992). All the high-ranking tombs from Sipán contained numerous versions of the spider beings in the form of bells, backflaps, and headdress ornaments. These artifacts display the legs of the spiders in exactly the same fashion as the ceramic bottle. The arms of the bottle figure are missing and may have been intention-ally separated from the sculpture, but they would, in all likelihood, have held a sacrificial knife in one hand and a severed human head in the other.

The complex roles shared between the spider, the octopus, and Individual D of the Sacrifice Ceremony are

FIGURE 15.27. Anthropomorphized crab from Tomb 3, Sipán. Photograph by Christopher B. Donnan.

FIGURE 15.28. Nose ornament with a depiction of a swimming crab (*Callinectes arcuatus*) from the site of La Mina. Private collection. Photograph by Christopher B. Donnan.

FIGURE 15.29. Bottle in the form of a Wrinkle Face with spider attributes and an octopus headdress. Museo del Banco Central de Reserva del Perú, Lima (ACE-507). Photograph by author.

beautifully illustrated in a fineline painting from Phase IV (Figure 15.30). It shows Individual A climbing a ladder with the help of five spider beings. Individual B, in a seated position to the left, appears to be overseeing the activity. Individual D, in the guise of an octopus being, is located to the lower right. He is in a splayed position and wears a fishing net complete with net sinkers as a train (Figure 15.31). Above the scene, Individual C, holding a cup, is seated inside a crescent-shaped form (Figure 15.32). This subject becomes especially widespread during Phase V. The crescent shape has been a matter of debate and has usually been associated with a reed boat or the crescent moon (Benson 1985; Cordy-Collins 1977). I would thus suggest that the Third Man at Sipán, in his incarnation as Individual D, might have been vested with a form of symbolism closely related to the world of the sea and the specific conditions that prevail during El Niño events.

This connection of the Old Lord to the sea and El Niño events does not rely solely upon a strict one-to-one correlation; the triad of octopus, spider, crab may actually evince a certain form of dialectical relationship. An El Niño event is primarily associated with the sea, bringing warm Ecuadorian currents deep into Peru, displacing the normally cold Humboldt Current and thus altering the biota of this ecosystem. Even the replacement of the cold current by the El Niño current could have been represented in Tomb 3 by a pectoral depicting a white wave overtaking a red wave (Figure 15.33). This double-wave design is also prominently depicted on a painted altar at Huaca de la Luna and on numerous vessels, including some depicting sexual activities (Bourget 2006).

On land, however, an El Niño event increases humidity on the coast, literally making the desert bloom and extending the reach of the lomas. This creates ideal conditions for the reproduction of a multitude of land snails (*Scutalus* sp.). In the iconography this land snail species is often morphed with a strombus seashell to create a strombus monster (Bourget 1990; Donnan 1978). This composite being is regularly associated with scenes of ritual warfare and captured warriors (Figure

FIGURE 15.30. Fineline painting of individuals in the Sacrifice Ceremony. Drawing by Donna McClelland.

FIGURE 15.31. Detail of Individual D, with fishing net and sinker train (Figure 15.30, *lower right*).

FIGURE 15.32. Detail of Individual C in a crescent moon (Figure 15.30, *top*).

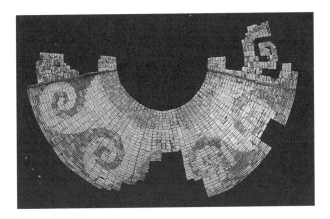

FIGURE 15.33. Pectoral in the form of a double-wave motif. Photograph by Christopher B. Donnan and Donald McClelland.

15.34). Strombus seashells (*Strombus galeatus*) come from Ecuador and the warm seas of El Niño to the north. They have been imported to the north coast region of Peru since at least 500 BC (Paulsen 1974). A strombus shell is often visually linked to images of Moche rulership and is consistently used as a musical instrument or as a prestigious offering. The rarity of this shell is underlined by the fact that shell trumpets are often copied in ceramic (Figure 15.35). On one ceramic vessel (Figure 15.36), it is interesting to note that while the *Strombus* shell (*pututo*) is being played by the modeled figure on top, the cup with blood is being offered to Individual D in the Sacrifice Ceremony (Figure 15.8). Again, this subject may be closely related to El Niño events, as may the sound produced by this instrument. In such a case, this ceramic representation would indicate that some of the rituals performed during the Sacrifice Ceremony—perhaps those that display Individual D as the recipient of the cup—may have been enacted at times of changing climatic conditions.

In summary, I propose that the animal species depicted on the main objects constituting the regalia of the Old Lord/Third Man—the catfish bracelet, the octopus pectoral, the spider necklace, and the swimming crab effigy—are indicators of the socio-symbolic nature of this individual. But why associate such a ruler with the El Niño phenomenon, whose warm sea current

FIGURE 15.34. Warriors in front of Strombus Being. By kind permission of the Trustees of the British Museum, London. Drawing by Donna McClelland.

FIGURE 15.35. Ceramic trumpet in the form of a strombus shell. Museo Nacional de Antropología, Arqueología e Historia, Lima (1-2622). Photograph by author.

FIGURE 15.36. Stirrup spout bottle with strombus shell (*pututo*) player standing on top and scene of Sacrifice Ceremony below. Museo Nacional de Antropología, Arqueología e Historia, Lima (C-03315). Photograph by author.

migrates from the north and invades the north coast of Peru only sporadically, every five to ten years? In order to conceptually understand this association, one must search for an answer less dependent on the Moche religion and system of representation than on the rise of social complexity and the justification of power of an early archaic state. Indeed, Moche visual culture and regalia are the conspicuous display of political and religious authority.

Power and Archaic State Formation

An aspect still poorly understood in the rise of social complexity is the legitimatization of power. How is a new and growing form of political authority perceived and acknowledged socially and ritually? In the first part of this chapter, I suggested that by specifically associating the Old Lord/Third Man with the warm seas and, by extension, the El Niño phenomenon, the Moche were associating his rulership and authority to an external origin and certain beings with supernatural attributes. Consequently, his political authority would have been proclaimed as originating from a divine and foreign source. It would appear that, like the torrential rainstorms accompanying an El Niño event, this ruler could have arrived with the hot sea current and imposed himself onto the Moche landscape.

In the case of the Third Man, I would argue that his authority resides on three distinct but interrelated aspects. The first step of this validating process is to link him to the past through the display of archaic subjects such as the spider. The second is to conceptualize him as sacred through depictions of this individual as a being with supernatural attributes. The third step is identifying a foreign origin through his association with the El Niño event.

The proposition of such a structural mode of power and governance must have found resonance elsewhere as well. In order to be effective, the rise of political authority in any early archaic state had to be validated and accepted by the population. Social, symbolic, and religious mechanisms must have been devised to facilitate, maintain, and perpetuate rulership. Therefore, in order to reflect on the evolutions of rulership and kingship in an early state formation, I will draw upon a Polynesian example. In his magisterial exploration of Captain Cook's death, *Island of History*, Marshall Sahlins brings

Dumézil's conception of the nature of archaic kingship to bear. He suggests that, in general:

> The kingship makes its appearance from outside the society. Initially a stranger and something of a terror, the king is absorbed and domesticated by the indigenous people, a process that passes by way of his symbolic death and consequent rebirth as a local god. (Sahlins 1985:73)

Sahlins makes a case that in Fiji, as in other parts of Polynesia, such as Hawaii, the origin myths of the paramount chiefs and their lineage place these individuals outside the natural world. They are "from the heavens or—in the very common case—they are of distinct ethnic stock. In either event royalty is the foreigner" (1985:78). Within this model, the royalty of an early archaic state, and its concomitant power structure, is conceived of as foreign, as alien both in nature and structure to the local population. In short the king and his consorts are conceptually foreigners:

> The rationalization of power is not at issue so much as the representation of a general scheme of social life: a total "structure of reproduction," including the complementary and antithetical relations between king and people, god and man, male and female, foreign and native, war and peace, heavens and earth. (Sahlins 1985:81)

I think that this general model fits rather nicely with the data presented so far. These animal representations as agents personify the nature of the Third Man's power. They not only legitimize the source of his rulership, but also associate him with one of the most awesome forces in the region: the periodic appearance of an El Niño event. This event is of a foreign nature and imposes itself upon the local scene. This imposition is directly experienced through the arrival of a warm northern sea current accompanied by a cohort of "supernatural" animals such as eagle rays (*Myliobatus peruvianus*), manta rays (*Manta hamiltoni*), sharks, gigantic swimming crabs (*Europhylax robustus*), and even leatherback turtles (*Dermochelys coriacea*). All of these species are clearly depicted in the iconography. In contrast, the local milieu is devastated or undergoes drastic changes: the usual

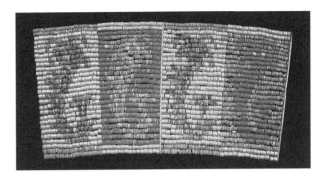

FIGURE 15.37. Bracelet with catfish design from Tomb 3, Sipán. Photograph by Ignacio Alva.

species of fish disappear, sea lions and sea birds die by the thousands, and beaches are littered by large masses of dead crabs and seashells. Yet amidst this marine holocaust, octopuses, borracho fishes, and catfishes thrive, betraying their true nature—in a sense, their real connection. As mentioned earlier, catfish representations abound in Tomb 3, and are depicted on some of the most prominent objects, including a nose ornament, two pectorals, and a bracelet (Figure 15.37).

On land, torrential El Niño rainfalls and floods destroy the labor of humans. Pests and insects invade fields and houses, spreading famine and diseases. Yet amidst this destruction, lomas and vast stretches of desert landscape bloom, and a multitude of land snails and arachnids take advantage of this bounty.

The attributes of the Third Man are of the land and of the sea—a foreign sea. His power source originates from outside the Moche world, and yet, because of its direct impact on the north coast, his authority is intimately tied to the local forces of social and biological reproduction. Again, the parallels with Fijian kingship are remarkable:

> The same, then, can be said of the ruling chief who, at once or alternately land and sea himself, functions as supreme mediator of the material interchange and great generator of the cultural totality. An immigrant by origin, he is a sea person relative to the people of the land, hence purveyor of sea and foreign goods in exchange for the indigenous land products. (Sahlins 1985:101)

I would suggest that the Third Man would also have served as a mediator between the people of the land, the Moche, and the powerful entity of the El Niño sea. These dialectical relations—between land and sea, between local and foreign, between humans and gods, and between the people and their rulers—indicate that in the domestication of nature and rulership, some solutions are better than others. In a structural mode, the dialectical solution created by the Moche addresses the invariance of mythical discourse but also the contingencies of historical conditions. The Sacrifice Ceremony, perhaps the one directly involving Individual D (Figure 15.8), would have maintained an atmosphere of predictability in the midst of severe ecological conditions. Of course, there is more to it than just the nature of Individual D. I would suggest that further research will eventually reveal connections between the other members of the Sacrifice Ceremony and concepts of Ancientry, the foreign and the divine.

The Legacy of the Moche and the Northern "Stranger King"

In the context of this foreign connection with power and rulership, it is worth mentioning that after the dissolution of Moche culture, around the ninth century AD, two distinct cultural traditions arose in the following two centuries. The first, to the south of the Pampa of Paiján, was the Chimú, centered on the capital of Chan Chan in the Moche Valley. The second, to the north of Paiján, was the Lambayeque (a cultural tradition also known as Sicán), concentrated at two main sites, Batan Grande and Tucume, in the region of Lambayeque.

The oral tradition of the north coast has retained two stories that may have initially been part of the origin myth of these two social formations. Interestingly, these stories describe first the arrival of the ruling elites. In both cases, these rulers originated from outside the region and came from the sea. I do not intend to analyze these myths in detail, but a succinct account of each one demonstrates that parts of them, conceptually speaking, may have originated during Moche times.

The first text, created around 1604, supposedly describes the history of the kingdom of Chimor. In Michael Moseley's condensed narration of the text, it is said that:

> Arriving by balsa watercraft, a man called Tacaynamo settles in the lower Moche Valley, saying he was sent

from over the sea to govern this land. His son Guacricaur conquers leaders of the valley. In turn, his son Ñançenpingo completes the upstream consolidation of the valley, then initiates the first stage of external expansion, extending the imperial frontiers to the Rio Santa in the south and the Rio Jequetepeque in the north. (Moseley 1990:4)

In this account, the maritime and foreign origin of the ruling line is stated at the very beginning: Tacaynamo was sent from over the sea to rule this region.

The account of the Naymlap dynasty dates from 1586 and frames the action to the north, in the Lambayeque Valley. Again, the arrival of this ruler is from the sea, but additional cataclysmic conditions, perhaps brought by an El Niño event, are woven into the narrative. This second text has been adapted from Donnan:

> The people of Lambayeque say that in times so very ancient that they do not know how to express them, a man of much valor and quality came to that valley on a fleet of balsa rafts. His name was Naymlap. With him he brought many concubines and a chief wife named Ceterni. . . . Naymlap and his people lived for many years and had many children. Eventually he knew that the time of his death had arrived. In order that his vassals should not learn that death had jurisdiction over him, his immediate attendants buried him secretly in the same room where he had lived. They then proclaimed it throughout the land that he had taken wings and flown away. . . . Subsequently (after the death of Cium, Naymlap's oldest son) there were nine rulers in succession, followed by Fempellec, the last and most unfortunate member of the dynasty. He decided to move the idol that Naymlap had placed at Chot. After several unsuccessful attempts to do this, the devil appeared to him in the form of a beautiful woman. He slept with her and as soon as the union had been consummated the rains began to fall, a thing which had never been seen upon these plains. These floods lasted for thirty days, after which followed a year of much sterility and famine. Because the priests knew that their lord had committed this grave crime, they understood that it was punishment for his fault that his people were suffering with hunger, rain, and want. In order

to take vengeance upon him, forgetful of the fidelity that is owed by vassals, they took him prisoner and, tying his feet and hands, threw him into the deep sea. (Donnan 1990:243–244)

In both the Chimú and Lambayeque mythic accounts, the ruling dynasties came by boats from a distant land. Furthermore, in the Naymlap story a transgression brought torrential rains followed by a period of drought. This climatic devastation was only stopped by the casting of the lord's body to the bottom of the ocean. In the same text, but not described here, there is mention of material of a northern origin such as *Strombus* in the form of a shell trumpet and *Spondylus* seashells. The rains and drought are of course indicative of El Niño and La Niña events.

Final Remarks

The remarkable consistency between the iconographical representations and the impersonators of these individuals found at Sipán and elsewhere reveals the pervasiveness and importance of the Sacrifice Ceremony. It further implies that ceremonies involving human sacrifice, especially the taking and partaking of human blood, were central to Moche religion and ideology. Such iconographic and ritual conservatism witnessed in the above examples of the same ceremony reinforce the view that Moche iconography maintained a high degree of coherency, providing ample justification for detailed analyses of further related scenes and subjects.

The identifications between real individuals and subjects depicted in the iconography suggest a much closer relationship between these two systems than previously realized. New paradigms will need to be developed and new explorations conducted to understand the ramifications of these implications. Some actions depicted in the iconography may appear to be of a supernatural nature, and yet how would they have been perceived by the Moche?

By providing a tentative identification for the Old Lord/Third Man at Sipán as Individual D of the Sacrifice Ceremony, I hope to have answered part of Walter Alva and Christopher Donnan's plea, when in 1993 they wished that "Perhaps someday we will know the identification of the man who was buried in such splendor in Tomb 3 and be able to understand and appreciate his role in Moche society" (1993:217).

Bibliography

Alva, Walter, and Christopher B. Donnan
1993   *Royal Tombs of Sipán*. Fowler Museum of Cultural History, University of California, Los Angeles.

Arntz, Wolf E., and Eberhard Fahrbach
1996   *El Niño: Experimento climático de la naturaleza*. Fondo de Cultura Económica, México.

Arsenault, Daniel
1994   Symbolisme, rapports sociaux et pouvoir dans les contextes sacrificiels de la société mochica (Pérou précolombien): Une étude archéologique et iconographique. Ph.D. dissertation, Département d'anthropologie, Université de Montréal, Montréal.

Benson, Elizabeth P.
1985   The Moche Moon. In *Recent Studies in Andean Prehistory and Protohistory*. Papers of the Second Annual Northeast Conference on Andean Archaeology and Ethnohistory. Edited by D. Peter Kvietok and Daniel H. Sandweiss, 121–135. Latin American Studies Program, Cornell University, New York.

Bourget, Steve
1990   Des tubercules pour la mort: Analyses préliminaires des relations entre l'ordre naturel et l'ordre culturel dans l'iconographie mochica. *Bulletin de l'Institut Français d'Études Andines* 19 (1):45–85.

1994   Los sacerdotes a la sombra del Cerro Blanco y del arco bicéfalo. *Revista del Museo de Arqueología, Antropología e Historia* 5:81–125. Universidad Nacional de Trujillo, Perú.

2001   Rituals of Sacrifice: Its Practice at Huaca de la Luna and Its Representation in Moche Iconography. In *Moche Art and Archaeology in Ancient Peru*, 88–109. Edited by Joanne Pillsbury. National Gallery of Art and Yale University Press, Washington, D.C.

2006   *Sex, Death and Sacrifice in Moche Religion and Visual Culture*. University of Texas Press, Austin.

Bourget, Steve, and Margaret E. Newman
1998   A Toast to the Ancestors: Ritual Warfare and Sacrificial Blood in Moche Culture. *Baessler-Archiv*, Neue Folge, 46:85–106. Berlin.

Cordy-Collins, Alana
1977   The Moon is a Boat! A Study in Iconographic Methodology. In *Pre-Columbian Art History: Selected Readings*, 421–434. Edited by Alana Cordy-Collins and Jean Stern. Peek Publications, Palo Alto, California.

1992   Archaism or Continuing Cultural Tradition: The Decapitator Theme in Cupisnique and Moche Iconography. *Latin American Antiquity* 3 (33):206–220.

Donnan, Christopher B.

1975   The Thematic Approach to Moche Iconography. *Journal of Latin American Lore* 1 (2):147–162.

1978   *Moche Art of Perú: Pre-Columbian Symbolic Communication.* Museum of Cultural History, University of California, Los Angeles.

1985   Archaeological Confirmation of a Moche Ceremony. *Indiana* 10:371–381.

1990   An Assessment of the Validity of the Naymlap Dynasty. In *The Northern and Southern Dynasties: Kingship and Statecraft in Chimor*, 243–274. Edited by Michael Moseley and Alana Cordy-Collins. Dumbarton Oaks Library and Collection, Washington, D.C.

2003   Tumbas con entierros en miniatura: Un nuevo tipo funerario Moche. In *Moche: Hacia el Final del Milenio*, Tomo 1, 43–48. Actas del Segundo Coloquio sobre la Cultura Moche, Trujillo, 1 al 7 de agosto de 1999. Edited by Santiago Uceda and Elías Mujico. Universidad Nacional de Trujillo and Pontifícia Universidad Católica del Perú, Lima.

Donnan, Christopher B., and Luis Jaime Castillo

1992   Finding the Tomb of a Moche Priestess. *Archaeology* 45 (6):38–42.

1994   Excavaciones de tumbas de sacerdotisas Moche en San José de Moro, Jequetepeque. In *Moche: Propuestas y perspectivas*, 415–425. Actas del Primer Coloquio sobre la Cultura Moche, Trujillo, 12 a 16 de abril de 1993. Edited by Santiago Uceda and Elías Mujica. Travaux de l'Institut Français d'Études Andines 79. Universidad Nacional de la Libertad, Trujillo, Perú.

Donnan, Christopher B., and Carol J. Mackey

1978   *Ancient Burial Patterns of the Moche Valley, Peru.* University of Texas Press, Austin.

Kutscher, Gerdt

1958   Ceremonial "Badminton" in the Ancient Culture of Moche (North Peru). In *Proceedings of the XXXII International Congress of Americanists*, 422–432. Munks Gaard, Copenhagen.

Moseley, Michael E.

1990   Structure and History in the Dynastic Lore of Chimor. In *The Northern and Southern Dynasties: Kingship and Statecraft in Chimor*, 1–41. Edited by Michael Moseley and Alana Cordy-Collins. Dumbarton Oaks Library and Collection, Washington, D.C.

Paulsen, Alison C.

1974   The Thorny Oyster and the Voice of God: *Spondylus* and *Strombus* in Andean Prehistory. *American Antiquity* 39 (4):597–607.

Sahlins, Marshall

1985   *Islands of History.* University of Chicago Press.

Shimada, I., K. Shinoda, S. Bourget, W. Alva, and S. Uceda

2005   MtDNA Analysis of Mochica and Sicán Populations of Pre-Hispanic Peru. *Biomolecular Archaeology: Genetic Approaches to the Past* 32:61–92.

Strong, William D.

1947   Finding the Tomb of a Warrior-God. *National Geographic Magazine* 91:453–482.

Strong, William D., and Clifford Evans

1952   *Cultural Stratigraphy in the Virú Valley, Northern Peru: The Formative and Florescent Epochs.* Columbia Studies in Archaeology and Ethnology IV. Columbia University Press, New York.

Index